THE CRUSADE OF 1456

The Crusade of 1456

Texts and Documentation
in Translation

JAMES D. MIXSON

UNIVERSITY OF TORONTO PRESS
Toronto Buffalo London

© University of Toronto Press 2022
Toronto Buffalo London
utorontopress.com

ISBN 978-1-4875-0576-9 (cloth)   ISBN 978-1-4875-3263-5 (EPUB)
ISBN 978-1-4875-2393-0 (paper)   ISBN 978-1-4875-3262-8 (PDF)

All rights reserved. The use of any part of this publication reproduced, transmitted in any form or by any means, electronic, mechanical, photocopying, recording, or otherwise, or stored in a retrieval system, without prior written consent of the publisher – or in the case of photocopying, a license from Access Copyright, the Canadian Copyright Licensing Agency – is an infringement of the copyright law.

Library and Archives Canada Cataloguing in Publication

Title: The crusade of 1456 : texts and documentation in translation / James D. Mixson.
Names: Mixson, James D., author.
Description: Includes bibliographical references and index.
Identifiers: Canadiana (print) 20220137293 | Canadiana (ebook) 20220137331 |
   ISBN 9781487505769 (cloth) | ISBN 9781487523930 (paper) |
   ISBN 9781487532635 (EPUB) | ISBN 9781487532628 (PDF)
Subjects: LCSH: Belgrade (Serbia) – History – Siege, 1456 – Sources.
Classification: LCC DR2119 .M59 2022 | DDC 949.71/013 – dc23

We welcome comments and suggestions regarding any aspect of our publications – please feel free to contact us at news@utorontopress.com or visit us at utorontopress.com.

Every effort has been made to contact copyright holders; in the event of an error or omission, please notify the publisher.

We wish to acknowledge the land on which the University of Toronto Press operates. This land is the traditional territory of the Wendat, the Anishnaabeg, the Haudenosaunee, the Métis, and the Mississaugas of the Credit First Nation.

University of Toronto Press acknowledges the financial support of the Government of Canada and the Ontario Arts Council, an agency of the Government of Ontario, for its publishing activities.

For my students

Contents

List of Maps xi

Acknowledgments xiii

A Note on Names and Places xvii

Introduction

Historical Frames: Political and Military Developments 2
Sources in Scholarly Context: The Middle Ages, the Crusades, and the Problem of "Lateness" 14
Framing the Sources: Selection, Structure, and Significance 21
Conclusion: Belgrade as a Fifteenth-Century Event 28

Part One: Preparations for Crusade, 1453–1456

1. Pope Nicholas V, *Etsi Ecclesia Christi* 39
2. Aeneas Silvius Piccolomini, *Constantinopolitana Clades* 46
3. Correspondence of 1455–1456 51
    3.1. The City of Ragusa to John Hunyadi 51
    3.2. John of Capistrano to Pope Callixtus III 53
    3.3. John of Capistrano to Pope Callixtus III 57
    3.4. Juan Carvajal to John of Capistrano 58
    3.5. John of Capistrano to Juan Carvajal 60

3.6. Juan Carvajal to John of Capistrano   62
3.7. Juan Carvajal to John of Capistrano   64
3.8. Juan Carvajal to John of Capistrano   65
3.9. John Hunyadi to Francis Oddi, Bishop of Assisi   65
3.10. John of Capistrano to Francis Oddi, Bishop of Assisi   66
4. Liturgy for Taking the Cross   68
5. A Pope's Call to Prayer   71
    5.1. Callixtus III, *Cum his superioribus*   72
    5.2. *Bulla Turcorum / "Türkenbulle"*   80
6. Pope Callixtus III, *Omnipotentis dei misericordia*   82

Part Two: The Earliest Accounts

7. John of Capistrano to Pope Callixtus III   87
8. John of Capistrano to Pope Callixtus III   88
9. John Hunyadi to Denis Szécsi, Archbishop of Esztergom   91
10. John Hunyadi to Ladislaus Garai, Palatine of Hungary   91
11. John Hunyadi to King Ladislaus V   93
12. John of Tagliacozzo to a Fellow Franciscan   95
13. John of Capistrano to Pope Callixtus III   104

Part Three: News and Propaganda

14. Ambassador of the Bishop of Šibenik to Pope Callixtus III   109
15. Cardinal Juan Carvajal to Francesco Sforza   112
16. Letters of John Goldener   113
    16.1. John Goldener to Franz Schlick   114
    16.2. John Goldener to Matthew Schlick   116
17. Ladislaus V to Duke Francesco Sforza of Milan   118
18. The City of Nuremberg to the City of Weissenburg   121
19. Pope Callixtus III to Francesco Sforza, Duke of Milan   122
20. Letters of Bernard of Kraiburg   125
    20.1. Bernard of Kraiburg to Sigismund, Archbishop of Salzburg   126
    20.2. Bernard of Kraiburg to Henry Rüger of Pegnitz   128
21. Pope Callixtus III, Letter to Juan Soler   130
22. Anonymous (Pseudo-John of Capistrano), to All Christians   133
23. Anonymous, Letter to Henry of Eckenfelt   137

24. Liturgical Commemorations of Belgrade   142
    24.1. Pope Callixtus III, *Inter divinae dispensationis*   142
    24.2. John Burchard, *Liber notarum*   144

Part Four: John of Tagliacozzo's *Story of the Victory of Belgrade*

25. John of Tagliacozzo, *The Story of the Victory of Belgrade*   147

Part Five: Memoir and Chronicle

26. Thomas Ebendorfer, *Chronicle of Austria*   217
27. Laonikos Chalkokondyles, *The Histories*   222
28. Michael Kritopoulos (Kritoboulos), *History of Mehmed the Conqueror*   228
29. Jacopo Promontorio, *Recollecta*   232
30. Âşıkpaşazade, *Memories and Chronicles of the House of Osman*   235
31. John Thurocz, *Chronicle of the Hungarians*   237
32. Tursun Beg, *History of the Conqueror*   249
33. *The Oxford Anonymous Chronicle*   256
34. Konstantin Mihailović, *Memoirs*   259

Cast of Characters   269

General Timeline   275

Timeline of the Crusade of 1456   279

Maps   281

Index   285

Maps

1 Central and Southeastern Europe, c. 1450   282
2 The City and Fortress of Belgrade, c. 1450   283
3 The Siege and Relief of Belgrade, 1456   284

Acknowledgments

The origins of this book reach back some twenty years, when as a graduate student specializing in late-medieval religion I first encountered the story of John of Capistrano and Belgrade. Not long after, I found myself as a novice teacher trying to help students make sense of the world in the early years of a new millennium, and like so many others, I was drawn anew to the teaching and study of the crusades. In that setting I became, again like so many others, more and more aware of the richness of the later medieval period for the study of the crusades, but at the same time aware of the comparative lack of affordable, widely available translations of the period's source material.

As the idea of this project began to take on a clearer shape, it came to enjoy generous institutional support. Leave time and funding from the University of Alabama helped both launch and finish it. My thanks especially to the Research Advisory Council grants program of the Office of Academic Affairs, and to the College Academy of Research, Scholarship, and Creative Activity (CARSCA) in the university's College of Arts and Sciences. Along the way the faculty and staff of several libraries helped me immensely in accessing both manuscript and printed editions for the volume, especially the staff at the Hill Monastic Manuscript Library at St. John's University in Collegeville, Minnesota; the Vatican Secret Archive in Rome; the Bavarian State Library in Munich; and the Amelia Gayle Gorgas library at the University of Alabama.

The project has also enjoyed the generous support of a wide circle of specialists, colleagues, and friends. Norman Housley offered early encouragement and advice and helped me think through first approaches to the project. Mark Whelan read and carefully critiqued an early draft of the Introduction. Paul Cobb and Dimitri Kastritsis kindly helped an awkward interloper negotiate the rich world of early Ottoman historiography and sources, which is unfortunately still only dimly captured in the work presented here. With the same collegiality, Aleksandar Fotic and Ognjen Krešić kindly helped with first approaches to Serbia and its wider region, and especially to the later-medieval history of Belgrade. Letizia Pellegrini, Filippo Sedda, and Marco Bartoli offered warm welcomes in Italy when I first began to think about this kind of a project. Gábor Klaniczay, Stanko Andrić, and Otto Gecser were always helpful in their responses to my many emails and have kindly provided me early access to their new editions of Capistrano's letters. Closer to home, Christine Caldwell Ames, David Bachrach, Michael Bailey, and Laura Smoller all offered their insight and encouragement at key points. But among my greatest debts are those I owe to my colleagues at the University of Alabama. Daniel Riches, Tanja Jones, and the members of our interdisciplinary community of medieval and early modern scholars offered support all along the way. I also owe a special debt to those who helped save me from myself as I fought through so many intractable passages – thanks to Daniel Riches, Kirk Summers, and Kelly Shannon Henderson for the Latin ones; Jessica Goethals for the Italian; and Rasma Lazda-Cazers for the German. Two former students, Michael Cervera and Gray Wood, read the completed draft carefully and offered valuable insights as veterans of my courses. Thanks as well to Craig Caldwell and the talented staff of the cartography lab of the University of Alabama, and especially to Alex Fries and Amber Chan for their work in preparing the maps. Yet for all this vital assistance and support, any mistakes found lurking in the volume of course remain entirely my own responsibility.

My guides through the publication process have also been invaluable. George Thompson has remained a steady and encouraging guide from the beginning. Natalie Fingerhut, Janice Evans, and the staff at the University of Toronto Press have been kind advocates and efficient colleagues on the long road to publication. I owe special thanks as well to the anonymous reviewers for the University of Toronto Press, who as specialists in crusade studies, Ottoman history, and Byzantine history offered perspective, critiques, and insights that strengthened the volume as a whole. My thanks as well to the scholars whose translations appear here alongside my own, and to all who have granted permission for the reproduction of their work.

As always, I am grateful to my wife Ashley and our family for their continued support during extended projects such as these. But above all, for this volume I am grateful to the now hundreds of students who have inspired me over so many years. They have lived through times that might seem to rival the Middle Ages for their chaos – seemingly endless wars, economic and political crises, and now a world-wide pandemic, with all of its bitter consequences. They have survived it all with resilience, diligence, and enthusiasm. It is to them, and especially to the seasoned veterans of HY 300, 388, and 442, that I dedicate these translations.

A Note on Names and Places

This volume, like so many others of its kind, presents a kaleidoscope of premodern names and places that are often difficult to render consistently in modern English. Centuries of change, so many linguistic divides, modern scholarly conventions, and a range of other factors make for a variety of possibilities. For the most part I have sought to render that variety in standard English (e.g., John for Johannes, Giovanni, János, and so on), and also to establish as much consistency and uniformity as possible among so many modern standards (so Ladislaus for Ladislas or Vladislav, Callixtus for Calixtus, Callistus, and so on). There are exceptions for translations reprinted here under copyright, where the original text remains unchanged, as well as other instances where my efforts at consistency have no doubt failed. In any event it is my hope that the text remains, above all else, readable and useful for its audience.

Introduction

This volume offers its readers access to one of the most interesting yet neglected stories in the later chapters of the history of the crusades: the events that led to the siege of the city of Belgrade in 1456, and how those events lived on in European narrative and memory. The sources collected here, some of them made available for the first time directly from archives and manuscripts, tell a compelling story. They reveal how fifteenth-century popes, like so many of their predecessors, shaped and disseminated crusading propaganda; how the princes of Europe both appropriated and resisted the energies of that same message; how ordinary people responded to the call to crusade, thousands of them soon the followers of an Italian friar of remarkable zeal and energy; how a warrior from Transylvania rose from relative obscurity to govern, for a time, Central Europe's greatest kingdom and lead the battle for Belgrade; how an ambitious young sultan, the conqueror of Constantinople itself, ground a modest but strategically crucial city to dust with his great cannons yet still somehow failed to capture it; how those who lived through the fight remembered and shaped the stories of its horrors; and how and why all the texts and memories that emerged from the campaign mattered in ways far removed from the battlefield itself.

But even more important than the story they tell, these sources also present their readers with compelling challenges of interpretation. They raise questions, for example, about the production and resonance of crusade propaganda – why and how it took the shape that it did; whether contemporaries responded to it; and how and why they made use of it. These texts also reveal much about the complex dynamics of travel and communication in premodern settings, and how difficult it could be to stay on top of the fast-moving events of a military campaign. They force readers to confront how seemingly straightforward "eyewitness" accounts of events are in fact produced, from their very origins, through a complex process that moves from human experience to narrative and text, and how texts in turn helped shape long-term cultural memory.

To render each of these aspects of the following collection more visible, this introduction will first offer a general overview of events leading up to the battle for Belgrade in 1456. It will then turn to the historiographical frames within which scholars have recently sought to make sense of the crusades generally, and of crusading in the fifteenth century in particular. Within that context it then turns to the story of Belgrade as seen through the texts themselves, and to an exposition of some of the main issues of method and interpretation those texts raise.

Historical Frames: Political and Military Developments

The events of 1456 had their origins in developments that reached back a century and more, to the rise of the Ottoman Turks in Anatolia. Later chroniclers shrouded those origins in foundation myths: the warrior Osman (d. 1324), so they recalled around 1500, had a vivid dream foretelling the rise of his descendants to dominance. Meanwhile, Western chroniclers and humanists cast the same story in a more ominous light, presenting the Turks as a bloodthirsty, warlike people ruled by tyrants. But the myths and propaganda only concealed a much more complex and much more interesting historical reality.[1]

In the early fourteenth century the Ottomans were just one of many Turkish tribes active across Anatolia, their leaders only the most successful of many chieftains fighting along a fragmented frontier that for them marked the far western reaches of the Islamic world. Their presence comes more clearly into historical view in the middle decades of the fourteenth century, when, under their emir Orhan, we can see them expanding from a new center of power in Bursa in northwestern Asia minor. A turning point came at mid-century, when Orhan made the most of the opportunities afforded him by the intrigues of the nearby Byzantine court. When the emperor Andronicus III died in 1341, he left a nine-year-old child, John V, as heir to the throne, with the courtier and general John Kantakouzenos as regent. Tensions over the regency soon broke out into a cycle of court strife and civil war that lasted until Kantakouzenos abdicated in 1354. The next year Orhan and his followers, who had served Kantakouzenos ably as mercenaries, settled and fortified the Gallipoli peninsula on the Dardanelles.

Following Orhan's death in 1362, his son and successor Murad I faced the challenge of consolidating what was still a very tenuous position. The new emir's interests looked out along two frontiers: eastward into Anatolia and now also westward into the Balkan peninsula. Murad patiently secured the former against rival Turkish clans and established a new European center of power at Edirne (the old Roman city of Adrianople). From there his warriors came into steady conflict with both the tsars of Bulgaria and the princes of Serbia, and subjugated both over the next generation. An early and decisive battle came in September 1371, when the Ottomans dealt the Serbian nobility a crushing blow near the village of Černomen on the Maritsa River. Sofia fell in 1385, Niš in 1386. But easily the most famous battle came on June 15, 1389, at Kosovo. There Murad faced a coalition led by Prince Lazar of Serbia and his Bosnian allies. From the earliest days after the battle, accounts of the events were wildly divergent, even contradictory, some of them fueling a powerful tradition of Serbian epic poetry and cultural memory that remains alive, even hotly political, still today. In any event the immediate outcome was clear: though both Lazar and Murad I died in the conflict, the battle was an Ottoman victory, and it consolidated an Ottoman presence in Europe that would last for more than five centuries.

Leading up to Kosovo, Murad and his followers had justly earned their reputation as fierce fighters. But they had also more quietly begun to prove themselves as both shrewd and flexible rulers. Rather than put conquered peoples to the sword, Murad had left them in place as protected peoples (*dhimmi*), who were expected to provide tribute and troops. The arrangements extended to the Byzantines, who had been forced to submit to Murad as early as the 1370s. The experience of Ottoman power could be brutal: coerced extractions of revenue; devastating reprisals for resistance; summons to war; youth taken captive in raids or levied in "collections" (*devşirme*) from newly subject territories, now forced to serve the ones who had invaded and conquered them. But it should be made clear that these experiences were not terribly different from experiences under the power of countless other regimes across Europe's long history. Moreover, it deserves emphasis that Ottoman rule had certain advantages. To many, it brought peace and stability, fostered trade and communication across what were often permeable cultural boundaries, and created opportunities for enrichment and advancement among those enterprising figures, many of them former Christians, who were eager to deploy their talents in the service of a new order.

In the years after the battle of Kosovo, Murad's son and successor Bayezid continued Ottoman expansion with a swiftness and boldness that earned him the compelling nickname *Yıldırım*, "Thunderbolt." He suppressed longstanding rivals in Anatolia. He married the daughter of Lazar Hrebeljanović of Serbia and recognized Lazar's son, Stefan Lazarević, as a vassal. With support from these new Christian Serbian troops Bayezid's raiders continued to subdue Bulgaria and Wallachia, and through the 1390s he worked to secure the southern shores of the Danube with a string of new fortifications. He also turned his full attention to Constantinople. Already in the early 1390s the city's hinterlands were almost entirely in the hands of Ottoman forces. In 1394 Bayezid then launched a full siege of the city. His troops blocked all entrance and exit along its ancient land walls and deployed a small fleet to interfere with any relief by sea. Food shortages, skyrocketing prices, profiteering, and all of the other sufferings of a protracted siege soon began to devastate those who remained in the beleaguered capital.[2]

During the siege, in the summer of 1396, Bayezid learned of the arrival of a crusading army from the West. A force of as many as twenty thousand troops, led by King Sigismund of Hungary, had begun to lay siege to the city of Nicopolis (modern Pleven, Bulgaria) on the Danube. The "Thunderbolt" now hastened there with ten to twenty thousand troops of his own. The armies met on September 25, the battle still one of the most famous in all of later crusading history: the valor and ambition of the heavily armed Western knights proved their undoing, as their bold advances against the sultan's infantry and archers led them right into the hands of the sultan's cavalry, Bayezid's vassal Stefan Lazarević and his Serbians among them. King Sigismund himself barely escaped with his life.

The string of conquests that culminated in the victory at Nicopolis were dramatic, but they both fostered and signaled the beginnings of a much quieter and equally decisive process of institutional growth. The precise chronology of the changes is often unclear and still contested, but the broad lines of development are clear enough: an emerging Ottoman polity was centered on the person of the Ottoman ruler – for his dominance now recognized as a sultan – who was surrounded by a court that included his extended family and an array of functionaries. An imperial council of viziers, judges, treasurers, and a chancellor all advised the sultan on major decisions regarding war and other matters of policy and administration. These deliberations were often inseparable from the affairs of the empire's new network of provinces, already taking root under Bayezid. Subject peoples who had been paying tribute and supplying troops were increasingly brought under direct Ottoman rule. Provincial governors-general (*beylerbeys*) administered justice and granted estates to the overlords of smaller districts (*sanjaks*). The oldest anchors of power remained centered on Anatolia, and above all Bursa. But the territories to the west were now of equal if not greater importance. With Edirne as its capital, the province the Ottomans called Rumelia, the "land of the Romans," would be vital for generations. The Danube and its tributaries; the old Via Egnatia and its string of cities and fortifications; their peoples, who became so many laborers, traders, and captives; and perhaps above all the region's crops, timber, and mineral resources – all of these made the region, as it had long been, a place worth fighting to keep.

The institutions and resources of the provinces in turn supported the annual advance of the sultan's growing army.[3] Older traditions of the early *gazi* warriors remained, above all in the work of the "raiders" (*akınjıs*) who sought plunder and captives along the provincial frontiers. But the heart of the sultan's force was increasingly built around several corps of elite provincial cavalry from Anatolia and Rumelia, and around a new elite infantry force, the janissaries (*yeñi çeri*). At the same time the Ottoman military had begun to learn from, and to adapt for its own purposes, the full range of tactics and technologies characteristic of "Renaissance" warfare: the art of blockades, of mining, of urban siege, as well as naval combat, at first on the waters of Central Europe's largest rivers, and eventually on the Aegean and the Mediterranean.

From the middle of the fifteenth century Ottoman forces also increasingly adopted and refined the art of combat with gunpowder weapons, their efforts often aided by founders and combat engineers from Central and Western Europe. Alongside increasingly large (if cumbersome and inefficient) cannons for destroying walls, a range of smaller mortars rained down their shells unpredictably on urban populations, while janissaries and others deployed a range of smaller firearms. One account from the later fifteenth century likely reflects what had much earlier become a standard order of battle and standard tactics: janissaries, by mid-century outfitted with handguns and other firearms, guarded a central position (and also the sultan, if he had taken the field personally). Rumelian and Anatolian cavalry guarded the wings. Regular infantry (*azaps*) occupied the most forward positions, often along with raiders who sought to draw the enemy into contact.[4]

Yet like so many other polities of the era, for all its power this early Ottoman regime in many ways remained fragile, its fate highly contingent and susceptible to sharp reversals of fortune. Only a few years after his victory at Nicopolis, Bayezid found himself facing ruin at the hands of a rival from the East. Timur (whose name, appropriately, meant "iron") arose from the Turkish and Mongol world centered on Samarkand in Transoxiana (modern Uzbekistan). By 1400 his conquests reached from India to Syria, and after he had captured Baghdad, Aleppo, and Damascus from the Mamluks, he set his sights on Bayezid. The decisive blow came at Ankara in July 1402. Timur captured Bayezid, and the Thunderbolt died in captivity. The decade and more of civil war and instability that followed not only threatened to bring an end to early Ottoman successes but also proved a decisive time of recovery and retrenchment for the Ottomans' main rival along the Danube frontier, the Christian kingdom of Hungary.[5]

Stung by his bitter defeat at Nicopolis, King Sigismund of Hungary now learned from the experience and took advantage of a season of Ottoman division and weakness. He worked to make Western European powers more aware of the Ottoman advance, especially in the era of the Council of Constance (1414–18), and lobbied successfully for aid from the Venetians and figures like Portugal's Pedro of Coimbra. Closer to home, he undertook a series of sophisticated, interwoven, longer-lasting reforms intended to establish a firm line of defense against Ottoman advances.[6] He also cultivated alliances with both his own nobility and key families in Serbia, Bosnia, and elsewhere, hoping to create a diplomatic buffer zone against Ottoman influence.[7] To that end the king's Order of the Dragon, established in 1408, proved a useful means of patronage. Sigismund also outlined a detailed system for organizing and funding troops, as well as an auxiliary force of commoners funded by peasant holdings (*portae*) across the kingdom (the *militia portialis*).[8]

But above all, Sigismund worked to strengthen his southern frontier. A key figure in that construction effort was Pipo Scolari, a Florentine merchant whose career mirrored those of the best *condottieri*, the Renaissance mercenary generals of his Italian homeland.[9] Gifted in both finance and war, he came to Hungary through his commercial ties, rose to become a valued administrator of its royal salt monopoly, and was eventually made Count of Temesvár. He was also a veteran of Nicopolis who laid claim to leading a string of victories against the Ottomans. By his death in 1426, Pipo had used his military and financial experience to help design and construct or remodel a network of modernized fortifications stretching from southeastern Hungary to the Adriatic, many of which would protect the region through the end of the fifteenth century. Perhaps more than any other military or political measure, this project made good on Hungary's claim to stand as the *antemurale Christianitatis* – the "bulwark of Christendom" against the Ottoman advance.

Among the many strategic locations across that region, Belgrade was one of the most crucial.[10] Settled atop a rocky promontory at the confluence of the Danube and the Sava rivers, the city had for centuries been a key site of settlement and fortification, reaching back to the days of Roman Singidunum. By the later Middle Ages, it was known as the "White City" to the many who fought for it, traveled through it, or lived in its streets – Latin Nandor Alba or Alba Graeca; Byzantine Veligradon; Hungarian Nándorfehérvár; German Griechisch Weissenburg; Serbian Beograd. By 1400 it was a Hungarian outpost on the Danube frontier of a border region known as the banate of Macsó, but for a time thereafter it was once again in Serbian hands. After Bayezid's capture and defeat in 1402, the Serbian prince Stefan Lazarević – whose father King Lazar had died with Murad at Kosovo, and who had fought for his new Ottoman overlord at Nicopolis – renounced the Ottomans and sought favor with both Constantinople and Hungary. He was granted the title of despot in 1402, and a year later King Sigismund of Hungary recognized him as overlord of Macsó and Belgrade. Stefan was also soon granted membership in the king's new Order of the Dragon, as well as extensive lands and privileges in Hungary.[11] In return, the prince recognized the crown of Hungary as his suzerain, worked to reorganize the banate of

Macsó in ways that rendered its military support stronger and more efficient, and served as Sigismund's watchful ally on the Danube.

Despot Stefan also shrewdly exploited his titles and privileges to establish Belgrade as a shining Serbian capital.[12] He launched an ambitious program of patronage whose many elements framed his city as a new Jerusalem. Remodeled churches and chapels in Belgrade's Lower Town recalled the Kidron Valley and Gethsemane. Relics of Constantine and of a ninth-century sainted empress, Theophano, tied it to the Holy Land and imperial glory. The literary works of figures like Constantine the Philosopher clothed the city in a sacred light.[13] But above all Stefan built up Belgrade militarily.[14] Archaeologists have now recovered his extensive restructuring of the city's defenses, an undertaking that unfolded in several phases. Stefan first had a new palace constructed on the site of older Byzantine fortifications. The same phase also saw the refurbishment of walls along the banks of the Danube and the construction of a new tower and walls to protect a small inlet on the Sava. Engineers also enclosed the site of the old Roman camp with the latest in military architecture: a ring of towers and seven-meter walls atop a stone escarpment that loomed over a deep dry moat and was armed at key positions with the latest gunpowder weapons. The new enclosure, some fifty thousand square meters in all, came to be known as the Upper Town, a settlement for local elites drawn to the despot's protection and patronage. Merchants and commoners, too, were brought to the despot's new capital, and the rapid growth of their communities fostered still more construction. As the Lower Town began to fill with these new settlers, a new run of some three hundred meters of towers and walls and escarpments enclosed it. The churches of the city were refurbished as well, above all an episcopal complex dedicated to the Dormition of Mary.[15]

Despot Stefan's death in July 1427 ushered in a period of still more transformation, both for Belgrade and for its region. By treaty, the fortress and garrison came once again under the control of King Sigismund and Hungary and were thus integrated into the king's network of Danubian fortifications.[16] In return, Hungary recognized Stefan's nephew George Branković as heir to his titles and lands in both Serbia and Hungary. A little more than a decade thereafter Serbia was all but gone, Branković on the run, Hungary on the verge of civil war, and the walls of the White City under Ottoman siege.

The most important catalyst for these rapid changes was renewed Ottoman pressure under the banners of Bayezid's grandson, Sultan Murad II. Though he seems to have been something of an ascetic figure, more inclined to literature and art than war, Murad II was nevertheless a capable and often shrewd ruler who took his position seriously and could move decisively. When the Byzantine emperor Manuel II released Murad's uncle Mustafa and supported him as an Ottoman rival, Mehmed responded with a bold, if brief, siege of Constantinople in June of 1422.[17] By 1430 Murad had captured the key Aegean port of Thessalonica. He then turned his attention more fully to Albania and to the remnants of a fragmented Serbia, now ripe for renewed exploitation.

The new despot George Branković now found himself in increasingly precarious circumstances. He continued to maintain his ties to the North, above all through the marriage of his daughter Katarina to Ulrich II of Celje in 1434. At the same time, exiled after the loss of Belgrade to the Hungarians, he sought to create another cultural capital on the Danube, this one at his new home of Smederevo. Now a home to refugees from Murad's advances to the south, the new despot's city soon boasted a remarkable library of Latin, Greek, and Slavonic texts whose coterie of readers had connections with Italian humanists. But Branković had also to yield to the constant pressure of Ottoman raids, and in 1435 he married his daughter Mara to Murad, offering Serbian territory as her dowry.[18]

The balancing act worked only for so long. In August 1439 Murad attacked and captured Smederevo and drove Branković into exile in Hungary. The next year, in early June of 1440, the sultan then launched an attack against Belgrade.[19] The Hungarians had entrusted the city to the ban (vice-regent) of Croatia, Matthew Talovac, who along with his two brothers had a prominent role in defending the region. It was Matthew's brother John, a Hospitaler and prior of Vrana on the Adriatic coast, who was now in charge as castellan, and who organized a defense against Murad. The siege, according to the brief surviving accounts of it, seems to have lasted at least until the middle of June. Murad himself took the field with his janissaries and the Rumelian guard, deployed a fleet of ships on the Danube, bombarded the city, and worked to undermine its walls. Though the sultan ultimately withdrew, his effort was a success, insofar as it seems to have been shrewdly timed to coincide with what was becoming a deep political crisis in Hungary.

King Sigismund had died in December 1437. His successor Albert II of Hapsburg had ruled for only two years, and he died suddenly in October 1439, leaving behind a pregnant widow, Elizabeth. She gave birth to their son Ladislaus (known, in the wake of his father's death, as "the Posthumous") in February 1440. Elizabeth had the infant boy crowned in May. But by June, as Sultan Murad's troops surrounded Belgrade, the Hungarian magnates rejected the child king and moved to crown Ladislaus III Jagiello of Poland as their king. Elizabeth and her son fled to the court of Holy Roman Emperor Frederick III, and the two factions went to war.

The intrigue and intricacies of these crucial months and years are less important here than they were for the career of arguably the most important figure in the events of 1456, John Hunyadi. Not least because of his role in those events, the centuries of cultural memory they inspired have transformed Hunyadi into a seemingly timeless hero. Perhaps more than any other character in Belgrade's drama he remains a hero today, shaped and reshaped by creative, sometimes divisive projects of myth and memory that have been fueled by modern ethnic and national identity. But the story of Hunyadi as a fifteenth-century figure, understood properly in his own context, is the more interesting one by far.[20]

Born around 1406, John was the son of a lesser Wallachian nobleman who in return for his service to Sigismund of Hungary had received an estate in Hunedoara (in modern Romania). By around 1430 John's own service to Sigismund had earned him access to royal circles, and in 1433 he had risen high enough to accompany the king as far as Milan on his coronation journey to Italy. There he is said to have studied the art of war in the circles of the Visconti, providing the foundation for what became his legendary military career. His earliest victories came in the civil war of 1440–1 when he sided with the magnates and Ladislaus III against Elizabeth and her infant son. With the support of the young Nicholas of Ilok, ban of Macsó from 1438 and one of the wealthiest magnates in Hungary, Hunyadi took to the field and gradually defeated the queen's forces across the kingdom's southern territories. In return, Ladislaus III granted Hunyadi titles and estates that gave him joint authority (with Nicholas of Ilok) over Transylvania and the southern counties of Hungary, as well as command over the network of fortifications protecting the Danube frontier, including Belgrade. From that position of strength Hunyadi helped bring papal negotiators to Hungary, and an end to the civil war by 1442. Hunyadi also continued to take the fight to the Ottomans. In the spring of 1442 he defeated a major offensive led by Mezid Bey, and also dealt a major defeat to Şehabeddin Pasha, beylerbey of Rumelia, in Wallachia later that same year.[21] Soon after, and more famously, Hunyadi then played a leading role in a crusade proclaimed by Eugenius IV.

Events leading to that crusade were set in motion some years before, in 1437, when a Byzantine delegation led by Emperor John VIII himself departed to Italy to negotiate a reconciliation of the centuries-old theological divisions between the Latin and Greek churches. The ultimate aim of the Byzantine delegation was to secure, in return for an agreement to unite their churches, Latin military aid for the Greeks.[22] Months of vigorous exchange and negotiation followed the delegation's arrival in Italy in 1438, much of it focused on matters that extended far beyond theology. While John VIII and others renegotiated vital commercial treaties with the Florentines, and while scholars and bookmen like Archbishop Bessarion of Nicaea and the humanist Traversari exchanged ideas and texts, theologians debated papal authority, the procession of the Holy Spirit, and the doctrine of purgatory. The negotiated settlement they reached, proclaimed on July 6, 1439, in the solemn decree *Laetentur coeli*, was worded carefully enough to allow all sides some room for preserving their own interpretations. But the decree was clear enough in its recognition of papal primacy that Eugenius IV was willing to call for a new crusade against Murad II.

By October of 1443, the campaign was underway. Led by King Ladislaus III of Poland and Hungary and John Hunyadi, an army of some twenty-five thousand Transylvanians, Hungarians, Poles, and others had moved across the Danube in a rapid, late-season campaign designed to catch the Ottomans off guard. Though the army was eventually driven back after a battle in the frozen Zlatitsa pass in December, the stories that made their way back to Buda and beyond – along with a few captured banners – were enough to inspire hope. Summer peace negotiations proved illusory, and by the fall of 1444 another land force of some twenty thousand had crossed the Danube. The decisive battle came on November 10 at Varna on the shores of the Black Sea, where a force under Murad II vastly outnumbered and soon outflanked and overwhelmed the crusaders. King Ladislaus III, who led a final charge before being captured and beheaded, was among them.[23]

But even in defeat, it had become impossible not to recognize Hunyadi's importance as an aggressive and agile leader. He had proven himself to be always willing to take his troops on the offensive, able to learn from experience, and able to adapt. At Varna and then at a second major battle at Kosovo (the site of Serbia's defeat and Murad I's death in 1389), Hunyadi continued to develop an intimate familiarity with Ottoman ways of war, including the famous tactic of feigned retreat that would play an important role in the outcome at Belgrade in 1456.[24]

It was above all this reputation as a commander that brought Hunyadi ever more political recognition.[25] In June of 1446 the Hungarian estates had appointed him as regent for the young Ladislaus V, who was at that time still the ward of Frederick III in Vienna. And even after his release and recognition as king, Ladislaus V recognized Hunyadi as "captain-general," a title that conferred broad military, financial, and administrative powers. Hunyadi was also granted the title of "perpetual count" of Beszterce (Bistrița in modern Romania). Hunyadi thereby retained his position as the de facto leader of the armies stationed along the frontiers of the "bulwark of Christendom."

In 1451, while Hunyadi was still regent, Ottoman diplomats brought offers of peace to those frontiers. They came in the name of a new sultan, Murad's son and successor Mehmed II. The terms established a three-year truce with Hungary, and with Serbia not only a truce but the return of the Serbian princess Mara – daughter of the Despot Branković, Murad II's widow after some fifteen years of marriage, and Mehmed II's mother. Hunyadi and Branković no doubt welcomed a respite from years of Ottoman pressure. But for Mehmed II the gestures of peace were only one part of a larger strategy that combined well-timed diplomacy and targeted military action, all of it a prelude to the young sultan's greatest ambition: to capture the city of Constantinople.[26]

Mehmed's first moves were to subdue the encroachments of his rival Karaman in Anatolia and to send his ambassadors to Serbia and Hungary to secure a truce along Rumelia's northern borders. He then launched a series of raids in the Peloponnesus to secure his southern flank. By August of 1452, his engineers had finished their construction of a fortress on the European shores of the Bosporus. Rumeli Hisarı (the "European castle"), also called (perhaps more descriptively) Boğazkesen, the "strait cutter" or "throat cutter," towered some two hundred feet over the waters below, as it still does today, its cannons securing control of all traffic through the crucial waterway between Europe and Asia Minor. Final preparations for the siege then began in earnest in early 1453, above all with the forging of the sultan's massive bombards. These weapons, which terrified the defenders of Constantinople and have fascinated ever since, were a marvel. The largest among them was nearly ten yards long and could cast stones weighing nearly two thousand pounds. The massive weapon, a "monster" in the words of the chronicler Doukas, was forged in Edirne, and for an arduous two months, hundreds of men and scores of oxen hauled it some 150 miles to Constantinople.[27] Mehmed II awaited its arrival there, flanked by his Rumelian and Anatolian guards and surrounded by his janissaries. It was placed in front of the Saint Romanos gate, along with three smaller guns. Nine other guns faced Constantinople's other main entrances. They began their fateful work on April 12, and within days large sections of the walls, unscathed for a thousand years, begun to crumble.

Yet for all of the sultan's might, the outcome of the siege he had begun was far from inevitable. Though the defenders of the city were far too few – some six thousand Byzantine defenders under Emperor Constantine XI, some three thousand Venetians under Giovanni Giustiniani, and a small fleet of Venetian and Genoese ships – they put up a valiant defense. They countered repeated attempts by Ottoman sappers to undermine the walls near the Blachernae palace. They worked tirelessly to repair the walls and towers ruined by the sultan's cannons. They took aim, too, with their own gunpowder weapons, many of them smaller cannons that were as accurate as they were lethal. Genoese sailors repeatedly ran the sultan's blockades to bring in supplies. Even the sultan's cannons had their limits. For all the terror they inspired, the latest weapons were inefficient and fragile – they took hours to load, fire, cool, and reload, and their overheated bronze barrels were constantly in danger of fracturing. For nearly a month, the Ottomans made relatively little progress. Only the sultan's determination, the creativity of his combat engineers, and some good fortune eventually broke the stalemate. Laborers cleared a path through the forested hills of Pera to the north, laid down tracks with greased rollers and railings, and hauled six dozen warships overland from the Bosporus Strait and down into the waters of the Golden Horn. They also constructed a pontoon bridge – some one thousand barrels tied together with iron hooks and topped with planks – across the waters of the Golden Horn to the siege army's positions outside the city. The dramatic move served its purpose as part of the sultan's larger strategy: it forced the city's defenders to stretch themselves still more thinly along its walls. Meanwhile the cannons continued their steady, grinding work. By late May the walls had been broken up enough to be scaled, the moats before them filled. The hour came for a final assault.

Early on the morning of May 29, 1453, a first wave of troops – the sultan's more expendable Christian vassals – charged the walls. A second wave of Anatolian troops followed, then a third and final wave led by Mehmed's janissaries. Amid the final charges the Venetian captain Giustiniani was wounded, and a small contingent of Ottomans slipped in a small gate near the Blachernae palace. The vivid (and often conflicting) accounts of what happened next, many of which soon evolved into myth and legend, have fueled the fascination with the story ever since: how the janissaries plundered the city's houses and churches; the flight to Hagia Sophia, where crowds of refugees awaited their deliverance at the hands of angels; how a desperate Byzantine emperor himself rushed headlong into the fight – his corpse, clad in purple shoes, later pulled from a pile of bodies, his head displayed in the center of the city until nightfall.[28] But for all of the drama of the narratives, in reality the number of casualties from the fall of the city was no more than a few thousand. A few thousand more, at most, escaped by Venetian and Genoese ships. The rest were captured and sold into slavery or left in the city to do the hard work of building a conquering sultan's new imperial capital.

Sources in Scholarly Context: The Middle Ages, the Crusades, and the Problem of "Lateness"

The craft of historical interpretation presents its practitioners – masters and apprentices alike – with a multifaceted and often paradoxical challenge of representation. As John Gaddis has noted, the historian is at once working within and as an heir to history, yet somehow positioned above and beyond it, surveying it from a supposedly impartial, detached, even "scientific" perch, yet in a way that is always culturally and personally engaged. From that position, the historian must make crucial choices about subject matter, representation, and interpretation – about where and why to focus a given inquiry; about what (or how much) to leave in or out; about proportion, scale and scope, purpose and perspective; about where and how to assign causation and meaning. All of this means that we are compelled, like a fine clothier (in Gaddis's apt metaphor), to "tailor" our representations into "fitting" representations, however partial or imperfect, of the many pasts that interest us. It means that any given work, inevitably, is both shaped by and reflective of an author's own circumstance and perspective.[29]

Historical eras, too, are subject to similar dynamics of representation. Students of early European history do well to remember that the entire structure of their field of study is predicated on a certain narrative artifice. The very concept of the "Middle Ages," after all, emerged only slowly, in the wake of so many thinkers whose partisan representations worked in some way to define their present ("reborn," "reformed," "enlightened") against a "medieval" past.[30] Each generation has done the same since, and we remain heirs, often unwittingly, to the tenacious and sometimes contradictory narratives they have left behind. Europe's formative thousand years, as it has been called, thus appears by turns as an era of darkness and semi-pagan superstition, an age of pristine faith, or as the foundation that shaped the modern world until the eighteenth century.[31]

As with the Middle Ages generally, so too with the crusades. From the earliest years of the twelfth century to our own day, each generation has read the phenomenon unleashed in 1095 through the lens of its distinct historical moment.[32] Medieval chroniclers and Renaissance historians preserved accounts of every campaign, collecting and often reshaping them in ways that reflected their own needs and experiences. In the wake of the Reformation, Protestant polemicists like John Foxe presented the crusades as a superstitious corruption of Christian ideals, while Catholics countered this understanding by holding the crusades up as an institution established in defense of the faith. Already by the seventeenth century the crusades had inspired a cacophony of competing, often contradictory interpretations: they were an expression of heroic idealism; a grand, uniting European enterprise; a marker of progress and civilization; an example of barbaric superstition, of sinful, wasteful, violent folly. It was that last strain of thought, famously, that won out in the eighteenth century.

Looking back on what had come to be called Europe's "Middle Age," leading lights of an Age of Reason poured out their vitriol on the whole era, and the crusades in particular. David Hume denounced them as "the most signal and most durable monument of human folly that has yet appeared in any age or nation," a movement that reflected a continent "sunk into profound ignorance and superstition."[33] Nineteenth-century Romantics then took their turn, recovering what they saw as the pure faith and noble idealism of the crusaders. In the twentieth century, the legacies of colonialism and two world wars, the 1960s, the Cold War and its aftermath all shaped a range of debates that remained vital through the end of the century and beyond: how to define a crusade; how to assess matters of crusader piety, intentions, and motivations; how to assess the nature of Latin rule in the Levant; how to understand ties between crusading and European culture generally.[34]

The events of September 2001 and their long global aftermath then reshaped the study of the crusades yet again. A history of armed combat between Christians and Muslims took on a new energy and urgency, not least because of so much misplaced popular enthusiasm and the inevitably distorted appropriations of crusading in the public sphere.[35] Nearly every military campaign from Urban II's call to the First Crusade in 1095 to the fall of Acre in 1291 soon received fresh treatment, and these appeared alongside a flood of new synthetic surveys, historiographical studies, textbooks, and source translations. At the same time, scholars launched a series of thematic investigations that explored the world of the crusades from fundamentally new angles, again in ways that reflected their own time. The rise of postcolonial studies and Edward Said's influential theory of Orientalism, for example, highlighted the importance of balancing Western and Christian sources and perspectives with careful studies grounded in Islamic sources and the many complex local environments of the Levant.[36] New work on a range of other themes signaled analogous shifts in other areas of crusade scholarship: in an age of revolutionary transformations in communication, for example, a fresh emphasis on preaching and propaganda, narrative and memory; in an age of performance, a turn to liturgy; and amid ongoing contemporary struggles over equality, fresh work on questions of gender.[37]

Many of these scholarly transformations are ongoing. Some have hardly only begun, or have only begun to intensify, over the last twenty years. It would be impossible to do justice to the full range of all the latest scholarly findings here. But a discussion of a few salient themes can help clarify some of the most important developments and underscore the particular contribution of this volume. The most important issue at stake concerns how scholars have come to approach the period after the supposed "end" of crusading.[38] With so much crusade scholarship having been focused – and often still focused – on the traditional topic of the campaigns of the "classical" era of the twelfth and thirteenth centuries, the story of what came after – the "crusades after the crusades," as one Italian scholar has cleverly called them – long remained in the shadows.[39] For most, the neglect was (and remains) rooted in older, half-conscious prejudices about the "later" Middle Ages generally. Just as the era was long dismissed as one of waning and crisis, so too did this perception hold with the crusade: its ideals were supposedly increasingly secularized, its institutions ineffective, its enthusiasm faltering.[40]

But from very early on, a few pioneering scholars were aware of the richness and potential of this later period. At the end of the nineteenth century, the prodigiously energetic Romanian nationalist and politician Nicolai Iorga drew together collections of key fifteenth-century documents from European libraries and archives. In the 1930s the Egyptian Aziz Atiya authored a first survey of the period in English, and in the 1970s Kenneth Setton turned to unexploited archival materials in Rome and Venice as the main sources for *The Papacy and the Levant (1204–1571)*, a massive four-volume treatment of later crusading.[41] Building on these foundations, by the 1990s a generation of scholars began to extend and refine our understanding of later crusading through at least three independent but broadly related and fruitfully overlapping scholarly efforts.

The first and most fundamental set of projects has been inspired by Norman Housley, whose early monographs on the papacy and crusading laid the foundation for two broad surveys, *The Later Crusades* and *Religious Warfare in Europe*.[42] More recently, and more directly relevant to the sources collected here, Housley and others then turned to more detailed investigations of the fifteenth century in particular. A pioneering volume of collected essays highlighted crusading propaganda and its reception and implementation.[43] Another milestone followed with Housley's *Crusading and the Ottoman Threat*, which offered a broad analysis of ideology, strategy, finance, communication, and more, each theme read against the particulars of distinct chronological periods and settings.[44] An international collaboration under Housley's direction also brought together a network of scholars from across Europe to produce a series of innovative conferences and edited volumes. Even a cursory survey of the themes treated in this corpus of essays suggests the creativity and significance of this new work and its questions: how popes, princes, cities, and other constituencies shaped and pursued goals that reflected their various perspectives and regional circumstances; how ideals became action, or failed to, with detailed attention to matters of communication, logistics, finance, and diplomacy; how crusades resonated, or failed to, through the full range of medieval culture, from liturgy and pageantry to art and literature.[45] Meanwhile, both in concert with and independently of these networks and their publications, scholars continue to fill in the broader picture with studies dedicated to a wide range of topics. Daniel Baloup has led a team of colleagues who have investigated topics ranging from strategy, logistics, and diplomacy to liturgy and memory. Benjamin Weber has authored a monumental study of the fifteenth-century papal efforts at crusade. Iulian Damian has published a monograph and several articles focused on the key figure of John of Capistrano.[46]

A second set of projects emerged from a small cohort of scholars of the Italian Renaissance. In 1995 James Hankins noted that crusading, though at the time hardly a field associated with the Renaissance, was a prominent theme in Quattrocento humanist literature, especially in the wake of Mehmed II's conquest of Constantinople. Hankins argued compellingly for what made that literature distinct: not only its classicizing style and tone, but its settings, themes, and uses, and above all its importance as a means of articulating an emerging European identity.[47] A decade later, Margaret Meserve traced the complexity of relationships between oral reports and early print for the dissemination of news surrounding the fall of Negroponte and authored a seminal monograph on the history of Islam in the writings of Renaissance humanists.[48] In a similar vein, Nancy Bisaha placed the crusades at the center of Renaissance humanists' project of shaping images of Greeks and Turks in ways that reflected and reinforced Western identity. She also authored important essays on the work of the crusading pope Pius II, and on the place of "late" crusading in the long-term development of human rights.[49] Historians of Italian Renaissance art, too, have detected crusading themes in the cultural production of the 1440s and 1450s emerging from the courts of Mantua and Ferrara.[50] Such work has helped historians further escape tired generalizations about the sterility, ineptitude, and decline of later crusading. The place of the crusades in the treatises, histories, images, objects, and other cultural products of the Renaissance reveals complex and fruitful interaction of old and new, and the resonance of crusading quite apart from its geopolitical and military failures.

Recent advances in late Byzantine and early Ottoman scholarship, to note a third cluster of projects, have also helped transform our view of fifteenth-century crusading. Well into the twentieth century, reflecting lines of interpretation that reached back to the medieval and Renaissance sources themselves, scholars often read the Latin, Byzantine, and Ottoman worlds against one another, and the story of the later crusades as an inevitable clash between mutually antagonistic civilizations.[51] But for many years now our best scholarship has fundamentally rejected such extremes and sought a more nuanced, less prejudicial account. The work of Jonathan Harris, among many others, has explored the complexities of the story that culminated in 1453. The "end of Byzantium" was something other than a story of the clash of civilizations. It was rooted precisely in the intimate connections between the Ottoman and Byzantine worlds, generations old by the middle of the fifteenth century, the result of a complex set of historical accidents, and driven by geopolitical concerns and self-interest. Meanwhile Cemal Kafadar, Daniel Goffman, and Colin Imber have made possible what Goffman has called an "Ottomancentric" scholarly view, one that seeks to reclaim the full nuance and complexity of the Ottoman world, and of its ties with Europe.[52] As Goffman has noted, the Ottoman sultans were no more or less warlike or brutal than their fifteenth-century counterparts in England, France, or Germany. The Ottomans' commercial and diplomatic ties, their cultural ambitions as heirs of Rome, even their common ground in the Abrahamic faiths, all tied them back to the "Greater Western World," even as the Ottomans also maintained a certain "responsive plasticity" that allowed them to co-opt and adapt elements from all parts of their empire, creating an enduring "Euro-Ottoman symbiosis."[53]

Amid these broader reconsiderations, scholars have turned with particular energy and focus to Eastern Europe, and especially to the region still known, however problematically, as the "Balkans." Once dismissed as backward and marginal, the region is now central to new projects that seek to decenter and rethink traditional geographies. The cultural zone that reached from Rome and central Italy across the Adriatic toward Hungary, Serbia, Romania, and the Black Sea was long a crossroads for the Latin, Greek, Slavic, and Ottoman worlds, a frontier whose complex interactions are now being sorted out more fully. It is a setting that remains difficult to access for most, not least because nationalist and Cold War legacies long shaped scholarship in the West, and especially graduate training, in ways that militated against scholarly collaboration. Discussion of the Middle Ages and the Renaissance were (and remain) for most scholars a conversation conducted in English, French, German, or Italian, not Hungarian, Romanian, Serbian, or Turkish.

More fundamentally, the "Balkans" remain in the shadows of a stubborn, lingering prejudice. Though we have worked to recover Byzantium and the Muslim world from Orientalism, scholarship on southeastern Europe has not yet been accessible enough to break the stereotype of the region as somehow backward, dark, exotic, and ambiguous. But a number of studies, many in English, have now shed light on the region in the crucial period of the fourteenth and fifteenth centuries, and the complexities of the story of the growing Ottoman presence there.[54] Debate surrounds even the most basic concepts – conquest, transition, and integration each captures something of the changes, but each also has its limits. Scholars struggle to balance evidence of accommodation (*istimalet*) and interaction with the harsh realities of raiding, warfare, enslavement and deportation, rebellion and resistance.[55] In that setting, a frontier so vibrant with new winners and losers, crusading appears as only one of the region's many possibilities for military and diplomatic engagement; a symbolically and ideologically charged option, but one whose tremendous potential energy nevertheless had to be set off by particular circumstances. Within such a framework, the career of John Hunyadi and the Crusade of Varna (1444) have recently received more detailed treatment, as has the broad sweep of Ottoman-Hungarian conflict from the fourteenth through the sixteenth centuries.[56]

In light of these new directions, the history of crusading has become one of the most energized and challenging fields in the study of medieval history overall. This volume offers itself as a modest contribution to that field. In one sense, it makes no claim to originality. At its center is a story whose main outlines, main characters, and challenges of interpretation have been well known for a very long time.[57] But these sources have never been fully drawn together for a wider audience in quite the way they have been here. They are presented as a focused case study that both renders Belgrade's story more accessible and in doing so also raises a number of broad issues of method and interpretation. The final section of this introduction articulates how the sources and structure of this volume engage many of these issues.

Framing the Sources: Selection, Structure, and Significance

Source collections, like all works of scholarship, position themselves within certain debates and frame their own issues and arguments. Their selection of materials, the manner in which the material is excerpted and arranged, introduced and annotated, all reflect an effort to raise issues and stake claims, implicitly or otherwise. This collection is no exception. It seeks to make clear through source material on Belgrade how this crusade reflected the full range and vitality of fifteenth-century culture. The collection also highlights the ways in which Belgrade, perhaps more than any other crusade of its era, poses distinct challenges of interpretation. A survey of the sources presented here, the story they tell, and the structure of their presentation will prepare the way for readers to make sense of it all for themselves.

On June 29, 1453, one month to the day after the start of the siege of Constantinople, refugees brought word of the sultan's victory to Venice. By early July, Serbians and Venetians had brought the news to Austria, and soon after the news finally reached Rome itself. Among the most powerful reactions was that of the humanist churchman Aeneas Silvius Piccolomini, the future Pope Pius II, who wrote to Pope Nicholas V from Austria. "I grieve that Saint Sophia, the most famous church in all the world has been ruined or polluted," Aeneas famously lamented. "Here is a second death for Homer, and for Plato too."[58] By early fall, Pope Nicholas V, the former Tomasso Parentucelli, whose love of books and buildings helped shape his reputation as the famed "Renaissance" pope, was at work on the formal call to crusade *Etsi ecclesia Christi*, issued on September 30, 1453 (document 1).[59] In February 1454, Duke Philip of Burgundy responded by staging an elaborate feast, the famous "Feast of the Pheasant," in which he demonstrated – at least by way of a splendid performance – his serious intention to uphold his family's tradition of crusading.[60]

Meanwhile diplomats made their way to other courts across Western Europe in the hopes of organizing whatever response to the call might be forthcoming. Their efforts had met with fragile success in Italy by the following April, when the rival powers of the peninsula agreed to the Peace of Lodi.[61] To the north, a series of three diets met over the next year.[62] At Regensburg in May the results were ephemeral. Nicholas V, wary of councils, and Emperor Frederick III, wary of both the pope and his many other rivals, both stayed away. Those who did attend – Philip the Good of Burgundy and Margrave, Albrecht Achilles, among others – could agree only to hold another meeting at Frankfurt in October. At that meeting Piccolomini, a leading humanist of the day, delivered the stunning oration "The Fall of Constantinople" (*Constantinopolitana clades*) (document 2).[63] But the complexities of collective mobilization strangled any real results, and only preliminary agreements could be made at the second diet, among them to hold a third assembly at Wiener Neustadt in February of 1455. As that diet concluded in April, word arrived that Nicholas V had died after a long illness. Shortly after, news came that Mehmed II had conquered the Serbian city of Novo Brdo, along with its silver mines (document 3.1). Nearly two years of planning seemed to be getting nowhere.

The election of Nicholas V's successor reinvigorated the faltering enterprise. On April 8, 1455, the college of cardinals chose an aging Catalan bishop, Alfonso de Borja, as a compromise candidate. Many thought the seventy-seven-year-old would be an easy mark for political manipulation.[64] But as Pope Callixtus III, he took to the cause of crusading with surprising vigor and conviction. In May 1455 he reissued Nicholas V's call from the previous September, adding practical clarifications regarding its provisions. He took firm control of a reformed and refocused institutional apparatus of preachers and indulgence collectors, especially those active in Italy.[65] He sent legates to the courts of Western Europe's major powers, funded and built a crusading fleet to operate in the Aegean, and set a departure date of March 1, 1456.

Among the new pope's most important allies in this renewed effort was John of Capistrano, a Franciscan friar from central Italy who more than any other figure became the most visible and vocal leader of the new crusade.[66] Friar John was at the height of his career in Italy as a reformer and popular preacher in April of 1451, when his reputation drew the attention of Emperor Frederick III and his secretary

Piccolomini. They invited Friar John to come north to Vienna. He was armed not only with his own forceful personality and intellectual skill but also with the relics of his recently sainted mentor Bernardino of Siena, whose canonization Capistrano himself had largely orchestrated. The friar preached to crowds in the thousands, and his popularity quickly propelled him on a tour that ensured he would never return to his homeland. Over the next two years he traveled from Austria and the borders of Bohemia across Saxony, Silesia, Poland, and Moravia, preaching hundreds of sermons (with the aid of his interpreters) whose full cycles sometimes lasted days on end.

By 1455 events had transformed the friar's mission into a crusade. In the summer of that year, he began an ambitious preaching tour that took him through Hungary, Transylvania, and Romania – "to the farthest frontiers of Christendom," as he himself put it in one letter (document 3.5). Throughout the journey, over some twelve months and perhaps four hundred miles in all, Capistrano channeled all of his considerable talent and energy – and his often irascible temperament – into recruiting and organizing a volunteer army that could serve effectively in the field. Together with Cardinal Juan Carvajal, papal legate to Hungary, he worked to negotiate the fraught relationships among the Hungarian princes and others along Europe's southeastern frontier (documents 3.5–3.8). Capistrano had also to work with Hunyadi, who as a seasoned warrior was understandably skeptical of, and on occasion openly irritated at, the prospect of so many untrained volunteers thrusting their way onto the battlefield (document 3.9). An assembly for planning the campaign against Mehmed opened at Buda on February 6, 1456, and on February 14 Carvajal solemnly proclaimed Callixtus III's crusading bull to the crowd. Capistrano himself proudly took the cross from the legate, and over the next months he worked tirelessly to raise an army of volunteers. By late June, as the armies began to gather before Belgrade, Callixtus III issued a solemn bull, *Cum his superioribus* (document 5.1), calling all of Europe to prayer, and offering generous indulgences in return for their devotion. Soon after, Capistrano wrote a hurried appeal to the region's princes: if they did not want to fight the Turks in their very homes, they should hasten to Belgrade to join the fight there (document 3.10).

The evidence of that fight, which began only days after Capistrano's last letter, is at once abundant and problematic. Part II of this volume presents a collection of seven accounts from three eyewitnesses to the events: John of Capistrano, John Hunyadi, and John of Tagliacozzo, one of Capistrano's closest followers. Capistrano and Hunyadi wrote three letters each (documents 7–11 and 13), all but one of them within days of the battle – and one of them, Capistrano's first, written within hours after its conclusion. Though brief, these letters thus seem to provide remarkably immediate access to the battle for Belgrade through the eyes of its two leading protagonists. Tagliacozzo's letter, somewhat longer and composed only a week after the battle, provides still another direct witness (document 12).

Part III then follows the news of the events as it echoed across Central and Western Europe. Its mix of private letters and public diplomatic correspondence illustrates the complex short-term dynamics of communication and flow of information after Belgrade, which in principle remained an active campaign after the raising of the siege. In these texts we see a pope and a king basking in the glow of a shocking underdog victory (document 21), a legate's pleas for secular powers to capitalize on the victory's momentum (document 15), a city council spreading joyous news (document 18), and private correspondents caught in a swirl of rumor and lamenting the confusion of a campaign whose sudden and unexpected victory caught everyone by surprise (document 14).

Following these brief accounts, Part IV contains John of Tagliacozzo's *Story of the Victory of Belgrade* (document 25). This text, too, is a letter, sent to John's Franciscan brother, James of the Marches, on the fourth anniversary of the battle for Belgrade. In one respect its basic structure and many elements of its account share much with Tagliacozzo's early report from the immediate aftermath of the battle. But this later account is also quite different, and much more complex. It is a long, richly detailed, and dramatic account that has long stood as easily the most important single source for the battle itself.[67]

Collectively the documents in Parts II–IV thus provide the main outlines of the key events of 1456. By the first week in July a large Ottoman force had encircled Belgrade. A flotilla of two hundred ships and over sixty galleys positioned itself on the Danube. On the land before the walls of the city, a force of perhaps as many as sixty thousand was digging in, so many in number that their white tents seemed (as Tagliacozzo put it) to cover the land "like snow." Their formation most likely reflected the standard Ottoman deployment for a siege – the sultan, on higher ground and guarded by his janissaries, at the center, with Rumelian and Anatolian cavalry guarding the wings. Meanwhile combat engineers erected the series of earthworks and artillery positions that would take down the walls of the fortress. The defenders of Belgrade, watching it all unfold, numbered a pitiful fraction of their besiegers: a garrison of some seven thousand soldiers under the command of Hunyadi's brother-in-law, Michael Szilágyi.

In early July, the sultan's guns roared to life. The walls of the ancient Danube town in the end stood no chance. Soon after, Hunyadi made his way down to the city with a flotilla on the Danube, supported by a relief army moving along the shore. The overall numbers are difficult to pin down, not least because the flow of troops caused the force to fluctuate considerably – estimates range from ten to thirty thousand.[68] In any event, Hunyadi's own hardened veterans and mercenaries formed the core of the force. The rest were Capistrano's untrained mob of volunteers: the farmers, artisans, and clerics he had recruited in the spring and early summer of 1456 across southern Hungary.

The first combat came on July 14, when Hunyadi's ships, supported by locals from the port at Belgrade, engaged the Ottoman blockade northwest of the city. Hunyadi's ships broke through, and after several hours of fighting on the water they had captured or sunk most of the ships in the Ottoman fleet. The relief army moved into Belgrade, and Capistrano's followers camped across the Sava River at Semlin. Over the next days, Ottoman cannons continued to blast away at Belgrade's walls, and mortars terrified the inhabitants of the city. The guns fell silent on July 20, and on the evening of July 21 the sultan launched a full ground assault. Light infantry led the way, followed by the elite janissaries. They were soon able to break through the many gaps in the walls that had been opened up by the cannons. In part their advance may have been possible because Hunyadi had deliberately withdrawn to the citadel that Stefan Lazarević had refurbished decades before. From there the garrison's defenders launched a counterattack that drove the Ottomans from the Upper Town. The fighting among the ruined walls was fierce – as Hunyadi later recalled, in an oft-repeated line, it unfolded "not in a fortress, but in a field" – and seems to have lasted well into the next day.

Mehmed and his generals soon realized that the city would not fall so easily, and they changed tactics. The sultan ordered a feigned retreat, hoping to draw the defenders out for a battle in the open field. It was a tactic Hunyadi knew well, and he ordered his troops to hold back. Capistrano's followers, though, seem not to have known, or not to have cared. They advanced across the Sava, by some accounts under Capistrano's direction, and began pillaging the abandoned Ottoman positions. A full counterattack soon erupted. Whether by accident or by design, the end result was the same: Belgrade's defenders captured the Ottoman artillery positions and drove the sultan's troops all the way back to his own tents. There, again, Mehmed himself is said by at least some accounts to have been wounded, and to have killed many with his own hands. Reinforcements soon arrived to prevent a total rout, but by nightfall the conqueror of Constantinople had been forced to retreat.

Such is the basic story in broad, often vivid outline. Yet even as they reveal that story, the sources in Parts II–IV in other respects repeatedly undermine its coherence. Careful reading shows these accounts to be by turns incomplete, competing, even contradictory on key points. In part the issue is as old as Thucydides: in the chaos of battle, inevitably, accounts of what happened, even from eyewitnesses, are partial and confused. But the problem is also rooted in the fact that so many stakeholders sought, from the earliest moments after the battle, to appropriate its events for their various purposes. Capistrano's first letters are radically different, in some ways, from Hunyadi's. Other reports in the days and weeks that followed were shaped by the complex intersection of fact and rumor, of oral and written reports. In that respect they also represent another instance of the rapid dissemination (and distortions) of information via what for this era can properly be called "news."[69] These sources thus present a rich paradox: on the one hand, we have an abundance of detailed accounts of an event, many from those who lived through them and who wrote only days, even hours, after its unfolding. On the other hand, we have so many perspectives, and so many different accounts, that the exact course of some of the crucial moments of the siege has never been fully understood. As one leading scholar put it over sixty years ago, Belgrade "is one of those historical events that remain inadequately known despite an abundance of source material, because from the very outset the eyewitness reports were used as partisan documents."[70] Figuring out "what happened" has therefore long proven tenaciously difficult.

Recent scholarship has begun to ask different questions, however, and thus to change what is at stake in these texts. For decades now historians have developed more sophisticated theoretical frameworks around the idea of history as narrative representation, and in that context Marcus Bull has recently framed a new interpretive challenge for crusade studies: greater awareness of the complexities involved in moving from personal experience of an event to a supposedly unmediated "eyewitness" narrative.[71] Meanwhile others have emphasized the role of history and historical narrative in shaping collective cultural memory. In light of this work, students of the crusades now confront the idea that our sources never merely narrate facts; those sources are also themselves culturally positioned representations, each of which reflects the distinct perspectives, needs, and experiences – whether on the battlefield or far from it – of those who lived through the crusading era.[72]

These kinds of approaches have begun to shape recent scholarship on crusading narratives, such as those about Mehmed II's siege of Rhodes in 1480, which have now been edited and studied with great care.[73] These new approaches are of clear relevance in our readings on Belgrade. In part they help explain – and enliven – the many gaps and contradictions across the patchwork of evidence found in the sources gathered in Parts II and III of this volume. They help make sense of the ways in which key facts of the battle were not only contested, but shaped and appropriated for self-serving purposes. Callixtus III, for example, who called Europe to prayer on the eve of the battle (document 5), who trumpeted the victory in so many letters afterward (document 21), and who commemorated it with an elaborate new liturgical feast whose legacy remains alive in modern Hungary (document 24), was only one of many figures who sought to make the most of the story. Attentiveness to the dynamics of narrative, memory, and propaganda also help explain how these sources can so effortlessly combine "eyewitness" experience and compellingly vivid, realistic detail with propaganda rooted in omens and pious miracle stories. Scholars long sought to separate "fact" from "pious fiction" in these accounts, the real and reliable from the fantastical. In light of recent work, however, that is perhaps a somewhat misguided line of inquiry. The sources collected in Parts II–IV allow readers to puzzle over the evidence and wrestle with the interpretative challenge for themselves.

A final section, Part V, extends these readings into the realm of long-term cultural memory. In the years and decades after 1456, a diverse cohort of authors recycled, revised, and reshaped the earliest accounts of the battle and brought its story to life anew in a range of genres: chronicles, memoirs, letters, sermons, liturgies, poems, images, and sculptures. Only a small portion of this material can be presented in Part V, which focuses mainly on passages from a few of the most familiar chronicles of the fifteenth century. While the clerical perspectives of an Austrian priest shaped the work of a figure like Thomas Ebendorfer (document 26), the cultural aspirations of the "Renaissance" royal court of Hunyadi's son Matthias Corvinus shaped the account of the notary John Thurocz (document 31). In the same years a range of chroniclers from the Ottoman world stitched the story of Belgrade into their larger accounts. Eyewitnesses like the merchant Jacopo Promontorio (document 29) and the Serbian janissary Konstantin Mihailović (document 34) offered brief but vivid accounts of the events in their memoirs. Greek authors like Chalkokondyles (document 27) and Kritoboulos (document 28) clothed Mehmed II's loss in a classical light, while Ottoman chroniclers (documents 30, 32, and 33) subsumed the sultan's defeat into a larger story of the inevitable rise of a new and glorious Ottoman regime.[74] Even these few selections are enough to show how strongly the story of the battle continued to resonate long after the summer of 1456, and how forcefully the era's dynamics of narrative, memory, and propaganda remained at work.

Conclusion: Belgrade as a Fifteenth-Century Event

The era of "later" crusading has long been somewhat peripheral to a story grounded in an earlier, supposedly golden, age of Urban II and Bohemond, Richard and Saladin, Enrico Dandalo and Louis IX. To the extent that this may still be true, this volume offers itself as another resource for integrating the later story with the earlier. Its texts provide another space for students and scholars to explore the richness of the "later" period on its own terms, and to work through points of comparison and contrast, continuity and change. Readers may discern in these sources a range of issues of organization and logistics, for example, that are in one sense familiar carryovers from earlier campaigns: the call to crusade, indulgences, diplomacy, preaching, rituals of taking the cross. They may also discern evidence of what military historians have called the "face of battle."[75] Tagliacozzo's extended narrative, in particular, offers up striking representations of what must have been the human experience, and heavy human cost, of armed combat: the confusion and horrors of the fight; women caring for the wounded and dying, and sometimes pressed into desperate battlefield roles; harried refugees and humiliated captives; bodies burned, lacerated, ritually humiliated, rotting. There are other glimpses of the experience as well: the sultan's massive army and its janissaries, to say nothing of his thunderous cannons; innocents terrified by his mortar rounds; the resonance of humanist oratory and historiography; the energies of fifteenth-century piety and prophecy; and perhaps above all the energy of a crusader camp filled with commoners, by turns raucous, violent, populist, and pious, even musical – all of it shaped and harnessed by a stern Observant Franciscan who was both powerfully steeped in and also unafraid to manipulate its loyalty.

More broadly than these issues of continuity and change in the history of crusading itself, these sources also speak to the distinctiveness of the era of Belgrade generally. Students still too often encounter that era in fragmented and competing ways. For some, it is the heart of the "late" Middle Ages: an era of famine, plague, and war, of peasant rebellion and crisis in the church, all of it ending in reforms that anticipated the Reformation. For others, it is the Quattrocento, an age of humanists and their love of the Ancients. For still others it is the beginning of the "early modern," an elusive time of transition from Christendom to Europe, to sovereignty, secular diplomacy, and revolutionary changes in military affairs.[76] Amid so many competing narratives, each with its own compellingly broad vistas, these sources have the power to draw the era's many strands together. Belgrade emerges as a story that reflects the multiplicity of the "late-medieval," with its indulgences and war masses, Capistrano's revivalist preaching, and the populist piety of the Holy Name of Jesus among his poor followers. Yet it is also a story whose dynamics intersect with traditionally "Renaissance" themes – a future pope's humanist oratory; Gutenberg's earliest typesetting, used for Callixtus's bulls; the frenetic travel, diplomacy, and communication among fifteenth-century cultural brokers; the textual communities of northern European monks, scholastics, humanists, and historians who remembered Belgrade, and many crusades besides, for generations after 1456. All of this is reflective of what scholars now recognize as a distinctly vibrant fifteenth-century religious and cultural landscape.[77]

NOTES

1. For an accessible but substantive overview of the material surveyed here, see Paul Cobb, *The Race for Paradise: An Islamic History of the Crusades* (Oxford: Oxford University Press, 2014), especially ch. 9. See also Colin Imber, *The Ottoman Empire, 1300–1481* (Istanbul: Isis Press, 1990); Daniel Goffman, *The Ottoman Empire and Early Modern Europe* (Cambridge: Cambridge University Press, 2002); and Cemal Kafadar, *Between Two Worlds: The Construction of the Ottoman State* (Berkeley: University of California Press, 1995). For Byzantine perspectives, an accessible overview is Jonathan Harris, *The End of Byzantium* (New Haven, CT: Yale University Press, 2010). For the Balkan world, John Fine's *The Late Medieval Balkans: A Critical Survey from the Late Twelfth Century to the Ottoman Conquest* (Ann Arbor: University of Michigan Press, 1994) remains an important starting point. See also Nikolay Antov, *The Ottoman "Wild West": The Balkan Frontier in the Fifteenth and Sixteenth Centuries* (Cambridge: Cambridge University Press, 2017).
2. For a brief survey, see Harris, *End of Byzantium*, 7–14. See n. 1 above in this introduction. For more details on the devastating economic consequences of the siege, see Nevra Necipoğlu, *Byzantium between the Ottomans and the Latins: Politics and Society in the Late Empire* (Cambridge: Cambridge University Press, 2009), ch. 7.
3. The best overview remains Imber, *Ottoman Empire*, ch. 7, especially 252–80. See n. 1 above in this introduction.
4. Imber, *Ottoman Empire*, 276–7. See n. 1 above in this introduction.
5. Pál Engel, *The Realm of St. Stephen: A History of Medieval Hungary, 895–1526*, trans. Tamás Pálosfalvi (London: Tauris, 2005). For military affairs, also see Tamás Pálosfalvi, *From Nicopolis to Mohács: A History of Ottoman-Hungarian Warfare, 1389–1526* (Leiden: Brill, 2018), especially chs. 1–2.
6. Mark Whelan, "Catastrophe or Consolidation? Sigismund's Response to Defeat after the Crusade of Nicopolis (1396)," in *Between Worlds: The Age of the Jagiellonians*, ed. Christopher Nicholson, Johannes Preiser-Kapeller, and Florin Ardelean (Frankfurt: Peter Lang, 2013), 215–27; Pálosfalvi, *From Nicopolis to Mohács*, 18–25. See n. 5 above in this introduction.
7. Fine, *Late Medieval Balkans*, 457–66. See n. 1 above in this introduction.
8. András Borosy, "The *Militia Portalis* in Hungary Before 1526," in *From Hunyadi to Rákóczi. War and Society in Late Medieval and Early Modern Hungary*, ed. János M. Bak and Béla K. Király (New York: Brooklyn College Press, 1982), 63–80.
9. For basic biographical information on Pipo Scolari, see "Pipo of Ozora (1369–1426)," in *The Oxford Encyclopedia of Medieval Warfare and Military Technology*, ed. Clifford Rogers (Oxford: Oxford University Press, 2010). See also Katalin Prajda, "The Florentine Scolari Family at the Court of Sigismund of Luxemburg in Buda," *Journal of Early Modern History* 14 (2010): 513–33.
10. The best general overview of the city of Belgrade remains the account of Marko Popović, *Beogradska Tvrdjava* [*The Fortress of Belgrade*] (Belgrade: Beograd Arheološki Institut, 2006), with a helpful English summary at 321–31.
11. Fine, *Late Medieval Balkans*, 500–2, 509–10. See n. 1 above in this introduction. See also Mihailo Popović, "The Order of the Dragon and the Serbian Despot

Stefan Lazarević," in *Emperor Sigismund and the Orthodox World*, ed. Ekaterini Mitsiou (Vienna: Austrian Academy of Sciences, 2010), 103–6.
12 Popović, *Beogradska Tvrdjava*, especially the English summary at 320–25. See n. 10 above in this introduction.
13 For accessible English-language treatments of art and culture in the age of Stefan Lazarević, see the recent work of Jelena Erdeljan, e.g., *Chosen Places: Constructing New Jerusalems in Slavia Orthodoxa* (Leiden: Brill, 2017), especially 178–87, and "Strategies of Constructing Jerusalem in Medieval Serbia," in *Visual Constructs of Jerusalem*, ed. Bianca Kühnel, Galit Noga-Banai, and Hanna Vorholt (Turnhout: Brepols, 2014), 231–40.
14 Miloš Ivanović, "Militarization of the Serbian State under Ottoman Pressure," *Hungarian Historical Review* 8 (2019): 390–410; Marko Šuica, "Effects of the Early Ottoman Conquests on the State and Social Structure of the Lazarević Principality," in *State and Society in the Balkans before and after Establishment of Ottoman Rule*, ed. Srđan Rudić and Selim Aslantaş (Belgrade: Belgrade Institute of History, 2017), 7–19.
15 Popović, *Beogradska Tvrdjava*, 324. See n. 10 above in this introduction.
16 See Pálosfalvi, *From Nicopolis to Mohács*, 70 and n62 for the disputes surrounding this turn of events. See n. 5 above in this introduction.
17 For a brief but vivid portrait of Murad II, and a survey of the events of 1422, see Harris, *End of Byzantium*, 90–6. See n. 1 above in this introduction. See also Franz Babinger, *Mehmed the Conqueror and His Time* (Princeton, NJ: Princeton University Press, 1978), 5–10.
18 Fine, *Late Medieval Balkans*, 529–30. See n. 1 above in this introduction. For Mara's remarkable story see Mihailo St. Popović, *Mara Branković: Eine Frau zwischen dem christlichen und dem islamischen Kulturkreis im 15. Jahrhundert* (Mainz: Rutzen, 2010).
19 For a succinct recent summary of the siege and its sources, see John Jefferson, *The Holy Wars of King Wladislas and Sultan Murad: The Ottoman-Christian Conflict from 1438–1444* (Leiden: Brill, 2012), 235–46.
20 For a general overview, see the essays in *Extincta est lucerna orbis: John Hunyadi and His Time*, ed. Ana Dumitran, Lajos-Loránd Mádly, and Alexandru Simon (Cluj-Napoca: IDC Press, 2009).
21 Pálosfalvi, *From Nicopolis to Mohács*, 92–105, is attentive to the challenge of the scant or otherwise problematic source material for these events. See n. 5 above in this introduction.
22 Harris, *End of Byzantium*, ch. 6. See n. 1 above in this introduction. See also the essays in Giuseppe Alberigo, ed., *Christian Unity. The Council of Ferrara-Florence* (Leuven: Leuven University Press, 1991).
23 Primary sources for the campaign as a whole are found in Colin Imber, *The Crusade of Varna, 1443–45* (Aldershot, UK: Ashgate, 2006). The introduction to Imber's volume also provides excellent context. See also Imber, "The Crusade of Varna, 1443–1445: What Motivated the Crusaders?," in *The Religions of the Book. Christian Perceptions, 1400–1660*, ed. Matthew Dimmock and Andrew Hadfield

(London: Palgrave Macmillan, 2008), 45–65. See also the comprehensive campaign history by Jefferson, *The Holy Wars of King Wladislas and Sultan Murad*. See n. 19 above in this introduction.

24 Pálosfalvi, *From Nicopolis to Mohács*, 141–66 (see n. 5 above in this introduction); Emanuel Antoche, "Hunyadi's Campaign of 1448 and the Second Battle of Kosovo Polje (October 17–20)," in *Reconfiguring the Fifteenth-Century Crusade*, ed. Norman Housley (London: Palgrave McMillan, 2017), 245–84.

25 See the succinct summary of Hunyadi's rise in Pálosfalvi, *From Nicopolis to Mohács*, 92–105. See n. 5 above in this introduction.

26 For this famous campaign, in addition to the older account of Babinger, *Mehmed the Conqueror*, 75–101 (see n. 17 above in this introduction), see both the accessible account of Harris, *The End of Byzantium*, especially chs. 8–9 (see n. 1 above in this introduction), and above all the monumental study of Marios Philippides and Walter K. Hanak, *The Siege and the Fall of Constantinople in 1453: Historiography, Topography, and Military Studies* (London: Routledge, 2011).

27 Philippides and Hanak, *Siege and Fall*, 413–29. See n. 26 above in this introduction. For general context see also Imber, *Ottoman Empire*, 269–71 (see n. 1 above in this introduction) and more fully Gábor Ágoston, *Guns for the Sultan: Military Power and the Weapons Industry in the Ottoman Empire* (Cambridge: Cambridge University Press, 2009).

28 For a sampling of the stories see Babinger, *Mehmed the Conqueror*, 93–4 (see n. 17 above in this introduction), and for a comprehensive analysis see Phillipides and Hanak, *Siege and Fall*, ch. 4, especially 231–9 (see n. 26 above in this introduction).

29 John Lewis Gaddis, *The Landscape of History: How Historians Map the Past* (Oxford: Oxford University Press, 2002).

30 A useful scholarly appraisal appears in Timothy Reuter, "Medieval: Another Tyrannous Construct?" *The Medieval History Journal* 1 (1998): 25–45. A more popular appraisal is in Jacques LeGoff, *Must We Divide History into Periods?*, trans. M. B. DeBevoise (New York: Columbia University Press, 2015).

31 On this complex dynamic with respect to issues of religious history, see the still foundational essay by John Van Engen, "The Christian Middle Ages as an Historiographical Problem," *The American Historical Review* 91 (1986): 519–52. For a North American perspective see also the reflections of Paul Freedman and Gabrielle M. Spiegel, "Medievalisms Old and New: The Rediscovery of Alterity in North American Medieval Studies," *The American Historical Review* 103, no. 3 (1998): 677–704. For a challenging reconsideration of periodization see Constantin Fasolt, "Hegel's Ghost: Europe, the Reformation, and the Middle Ages," *Viator* 39 (2008): 345–86.

32 A strong account of this rich history is available in Christopher Tyerman, *The Debate on the Crusades* (Manchester: Manchester University Press, 2011).

33 Accessible selections from Hume can be found in *The Crusades: A Reader*, ed. S.J. Allen and Emilie Amt, 2nd ed. (Toronto: University of Toronto Press, 2014), 388–92 (here 388 and 390).

34 A good synthesis up to the early 2000s is available in Norman Housley, *Contesting the Crusades* (Oxford: Blackwell, 2006). See also the essays collected in the multivolume survey edited by Andrew Jotischky, *The Crusades* (London: Routledge, 2008).

35 See generally the essays collected in Andrew Albin, Mary Carpenter Erler, Thomas O'Donnell, Nicholas L. Paul, and Nina Rowe, eds., *Whose Middle Ages? Teachable Moments for an Ill-Used Past* (New York: Fordham University Press, 2019), and for the crusades especially, see the contributions of Nicholas Paul ("Modern Intolerance and the Medieval Crusades," at 34–43) and Adam Bishop ("#DeusVult," at 256–64), both with suggestions for further reading. See also Jonathan Phillips and Mike Horswell, eds., *Perceptions of the Crusades from the Nineteenth to the Twenty-First Century* (Andover: Routledge, 2018) and Mike Horswell and Akil N. Awan, eds., *The Crusades in the Modern World* (Andover: Routledge, 2018).

36 Carole Hillenbrand, *The Crusades: Islamic Perspectives* (Edinburgh: Edinburgh University Press, 2012) and Cobb, *The Race for Paradise* (see n. 1 above in this introduction).

37 Foundational works on preaching include Penny J. Cole, *The Preaching of the Crusades to the Holy Land, 1095–1270* (Cambridge, MA: Medieval Academy of America, 1991) and Christoph T. Maier, *Preaching the Crusades: Mendicant Friars and the Cross in the Thirteenth Century* (Cambridge: Cambridge University Press, 2003). On the importance of narrative, see Marcus Bull and Damien Kempf, eds., *Writing the Early Crusades: Text, Transmission and Memory* (Woodbridge, UK: Boydell, 2014), and on memory, Megan Cassidy-Welch, ed., *Remembering the Crusades and Crusading* (London: Routledge, 2017). On liturgy see M. Cecilia Gaposchkin, *Invisible Weapons: Liturgy and the Making of Crusade Ideology* (Ithaca, NY: Cornell University Press, 2017), and on gender Susan Edgington and Sarah Lambert, eds., *Gendering the Crusades* (New York: Columbia University Press, 2002) and also Natasha R. Hodgson, Katherine J. Lewis, and Matthew M. Mesley, eds., *Crusading and Masculinities* (London: Routledge, 2019).

38 Housley, *Contesting the Crusades*, ch. 6. See n. 34 above in this introduction.

39 Marco Pellegrini, *Le crociate dopo le crociate: da Nicopoli a Belgrado (1396–1456)* (Bologna: Il mulino, 2013).

40 For a general assessment of the era, see Howard Kaminsky, "From Lateness to Waning to Crisis. The Burden of the Later Middle Ages," *Journal of Early Modern History* 4 (2000): 85–125. Revealing for contemporary scholars' approaches to periodization and the crusades is a recent online bibliographical project, which asked this generation's leading historians to reflect on "the most important books on the crusades" (https://apholt.com/2017/07/27/historians-rank-the-most-important-books-on-the-crusades). A cursory survey of their reflections suggests that only around two percent of the titles that came to mind concerned themselves with the period after 1291. I am grateful to my colleague Michael Cervera for this reference.

41 Nicolai Iorga, *Notes et extraits pour servir à l'histoire des croisades au XV. siècle*, vol. 4, 1453–1476 (Bucharest: Acad. Roumaine, 1915); Aziz Suryal Atiya, *The Crusade in the Later Middle Ages* (London: Meuthen, 1938; repr., New York: Kraus, 1970); Kenneth M. Setton, *The Papacy and the Levant (1204–1571)*, 4 vols. (Philadelphia: American Philosophical Society, 1976–8). For an appraisal of these works in the larger arc of historiography, see Tyerman, *The Debate on the Crusades*, 200–11 and especially 208–11. See n. 32 above in this introduction.

42 Norman Housley, *The Later Crusades, 1274-1580: From Lyons to Alcazar* (New York: Oxford University Press, 1992) and *Religious Warfare in Europe, 1400-1536* (Oxford: Oxford University Press, 2002).
43 Norman Housley, ed. *Crusading in the Fifteenth Century: Message and Impact* (Basingstoke, UK: Macmillan, 2004). The introduction is especially useful for its broad appraisal of the field of "late" crusading to the end of the twentieth century, and especially of the foundational work of Iorga and Setton.
44 Norman Housley, *Crusading and the Ottoman Threat, 1453-1505* (Oxford: Oxford University Press, 2012).
45 Norman Housley, ed., *The Crusade in the Fifteenth Century: Converging and Competing Cultures* (London: Routledge, 2017) and Housley, ed., *Reconfiguring the Fifteenth-Century Crusade* (see n. 24 above in this introduction).
46 Daniel Baloup and Manuel Sánchez Martínez, eds., *Partir en croisade à la fin du Moyen Âge: financement et logistique* (Toulouse: Presses universitaires du Midi, 2015); Daniel Baloup, Benoît Joudiou, and Jacques Paviot, eds., *Les projets de croisade: géostratégie et diplomatie européenne du XIVe au XVIIe siècle* (Toulouse: Presses Universitaires du Mirail, 2014); Benjamin Weber, *Lutter contre les Turcs: les formes nouvelles de la croisade pontificale au XVe siècle* (Rome: École française de Rome, 2013); Iulian M. Damian, *Ioan de Capestrano și Cruciada Târzie* (Cluj-Napoca: Academia Română/Centrul de Studii Transilvane, 2011).
47 James Hankins, "Renaissance Crusaders: Humanist Crusade Literature in the Age of Mehmed II," *Dumbarton Oaks Papers* 49 (1995): 111-207. Hankins credits humanist crusading literature with an "articulation of a new secular identity for western Europe" (123) and with the development of the idea of the West as the "true heir to Greek and Latin antiquity, and therefore the heartland of civilization" (124).
48 Margaret Meserve, "News from Negroponte: Politics, Popular Opinion, and Information Exchange in the First Decade of the Italian Press," *Renaissance Quarterly* 59 (2006): 440-80; and *Empires of Islam in Renaissance Historical Thought* (Cambridge, MA: Harvard University Press, 2008).
49 Nancy Bisaha, *Creating East and West: Renaissance Humanists and the Ottoman Turks* (Philadelphia: University of Pennsylvania Press, 2004). See also her essays "Pope Pius II and the Crusade," in *Crusading in the Fifteenth Century*, 39-52 (see n. 43 above in this introduction); and "Reactions to the Fall of Constantinople and the Concept of Human Rights," in *Reconfiguring the Fifteenth-Century Crusade*, 285-324 (see n. 24 above in this introduction).
50 Tanja L. Jones, "Ludovico Gonzaga and Pisanello: A Visual Campaign, Political Legitimacy, and Crusader Ideology," *Civiltà Mantovana* 49 (2014): 40-57.
51 The most spectacular expression of this model is found in Samuel P. Huntington, *The Clash of Civilizations and the Remaking of World Order* (London: Penguin, 1996). For one of many rebuttals see "Umej Bhatia's Analysis of the Crusades and Modern Muslim Memory," in *The Crusades: A Reader*, 422-5. See n. 33 above in this introduction.
52 See the introduction to Goffman, *Ottoman Empire*, especially 4-8, for a discussion of Orientalist legacies. See n. 1 above in this introduction for this and other titles.

53 Goffman, *Ottoman Empire*, 7–9. See n. 1 above in this introduction.
54 See the essays in Oliver Jens Schmitt, ed., *The Ottoman Conquest of the Balkans: Interpretations and Research Debates* (Vienna: Austrian Academy of Sciences, 2016). The extensive introductory remarks by Schmitt (7–46) are especially useful for addressing problems of conceptualization and method. See also Antov, *The Ottoman "Wild West."* See n. 1 above in this introduction.
55 For sophisticated theoretical reflections on the problem of "Balkanism," see the introduction to Mariâ Nikolaeva Todorova, *Imagining the Balkans* (Oxford: Oxford University Press, 2009).
56 See the works of Imber (see n. 1 above in this introduction), Jefferson (see n. 19 above in this introduction), and Pálosfalvi (see n. 5 above in this introduction).
57 In the nineteenth century, the story of Belgrade was central to Ludwig Pastor's classic narrative of the history of the papacy, *The History of the Popes, from the Close of the Middle Ages. Drawn from the Secret Archives of the Vatican and Other Original Sources*, 4th ed. (St. Louis: Herder, 1923), 2: 389–428. In early-twentieth-century studies, the battle for Belgrade was the climactic moment of Johannes Hofer's biography of John of Capistrano: *Johannes Kapistran. Ein Leben im Kampf um die Reform der Kirche*, 2 vols., 2nd ed. (Rome-Heidelberg: Kerle, 1964), especially vol. 2, chs. 13–14. The siege also received brief attention as part of Franz Babinger's biography of Mehmed II (see n. 17 above in this introduction). The best recent treatments are in Italian: Gábor Ágoston, "La strada che conduceva a Nándorfehérvár (Belgrade): L'Ungheria, l'espansione Ottomana nei Balcani e la vittoria di Nándorfehérvár," in *La campana di Mezzogiorno. Saggi per il quinto centenario della bolla papale*, ed. Zsolt Visy and Mihály Zöldi (Budapest: Edizioni Universitarie Mundus, 2000), 203–50; and Pellegrini, *Le crociate*, 272–315 (see n. 39 above in this introduction). For the most accessible English treatments, see Kenneth Setton's *Papacy and the Levant*, 179–89 (see n. 41 above in this introduction), and Norman Housley, "Giovanni da Capestrano and the Crusade of 1456," in *Crusading in the Fifteenth Century*, 94–115 (see n. 43 above in this introduction). For a concise summary see also Pálosfalvi, *From Nicopolis to Mohács*, 179–87 (see n. 5 above in this introduction).
58 Setton, *The Papacy and the Levant*, 2: 150. See n. 41 above in this introduction. For broader context on Piccolomini, see the works of Meserve and Bisaha cited in n. 48 and n. 49 above in this introduction.
59 Lawrence G. Duggan, "Were Nicholas V and Pius II Really Renaissance Popes?," in *Where Heaven and Earth Meet: Essays on Medieval Europe in Honor of Daniel F. Callahan*, ed. Michael Frassetto, Matthew Gabriele, and John D. Hosler (Leiden: Brill, 2014), 63–80.
60 There is a massive literature on this topic, but see the useful overview of Jacques Paviot, "Burgundy and the Crusade," in *Crusading in the Fifteenth Century*, 70–80. See n. 42 above in this introduction.
61 For a succinct and still reliable presentation of context and negotiations, see Garrett Mattingly, *Renaissance Diplomacy* (New York: Cosimo Classics, 2009), especially ch. 1.
62 The sources are available as part of the monumental editorial project focused on the German imperial diets of the later medieval and early modern eras. For

Regensburg see Helmut Weigel and Henny Grüneisen, eds., *Deutsche Reichstagsakten. Ältere Reihe. XIX/I* (Göttingen: Vandenhoeck and Ruprecht, 1969). For the sources for Frankfurt and Wiener Neustadt, see Johannes Helmrath and Gabriele Annas, eds., *Deutsche Reichstagsakten unter Kaiser Friedrich III. Reichsversammlung zu Frankfurt 1454* (=Deutsche Reichstagsakten. Ältere Reihe. *XIX/2*) and *Reichsversammlung zu Wiener Neustadt 1455* (=XIX/3) (Munich: Oldenbourg, 2013).

63 See Norman Housley, "Pope Pius II and Crusading," *Crusades* 11 (2012): 209–47, and *Crusading and the Ottoman Threat*, ch. 5 (see n. 44 above in this introduction), for the wider cultural contexts of oratory and communication. See also Duggan, "Were Nicholas V and Pius II Really Renaissance Popes?" (see n. 59 above in this introduction).

64 Miguel Navarro Sorní, "Calixto III y la cruzada contra el Turco," in *Alessandro VI dal Mediterraneo all'Atlantico*, ed. Maria Chiabò, Anna Maria Oliva, and Olivetta Schena (Rome: Roma nel Rinascimento, 2004), 147–67.

65 Weber, *Lutter contre les Turcs*, especially ch. 4. See n. 46 above in this introduction.

66 The standard biography remains Hofer (see n. 57 above in this introduction); but for an accessible overview of Capistrano's travels after 1451, see Kaspar Elm, "John of Capistrano's Preaching Tour North of the Alps," in *Religious Life between Jerusalem, the Desert, and the World: Selected Essays by Kaspar Elm*, trans. James Mixson (Leiden: Brill, 2016), ch. 7. More recently there has emerged an international collaborative project to edit Capistrano's correspondence led by Letizia Pellegrini, its aims and stakes surveyed in Letizia Pellegrini and Ludovic Viallet, "Between *Christianitas* and Europe: Giovanni of Capestrano as an Historical Issue," *Franciscan Studies* 75 (2017): 5–26. The first volumes have now appeared: Paweł Kras and James D. Mixson, eds., *The Grand Tour of John of Capistrano in Central and Eastern Europe (1451–1456)* (Lublin: Catholic University of Lublin, 2018) and Paweł Kras et al., eds., *Corpus epistolarum Ioannis de Capistrano*, t. 1: *Epistolae annis MCDLI–MCDLVI scriptae quae ad res gestas Poloniae et Silesiae spectant* (Warsaw-Lublin: Polish Academy of Science, 2018). Another volume of the epistolary focused on Capistrano's Hungarian letters, under the direction of György Galamb and Otto Gecser, is in preparation. For Belgrade and its aftermath specifically, see Housley, "Giovanni da Capestrano" (see n. 57 above in this introduction) as well as Stanko Andrić, *The Miracles of St. John Capistran* (Budapest: Central European University Press, 2000).

67 The issues were first surveyed thoroughly in Johannes Hofer, "Der Sieger von Belgrad 1456," *Historisches Jahrbuch* 51 (1931): 163–212. See also the appendix (Excursus 24) to Hofer's biography of Capistrano (see n. 57 above in this introduction); and Franz Babinger, "Der Quellenwert der Berichte über den Entsatz von Belgrad 1456," in *Sitzungsberichte der Bayerischen Akademie der Wissenschaften* (Munich: Bayerische Akademie der Wissenschaften, 1957), 1–69.

68 See the remarks of Housley, "Giovanni da Capestrano," 99–100 (see n. 57 above in this introduction); Ágoston, "La strada che conduceva a Nándorfehérvár," 242–4 (see n. 57 above in this introduction); and Pálosfalvi, *From Nicopolis to Mohács*, 180 (see n. 5 above in this introduction).

69 For these dynamics at work around the story of Joan of Arc, see Daniel Hobbins, "Jean Gerson's Authentic Tract on Joan of Arc: *Super facto puellae et credulitate sibi*

praestanda (14 May 1429)," *Mediaeval Studies* 67 (2005): 99–156. For the nature of news in an environment of early print after the siege of Negroponte in 1470, see Margaret Meserve, "News from Negroponte" (see n. 48 above in this introduction).
70 Babinger, *Mehmed the Conqueror and His Time*, 143–4. See n. 17 above in this introduction.
71 Marcus Bull, *Eyewitness and Crusade Narrative: Perception and Narration in Accounts of the Second, Third and Fourth Crusades* (Woodbridge, UK: Boydell, 2019). See also Bull's "Eyewitness and Medieval Historical Narrative," *The Medieval Chronicle* 11 (2017): 1–22, and "Narratological Readings of Crusade Texts," in *The Crusader World*, ed. Adrian Boas (London: Routledge, 2016), 646–60.
72 On the theme of crusading memory specifically, see Megan Cassidy-Welch and Anne Lester, "Memory and Interpretation: New Approaches to the Study of the Crusades," *Journal of Medieval History* 40 (2014): 225–36, building on the work of Nicholas L. Paul and Suzanne M. Yeager, eds., *Remembering the Crusades: Myth, Image, and Identity* (Baltimore: Johns Hopkins University Press, 2012). See also Nicholas Paul, *To Follow in Their Footsteps: The Crusades and Family Memory in the High Middle Ages* (Ithaca, NY: Cornell University Press, 2012).
73 See the sources translated in Theresa M. Vann and Donald J. Kagay, *Hospitaller Piety and Crusader Propaganda: Guillaume Caoursin's Description of the Ottoman Siege of Rhodes, 1480* (Burlington, VT: Ashgate, 2015).
74 The fields of Byzantine and early Ottoman historiography are rich, challenging, and now the subject of a rapidly expanding literature. They are also well beyond my own expertise. I have therefore had to rely here on the work of others, or on partial modern translations of original sources. The introductions to the texts reproduced here, especially the works of Kaldellis (document 27) and Kastritsis (document 33), provide useful orientations to these wider fields.
75 An invocation of John Keegan's famous title, *The Face of Battle* (London: Jonathan Cape, 1976).
76 To note only one useful recent title in this vast field, see the essay collection edited by Philippe Contamine, *War and Competition between States* (Oxford: Clarendon Press, 2001).
77 See in this regard the concluding remarks to Housley, *Reconfiguring the Fifteenth-Century Crusade*, 325–31. See n. 24 above in this introduction. For broader context see Daniel Hobbins, *Authorship and Publicity Before Print: Jean Gerson and the Transformation of Late Medieval Learning* (Philadelphia: University of Pennsylvania Press, 2009), and John Van Engen, "Multiple Options: The World of the Fifteenth-Century Church," *Church History* 77 (2008): 257–84.

PART ONE

Preparations for Crusade, 1453–1456

1. POPE NICHOLAS V, *ETSI ECCLESIA CHRISTI*
September 30, 1453 (Rome)

Sultan Mehmed II captured Constantinople on May 29, 1453. News of the event made its way to Western Europe over the summer, and by September, Pope Nicholas V had prepared the call to crusade presented here. The decree reflects, on the one hand, a long tradition of crusade propaganda: the theology and piety that informed the practice of crusade indulgences; scriptural allusions reflecting a long tradition of crusading; detailed provisions for fundraising. On the other hand, it signals developments more reflective of the fifteenth century, above all in its anti-Turkish sentiment, which here frames Mehmed II as a bloodthirsty tyrant and highlights the atrocities committed in his name. The decree became in many respects a model document for subsequent calls to crusade through the end of the century.

Source: Trans. J. Mixson, from the partial editions available in Cesare Baronio, ed., *Annales ecclesiastici* (Bar-le-Duc, 1864), 28: 599–601, and L. M. Bååth, ed., *Diplomatarium Svecanum appendix. Acta pontificum svecia I. Acta cameralia*. vol. 2: 1371–1492 (Stockholm, 1957), 385–7 (no. 1243). These editions are supplemented here with readings from Vatican, Archivio Segreto Vaticano, Arm. XXXII, vol. 12, fols. 75–80r.

Nicholas, servant of the servants of God, for perpetual memory.

Although the church of Christ is governed, protected, and defended ceaselessly through Jesus Christ our Lord, the only begotten Son of God and our eternal pontiff, lest the roaring enemy should prevail against her (and indeed it is Jesus who, by his own words in the presence of his apostles, promised to all the church that he would always be present, saying, "Behold I am with you all, until the end of the age";[1] and it was Jesus who gave the church assurance that she would never be overcome by her persecutors, saying, "Fear not! I have overcome the world"[2]); nevertheless, he is forever calling back his faithful, who so often break his laws and wander from the way of his commands, and through their tribulations and difficulties he never ceases from calling them back to the power of salvation.

Thus, it has been established through God's most merciful providence that although mankind's life here on earth is one of struggle and temptation (and there is not one who does not face it, from the mother's womb to the grave); nevertheless, divine Providence desired that mankind should place all of its hope in God's aid and protection (because "unless the Lord build the house, its builders labor in vain" and "unless the Lord guard the city, the watchmen guard it in vain");[3] and that mankind should put forth every care and effort to cooperate with divine grace, so that there would be triumph, and not defeat. He cooperates in every good work of the faithful, and grants that, by his merciful piety, their strength prevails. For as the most blessed [Pope] Leo says, "the gifts of God's grace are indeed sweeter to us whenever they are gained with great effort; and an uninterrupted peace obtained through ease can seem a lesser good than one that is earned through labor."[4] For the victory that Christ our God granted to the church while we are in this world, though it is grounded in great faith, still does not come without effort; and it has not been given so that we might sleep, but that we might work all the more cheerfully. "Through many tribulations," says the Apostle, "we must enter into the kingdom of God."[5]

---

1 Matthew 28:20.
2 John 16:33.
3 Psalm 126 (127):1.
4 Pope Leo I (d. 461), Letter 120, to Bishop Theodoret of Cyrus. Adapted here from Philip Schaff and Henry Wace, eds., *Nicene and Post-Nicene Fathers*, Second Series, vol. 12 (1895; repr., Grand Rapids, MI: Eerdmans, 1989), 87.
5 Acts 14:21.

There was once a most bitter enemy of the church of Christ, the cruelest of persecutors, Muhammad, son of Satan, son of perdition, son of death – who longed with his father, the Devil, to devour both souls and bodies, thirsting for Christian blood, a savage and bloodstained enemy of the salvation wrought by our Savior and Redeemer Jesus Christ our Lord; who is thought certainly to have been that great red dragon having seven heads and ten horns and seven crowns on its head that John saw in Revelation, whose fall brought down a third part of the stars of heaven and sent them to the earth; who occupied almost all of the East and Egypt and Africa; and who compelled others to imitate his impiety, as he profaned the holy city of Jerusalem, destroyed its sanctuaries, inflicted injuries, shame, blows, prison, and death upon the faithful of Christ. And yet divine Providence preserved the church of the faithful who (in his most inscrutable judgment) were pleasing to him, and up to this day he has not allowed the enemy to prevail.

But very recently, in our times, a second Muhammad has risen up, an imitator of his impiety, burning with a thirsty passion for pouring out the blood of Christians, burning against the name of Christ, forgetful of all humanity, like a rabid beast who, since he can only attack the head [of the church] with empty words, now tries to sprinkle, to pour, and to spew out his furor and wrath as if from a vomiting stomach upon the members, that is the faithful.[6]

And now in most recent days he has brought under his dominion the city of Constantinople, overcome by a brutal siege and a fight to the bitter end, with a great slaughter of Christian people. All of the churches and sanctuaries there have been profaned; the reliquaries of the saints trampled underfoot; the sacred images of our Lord Jesus Christ and his most glorious Mother and of the living cross subject to insults and taunts, cast down, knocked over, torn to the ground, stained with mud and other vile matter, and thrown away as objects of shame and hatred. Here, truly, is a herald of the Antichrist, who like a second Sennacherib[7] glories in his strength and in the number of his people,

---

[6] The reference here is to the traditional bodily metaphor for the medieval church, with the papacy as the "head" and the faithful as the "members."

[7] King of Assyria whose armies besieged Jerusalem under King Hezekiah. In the biblical narrative (see 2 Kings 18–19), 185,000 of Sennacherib's troops were killed by an angel. The story became integral to liturgies of crusade and narratives of Christian victory against overwhelming odds. See also 2 Chronicles 32:20–1. For context see Gaposchkin, *Invisible Weapons*. See the introduction, n. 37.

that he might obtain all of the West by his hand and erase the name of Christian from all the world. He is out of his mind, obsessed with the idea that he can prevail against the power of God.

Therefore we who, though unworthy, hold the place of the one to whom Christ commended his church: the one who has worked to ensure that "the gates of hell should not prevail against it";[8] and the one to whom Christ gave the command that he should support his faltering brothers in their commitment, saying, "I have prayed for you, Peter, that your faith may not fail. And when you have repented, strengthen your brothers"[9] – in this moment we look to the duties of our office as is required of necessity by the church. And so, by the advice and assent of our venerable brothers, the cardinals in the holy Roman Church, we have undertaken to arrange the following:

First, we encourage, require, and command all Christian princes, whatever imperial, kingly, queenly, ducal or other worldly dignity they might hold, by virtue of the profession they made in taking on holy baptism, and by virtue of the oath they offered when they took up the insignia of their dignities, to come to the defense of the Christian religion and of the faith with their goods and persons, as genuinely and insistently as is possible. In doing so they will receive an eternal reward from the one whose cause they advance, both in the present life and in the future, since in the present moment we believe it to be incumbent upon each of them, as a necessity of salvation and a necessity from which no one may legitimately excuse themselves. As for other lords or communities or anyone having whatsoever other dominions, we also exhort, require, and admonish them, commanding similarly by the force of the faith which they have professed, to strongly and perseveringly assist in the defense of the religion and of the faith with all their strength and all their power, remembering that they have alongside them that champion who, through his angel, in one night killed 185,000 from the army of Sennacherib,[10] and who has otherwise never abandoned his church, nor allowed its enemies to glory in their impiety.

Thus, to all of whatsoever estate, rank, condition, or order who, in the face of such a great emergency for the church and the faith, shall

---

8 Matthew 16:18.
9 Luke 22:32.
10 See n. 7 above in this document.

be present and serve for six months from February 1, whether clergy or laity, whatever ecclesiastical or worldly dignity may distinguish them, by the authority of almighty God and of the blessed apostles Peter and Paul as well as the plenitude of heavenly power given to us, we grant full remission and pardon of all sins. We also grant all that has been customarily given by our predecessors in aid of the Holy Land, as well as all things which our predecessors and we as well have granted to the Christian people for the Jubilee year [...].[11] And by apostolic authority we command that however many of the aforesaid holy works to which they may obligate themselves by vow, they should also place on their clothing the saving sign of the living cross, carrying on their shoulders the memory of the one by whose suffering they have been saved from eternal damnation and imitating the one who, for our redemption, had "the government of the world placed on his shoulders," who admonished us to follow in his footsteps, saying, "Whoever wants to be my disciple must deny themselves and take up their cross and follow me."[12]

But since an almost incalculable amount of money is needed in order to carry out this task successfully, in order to make arrangements for those things that necessity will require, and since this is a matter involving the faith, and of all the Christian religion, to which all are held accountable without exception, as a matter of their salvation, we therefore first ordain, decree, and order it to be sacredly observed, that all fruits, revenues, and profits coming to the apostolic camera,[13] from whatever benefice, whether greater or lesser, whether archiepiscopal, episcopal, abbatial, or whatever other kind, by whatever name they might be deemed to belong to us, be put in the service of this holy task – totally, fully, and without being lessened in any way. And so that this may be put into effect precisely as we desire, we wish and command that these revenues should be assigned by our chamberlain (or his representative, our treasurer) to our venerable brothers and cardinals of the holy Roman Church [...] all of whom will ensure that the money is held by a depositor to be chosen by them for the use of this holy expedition.

By the same rationale we wish and command that a tenth portion of all revenues that come to our camera from the temporal holdings of

---

11   A series of detailed prescriptions regarding indulgences follows.
12   Isaiah 9:6 and Matthew 16:24.
13   That is, the papal treasury.

the Roman Church should be assigned to the aforementioned cardinals through the same chamberlain or his representative and treasurer, and we dedicate this along with the above sum to this holy work as well. Moreover, our venerable brother cardinals of the holy Roman Church should willingly and freely offer to pay for such a holy and pious task, fully and without any reduction, an entire tenth from common incomes from their chapel and all their churches and benefices. And since it is a shameful thing for anyone of a lesser rank or order to retreat from observing the law to which the highest pontiff has obligated himself out of charity, and on the other hand since it is a decent and fitting thing that all, whether prelates or those of a lesser rank, should be participants in bearing the same burden, we wish (and by this present constitution decree) that for such a holy work a tenth portion should be paid in full from the incomes of all of the offices of the Roman curia, whatever their titles, even those administered by the aforesaid vice-chancellor, chamberlain, and major penitentiary, cardinals of the holy Roman Church (as these same cardinals have willingly offered to do).

And so that all of this might be strictly observed by those of lesser rank, we wish and decree that anyone who is fraudulent and does not pay the aforesaid tenth in full will be subject to excommunication and removal from office. And since all of this would still not suffice for only a modest part of the needs of such a great undertaking, unless the prelates and other ecclesiastics of all of the churches which are spread across the whole Christian world should also lend their aid and effort, by the counsel and also the assent of our venerable brother cardinals of the holy Roman Church, by virtue of the fullness of apostolic power we hereby reserve for such a holy effort a full tenth of all ecclesiastical incomes throughout all the world, according to their true value, without any exception – those of patriarchs, archbishops, bishops, abbots, and whatsoever other incomes, whatsoever their titles, greater or lesser, with or without pastoral duties attached, exempt or nonexempt, whether bound by religious rule or not, of whatsoever order, status, or condition they may be.

So that this measure might be carried out more efficiently, we wish to place under the sentence of excommunication those who resist or disobey or defraud, so that those who are disobedient or who knowingly commit fraud, whatever their estate or condition, should incur the sentence of excommunication. By the same authority we also decree that, until this holy undertaking should see a happy outcome, all who hold offices in lands subject to the temporal rule of the Roman Church, whether in the present or in the future, whether clergy or laity governing cities or provinces, public or civil governors or treasurers, whether holding their offices for life or for a term, if they are owed a salary, should pay a tenth of all pay and other incomes that are due to them or to their ministers, without any reduction. And they should do this according to the manner and form established by our venerable brothers [...] whom we have assigned especially to this task. If they should do otherwise, let them incur excommunication, and also be rendered unable and unworthy to hold any office in the future.

And clearly since those who dedicate themselves to the services of the heavenly emperor ought to enjoy a special privilege, we decree that all those who sign themselves with the cross for this holy expedition should be exempt from collections, taxation, or other burdens, commanding each and all, whatever dignity they enjoy, that they not require anything from those under the sign of the cross. After they have taken the cross, we take their persons and goods under Saint Peter's protection, and ours.

Should anyone stubbornly refuse to obey this command, let them incur excommunication. Moreover, so that those maritime predators called pirates or others accustomed to committing robbery on land and sea should not dare to impede this expedition, we bind all of them with the chains of excommunication, along with their accomplices, protectors, and harborers. We strictly forbid anyone to enter into any contract for selling or buying, to make concessions for any port or locale, or to interact with them publicly or in private, also commanding the leaders of cities and locales that they prohibit anyone from committing such impiety. Moreover, as blessed Felix our predecessor said to Acacius, "to not disturb the perverted is nothing other than to support them," and "let those not shy away from hidden association who refuse to confront manifest crimes."[14] Therefore we inflict on these persons the sentence of excommunication, and we command that the prelates of their lands strike them with the sentence of interdict. We furthermore excommunicate and condemn those pseudo-Christians who carry to the aforesaid enemy of Christ (or to their allies) iron weapons and wood; those who sell war galleys or cargo ships or any other vessels to them; those who

---

14 Acacius, patriarch of Constantinople (d. 489), was involved in a series of controversies with Pope Felix III and eventually excommunicated.

build ships for their use; and those who take command of their ships; as well as any who offer any aid or counsel with machines of war or in any other acts. They are also to be punished by the privation of their goods and declared the servants of their captives. We command that sentences of this kind should be publicized in all maritime cities on every Sunday and feast day, and that the bosom of the church should not be open to those punished in this way unless they should offer both all that they gained from this damnable commerce as well as their own resources in support of this praiseworthy and most holy undertaking.

But since for the advance of such a holy task we discern it most fitting that kings and princes and all others who hold dominion among the Christian people should have and observe peace, by the authority of almighty God we establish and order that throughout the Christian world peace should be generally observed, so that through the prelates of the church those who are at odds might be returned to peace, or if there is no way at all to find peace then at least truces might be strictly observed. And if someone should refuse to yield, then let them be compelled to obey individually by way of excommunication, or as a community by way of interdict. Therefore let no one infringe on our exhortation, requirement, admonition, mandate, concession, gift, will, decree, reservation, transfer, assignment, or command. But if someone should presume to do so, let them know that they have incurred the wrath of almighty God and of his apostles, the blessed Peter and Paul.

Given in Rome in 1453, on September 30, in the seventh year of our pontificate.

2. AENEAS SILVIUS PICCOLOMINI, *CONSTANTINOPOLITANA CLADES*
October 15, 1454 (Frankfurt)

In the wake of Nicholas V's call to crusade, papal diplomats sought to persuade the powers of Western Europe to coordinate a military response. Their efforts resulted in what became a longstanding truce in Italy (April 1454) and in Germany a series of diets at Regensburg (April 1454), Frankfurt (October 1454), and Wiener Neustadt (February 1455). One of the most important figures at these diets was Aeneas Silvius Piccolomini. Born near Siena to an impoverished noble family and trained as a humanist in Florence, Piccolomini's skill as a writer and orator drew him into the circles of several leading Italian cardinals as well as to the assemblies of the Council of Basel (1431–49), as they worked to reform and govern the church. He also came to the attention of Germany's Frederick III, who appointed him imperial secretary. As the Council of Basel's fortunes waned, Piccolomini eventually came to side with the papacy. Ordained as a priest in 1446, he worked on behalf of Eugenius IV and then Nicholas V, who appointed him bishop of Trieste (1447) and Siena (1450). Piccolomini was one of many humanists who in their writings responded forcefully to the fate of Constantinople in 1453. He authored a series of eloquent letters lamenting the fall of the city, as well as the famous oration whose opening lines are translated here. Delivered on behalf of Frederick III at the Diet of Frankfurt in 1454, Constantinopolitana clades *("The Fall of Constantinople") was a strikingly effective deployment of humanist style in a crusading context. The address became in many ways a touchstone and a model for the formal crusade oration, a new genre that came to complement the traditional sermon as a key element of crusade propaganda.*

Source: Michael Cotta-Schønberg, ed. and trans., "Oration *Constantinopolitana clades* of Enea Silvio Piccolomini (15 October 1454, Frankfurt), 6th version," in *Collected Orations of Pope Pius II* (Saarbrücken Scholars' Press, 2019), vol. 5, no. 22, pp. 98–223.[1]

Reverend fathers, illustrious princes, and you others, noble and respectable men:

The Fall of Constantinople was a great victory for the Turks, a total disaster for the Greeks, and a complete disgrace for the Latins. Therefore, I believe, it must pain and hurt each of you – and the more so the more noble and good you are. For what is more proper for a good and noble man than to care for the true Faith, to favor religion, and to extol and spread the name of Christ, Our Savior, as much as possible? But now that Constantinople is lost, and this great city has fallen into the power of our enemies, now that so much Christian blood has been shed, and so many people[2] have been carried off into slavery, the Catholic Faith has been grievously injured, our religion has suffered a shameful reverse, and the name of Christ has been grievously damned and abused.

---

1 Only the opening passage of the text is presented here, with the permission of the author. Note that the full text (in Latin and English, with a substantial introduction and apparatus) is also available in the public domain (https://hal.archives-ouvertes.fr/hal-01097147/document).

2 Here *animae*, or "souls."

Truly, for many centuries the Christian commonwealth has suffered no greater disgrace than today. Our forefathers often experienced setbacks in Asia and Africa, that is in other regions, but we, today, have been smitten and struck in Europe[3] itself, in our fatherland, in our own home and seat. If somebody says that it is many years since the Turks came from Asia[4] to Greece, the Tartars settled in Europe on this side of Tanais,[5] and the Saracens crossed the Herculean Sea,[6] occupied a part of Spain,[7] and inflicted many defeats on the Christians, [my answer is that] until now we have never lost a city or a place equal to Constantinople, and never have we, in Europe, lost so much Christian and noble blood to the infidels as now.

Constantinople is almost at the center of all the lands that may be easily cultivated, and it has a very large and safe harbor where ships, nay immense fleets can be armed and provisioned. In one direction, the way is open through the Bosporus to the Euxine Sea, that we today call the Great Sea,[8] and all its Northern and Eastern coasts. And in the other direction, you may easily go through the Hellespont,[9] that we now call the Arm of Saint George, to the West and to the coasts of the Mediterranean. This place, so advantageous, so useful, and so essential, has now been lost to Christ, Our Savior, and gained by Muhammad, the Seducer, while we were silent, not to say asleep.

Moreover, the Christians had two emperors, one Latin and one Greek. Now that the Greek emperor has been killed together with his nobles, can we not say that one of the two eyes of Christianity[10] has been plucked out and one of its two hands cut off? In the whole world, four empires have been considered great and outstanding: the empire of the Assyrians, the empire of the Greeks, the empire of the Carthaginians, and the empire of the Romans. The first one may be called the Eastern Empire, the second the Northern Empire, the third the Southern Empire, and the fourth the Western empire.

---

3   Note Piccolomini's geopolitical use of the concept of Europe.
4   Asia Minor. Reference here to the Battle of Gallipoli in 1354.
5   The Don River, in antiquity considered to be the frontier river between Asia and Europe. Reference here to the Battle of Liegnitz in 1241 against the Mongols.
6   The Strait of Gibraltar.
7   Reference to Arabic conquests of the eighth century.
8   The Black Sea.
9   The Dardanelles.
10 The image of Rome and Constantinople as the two "eyes" of the world was coined by Themistius in the fourth century.

In the same way, our forefathers established four patriarchal sees: the Antiochene See they gave to the Eastern people, the Constantinopolitan See to the Northern people, the Alexandrian See to the Southern people, and the Roman See to the Western people. The patriarchal sees of Jerusalem, Aquileia, and Grado that has now been translated to Venice, were founded long afterwards and are not considered as equal to the first four. Of the four principal patriarchates, our forefathers lost two, together with the See of Jerusalem, due to passivity and mutual conflicts.[11] Because of the same passivity, but to our greater shame, we ourselves have now lost the third one, the one that is followed by all the Ruthenians and many peoples to the North and East of Tanais. No wonder, nobles, that you are all mourning, shocked and stupefied by this great blow to Christianity, seeing that at one stroke the Greeks have fallen, the Turks are victorious, and the Latins have been thrown into confusion and disorder.

The grief of Holy Emperor Fredrick was just as great as yours. You should have seen him when he was first informed about this catastrophe, crying in his chamber, sorrowful in court, worried in council, praying in church, and everywhere downcast and anxious. For a long time, food gave him no pleasure and sleep no rest. But since the Turks are daily threatening Christendom with greater evils, it does not need moaning and tears as much as vigor and weapons. His Serene Highness has therefore found it worthwhile to summon an assembly of princes and cities of the German nation in order to take counsel on how to protect Christianity. Indeed he remembered the saying: "For, before you begin, there is need for deliberation, and for prompt action after you have deliberated."[12] The convention was asked to assemble in Regensburg, and you all know what happened there. The present meeting is held at the decision of that assembly. During the last days, it has been amply explained why this meeting is not held in Nuremberg, and why the emperor is unable to be present. For he would most certainly have come to the upper parts of the Empire in such an important matter if he had been able to leave his homeland at peace.

Though his desire was frustrated by those who benefit more from strife and war than from peace and tranquility, he did not want to

---

11 Alexandria (641), Jerusalem (1187), and Antioch (1268).
12 Sallust, *Bellum Catilinae*, 1.6.

disregard this assembly. Therefore, he sent these princes[13] to act in his place and to represent him, and he has given them full and ample powers. They are prepared to negotiate both on the affairs of the Empire and the common matter of the Faith. But since your primary task is to consider and discuss the articles discussed in Regensburg, you wish to know the emperor's mind on the matter. Therefore, by the authority of my colleagues I am now requested to set forth his mind, his opinion, and his intentions on these issues. As I would rather seem stupid through obedience than clever through defiance, I have taken this almost unbearable burden upon my shoulders, trusting in help from Him who would rather have obedience than sacrificial victims.[14] And I do not fear to falter under this great burden since some here will lend me a hand if I stumble.[15] And I obey so much more gladly that I see your numerous and kindly disposed assembly.

I am also moved by the fact that the matter on which I am to speak is important and urgent: should we go to war against the Turks who have unjustly conquered Constantinople; who have killed the Greek nobles and their emperor; who have polluted all the holy places; and who are threatening all Christians with chains, whips, murder, and atrocious punishments? If I convince you to do this, we shall easily settle the issues of how large a force is necessary, how the soldiers should be found, what wages to pay, which privileges to issue, how to provision the army, what war machines to prepare, as well as the time of departure, and the route to follow.[16] It will also be easy to appoint a captain or leader of the war whom the ancient Romans called *imperator*. You will not hesitate to choose someone who has expert "knowledge of military affairs, great bravery, evident authority, and luck,"[17] and who shows "application to duty, courage in danger, thoroughness in operation, rapidity in execution, wisdom in strategy."[18] I do not doubt that there is such a man among you. And as I shall explain later, you will not have to worry about keeping peace at home if you decide to go to war abroad.

---

13 Bishop Ulrich Sonnenberger of Gurk; Henry of Pappenheim; Hartung von Cappel; Margrave Albrecht of Brandenburg; Margrave Kar of Baden; and Piccolomini himself.
14 Cf. 1 Samuel 15:22.
15 Cf. Ecclesiasticus 7:36.
16 Cicero, *Pro lege Manilia* 1.1.
17 Cicero, *Pro lege Manilia* 2.6.
18 Cicero, *Pro lege Manilia* 11.29.

Now you understand, Princes, the substance of my oration and what the matter is all about:[19] the whole issue is whether or not to go to war. I have come to persuade you, in the name of the emperor, to go to war, and I have only accepted this burden because I see that the matter is clearly worthy of your courage, your nobility, and your nation. So, do now consider, hear, and examine the issue of undertaking this war for the sake of the Catholic Faith. Noble princes, every senate and every people that has to deliberate on going to war should discuss, carefully and stringently, three things so that it will not do something that it will later regret. For, as the saying of Scipio goes, it is shameful to err and then afterwards to say: "I had not thought of that!"[20] So, anyone who is going to war should first ask: is the war just? Secondly, is it useful? And thirdly: is it feasible?[21] If these conditions are not met, there is no reason for good men to go to war.[22]

3. CORRESPONDENCE OF 1455–1456

This section turns to the correspondence of those active along the Danube frontier and southern Hungary in 1455–6 who most directly confronted the Ottoman advance in the months, weeks, and days leading up to the siege of Belgrade. The letters translated here allow us to hear, however indirectly, the voices of a few of the key characters in that historical moment, and to access something of the moment's energy and anxiety.

3.1. THE CITY OF RAGUSA TO JOHN HUNYADI
June 11, 1455 (Ragusa)

The Adriatic port city of Ragusa (modern Dubrovnik, Croatia) was a former Byzantine and Serbian city that by the fifteenth century was under Venetian

---

19 Cicero, *De officiis* 2.12.
20 Cicero, *De officiis* 1.81.
21 Cf. Quintilian, *Institutio oratoria* 3.8.22.
22 The treatise continues by answering each of these questions affirmatively, at length, in sonorous humanist prose. The full text is available via the link provided in n. 1 above in this document.

influence. The city was crucial both commercially and diplomatically, as a point of contact between Italy, Central Europe, and the Balkans. In this letter the Ragusans relate to the Hungarian general John Hunyadi the fate of the Serbian city of Novo Brdo. Because of both its fortifications and its vital mining industry, Novo Brdo was a key center of commerce, communication, and military leverage, and thus an obvious target for Mehmed II, who captured it on June 1, 1455, after a forty-day siege. Mehmed executed most of the city's leaders, but he left its mining experts in place to continue their work, now on his behalf. He also conscripted many Serbian youth for his janissary corps, among them Konstantin Mihailović, whose later memoirs (see document 34) are a key source for the period, including the events of Belgrade.

Source: Trans. J. Mixson, from József Gelcich and Lajos Thallóczy, eds., *Diplomatarium Ragusanum* (Budapest, 1887), 580–1 (no. 332).

To the lord governor of Hungary, June 11, 1455:

Though there is no doubt that Your Lordship has scribes and ambassadors who are [aware] of everything that is happening across these lands, we might seem to fail in fulfilling our duty were we to neglect to signal to Your Highness in our letters those things which you yourself have scouted out most thoroughly. For who has not heard such great rumors, which we think, because of their magnitude, must have made their way to every land, from west to east?[1] Who does not react with horror, the voice stuck in the throat? Behold, the most savage emperor of the Turks, most fierce and common enemy of all, with his innumerable troops, with so many different and unheard-of instruments of war, has attacked the city of Novo Brdo, and strives to conquer it thoroughly. What is there to say about the city? He seeks through his lustful and ambitious will to bring all of the Christian religion under his rule. So, who could be of such a stubborn heart or so ignorant as not to see this great danger to the Christian people, or indeed more truly that the time of our destruction and death is at hand? What ought to be done with this letter, perhaps Your Excellency might say? We certainly wish that it might serve as a goad for Your Lordship to issue a call to arms against these Turks. For unless some aid be forthcoming from

---

1 Here a loose translation of an obscure phrase.

your kingdom [of Hungary], as we see it this evil will bring about grave injury. So: act quickly! No more delay, our great and unconquered leader! All of the Christian people turn their eyes to you and prefer you, who alone can and are able to bring aid against and to face down such furor – you who wish to avenge and to restore to her ancient dignity and freedom the Christian republic that is now so miserable and afflicted.

In this form [also] written to:

His Majesty the lord king [Ladislaus V]
Nicholas of Ilok
Ladislaus Garai
The bishop of Oradea [John Vitéz]

3.2. JOHN OF CAPISTRANO TO POPE CALLIXTUS III
June 21, 1455 (Győr)

As noted in the introduction, the Italian friar John of Capistrano was one of the central figures in the events surrounding Belgrade.[1] Already engaged in a sustained preaching mission across northern Europe after 1451, in the wake of the Diets of 1454–5 Capistrano's mission turned to the call to crusade. Unfortunately, no texts of his crusade sermons survive. But Capistrano was a prolific correspondent throughout his travels, and his letters provide important information about his itinerary and perspective. The letter translated here was authored at the height of an important early assembly of barons and princes in the Hungarian city of Győr, just as Capistrano's crusade recruitment was underway. Here the friar writes to Alfonso de Borja, who on the death of Nicholas V (see document 1) had been elected Pope Callixtus III. A native of Valencia with close ties to King Alfonso V of Naples, the new pope brought a distinct focus and intensity to the challenge of launching a crusade against Mehmed II. In this letter, Capistrano informs the pope of the deliberations of the assembly at Győr, the desperation of Serbia after the fall of Novo Brdo, and the urgent negotiations over John Hunyadi's grand plan for raising an army of some one hundred thousand troops.

---

1 See the introduction, pp. 38–40.

Source: Trans. J. Mixson, from Luke Wadding, ed., *Annales minorum*, 3rd ed. (Quaracchi, 1932), 12: 292–4.[2]

Most blessed father, I lie prostrate, humbly, to kiss the footprints of your sacred feet. Although in these last days I have sent Your Holiness two letters, nevertheless I will not pass over an opportunity – while the services of letter carriers are available – to write to Your Blessedness above all regarding those things that I deem to concern the honor of both God and Your Holiness. Two ambassadors of the holy Apostolic See recently came to me, one by the name of Rudolf, a confidant of the most reverend lord of Győr, carrying a letter from Your Holiness. The other was a courier of the reverend lord of Firmano[3] who, as he claimed, bore letters from the sacred college of the most reverend cardinals that announced the election of the Holy Spirit, namely that by divine disposition you, holy father, had been chosen as the true Vicar of Christ, not only to preserve but even to advance the holy Catholic faith. And since most of the barons of the distinguished kingdom of Hungary have gathered here to establish mutual harmony among themselves, having received a letter of this kind they have been filled with great gladness and delight, and are rejoicing intensely in the will of the divine.

But it was not without envy and grumbling that, in a meeting of such lords, there were letters presented on behalf of Your Holiness to certain lesser types that were not also given to the most powerful ones of the same kingdom; that is, to the bishops of Pécs, Oradea, and to certain more distinguished barons of the realm. It was easy to resolve this matter on your behalf. Thereafter, it pains me to say, just today a courier hastened here with a special message for the despot of Serbia [George Branković], who has desperately sought from these lords and barons support and defense of his territory. The courier announced to

---

[2] Wadding's editions of Capistrano's correspondence, though long standard, have come to be seen as problematic. Currently an international team of scholars led by Letizia Pellegrini is undertaking a new authoritative edition of the corpus (see the introduction, n. 66). An edition of the correspondence of John of Capistrano in Hungary, supervised by Gábor Klaniczay and Otto Gecser, is nearing completion but not yet in print. I am grateful to both scholars for allowing access to their team's ongoing editorial work. In this section and the next, where possible I have checked Wadding's edition of Capistrano's letters against drafts of the forthcoming editions.

[3] Domenico Capranica (d. 1458), Italian canonist, bishop of Fermo, papal diplomat, cardinal, and protector of the Franciscan order.

the same despot and barons that the most shameful enemy of Christ, Muhammad, emperor of the Turks, has occupied a most powerful Serbian city, called Hobordam,[4] where there is a gold and silver mine that brings annually to his coffers – so they say – 120,000 ducats. And all of the other cities and fortresses are said to be surrounded, soon to be cut off. Everyone, blessed father, is terrified of such terrible news, and of all the wicked deeds that have been committed – and we seem only to hear every day that there is more, God forbid, to come. So, it is no surprise that there is worry over whether, should the right kind of aid not arrive quickly, things might turn out even worse. Therefore, blessed father, since God has given you power to see to it (just as you have established other holy undertakings) to effectively preserve and grow the holy Catholic faith, I hold it as certain that God has brought you to this moment for no other purpose, than for you to guard what has been prepared for the appropriate time, restore what has been lost, and by your virtue and care to restore damaged members to the wholeness of your body.

I wrote yesterday to Your Holiness that you should adorn the most serene king [Alfonso V] of Aragon with spiritual and temporal weapons; and that although he is already most powerful, Your Holiness could help make him still more so. Indeed, I think it is necessary, and most advantageous, that we resist manfully and wage war strongly against this evil enemy of Christ, not only by sea but also by land. For since I conferred today with these lord prelates and barons, the magnificent and excellent governor [John Hunyadi], Count of Beszterce, offered himself as the first to take up arms at his own expense, along with ten thousand elite horse at his command. He said, moreover, that the most serene lord King Ladislaus would provide twenty thousand from the rest of the kingdom of Hungary. And though the despot of Serbia [George Branković] has suffered great loss, he has offered to provide ten thousand, even though he continues to adhere to his faith.[5] It falls to us, however, to take into consideration the dangers that we face, and to arrange for an appropriate remedy.

---

4   A garbled rendering of Novo Brdo (in modern Kosovo). See the first letter in this section.
5   The reference here is to the Greek Orthodox tradition of Serbia, deemed "schismatic" by the Latin church and by Capistrano.

The aforesaid magnificent Lord John [Hunyadi] has taken part in a second conference, saying that if our serene lord pope would provide twenty thousand horse, and if the serene king of Aragon ten thousand, and the other cities of Italy ten thousand, since the Duke of Burgundy offers that he would come with ten thousand horse and ten thousand foot soldiers, this John was confident that within three months we could take such a fight to the Turk that he would have nowhere in Europe to lay his head, especially since [Hunyadi] knows the power of the Turks in every detail, along with that of other infidels, and since he is the one who understands thoroughly the right way of waging war against them. So it was that in the presence of all of these lords and barons he asserted this today: that with such a great number of soldiers he would hope to regain even Jerusalem, and that he would not ask for any payment for the aforesaid cavalry beyond the first three months.

It would be expedient for Your Holiness to designate a cardinal for these lands, to act as a kind of supervisor for such an army, along with a sufficient amount of money. Or if it seems well to Your Holiness to commit this matter to the reverend lord cardinal of Esztergom (who is strong in virtue, foresight, and counsel), I think the consultation would turn out well.[6] Moreover, this John [Hunyadi] has offered himself – if he is given true warriors, not youths, but men who are vigorous and well trained in arms, well suited to pursue the enemies of Christ – from one year to the next, if need be, to persevere with such an army and to require no further financial support, trusting that he could reap from the goods and lands of the Turk so much that he could provide for his army more abundantly than the Turk himself pays his own troops. Therefore, in this way, with the most serene king of Aragon fighting on the sea and this John on land, there could be genuine hope of recuperating what has been lost and of acquiring the reign that Christian princes deserve, as well as capturing the wealth of the infidels and spreading widely the holy orthodox Catholic faith, unto the everlasting glory and immortal praise and eternal memory of the name of Your Holiness.

Thus, may Your Holiness, blessed father, discern what may be done in this matter, and may the Almighty preserve his holy church and the Christian people forever, to whom I commend my suppliant self, along

---

6 Denis Szécsi. See document 9.

with our [Franciscan] order. From the town of Győr in the kingdom of Hungary, June 21, 1455.

A worm and an unworthy little servant of Your Exalted Holiness, yet a most faithful orator, Brother John of Capistrano.

3.3. JOHN OF CAPISTRANO TO POPE CALLIXTUS III
September 17, 1455 (Csanád)

His contemporaries marveled at Capistrano's energy and dedication to the task of recruiting an army for crusade, which took the seventy-year-old friar on a journey of some four hundred miles across Hungary and Romania between May of 1455 and February of 1456. In this letter, only the introduction of which appears here, Capistrano sends a report to Pope Callixtus III from the church of Csanád in southern Hungary, not far from the advancing Ottoman forces.

Source: Trans. J. Mixson, from Luke Wadding, ed., *Annales minorum*, 3rd ed. (Quaracchi, 1932), 12: 326–8.

Most blessed father, with a kiss for the footprints of sacred feet, and with humble and eager obedience to your commands, unto the death of the cross[1] (and there is nothing more delightful to me): I have a most fervent desire to make my way to Your Most Merciful Holiness in person, if only the weight of old age would not hinder me, if the great distance of the journey did not deter me, and if these unsettled times did not hold me back. For I am at the moment stationed in Christendom's most distant cathedral church, called Csanád (at most fourteen miles, so they tell me, from the most treacherous Turks), whose diocese extends to the front lines. In recent times they have now not only come against this city twice but depopulated and ravaged the region with iron and fire. As an absent pilgrim I have thus visited you five times now with my humbled quill, and after other reports regarding the dangers facing the Christian republic I write to Your Serenity that the despot [George Branković] of Serbia has arranged peace with the enemy of Christ, the

---

1 The phrasing here seems to reference the possibility of Capistrano's martyrdom.

most savage Great Turk Mehmed. These are dangerous times, blessed father, and the days are evil. It is thus necessary to prepare for avoiding the dangers to come, and better to meet them ahead of time than to try to heal a wounded Christendom afterward. For after death, it is too late to offer medicine. And in fact, almost everyone in these parts lives in fear of the ferocious lions who now rise up against them. I will not repeat what I have already written to Your Serenity in other letters. It is your task to discern, in Jesus Christ, what ought to be done.

[The letter continues, first praising the office of pope as the head of the church and then asking Callixtus III to confirm the privileges his predecessors had issued for Capistrano's Franciscan order. It concludes by emphasizing the special bond between the Observant wing of the order and the papacy].

3.4. JUAN CARVAJAL TO JOHN OF CAPISTRANO
January 16, 1456 (Vienna)

Alongside Capistrano, the papal legate Juan Carvajal played an important role in the effort to mobilize an army against the Ottomans. Born to a noble family in Trujillo in the territory of Extremadura in western Iberia, Carvajal was a university-trained canon lawyer who rose to prominence at the papal court in the middle of the fifteenth century. As a papal legate to Germany in the conciliar era he became one of the most active and influential diplomats of his day, especially in Central Europe and in the circles of Ladislaus V. By 1456 he had been charged by Callixtus III with organizing the crusade against Mehmed II. His exchange with Capistrano in the next five letters offers a glimpse of the interweaving of theology and practical matters in these kinds of communications. The exchange also hints at the complex web of diplomatic relationships figures like Carvajal and Capistrano had to negotiate in order to advance their agenda, and at the urgent but also delicate matters of timing and logistics that all had to negotiate in the first months of 1456.

Source: Trans. J. Mixson, from Luke Wadding, ed., *Annales minorum*, 3rd ed. (Quaracchi, 1932), 12: 371.

To our esteemed reverend father in Christ,

Asking for your prayers, we inform Your Paternity that the most serene king of Hungary, as he told us today, intends with God's help to begin his journey toward Hungary this week. We hope through his arrival in that kingdom to be able to make good arrangements for the affairs of the faith, since the most serene lord king himself has no small amount of religious fervor, along with these lords who are with him. May almighty God see fit to keep Your Paternity safe from danger. We cannot express in words or letters how much joy and consolation we have taken from those things we have heard regarding the most illustrious lord governor [John Hunyadi], who we have heard has raised seven thousand troops. We reminded those among them who were wavering of all that God has done on our behalf: how Maccabeus, master of a holy army, routed the army of Nicanor and Gorgias with that number. But the people of Israel killed 120,000.[1] And so we hope in the Lord that this army of seven thousand, if all other human help should fail, under the aforesaid governor, the Maccabeus of our time, should be victorious, and that God will grant his people victory. We would wish that the same lord governor should write to those princes with whom he has close ties in this affair, including the emperor, the king of Aragon, the Duke of Burgundy, and others, that their troops should be sent to Hungary in the month of June, or July at the latest, and that the governor himself will be prepared by that time. Nor are they to be asked that they should provide this or that many thousands of troops, because they will soon clearly understand that the lord governor (in whose name they place great faith) ought to be properly prepared. Tell them also that the apostolic legate [i.e., Carvajal] is here with the cross, that "the curtain will draw the curtain,"[2] and that some will come for devotion, others for honor, in such great numbers (so we hope in the Lord) that we will fear not having enough food more than not having enough troops. Therefore, Your Paternity should consider carefully in this matter what to write to the lord governor, and that he should be prepared at the appointed time, because God will provide both the sacrifice and all that is needed for the offering.

A certain courtier, a very noble man, said to me that he has it from the curia that the reverend father in Christ, the patriarch and chamberlain Lord Ludovic, has been announced as legate to fight against the Turks

---

1 Cf. 2 Maccabees 8.
2 This phrase appears in quotation marks in the edition of the text; it seems to be a colloquial phrase whose resonance is now lost.

on the sea.³ You know what kind of a person he is, and how well suited to this service. And so, everything is properly arranged. May Your Paternity see to it that nothing is lacking in the province given to you by God. The most serene lord king is most eager to engage in this business, so much that we anticipate he will be a second David, and in his most pure innocence will slay the unbaptized Turk, killer of Christians. May Your Paternity remember the most serene king in your prayers, that God would give him an upright heart. Even the illustrious Count of Celje⁴ promises to do all he can. Again and again, may God bless Your Paternity.

From Vienna, January 16, 1456.

3.5. JOHN OF CAPISTRANO TO JUAN CARVAJAL
February 19, 1456 (Pest)

Source: Trans. J. Mixson, from Luke Wadding, ed., *Annales minorum*, 3rd ed. (Quaracchi, 1932), 12: 372–3.

To the most reverend father in Christ and lord to be most obeyed, Cardinal John of Sant'Angelo, apostolic legate, etc.

Most reverend father in Christ and lord, lord to be most obeyed, most distinguished protector and teacher, a humble commendation, with every obligation of deference. When I in my weakness was by God's grace engaged along the farthest frontiers of Christendom, in the kingdom of Transylvania, sowing the word of the one from whom an abundant crop has grown (for a multitude of infidels has been baptized there, and more are baptized daily!) note how, amid that harvest, by the command of the letters of Your Reverend Lordship, I postponed all things and immediately took up the journey toward this city of Pest. Although it pained me in no small measure to leave unfinished that work of harvesting souls, nothing could be more pleasing or joyful than to obey the Apostolic See with an eager spirit – something I have always

---

3   Ludovico Trevisan (d. 1465), patriarch of Aquileia, cardinal priest of San Lorenzo, and chief financial officer of the apostolic camera. By the 1450s Trevisan had behind him a long career of diplomatic and military service on behalf of the papacy in Italy. He was now charged with leading the papacy's naval campaign against the Ottomans.
4   Ulrich II, Count of Celje. See the cast of characters, p. 274.

done and will always do, unto my last breath. There was another time, when I was near Prague for an assembly, that I had in my writings so destroyed those biting ones, Rokyczana and his allies,[1] that they had fallen totally silent, and many among the heretics renounced their errors in throngs almost every single day. And so, the letters of the reverend lord cardinal of Saint Peter in Chains[2] called me to hasten to the assembly at Regensburg; I postponed everything and willingly complied. Then a third time, when I had gone down to Moravia from Poland to combat the heretics mentioned above, and was making good progress there, again I received word from the reverend lord [Aeneas Silvius Piccolomini, bishop] of Siena that I should make my way to the assembly at Frankfurt. I obeyed immediately. So many regions, so many provinces have I crossed, and encountered so many different languages, that the length of the journey and the difficulty of the labors would even wear down stones! But I have never shied away from nor succumbed to any labor for the growth of the holy Catholic faith, and for maintaining obedience to the holy Apostolic See.

I only say all of these things so that Your Reverend Lordship may understand: I desire nothing more fervently than to offer every service to Our Reverend Lordship [the pope] and his legates for the advancement of the Christian religion. And I do not think I should neglect to say that when I made my way to Frankfurt, by the words of his own mouth the aforementioned reverend lord of Siena [Piccolomini] asked me to come to the assembly at Vienna Neustadt, which I did, freely obeying his commands. I finally came to Pest, where the letters of Your Reverend Lordship summoned me. And here I stand ready for whatever you might command, ready to obey your orders most promptly. But I have received letters from our most serene lord [the pope] that I should under no circumstances depart from the kingdom of Hungary or the surrounding infidel lands without special command. Moreover, on the very day on which I made contact, the letters of Your Reverend Lordship were given to me, which very much inspired us to encourage

---

1 Jan Rokyczana (d. 1471), follower of Jan Hus and Capistrano's bitter opponent during the friar's mission across Central Europe. Their clashes took the form of an intense exchange of polemical letters and treatises, many of which were widely read across Central Europe in the second half of the fifteenth century.
2 Nicholas of Cusa (d. 1464).

the magnificent Lord John Hunyadi, Count of Beszterce. I can tell Your Reverend Lordship this one thing: he needed neither persuasion nor exhortation! He himself promised me, with his own mouth, seven thousand armed knights, equipped with all they needed for battle; that he would confirm more day by day; and that he would write to our serene lord the most unconquered Roman emperor, the most serene king of Aragon, the most illustrious Duke of Burgundy and other lords, informing them all that he would be ready with ten thousand troops, when the time was right, to move against the shameful enemy of Christ. Your Reverend Lordship should not think that he would for any reason back away from his promise. He is wearing his armor at every hour. I only fear that all of this delay will bring great danger to the Christians. The others promise that they will be ready this coming July. But the Turks do not sleep. Almost every day they invade the lands to the south, miserably plunder them, and also fortify them, such that we ought greatly to fear them [i.e., their advance] even before Easter. We therefore need a more urgent effort to resist the raging enemy, who enjoys nothing but the pouring out of blood, especially against Christians – the killing of whom, he thinks, is an offering to God.

Thus, whatever is to be done, may Your Reverend Lord decide. May Jesus Christ see fit to protect you into a generously old age, for the defense of his holy faith. From our convent in Pest, February 19, 1456. The useless little servant of Your Reverend Lordship, but also a faithful ambassador, Friar John of Capistrano.

3.6. JUAN CARVAJAL TO JOHN OF CAPISTRANO
May 14, 1456 (Buda)

Source: Trans. J. Mixson, from Luke Wadding, ed., *Annales minorum*, 3rd ed. (Quaracchi, 1932), 12: 385–6.

Reverend [father]. [We offer] greeting and [wishes for] every prosperity.

Your Reverend Paternity recalls the great insistence with which we have been urged to move south with the crusaders, and Your Reverend Paternity should do the same. But we, who have faith not in arms but in God (who when appeased by the prayers of his holy church softens his anger) promised to do so not so much in consideration of human strength but of divine power, and the Count of Beszterce [Hunyadi] wrote to us nothing against it. Thus, we went down to Szeged, where soon after the count (who has treated us with much humanity and honor) also arrived. We had many conversations about the service of Christ and the business of the faith, and in the end, it seemed best to the count that we should return to His Royal Majesty [Ladislaus V]. But we pressed on our way, making it as far as Petrovaradin.[1] The count not only condemned the move but also testified against us publicly, blaming us for all the losses that would follow, and openly adding that it would bring an enormous loss to Christendom as a whole. We thus yielded to his admonitions and returned to the most serene lord king. But since we have heard that other crusaders continue to make their way down, we have sent our reverend father in Christ, Lord Francis the bishop of Assisi,[2] who will receive them and deploy them to their proper positions. Among other reasons that the count opposed our move south was that it would above all harm the reputation and expectations that everyone had of the army that the legate of the Apostolic See was said to have gathered, that the enemy's fear of a strong force coming to our aid would thus be turned to mockery, and that [the enemy] would thereby be all the more bold. But for the gathering of so many knights and crusaders there is great need of your reverend father's assistance, and so we would gladly meet you somewhere that would allow us to be without the interference of others.

In the early days of the church the holy Roman pontiffs offered themselves to martyrdom, and we would do so freely now, just as we told the lord count; we also offered to stay in whatever place he might desire. And lest we seem to place any hope in arms, we have forbidden anyone of our household to bear the arms which they have purchased; for we have placed all of our hope in the prayers of the church, in which we place all of our hopes for defense. The day before yesterday a certain brother of the Order of Preachers whom we had sent to Venice came to

---

1 On the south bank of the Danube across from Novi Sad, approximately fifty miles upriver from Belgrade.
2 Francis Oddi, consecrated bishop of Assisi in 1444. A close confidant and collaborator with Capistrano, he had been given broad authority for the administration of affairs related to the crusade in these months. See documents 3.9 and 3.10.

us. He reported that he had heard from a Venetian nobleman (an ambassador or legate to Constantinople who had returned to Venice) that the captain of the fleet of the king of Aragon, Filomarinus, had been seen in those parts with a great multitude of galleys and ships, that the king was adding daily to the strength of the fleet, and that he had now sent twelve galleys to the captain. He also said that Lord Skanderbeg had taken the field, and that the king of Aragon had sent a thousand horse and other foot soldiers, and that he had seen a certain French knight and crusader making his way to Albania with five thousand armed crusaders wanting to serve in this war for a whole year. It is to be believed that on account of our delay here, as long as we are not drawn into the fight, a great gathering of crusaders will come together in Albania.

May our almighty God see fit to long protect Your Reverend Paternity. From Buda, May 14. Your devoted son, Cardinal John of Sant'Angelo, legate of the Apostolic See.

3.7. JUAN CARVAJAL TO JOHN OF CAPISTRANO
May 25, 1456 (Buda)

Source: Trans. J. Mixson, from Luke Wadding, ed., *Annales minorum*, 3rd ed. (Quaracchi, 1932), 12: 386–7.

Just this hour I have received the last of Your Reverend Paternity's letters, in which you advise us to handle the affairs of the crusaders promptly and with care. And we have done so with great care indeed. We have already written twice regarding our descent as far as Szeged, and our return to Buda at the counsel and insistence of the Count of Beszterce, and how we directed the reverend lord bishop of Assisi to go down to Petrovaradin to receive the crusaders and to scout the region and advise us regarding all things. It was not very pleasing [to Hunyadi] that we sent the bishop; and the count desires that we press the king and the princes of Germany to send military aid. Indeed, the count said to me that he had written to Your Reverend Paternity, telling you not to send any crusaders until he should advise that it be done. And having considered everything, it seems best to me that Your Paternity should go down to explore the region, and to inspire its men to war, so that they will be ready when the time comes. Then you can come to the lord king, and thereafter go to the emperor.

And if we work together here, we could accomplish much and prevail upon these princes. If the Holy Spirit should say otherwise to Your Paternity I pray that you would write, and if you cannot come I will make my way down to you. I have said much and proposed much but have accomplished nothing. I have heard some news from Rome that can be put neither well nor safely into writing. But if I am able to see Your Paternity, I will share it. Almighty God, etc. From Buda, May 25.

3.8. JUAN CARVAJAL TO JOHN OF CAPISTRANO
June 5, 1456 (Buda)

Source: Trans. J. Mixson, from Luke Wadding, ed., *Annales minorum*, 3rd ed. (Quaracchi, 1932), 12: 387.

By way of my own ambassador, I have sent to Your Reverend Paternity an apostolic brief and a copy of the letter of Count Hunyadi, in which he warns of the approach of the Turks. I ask Your Paternity to inform me about all that is being done there, and all that has been heard. The most serene lord king [Ladislaus] has gone hunting and has not returned. See to it, distinguished father, that the crusaders make their way down as quickly as possible. We will do the same, diligently. Almighty, etc. From Buda, June 5.

3.9. JOHN HUNYADI TO FRANCIS ODDI, BISHOP OF ASSISI
June 18, 1456 (Hollós)

This letter reflects John Hunyadi's efforts to coordinate troop movements and communicate strategy in the weeks leading up to Belgrade. It is addressed to Francis Oddi, bishop of Assisi, who had been given an important role in coordinating the campaign. The text is written in a hasty Italian that captures something of the urgency of the moment.

Source: Trans. J. Mixson, from L. Thallóczy and A. Antal, eds., *Codex diplomaticus partium regno Hungariae adnexarum*, Monumenta Hungariae Historica 33 (Budapest: Magyar Tudományos Akadémia, 1907), 2: 464–5.

Most reverend father in Christ, to be honored by us, etc.

We advise Your Lordship that this past Thursday we departed from Szeged and made our way toward Rumelia, as the land is called, where in every way and without any doubt we will arrive on the approaching feast of John the Baptist [June 24], insofar as once again we have now received certain news that the most cruel emperor of the Turks hastens and agitates for his arrival, and wants and is determined to come soon. And for this reason, we also hasten our movement to the place where the river called Morava passes or rather falls into the Danube, since by taking our stand against the Turks there he will not be able to sail his ships into that river.[1] We therefore ask Your Reverence to command all those who are signed with the sign of the cross to make their way, if possible, toward Rumelia. And this should be done quickly, because to delay their arrival any longer seems of little use, since they would not arrive before the Turks have put their ships into the Danube. We ask that Your Lordship send this letter to the bishop of Oradea, who will show it to the Palatine bishop.[2] From Hollós, on the sixth day after the feast of saints Vitus and Modestus, martyrs, in the year of our Lord 1456.

John Hunyadi, Count of Beszterce

3.10. JOHN OF CAPISTRANO TO FRANCIS ODDI, BISHOP OF ASSISI
July 3, 1456 (Belgrade)

This is among the very last of over six hundred letters that survive from John of Capistrano. Composed just as Mehmed II's troops were beginning to settle in before the city, it was also among the very last letters sent out before the opening of the battle for Belgrade. Like the previous letter by Hunyadi, this one is addressed to Francis Oddi, bishop of Assisi. It is also written in a style similar to Hunyadi's letter: a hasty Italian whose rapidly flowing prose captures the urgency of the moment. The translation here attempts to preserve that original style, even as its often run-on sentences at times overflow into what is an almost incoherent narrative.

---

1 This is eight miles northeast of Smederevo. The Morava was a crucial route for ships ferrying troops, weapons, and supplies northward from Ottoman-controlled territories in Serbia. See also the account of Jacopo Promontorio in document 29.
2 Oradea is in western Romania, on the Hungarian border, some 150 miles east of Buda. Bishop John Vitéz (d. 1472) was later cardinal archbishop of Esztergom, the position held at this time by Denis Szécsi. See document 9.

Source: Trans. J. Mixson, from L. Thallóczy and A. Antal, eds., *Codex diplomaticus partium regno Hungariae adnexarum*, Monumenta Hungariae Historica 33 (Budapest: Magyar Tudományos Akadémia, 1907), 2: 465–7.

To the reverend father and lord in Christ, Lord Francis bishop of Assisi, his most worthy protector and most honorable teacher.

Most reverend father and my most distinguished lord, etc. Just this hour I have received the letters of Your Lordship, and with them all that they command regarding those signed with the sign of the cross, and its admonitions which are most welcome to me. At this time the Turks already occupy all of the Danube, and their ships, which have made their way into the Danube, can easily make their way into Hungary, since as I said they hold and occupy all of the Danube, and today we await their siege of this fortress, because the Turks have never before been present in such power and strength. The Christian republic, the Catholic faith, and the Christian people and also the kingdom of Hungary are all under immediate danger, and Lord John the Count of Beszterce fights hand to hand with them in battle every day. But who could ever resist such an army and such a multitude without the help and aid of others? For this reason, I ask Your Lordship, if it please you by your faith, to send word by your trustworthy and speedy messenger to advise the most reverend lord legate [Carvajal] of this danger, attack, and occupation. Let them all look to the Danube, the most serene king and all ecclesiastical and secular princes who want to offer favor and aid to resist this great danger, since now is no longer the time to sleep and to stand around doing nothing, but rather the time and the hour "to rise from sleep."[1] See now that the one thing we worried about has already come to pass, in that the esteemed kingdom of Hungary, if it offers no resistance, will come under the hand of the Turks, under their subjection and command. And see now that if the king and the other princes, barons, and prelates of this land do not wish to be visited by the Turks, and if they seek and wish to defend their land, they should come themselves, or send their military contingents, and they should not wait for the day when they will have to drive the Turks from their own homes, since here is a proper and fitting place to resist them, here

---

1 Romans 13:11.

is the proper place to fight the battle with them, and here is the best place to fight them since after they have taken control of the water they will not stop before taking the land. Your Lordship must therefore write to the most reverend lord legate that His Lordship must work night and day with the king and other lords to stand up against this imminent threat and in the face of this pressing necessity they must provide aid and give help and support, and in the letters that Your Lordship sends to them, and may it please you to include this letter of ours along with them at the end, so that His Most Reverend Lordship may more clearly understand and confront this great and threatening storm. With the great affliction, pain, and weariness that I presently endure I am unable to write them, but Your Lordship can provide for what is lacking in me, always recommending me to His Most Reverend Lordship.

From the fortress of Belgrade, July 3, 1456.

Servant of Your Most Reverend Lordship, Brother John of Capistrano, by my own hand.

4. LITURGY FOR TAKING THE CROSS
1456 (Germany/Austria)

In recent years scholars have turned with great interest to church liturgy as a key source for understanding the history of the crusades. The ceremonies of the church, their words, music, and gestures, their theology and symbolism – all are now seen as crucial points of contact between the ideals and practices of crusade and medieval culture. Among the many liturgies of crusade, one of the most central was of course the ceremony for taking the cross, which survived in many varieties and remained a vibrant tradition throughout the later Middle Ages. One of those many ceremonies is preserved here, in a text translated directly from a fifteenth-century manuscript from the Austrian abbey of Saint Peter in Salzburg. The manuscript also contains Robert the Monk's famous Historia Hierosolymitana and other crusading materials, as well as brief narratives of the victory at Belgrade. This liturgy is copied into the manuscript alongside other materials associated with the Benedictine abbey of Benediktbeuern in Bavaria, suggesting their possible origin in that setting.

Source: Trans. J. Mixson, from Salzburg, Stiftsbibliothek St. Peter, MS B.IX.28, fols. 125a–b.

First, Let Them Take a Vow in This Manner:

I, N., promise to almighty God, the blessed Mary, forever virgin, and to all the saints, and to you, Father, that I will undertake the journey to fight against the Turks, freed of any legitimate impediment, offering myself to God, whether dead or alive. Amen.

The Form for Giving the Cross:

If anyone should desire to set out on campaign against the Turks, the cross should be imposed upon him in this way, since it is first blessed in this way and then imposed.

Blessing of the Cross:

First let the versicle "*Adiutorium nostrum*," etc., be said.[1] The Lord be with you. Prayer:

Almighty, eternal God, who gave the sign of the cross by the precious blood of your Son, and who through the same cross of your Son, our Lord Jesus Christ, desired to redeem the world, and through the power of the same venerable cross freed humankind from the bonds of the ancient enemy, we your suppliants ask that you see fit to +[2] bless these crosses with paternal piety, and impart unto them heavenly power and grace, so that whosoever might bear this sign of the Passion and the cross of your only begotten Son for the protection of body and soul would receive, through them, the fullness of heavenly grace, and the protection of your + blessing. And just as you blessed the rod of Aaron so he could put down a treacherous rebellion,[3] may you also bless these signs with your right hand and infuse them with your power to defend against all diabolical deceit, so that they might confer upon those who carry them saving prosperity of both soul and body and multiply their spiritual gifts. Through the same Christ.

---

1 A "versicle" is a short passage read by a worship leader, leading to a response by the congregation. The versicle noted here is "*Adiutorium nostrum in nomine Domini*," or "Our help is in the name of the Lord" (Psalm 123:8).

2 In the manuscript, this sign instructs the presiding cleric to make the gesture of the cross at various points in the liturgy.

3 Cf. Numbers 17.

Here They Kneel, and This Prayer Is Said Over Those Receiving the Cross:

Lord Jesus Christ, Son of the living God, who are true and almighty God, the splendor and image of the Father and eternal life, who said to your disciples that whoever wanted to follow after you should "deny himself and take up his cross and follow you,"[4] we seek your immense mercy, that you might always and everywhere protect and save from all dangers these your servants, who, in accordance with your word, desire to deny themselves and take up their cross and to follow you and fight against the Turks. May you also absolve them from the bond of sin and lead them from the vow they have taken to their desired goal. You, Lord, who are "the way, the truth, and the life," and the strength of those who hope in you[5] – we ask that you clear the way and grant prosperity to all, so that amid the trials of this passing world they may be always guided by your aid. Send them, Lord, your angel Raphael, who accompanied Tobias on his journey and freed his father from blindness, so that in going out and in returning he might be their defender against the treacheries of all enemies both visible and invisible.[6] And may you drive from them all blindness of mind and body.

After This Let Him Begin, Saying:

Accept this sign of the holy cross in the name of the Father + and the Son + and the Holy + Spirit, in the image of the Passion and the death of our Lord Jesus Christ and for the defense of your body and soul, so that by the grace of divine blessedness, after the completion of your journey, you may return to us healed and corrected. Through the Lord, etc.

---

4 Cf. Matthew 16:24.
5 Cf. John 14:6 and Isaiah 40:31.
6 The tradition of Christian pilgrimage, and eventually crusading liturgy, had deep roots in the story of Tobias and Raphael (from the Book of Tobit, ch. 5 ff.). See Gaposchkin, *Invisible Weapons*, ch. 1, especially p. 37 and nn. 42 and 43. See the introduction, n. 37.

Finally let him [the priest] sprinkle them with holy water.

Form of absolution for those marching personally against the Turks.

May our Lord Jesus Christ absolve you. And by his authority, and that of the most holy lord Pope Callixtus III granted specially to me in this region, I absolve you from all sins which you have now confessed to me, and which you would freely confess should they come to your mind. In the name of the Father, and the Son and the Holy Spirit, amen. By the same authority I grant to you full remission of all your sins and restore you to baptismal innocence. Know also that I commend your soul to the angels, so that should death befall you on your journey against the Turks, they will bear it away to the heavenly realms without delay, and without any taste of the pains of purgatory. Amen.

I impose nothing upon you for satisfaction except that you fight against the Turks without fraud or deceit, and that you persevere until the task is complete, or at least for the course of one year. In the name of the Father, the Son, and the Holy Spirit, amen.

Form of absolution for those remaining, that is contributing [financially], sending [support], or praying.

May our Lord Jesus Christ absolve you. And by his authority, and that of the most holy lord Pope Callixtus III granted specially to me in this region, I absolve you from all sins which you have now confessed to me, and which you would freely confess should they come to your mind. I also grant to you full remission of all your sins. In the name of the Father, and the Son, and the Holy Spirit, amen.

5. A POPE'S CALL TO PRAYER

As word reached Rome of the Ottoman advance toward Hungary, Pope Callixtus III issued a general call to prayer. After an initial publication of the decree on June 19, the pope then reissued it ten days later, on the feast of saints Peter and Paul in Rome, to broaden its reach. Though the battle for Belgrade was already over only weeks after its publication, the decree enjoyed a long afterlife. Copies of the text circulated relatively widely in both manuscript and print through the second half of the fifteenth century, and its provisions inspired both devotion and debate in the same period.

The text offers a strong example of several key themes in fifteenth-century crusading: the intersection of liturgy, piety, and memory; the intersection of communication and culture, and of preaching and pastoral care in a crusade context; and the deployment of longstanding tropes of crusade theology in a new fifteenth-century circumstance. As a solemn papal pronouncement, the language of the document is intentionally florid and intricate, its often paragraph-length sentences and their complex clauses intended to convey the gravity of the moment and the seriousness of the document's purpose.

5.1. CALLIXTUS III, CUM HIS SUPERIORIBUS
June 29, 1456 (Rome)

Source: Trans. J. Mixson, from Zsolt Visy, ed., *La campana di mezzogiorno: Saggi per il quinto centenario della bolla papale* (Budapest: Mundus, 2000), 192–201.

Bishop Callixtus, servant of the servants of God, to our venerable brother patriarchs, archbishops, and bishops, along with their beloved sons in spiritual affairs, vicars and abbots and other ecclesiastical persons, wherever they may be established in the Christian world, greetings and apostolic blessings.

Since in these last years the wicked persecutor of the Christian name, the tyrant of the Turks, has taken Constantinople, and in doing so carried out every kind of cruelty, burning against not only its people – because he could do nothing against our God – but also against the relics of his saints, striving with all of his might to persecute the faithful, whom he wished to oppress, striking them with such unceasing slaughter that every day now brings word of new plagues and new calamities;

And since – which is even more outrageous – he has not been content with all of this, but has instead climbed into a chariot of pride and put it into his mind that he should establish an empire over all of the Christian people and of the West, preparing himself day by day to invade it with violence, working to wipe the holy name of Christ from the earth and to establish the damnable and horrendous blasphemy of the dog Muhammad;

So it is that some time ago, amid such harsh times and circumstances, we (though of insufficient merit) were called to the pinnacle of the highest apostolate and had compassion for the Lord's flock as it fell everywhere under the sword of the infidel. The Lord our Savior thus charged us to guard and feed that flock, and we have tried up to this day (insofar as divine grace has seen fit to be generous) to fight back against such perniciousness as best we can, with all of our strength and that of the Roman Church.

To this end we press onward with an attentive mind and spirit. And indeed we have already imposed a tithe on all clergy throughout the Christian world; we have summoned the Christian people for the common cause of the faith through our letters; we have sent ambassadors to preach that all should gird themselves as best they can to come to the defense of the holy cross of the Lord, and to collect the aid offered by Christians; we have also sent our legates in part to pacify kingdoms, in part to inspire kings and princes, and also in part to gather and lead troops against this second Muhammad, who follows in the footsteps of the old; and not long ago we commanded our beloved son Ludovico, cardinal priest of San Lorenzo in Damaso and our chamberlain, to depart under the Lord's command with a maritime fleet.[1] In the end we have omitted nothing, insofar as the Lord has seen fit to help us, that might be of profit, on both land and sea, for this salutary expedition.

But since, as the Apostle says, it is for us to labor and for God alone to ensure that our actions have results,[2] we see that nothing will be accomplished in all of the effort of these great deeds unless we return to the Lord in fasting, weeping, and lamenting and prayer, so that God might return to us – who, with lashes of this kind, bruises the Christian people because our sins demand it, just like a slave who knows the master's will and does not do it.

For this reason, we think it necessary and especially appropriate that we beg for God's mercy with groans and cries; that we humble our souls in prayer, trusting not in our human strength alone, which is fragile and faltering, but in the army of the Lord, who is truly a "tower of strength,"[3] and who once gave to Abram and his small band, trusting in the Lord, victory over powerful kings.[4] For victory in war is his. "No king is saved by the size of his army; no warrior escapes by his great strength."[5] "Behold," says the Psalmist, "the eyes of the Lord are on those who fear him, on those whose hope is in his unfailing love, to deliver them from death and keep them alive in famine."[6]

---

1 Ludovico Trevisan. See document 3.4, n. 3.
2 Cf. 1 Corinthians 15:58.
3 Cf. Psalm 60:4.
4 Cf. Genesis 14.
5 Psalm 32 (33):16.
6 Psalm 32 (33):18–19.

Was it not more through prayer than through weapons that the people of Israel overcame the Amalekites, as divine scripture bears witness? And when Moses raised his hands, Israel conquered, but when he lowered them only a little, Amalek had the upper hand. And preparing to fight the Philistines, they also said to Samuel, "Do not stop crying out to the Lord our God for us, that he may rescue us from the hand of the Philistines."[7] And when he prayed and offered a sacrifice for them, the Lord "thundered with loud thunder against the Philistines and threw them into such a panic that they were routed before the Israelites."[8] And did not the humble and devout prayer of King Hezekiah destroy the pride of Sennacherib, king of Assyria, who gloried in all of his chariots and horses, until an angel's blows struck down 185,000 of his soldiers?[9]

For who is not admonished, amid troubles and challenges of this kind, to flee to prayer as if to an unconquerable fortress? Is not King Jehoshaphat more to be admired than any great victory, [a king] who, when surrounded by the neighboring Gentile nations and struck with fear, offered himself completely to the Lord and preached a fast for all of Judah, and with all of the people gathered together offered a most devout supplication to the Lord – who then sent his spirit on Jahaziel son of Zechariah, and so responded to him: "Listen, King Jehoshaphat and all who live in Judah and Jerusalem! This is what the Lord says to you: do not be afraid or discouraged because of this vast army. For the battle is not yours, but God's. It will not be you who will fight. Only be strong, and you will see the Lord coming to your aid."[10] Jehoshaphat then embraced fervent prayers and divine praises, and established singers who praised the Lord and who went before each of the army's divisions like a most firm and unassailable fortress, saying with a resounding voice: "Confess to the Lord, for his mercy endures forever." And as they began to sing praises, the Lord set ambushes against them, so that they turned against one another and began to wound and kill each other.[11]

By these same powers Judith, so illustrious among women, a woman sustained by prayer in tears of weakness, killed Holofernes and broke

---

7   1 Samuel 7:8.
8   1 Samuel 7:10.
9   2 Chronicles 32:20–1. See document 1, n. 7.
10 A paraphrase of 2 Chronicles 20:15–17.
11 A paraphrase of 2 Chronicles 20:21–2.

the swollen pride of the great king Nebuchadnezzar. "For thy power, Oh Lord, is not in a multitude, nor is thy pleasure in the strength of horses, nor from the beginning have the proud been acceptable to thee: but the prayer of the humble and the meek hath always pleased thee."[12]

And what shall we say about Maccabeus, the strongest of men, glorious for all ages, who as often as he went out in battle and was filled with prayer came back victorious? Yet when he neglected prayer and failed to call on God and went to fight with King Antiochus, he fled in defeat. He also neglected the protections of prayer in the war against Bacchides, and so was conquered and killed, and the people of God were defeated.[13]

We say then that you are just, oh Lord, and your judgments are proper. We deserve all that we suffer, because we have sinned against you and have not obeyed your commands. Divine mercy does not strike a sinful people with such a severe punishment without seeing them wander stubbornly from its commands. Achior of the Ammonites, though he was a pagan, offered this advice to Holofernes: "Now therefore, my lord, search if there be any iniquity of theirs in the sight of their God: let us go up to them, because their God will surely deliver them to thee, and they shall be brought under the yoke of thy power: but if there be no offense of this people in the sight of their God, we cannot resist them because their God will defend them: and we shall be a reproach to the whole."[14]

So it is that we ought to have fear and great dread, because the furor of the infidel could never prevail against the people of faith unless the Savior has seen something in them that offends the eyes of His Majesty. He often crushes and corrects the corrupt ways of mankind through war and avenges his enemies by way of their enemies. We should therefore hasten to penance and prayer, lest in putting off our emendation and our return to the Lord our God worse things should happen to us. For it is certain indeed that if we return to the Lord, he will return to us. Seeing the affliction of the sons of Israel in Egypt and hearing their cry, he gave them a most glorious triumph over the Egyptians, freed them, and led them with joy across both the sea and the vast solitude of the desert to the promised land. And when they joined new evils to old and found themselves oppressed at various times from all the surrounding

---

12 Judith 9:16.
13 1 Maccabees 9.
14 Judith 5:24–5.

nations, as often as they turned back to seek the help of the Lord, he freed them through divine mercy. God heard David himself, penitent and in tears, when he said, "I have sinned, Lord!" and immediately forgave his sin; when Ezekiel prayed, God extended his life and put off the hour of his death; and when those who were about to die under the just sentence of the Ninevites turned to him in weeping and prayer, God heard them in his mercy. And now, too, "the hand of the Lord is not shortened,"[15] for "he is gracious and merciful, patient and rich in mercy, and ready to repent of the evil"[16] of his people.

Moved by these witnesses of holy scripture and by many other examples, we therefore exhort you, brothers and sons, through the merciful heart of our Lord Jesus Christ, that by virtue of the pastoral duty with which you have been entrusted, you insist diligently on the moral reform of the people under your care, according to the canons and decrees of the holy fathers, since, as our predecessor blessed Gregory says, the wolf does not tear apart the Lord's flock secretly in the night, but in the light of day.[17] Let us be vigilant, therefore, that none are lost, and that if any are captured let us call them back to the Lord's flock with voices of divine eloquence; and let us not be afraid of the task, because we have taken up the title of pastor not for rest but for labor. For a pastor who refuses to reprove the errant surely kills them. But nothing is closer to our heart, and there is nothing we desire more (as we ought to do, according to God, and as we are obliged to do) than to reform the life and customs of the people. And with God's help we intend to do so in due time. But because at the present moment this storm of the Turks is the most urgent matter, we labor to confront it with all of our effort and strength. And just as we have required bodily aid from all the Christian faithful, both clergy and laity, through the bull we crafted for that reason[18] (so that we ourselves might not seem to be lacking in commitment) we now turn all the more fervently to spiritual matters, which are the greater ones.

---

15 Isaiah 59:1.
16 Joel 2:13.
17 Gregory the Great, *Epistolae* 2: 39. See *The Letters of Gregory the Great*, vol. 1: Books 1–4, trans. John R.C. Martyn (Toronto: Pontifical Institute of Mediaeval Studies, 2004), 218.
18 Under his own name, Callixtus III had reissued and revised Nicholas V's call to crusade with the bull *Ad summum pontificates apicem* (May 15, 1455).

We therefore admonish you in the name of the Lord, and by the authority granted to us by almighty God and by blessed Peter and Paul, his apostles, we direct and command, that each and every priest, even if a cardinal, or of whatever other dignity, whether secular or regular, exempt or nonexempt, whenever they may celebrate Mass, should remember and recite the established prayer against the pagans: "Almighty and eternal God, in whose hand are the power and rule of all kingdoms, in your mercy look upon the Christian armies, that the heathen who put trust in their own ferocity may be vanquished by the power of your right hand."[19]

For both those who celebrate this Mass and those who say this prayer, from the spiritual treasury of the church and in the name of the Lord we mercifully release them from one hundred days of any penance imposed upon them. And so that all people – of both sexes and all kinds – can participate in the prayers and indulgences offered here, we order and command that in each individual church, of whatever city, land, or locality, between nones and vespers (that is, before the ringing of vespers and separated from it by at least half an hour), on each day one or more bells should be rung three times – richly, that they might be heard well, just as the customary evening salutation for angelic protection.[20] And at that time each individual ought to say the Lord's Prayer (that is, the Our Father) and the angelic salutation ("Hail Mary, full of grace," etc.) three times. To those who do so once, we mercifully grant in the Lord forty days' indulgence; and for those who do it three times, with genuflections, one hundred days.

Moreover, we command and order that in each of the cities, lands, fortresses, and villages or locales of your dioceses, administrations, or jurisdictions, you should hold general processions on every first Sunday of each month. All of the people should come together for these, along with all of the clergy, whether secular or regular, mendicant or

---

19 For the origins of this traditional prayer, see Gaposchkin, *Invisible Weapons*, 198–9, where it is described as "one of the most important prayers in the history of crusade liturgy" (198). See the introduction, n. 37.

20 The tradition referenced here is that of the liturgy of the hours, specifically the afternoon hours between "nones," i.e., the ninth hour of the day (roughly 3:00 p.m.), and "vespers," at nightfall. These lines, along with later traditions of commemoration (see document 24) would eventually inspire the legend of a bell rung at noon in commemoration of the victory.

not mendicant, exempt and nonexempt, whether outside or inside the walls of the cities, lands, fortresses or towns, or in the suburbs. But those religious who dwell in solitude[21] and who are not accustomed to come together for such processions when they are found in cities, lands, fortresses, and towns or other locales, should not be compelled to do so. Rather, on these days let them gather either within their own monasteries, or around them, or in a nearby basilica – whatever will inspire greater devotion for them – and hold their processions there. As for nuns, whether they live within or outside their city walls, let them hold their processions within their convents, singing the seven penitential psalms with litanies. Moreover, if on any of these Sundays some legitimate obstacle should arise that would prevent these general processions from being done devoutly and peacefully, we ask that each parish or monastery or other church carry them out inside their churches or monasteries, or however else might be judged best for the devotion and peace of the people. We leave this matter to your conscience. But let the prayers, songs, and other ceremonies in these processions be done in whatever way is customary in each city, land, fortress, town, or locale, or however you think best to arrange devoutly for a matter so pious and necessary. Only make sure that the solemn Mass to be said in these processions is the one ordained by the church "against the pagans."[22]

But since the faith and its works come from hearing[23] – as the Apostle says – and no one can hear without preaching, we wish and command that in all cities, fortresses, towns, and locales that might be able to host a preacher of the word of God, he should preach a sermon to the people on the occasion of this solemn procession. In that sermon he should first work to confirm the faith, and to encourage patience in tribulations of this kind. Let him also teach how the "trying of faith works patience," and how "patience has its perfect work,"[24] and that (as blessed Augustine says) as often as we suffer some oppression or tribulation, we are given admonitions and corrections. For sacred scripture does not promise us peace, security, and rest, but warns of tribulation,

---

21 A reference to those who led the life of hermits, or who belonged to religious orders that emphasized solitude, such as the Carthusians.
22 For the origins of the *Contra paganos* mass, see Gaposchkin, *Invisible Weapons*, 222–5. See the introduction, n. 37.
23 Cf. Romans 10:17.
24 Cf. James 1:3–4.

oppression, and scandal. What unusual things does humankind suffer that our fathers did not suffer? The church is indeed (as Ambrose says) a ship sailing on the sea of this world, tossed by the winds and the waves (that is, the lashes of temptation) while the angry tides (that is, the powers of this world) try to drive it on to the rocks. But even if it is often cast about by waves and storms, there will never be a shipwreck, because on its mast (that is, the cross), Christ is raised up; the Father guides the rudder; and the comforter Spirit guards the prow. Twelve oarsmen guide the ship through the straits of this world, that is the twelve apostles and the same number of prophets. Here, I say, is the ship that, even though it might be tossed about by this world as if on the open sea, will never founder on the rocks or sink in to the deep. Divine Providence has arranged that it find consolation in prosperity, insofar as it was not destroyed by adversity; and that in adversity it should be tested, so that it will not be corrupted by prosperity. In this way the two circumstances compensate for one another.

Let the preacher also lead the people to penitence, since both the master of truth and his precursor John began their work of preaching by saying, "Do penance! The kingdom of heaven is near!"[25] Let them also consider, with an anxious mind, the day of eternal judgment and its terror, and embrace penance; and let them bathe in tears the stains of all of their sins, so that our pious Creator, when he comes for judgment, will console them all the more with grace, insofar as he now sees they are punished for their sins.

And so, in the end, as it becomes clear just how savage the Turks are and what great harm they try to bring to Christians, the prayers and pious vows of all are directed to God against them. To be sure, we (who are assured of the mercy of almighty God) have granted a generous indulgence entailing bodily labor, and we have also granted an indulgence to those who take up a spiritual task. Therefore, to all who are truly penitent and confessed and who take part in these processions, we grant seven years (and the same number of Lents) of true indulgence. To those who offer a pious vow and fulfill it, however, whether of prayer or pilgrimage or the offering of alms, so that almighty God might see fit to come to the aid of pious Christians, we offer two years (and the same number of Lents), as contained in our present apostolic letters or bulls,

---

25 Cf. Matthew 3:2.

to be valid for as long as our holy crusade should last, and until victory be granted – as we have faith it will – against the treacherous Turks and the other followers of the damnable sect of Muhammad in the East.

Therefore let no one diminish or with reckless daring presume to contradict this record of our warning, encouragement, command, release, grant, and concession. But if someone should presume to do this, let them know that they incur the wrath of almighty God and of the blessed apostles Peter and Paul.

Given in Rome, at Saint Peter's, in the year of our Lord's Incarnation one thousand fourteen hundred and fifty-six, on the third kalends of July,[26] in the second year of our pontificate.

5.2. BULLA TURCORUM / "TÜRKENBULLE"
Cum his superioribus in Gutenberg type (Mainz, 1456)

The text of Callixtus's call to prayer circulated widely in manuscript after 1456, especially across the regions of Central Europe (e.g., southern Germany and Austria) that were nearest the Ottoman advance. The publication of the text also coincided with the advent of the printing press, making it among the very earliest examples of what would become a long tradition of crusade indulgences and other papal propaganda in print.[1] In Erfurt in October 1454, an indulgence inspired by appeals from Cyprus and authorized by Pope Nicholas V came into print and circulated widely across Germany. Soon after, in December 1454, a German pamphlet exhorting European powers to action was published in Mainz in the circles of Johannes Gutenberg, its imprint in a rough version of the same type (the so-called DK) that Gutenberg would use for his famous 42-line Bible. In 1456, Gutenberg's circles in Mainz used the same type to publish Callixtus III's call to prayer, in both Latin and German.

Source: Catholic Church. Pope Callistus III (1455–1458), "Bulla Turcorum" (Mainz: Johann Gutenberg, 1456). (Donatus and Kalendar Type.) Princeton University Library, Scheide Collection. https://dpul.princeton.edu/scheide/catalog/0v8380652.

---

26 June 29.

***

1 For this broader context see Margaret Meserve, *Papal Bull: Print, Politics, and Propaganda in Renaissance Rome* (Baltimore: Johns Hopkins University Press, 2021).

❖ Bulla thurcoṛ ❖

Calistus ep̄s serū[9] seruoṛ dei venẽabilib[9] frib[9] p̄triarchis arc'ep̄is ep̄is electis necnõ dilectis filiis eoṛ in sp̄ualibus vicariis ac abbatib[9] rectis[que] eccãsticis p[er]sonis vbilibet p[er] orbẽ xp̄ianũ constitutis Salutẽ & ap[osto]lica b[e]n[e]diccionẽ Cum hiis sup[er]iorib[9] annis impius noı̃s xp̄iani p[er]secutor Thurcoṛ tyran[9] p[ost] oppressã constãtinopoli ciuitatẽ in qua om̃e gen[9] crudelitatis exec-cuit seuiẽs nõ solũ sed ex quo i deũ n[ost]r̃m nõ poteat in suos s[an]c[t]os q[ue] reliquias impij desiderii conatũ totũ virib[9] sit p[er]secut[9] fideles p[o]p[u]l[o]s ad q[uos] valuit aspirare assiduis cladibus affligẽdo ita vt noue plage i dies calamitates nũcient Cũq[ue] etiã q[uod]

Bulla Turcorum/"Türkenbulle"

6. POPE CALLIXTUS III, *OMNIPOTENTIS DEI MISERICORDIA*
March 26, 1457 (Rome)

This decree, issued in multiple versions between 1455 and 1460, served as a complement to the formal calls to crusade issued in 1453 and 1455. It opens with a rich statement of incarnational theology, here shaped by late-medieval traditions of Christ's suffering. It then turns to another sharply polemical denunciation of Mehmed II as a bloodthirsty tyrant, and a lament of the failure to respond to earlier calls to crusade, before concluding with the terms of a portfolio of indulgences (here specifically for territories in southeastern France, the Rhineland, and the Low Countries), as well as the procedures for their publication and for the collection of funds. At the end of the document, in the bottom margin, a scribe has also copied an additional paragraph with further variants on the same terms – a rare glimpse of the flexibility and negotiation that shaped these kinds of arrangements, as well as the reality that they might also circulate in multiple versions.

Source: Trans. J. Mixson, from Vatican, Archivio Segreto Vaticano, Reg. Vat. 446, fols. 269r–270r. The bull remains unedited and unprinted, but a preliminary census of surviving copies can be found in Benjamin Weber, *Lutter contre les Turcs: les formes nouvelles de la croisade pontificale au XVe siècle* (Rome: École française de Rome, 2013), 536. This document in particular is noted on p. 300.

The immeasurable mercy of almighty God toward the sons of mankind (who are held captive under the law of death and damnation by the sin of the first parent) ordained, by way of a profound and inscrutable plan, that the only-begotten Son of the Father, coequal and coeternal in the same substance, should take on the form of a servant and made to be obedient unto death on our behalf, bearing in his own body all of our frailty and pain. So great was his desire for us, and so great the magnitude of his love, that he, though righteous, did not shy from enduring torture for the unrighteous: flogged, spit upon, insulted and taunted, struck with blows, crowned with thorns, pierced by nails, stabbed by a lance, hung on the wood of the cross, so that he could justly say to the pilgrims of this world, "Oh all ye that pass by the way, look and see if there be any sorrow like to my sorrow!"[1] For our Redeemer has been

---

1 Lamentations 1:12.

wounded because of our sins, led to death because of our crimes: "he hath done no iniquity, neither was there deceit in his mouth."[2] Here is the one through whom we have been liberated from the gates of hell, and through whom the gates of paradise have been opened for us, the one who "laid down his life for his sheep."[3]

And since none of us can participate in his merits except by adhering to the faith of the Catholic truth, and also by risking life and goods in defense of the Christian religion, we, upon whose shoulders divine mercy has seen fit to place the burden of caring for all of the Christian people, have taken careful notice of how the enemy of our religion, Muhammad, prince of the Turks, has by his power not only subjugated Constantinople and many other Christian cities, lands, and locales, but also – thirsting for Christian blood – is now drawing near to us everywhere and waging horrible wars. He glories in depopulating Christian lands, and daily he rises up more and more pridefully, presuming to ascribe to his own strength what is in fact known to have happened because of the sins of the Christian people. And indeed, he labors daily with such cruelty, with unquenchable madness, to drink the very blood of Christians, sparing no one from his sword whatever their age, sex, or creed. He glories in settling his people and in depopulating the land of Christians, so much that unless we rise up quickly against him, we fear he will overcome us like a tempest's thunder.

Our predecessor, Pope Nicholas V of blessed memory, in whose time the city of Constantinople, alas, was lost, at that time exhorted, required, and commanded all Christian princes, whether emperors, kings, or whatever else their worldly titles might be, by the force of the profession made at their baptism and the oaths offered when they accepted their crowns, to come to the defense of the faith with their goods and their persons as much as possible, in reality and without delay. The same pope also granted the fullest of indulgences to all who come to the aid of the faith in this moment of such great necessity. But as we have heard, painfully, from the reports of trustworthy witnesses, the devotion of our faithful has grown colder by the day, and there are few who have prepared themselves to resist the power of this Muhammad, most bitter enemy of the Christian people.

---

2 Isaiah 53:9.
3 Cf. John 10:11.

Therefore, so that we do not fall under the fearful judgment of our Savior (because we, in our silence, did not see to it that the Christian religion should be protected from this foul Muhammad); but instead, so that by our effort the Christian faithful might be all the more fervently inspired to such a saving work, and thus find salvation for their souls; by the mercy of almighty God, and trusting in the authority of his apostles Peter and Paul, we grant to each and every faithful Christian of either sex who is truly penitent and confessed, in the whole dominion of the Dauphiné of Viennois, the duchy of Savoy, and all of the dominions of the same duke on both sides of the mountains, as well as on both sides of the Rhine all the way to the ocean, in the duchies of Cleves and Blois[4] and the cities and dioceses of Liège, Metz, Cambrai, and Utrecht, as well as other jurisdictions found in those parts, [the following]:

All who wish to do so may choose a suitable confessor, whether a secular cleric or a member of a religious order, if they make an offering from their resources that is proportionate to their estate and dignity; that is, for those who have greater resources, man and woman counted as one person, five or four florins of the camera; those who are of middling sort, three or two; those who are truly poor, one florin or even a half, or its equivalent true value, so that, even if any of them are joined in marriage, they can make payments of this kind separately. Upon listening diligently to their confessions, the chosen confessors shall [absolve them] from all of their sins, errors, and excesses, even if these are reserved for the Apostolic See, whether generally or in particular. The absolution should be granted only once. Moreover, confessors may in fact absolve penitents (if such is asked for in a spirit of humility) from whatever sentences and censures and lawful penalties might bind them, imposing a suitable penance and other things enjoined by law. They may then grant to each one who is truly penitent and confessed a plenary indulgence and remission of all sins, for one time at the point of death, insofar as they remain in sincerity of faith, in the unity of the holy Roman Church and obedience and devotion to our laws and those of our successors as Holy Roman pontiffs. Moreover, we grant that they may, by apostolic authority, freely and licitly commute vows, whether for Outremer, or to the blessed apostles Peter and Paul and James, as

---

4 Here perhaps a scribal error, in that Blois was a county, not a duchy.

well as vows of chastity, excepting only vows of religious life, to serve other works of piety, as may be appropriate for the salvation of souls.[5]

To all primates, archbishops, bishops, abbots, and other ecclesiastical prelates and metropolitans, or the canons of other cathedral churches established throughout all of the world, by virtue of holy obedience and under penalty of excommunication (which those who disobey will incur immediately), we strictly order and command that each of them (whether they themselves or through others) should by apostolic authority solemnly publish and explain (or have published and explained) the present document (or a copy of it) on Sundays and festival days in all metropolitan, cathedral, collegiate, parish, or other churches or places, wherever they might be. And from these there should be [sent out] collectors [or their deputies or substitutes] who should by apostolic authority solemnly publish and explain (or have published and explained) the present document in the vernacular tongue as well, so that it might be more clearly understood by all. Let them also promise to publish and promote [also through deputies or substitutes] as often as may be required, the exhortatory letters called *De placet*, which ought to be granted and held without any contradiction, fee, or payment.[6]

But because it will perhaps be difficult to carry these documents to all of the individual places where it might be necessary to have them, we wish and by the same authority decree that copies of these documents, authorized by a public hand and the seal of the aforesaid collector (or archbishop, bishop, or other ecclesiastical authority) ought to be granted the same full faith as the originals, and ought to have the same force as if the aforesaid originals were being presented or shown. Therefore let no one diminish or with reckless daring presume to contradict this record of our warning, encouragement, command, release, grant, and concession. But if someone should presume to do

---

5 The reference here is the release from vows of crusading or of pilgrimage to Rome and Santiago, with an exception for vows of entry into a religious order.

6 The reference here is to letters of approval granted by secular authorities prior to the publication of ecclesiastical enactments. These are also called "*Regium placet*" or "*Exequatur.*" See the article "*Exequatur*" in F.L. Cross and E.A. Livingstone, eds., *The Oxford Dictionary of the Christian Church*, 3rd rev. ed. (Oxford: Oxford University Press, 2005).

this, let them know that they incur the wrath of almighty God and of the blessed apostles Peter and Paul.

Given in Rome at Saint Peter, March 26, 1457, in the second year of our pontificate. (+

(+ Here is a variant: If of the rank of count, baron, or magnate, or other illustrious figure, [they should pay] one hundred papal ducats. Those who are of the rank of noble knights, burghers, or wealthy merchants of sufficient means should pay fifty ducats. Middling sorts of the same professions, however, should pay thirty ducats, wealthy burghers and artisans twenty-five, middling sorts of these professions fifteen or at least ten. Others of lesser rank, however, should pay five or three gold florins, or their true value. In another [version] the quantities have been changed: If of the rank of count, etc., fifty; knights, etc., thirty; middling sorts, etc., twenty; burghers, etc., fifteen; middling sorts, etc., ten or eight; lesser sorts, five or three. In other versions [of this decree] the quantities have been modified: If of the rank of count, etc., twenty-five; of the rank of knights, etc., thirty-five; middling sorts, etc., ten; burghers, etc., seven; others, etc., five or three, etc.

PART TWO

The Earliest Accounts

7. JOHN OF CAPISTRANO TO POPE CALLIXTUS III
July 22, 1456 (Belgrade)

This letter is the earliest surviving witness to the fight for Belgrade. John of Capistrano, whose preaching and correspondence were central to the organization of the crusade (see documents 3.2, 3.3, 3.5, 3.9, and 3.10) was also an eyewitness to and at least in part a participant in the battle. He drafted this letter in its immediate aftermath, perhaps only a few hours after its conclusion.

Source: Trans. J. Mixson, from Luke Wadding, ed., *Annales minorum*, 3rd ed. (Quaracchi, 1932), 12: 429–30.

Most blessed father, after kisses for your sacred feet, joy and exultation! Glory to God in the highest, by whose mercy it has happened that we have not been destroyed. We were in such tribulation, and in such dire straits, that everyone thought we could no longer resist the power of the Turks. Even general Hunyadi himself, truly the terror of the Turks and a most powerful defender of Christians, judged that it would be best to abandon the fortress of Belgrade. For the savage Muhammadans so strongly and incessantly assaulted the citadel, destroyed the walls with so many machines, and fought against us so fiercely that our strength began to fail, and that our soldiers, especially, began to lose heart. But amid tribulation the Lord revived us: after we had driven them from the city, our most savage enemy deceptively retreated, seeking to set an ambush for us as we pursued them. And though Lord Hunyadi commanded that none of our soldiers should leave the fortress, the crusaders cared nothing for his command and instead rushed upon the enemy, placing themselves in great danger. And when I, the least of the servants of Your Holiness, was unable to call them back from beyond the walls, I went forth into the field of battle and ran here and there, now calling them back, now encouraging them, and setting them in order so that they would not be surrounded by their enemies. And in the end the Lord, who can save through the few as well as through the many, mercifully granted victory to us, and put the most savage army of the Turks to flight. We captured all of their catapults and their diabolical machines,[1] through which they thought they would subjugate all of Christendom. Therefore, may Your Holiness rejoice in the Lord, and may he decree that praise, honor, and glory be offered to him, because he alone has done a great wonder. Neither I, an unarmed and useless servant, nor the poor and rough crusaders who are your devout servants, could have done this through our own strength. The Lord God of Hosts has done all of it. To him be the glory forever. I write this quickly and hastily, exhausted as I return from the battle. I will write again very soon to describe more clearly what has happened in detail.

From Belgrade on the feast of Saint Mary Magdalene, on the very day of the most glorious victory.

8. JOHN OF CAPISTRANO TO POPE CALLIXTUS III
July 23, 1456 (Slankamen)

This second letter from Capistrano, discovered only in the twentieth century, was composed only a day after the first letter. It was written in Slankamen, a town on the south bank of the Danube roughly a day's journey (some thirty miles or fifty kilometers) northwest of Belgrade. The letter offers more detail and context than

---

1 Capistrano's reference here is to the sultan's great bombards.

the first, including more about Capistrano's own role, which has been disputed from the day of the battle itself. Capistrano also notes that he will send by way of the emissary Jerome of Padua a "certain noble boy of Bosnia," who will bear witness to the outcome of the battle in person.

Source: Trans. J. Mixson, from Luke Wadding, ed., *Annales minorum*, 3rd ed. (Quaracchi, 1932), 12: 796. The letter was originally discovered by Michael Bihl in a manuscript in the Benedictine abbey of Salzburg (Salzburg, Erzabtei St. Peter, Benediktinerstift, Bibliothek, b XI 19).

Most blessed father, a kiss before your feet, and humble and devout obedience unto death. What praises and acts of grace we offer to almighty God and to our Lord Jesus Christ, by the invocation of whose name he has seen fit to give to us this, his glorious victory. Oh, most blessed father, if Your Holiness could have seen it with your own eyes, how many dangers, and how great, from which the Most High delivered the Christian people, I think there is no way Your Holiness could consider it all without coming to tears.

The most treacherous pagan Turks destroyed the walls, towers, and buildings of the fortress that was a first line of defense, meant to deter the invasion not only of the glorious kingdom of Hungary, but indeed of all Christendom. Now the Turks climbed through walls destroyed by siege engines and cannons. They breached the outer walls, lest I exaggerate, through perhaps thirty holes, after which they then worked to fill in the rampart and the moat surrounding the fortress of Belgrade. Having done this, they were more easily able to climb the destroyed towers and walls. They did as much as God allowed, and thus brought down great judgment upon themselves. They climbed their way into the fortress and thought that they could take it with their diabolical machines and inventions. But Christ Jesus our Lord, with his customary piety and mercy, protected us; I would say nothing but that they were hardly able to harm us, and many thousands of their number were killed. I counted forty-four [Turkish] galleys in the first of our attacks, all of which were destroyed by the same treacherous Turks, who set them on fire. But there were, as we later found out, sixty-four; all told, we had some twenty in hand. We had overcome ten in the first conflict of your crusade, three of which survive of the larger kind, and two of the smaller. And what would I say to Your Holiness regarding their land forces which, as those who fled from them now claim, numbered over one hundred thousand soldiers? Still others say that there were over 120,000. Oh, most blessed father, how great is the strength of our Lord Jesus Christ!

Since no one else arrived who could serve as a regent for Your Holiness, it fell to me alone to motivate the troops, to direct the battle line, and lead them to take up a strong position in the face of the Turks. I advised, and at first often instructed our troops, like a Joshua working among the ruins of the walls of Jericho, so that with my cries as I invoked the most holy name, all could cry "Jesus!" together in the loudest voice.[1] And so it was, most blessed father, that when I had gathered together what was no small number, and when I first began to cry "Jesus!" all responded to my voice – even if we could not easily attack the enemies of Christ, because we could not easily cross the Sava River (which stood between us) without the aid of small ships. When those enemies of Christ heard our loud voices and our resounding cries, those wicked and cursed ones, though no one pursued them, were for the first time put to flight. Our Lord and God Jesus Christ rose up, and his "enemies were scattered"; "as the smoke vanishes," his enemies vanished, and "as wax melts before the fire," so his enemies perished before the face of God.[2]

O most blessed father, how could all the people of the Christian religion be enough to return thanks and worthy praise to our Lord Jesus Christ, who alone, for his cause and for our protection, fought and drove out and destroyed the army of the Great Turk with such confusion and memorable shame, so that forever, as long as the present age will last, such a glorious victory of Christ Jesus will never cease to be on the lips of all Christians.

Hindered by many things, holy father, and tangled in the difficult business of the matters assigned to me by Your Holiness, I am not able to give a thorough account of all of these events. But note that I am sending the noble man Jerome of Padua to the feet of Your Holiness, who will present to Your Blessedness, as a testimony to this victory, a certain noble boy of Bosnia, who was carried to the Turks in his mother's womb and raised up in their royal court. He is of good character and prudent disposition, and he will tell Your Holiness many things concerning the status of the Great Turk and his present ruin. I commend them, both

---

1 Cf. Joshua 6:1–27.
2 Cf. Psalm 67 (68).

the one presenting and the one presented, to Your Blessedness. And although I, a weak little worm at your feet, am unworthy and undeserving of your grace and of the opportunities you have afforded me, nevertheless with Abraham's reverent humility, I might speak to you and ask you, my lord, insofar as it please Your Holiness, to support me with greater authority, at least insofar as it pertains to the salvation of souls and the protection of the Christian faith, for the glory and the honor of that name "which is above every name,"[3] Christ Jesus. May he see fit, happily, to long maintain Your Holiness within his holy church.

From Slankamen on the twenty-third day of July, 1456, after the flight of the Great Turk, against whom the Almighty saw fit to grant us victory on the previous day, that is, on the feast of Saint Mary Magdalene, in a fight that was terrible and terrifying in every way. Let all Christians give thanks to God. Concerning the thirty-two cannons of the great and diabolical Turk, I hold it as certain that we have captured nearly all of them. After my departure from the site of the victory, as we came to meet the most reverend lord legate [Juan Carvajal], the illustrious lord governor John [Hunyadi] wrote to me that with certainty half of the army of the Great Turk had been destroyed.

9. JOHN HUNYADI TO DENIS SZÉCSI, ARCHBISHOP OF ESZTERGOM
July 23, 1456 (Belgrade)

and

10. JOHN HUNYADI TO LADISLAUS GARAI, PALATINE OF HUNGARY
July 24, 1456 (Belgrade)

In the days after the battle for Belgrade, John Hunyadi sent two essentially identical letters to two different recipients. The first letter, sent on July 23, was addressed to Denis Szécsi, archbishop of Esztergom and cardinal. The second was sent to Ladislaus Garai, palatine of Hungary. Both were strong supporters of Ladislaus V, and

---

3 Philippians 2:9.

central figures in the circles around him: Szécsi was among the most important church prelates in Hungary, and Garai among the kingdom's most important barons. These two letters are significant because they, like those of Capistrano, are among the earliest accounts of the battle. And here again the rambling diction of a hurriedly composed communication captures the urgency of a moment. These letters also enjoyed (with minor variations) a wide circulation in subsequent decades, offering their copyists and readers a succinct, if partial, account of the events of July 22, 1456.

Sources: Hunyadi's letter to Szécsi is printed in Gelasius Dobner, *Monumenta Historica Boemiae* (Prague, 1768), 2: 417–18. His letter to Garai is printed in L. Thallóczy and A. Antal, eds., *Codex diplomaticus partium regno Hungariae adnexarum*, Monumenta Hungariae Historica 33 (Budapest: Magyar Tudományos Akadémia, 1907), 2: 208–9. Both letters, with a discussion of their German translations, are also printed in A. Bernoulli, ed., *Basler Chroniken* (Leipzig: Hirzel, 1890), 4: 391–2. The following is my translation of the core text, which is common to both letters.

Magnificent lord, to be honored by us! We are able to write of this news to Your Lordship: that the emperor of the Turks had come with his mighty power, and with many machines, to lay siege to the fortress of Belgrade. Indeed, he came with such power and skill as no human eye has ever seen, nor mind could comprehend, and in fact he so destroyed the fortress through the blows of his cannons such that it is no longer a fortress, but a field;[1] indeed the walls have been torn down to the ground. On the most recent Wednesday, after the hour of vespers,[2] they stormed the fortress in a marvelous way, such that it lasted all through the night and into the next day up to midday, such that we engaged them twice in the middle of the fortress, as if in an open field. Then at last we charged against them beyond the fortress and fought with them into the evening. With God's help we drove the emperor of the Turks himself from the aforesaid fortress. We captured all of his cannons and engines. And on this last Friday he took to flight with those who were left, alone, in the middle of the night, confused and defeated.

It is clear that if anyone should at present move militarily against that emperor, he would never be able to capture his kingdom more easily

---

1 Here and elsewhere, the letter offers a clever play on words in Latin: *non castrum sed campum*.
2 These events take place from the evening of July 21, through the night, and all through the day of July 22.

than at the present, since the princes and leaders of his people, and especially his foot soldiers, were utterly defeated before that fortress, and since the aforesaid soldiers of that emperor (who are normally a superior force among his people) have been utterly annihilated. And we were in the fortress, with our own leader,[3] at the time of the victory, and from that day on which the siege of the fortress began, we were there. Indeed, many of our household and our men have been wounded, and some have died. But with God's help, the emperor of the Turks never turned himself to flight from a battle with greater shame than now, as one totally defeated. For we first had a fight against them on the water, during which we captured many of their galleys. Of those ships that remained, when on the aforesaid Thursday we sought to move against them, they soon turned themselves in flight; their men rushed out from them and set the ships on fire. But for now, we do not know what we are to do with the aforesaid fortress, since it cannot be called a fortress, but an open field, because it is so broken apart and totally destroyed.

Given in the aforesaid place on the Friday before the feast of Saint James the Apostle, in the year 1456. John Hunyadi, Count of Transylvania.

11. JOHN HUNYADI TO KING LADISLAUS V
July 24, 1456 (Belgrade)

This third letter from Hunyadi recounts for the king of Hungary the news of the battle. Note that the phrasing of the account is often very similar (and sometimes identical) to Hunyadi's two previous letters.

Source: Trans. J. Mixson, from N. Iorga, ed., *Notes et extraits pour servir à l'histoire des croisades au XV. siècle* (Bucharest: Académie Roumaine, 1915), 4: 134–5 (no. 68). See also the alternative recension (with minor discrepancies) in A. Bernoulli, ed., *Basler Chroniken* (Leipzig: Hirzel, 1890), 4: 394–5.

To the most serene prince and lord, Lord Ladislaus, by the grace of God king of Hungary, Bohemia, Dalmatia, Croatia, etc., also Duke of Austria

---

3 A somewhat obscure phrase, though perhaps a reference to the castellan Szilágyi.

and Styria, as well as margrave of Moravia, our most gracious lord, the faithful servant of Your Distinguished Serenity, John Hunyadi, Count of Transylvania.

Most serene prince, our most gracious lord! Following the humble recommendation of my servants, we recount for Your Serenity how and in what way the emperor of the Turks, with certain clever schemes, lay siege to this fortress of Belgrade – indeed with such war machines that no human eyes have ever seen, nor any human could comprehend. For in the end we could not defend this fortress, and he was able to grind it down to the ground, along with the moat – so much so that we cannot call it a fortress, but a field. For we were in that fortress with our own leader from the beginning, as well as at the time of the assault, and we are there now.

Having broken and destroyed the fortress, early on Wednesday after the hour of vespers, the emperor of the Turks began the hand-to-hand fight for the castle (called "storming" in the vernacular tongue). It lasted through the whole night and into Thursday, up to the hour of the midday meal, so that two times we found ourselves fighting within the castle and face-to-face, as if on one field, due to the breaking and destruction of the walls. We won both battles, by God's will. Then with God's help we rushed out and rose up against those Turks. We drove the emperor of the Turks out from under the aforesaid fortress and field, and he was totally defeated. By God's will we even captured all of his machines and his cannons. We continued to fight on the fifth day [Friday] until just before nightfall. Then at last the emperor of the Turks turned and fled the battle by night, fumbling and in great shame. Indeed, no emperor of the Turks has ever faced such great destruction as he has just now, and he has endured such great shame as has [never] been read about in history.

Your Serenity should know that the greater part of his infantry has been destroyed, and certain wounded among them, who barely escaped, were among the strongest of his people. There are also many other leaders and princes of his that lie dead beneath this fortress. We, too, have suffered great losses of our men and our household through these enemies. But for now, Your Serenity must know that at present this emperor of the Turks has been so defeated and disordered that should the Christians rise up against him, as has been suggested, with God's permission they could gain all of the kingdom of the Turks quite easily, because he has lost all of his power beneath this castle. The more so because, before the aforesaid fight on land, we fought with their galleys on the river, and we were able to capture a number of these. But on the aforesaid Thursday, when we were about to move against them, those that remained soon turned in flight, and the Turks jumped from them and set them on fire.

Although Your Serenity wrote that all were to come [here] under our military authority for the defense of your kingdom, Your Serenity should know that none responded. There were only crusaders, and John Korogh.[1] Thus, we diligently ask Your Serenity that you send one of your faithful and a reliable German man who can see the destruction and the brokenness of Your Serenity's aforesaid fortress; and also that Your Serenity inform us of what to do about this place, since it cannot properly be called a fortress anymore, but a field. And we also are ready and prepared to uphold for Your Serenity that fidelity which we have promised, and now promise again.

Given at Belgrade, on the Saturday before the feast of Saint James the Apostle, in the year 1456.

12. JOHN OF TAGLIACOZZO TO A FELLOW FRANCISCAN
July 28, 1456 (Sava River)

A native of the Abruzzo region of central Italy, John of Tagliacozzo rose through the ranks of the rigorist Observant wing of the Franciscan order and by the 1440s had become a renowned preacher. In 1454 he was assigned to a small group of companions who were to accompany John of Capistrano on his mission to preach the call to crusade in Central Europe, and was present at its launch in Frankfurt. An eyewitness to Belgrade, he is the author of the most substantial single narrative account of the battle (document 25). This letter, addressed to a fellow Franciscan in the Abruzzo region of Italy, is a crucial early witness. Here we have another hurried, often seemingly stream-of-consciousness account, this one written in Tagliacozzo's lively Italian, as the friar was on board a ship on the Sava, at the foot of what was left of Belgrade.

---

1   As ban of Macsó, John Korogh played a key role in the defense of Belgrade. See document 25, pp. 172–3 and n. 32.

Source: Trans. J. Mixson, from G.B. Festa, "Cinque lettere intorno alla vita ed alla morte di s. Giovanni da Capestrano," *Bullettino della R. Deputazione abruzzese di storia patria*, ser. 3, 2 (1911): 18–58 (here 49–56).

Reverend father, by humble recommendation, though I am occupied by many things and hindered by the cares of the present moment, nevertheless I thought to write about other things which have come to pass after my last letter was sent to Your Paternity, knowing that you will pass along what I write to you to all the fathers, for their consolation. I am not beset by any desire to note every detail; rather, I have decided to select, with care, a few things from among many. And so that the unlettered may delight in what is written here, and so that the joy may be common to all, I will write in our mother tongue.[1]

Through the letter which I sent to Your Paternity during the most recent month of May, I advised you of all that had happened and what had then been planned. It was rumored among all of us that the Turks with all their power would come to besiege Albandander,[2] or Belgrade, the farthermost city in Hungary, most famous and the key point for entering Hungary and a gateway to Serbia, situated in the middle of the two most famous and grand rivers, the Danube and the Sava. The city also has a stronghold, which we call the citadel, which is like a good Italian castle. We made our way toward the aforesaid city, our father [John of Capistrano][3] on the land, preaching and signing with the cross, and we on the Danube on a large ship that carried provisions, as well as some books. The governor of Hungary, John [Hunyadi], wrote continually to the father that he should hasten toward the city, since the Turks were approaching by land and sea, but he offered no more detail. We wrote letters to prelates, to princes and lords of the kingdom, that they should command the crusaders to come, that they should come themselves, and that they ought to carry out the command of the

---

1 Tagliacozzo here distinguishes between those trained in Latin and a broader public that is not, and therefore "unlettered." This broader population was still possessed of varying degrees of vernacular literacy, however, and the letter might in any case have been read aloud. After his opening lines in Latin, Tagliacozzo from this point writes in Italian in order to allow his account to reach that wider audience.
2 Here a garbled articulation of Nandor Alba, one of several names for the city.
3 Here and throughout this letter (as well as in his later account), Tagliacozzo uses "father" as a term of deference for Capistrano.

king (which was with common assent of all the kingdom) and that for every one hundred people there ought to be ten men-at-arms and two foot soldiers in the field against the Turks.[4]

We arrived in great haste with five ships full of crusaders on the second day of this month, that is on the feast of the Visitation of Our Lady, and early that morning we entered the city with great solemnity and celebration. On this day, after Mass and a sermon and then a meal, the father thought to go to the aforesaid John, who was more than ten miles toward the front with the Turks. Going by way of the Danube with three ships and a few brothers, he encountered a great storm of wind and water on the Danube. It was necessary for them to pause on land and with great fatigue, not being able to go any farther, because they could not even see one another. It was thus necessary that they turn back toward where they had left. Oh God, who does not allow your servant to perish! Had they gone but a half of an Italian mile[5] farther, they would have encountered the galleys and ships of the Turks, and their army on land, and they would not have been able to escape, and would have been captured and killed. On the following morning, a Sunday, it was decided that the father should go back for reinforcements and rouse the crusaders to defense of the city. Some twenty-seven thousand had taken the cross from the father in Hungary, all of them quite ready for battle. Many others also received the cross from the legate [Carvajal] and the other preachers and prelates. After the father had left, the Turkish army began to arrive in such numbers that within three days the Great Turk had one hundred thousand troops and, between his ships and galleys, some two hundred sails. He also had nineteen cannons so large and destructive that truly nothing in human history had ever been made like them – some to destroy the walls, and some to cast great stones upon people. The length of these nineteen cannons is incredible. The larger is two ells and around five palms long.[6] The stones are so large that they are some two or three palms larger than a man's embrace. Of the smaller cannons

---

4 The Italian of this phrase ("*x homini armati et dui ad pedi*") is somewhat obscure.
5 Here and elsewhere, distances described as "miles" in the sources could vary widely by region. In this case, across the Italian peninsula, a mile was typically around 1.5–1.8 km.
6 "Ells" (for the Italian *canna*) and "palms" are again units that varied regionally across Tagliacozzo's Italy, but his estimate here totals approximately five meters, or sixteen feet. The surviving Turkish cannon known as the "Dardanelles gun," cast in 1464, is almost exactly this length.

there is no number, though it is said there were two hundred; there is no counting the arquebuses to be found on land and in the water.[7] And of all the expert bombardiers in the world – and there are many – four [in the service of the sultan] are the most excellent: one a Venetian, one a German, another a Hungarian, and the fourth a Bosnian.

While the father made his way among the troops, I remained behind with the brothers and the books and the provisions in the citadel. The field was now filled nearly up to the gate with many astonishing machines, which the cannons on the ground could not harm.[8] Those who could have seen what I saw would have said that everything was covered in snow, so many were the pavilions. But the common rumor was that there were one hundred thousand people gathered there. Christian refugees would often come to us, and we received them kindly. I believe fifty people of various Christian nations fled to us from their army. After three days their galleys took the Danube and blocked the passage, so that the supplies and reinforcements we were waiting for could no longer reach us. And the governor [Hunyadi] was with his army on the far side of the Danube. We were closed in and surrounded by land and by water; every day we waited for death, and the cannons knocked the walls down flat to the ground. If it had not been for the large and wide moat, the Turks would have entered at any time. We placed our only hope in our governor John [Hunyadi], who often comforted us, and came to support us. We placed our hope in the father, who did not sleep day or night. I fell seriously ill, and we had no safe place to hide from the cannons. He [Capistrano] often went along the walls, and especially to those who were ill and to those who manned the cannons.

Let no one think that I or any other friar of the Observance touched a single stone or did anything else to attack, nor that a single Turk was ever killed at our command. With a clear conscience we said, "Defend

---

7 Here and also in his later and longer account of Belgrade (document 25), Tagliacozzo uses a variety of terms to describe the firearms of his day. These terms are not easy to translate, above all because they had not yet settled into the more consistent patterns of use characteristic of later centuries. Here the word *scopetto* is translated as "arquebus," designating a variety of early, hand-held long guns that were in widespread use across Europe by the middle of the fifteenth century. For context see Kelly DeVries and Robert Douglas Smith, *Medieval Military Technology*, 2nd ed. (Toronto: University of Toronto Press, 2012), 145–56.

8 Another somewhat obscure phrase: "*che le bommarde de la terra non le potevano offendere.*"

the name of Christ and the Catholic faith; repel the enemies of the cross of Christ; do not fear death, because you will be martyrs and fly to heaven,"[9] and similar things. We visited the sick, we said Masses. We shared with the poor from such provisions as we had: three barrels of wine and plenty of biscuits, a barrel of flour in many sacks and a barrel of wheat, salted meat, and cheese and other things of this sort, dispensed as seemed appropriate to me. But nearly all of us were ill. Brother Ambrose argued with the father.[10]

We were in this circumstance for thirteen days, and the famine and death in the city were severe. Then after those thirteen days of siege, that is, on the fourteenth day of the month, there came more than two hundred ships and in them were more than three thousand people and many cannons, and on land from both sides of the Danube. These were almost all crusaders. There were on land and water around eighteen thousand people altogether, and [the army of?] the two Johns [also] sent by land. The Turkish galleys were about an Italian mile[11] upriver from the city, and from the city more than forty well-armed men were set in order;[12] some came upriver and others down, trapping the galleys of the Turks in the middle. The battle lasted about ten hours, and the Turkish galleys were driven back by our ships, suffering great losses. Three of them were rammed by ours, and more than a thousand Turks drowned in the Danube, with untold numbers wounded. And if it had not been for a fire on our ship that was set off from the powder of a cannon (caused by a careless bombardier), all of the galleys would have been taken. Thus it was necessary for our ship to retreat. But the fire was put out quickly and caused no damage to either our ship or our men. Some galleys went down; we suffered thirty dead in our ranks. I saw more than ten decapitated who were carried back to land. We also captured three of the Turkish ships, their crew and spoils, and recaptured the passage of the Danube and our ships anchored where the

---

9 These phrases in the text are in Latin, perhaps to reflect dialogue among clerics over issues of violence and martyrdom.
10 In the text *calivicava*, taken here as a garbled form of *cavillare*. The Brother Ambrose referenced here is Ambrose of Aquila, a close companion of both Capistrano and Tagliacozzo, mentioned many times in Tagliacozzo's accounts of the events.
11 Approximately 1.5–1.8 km. See n. 5 above in this document.
12 A seemingly low number. Perhaps "forty" for "four hundred," or in this context, perhaps forty "men" (*homini*) for forty "ships" (*navi*)?

[Turkish] galleys had been, along with the army with the two Johns. And in a short time, there were more than forty thousand there, almost all of them crusaders.

The Turks worked on destroying the walls. And on the following day, the day after the victory of the ships and the galleys, the two Johns entered the citadel with more than three thousand soldiers, and one hundred Polish crossbowmen. Thereafter they went out and fought hand-to-hand with the Turks, many of whom were killed and wounded, while only three of ours died. We watched this from the walls together with the father. Also, many spoils were taken from the galleys. On this day I went with the father to the army where our ships were. The number of our troops was growing every day. And the father, now with ambassadors, now with letters, moved all the kingdom to offer support. And every day the Turk grew in anger because he could not for all of his ingenuity obtain what he desired. And I do not want to pass over in silence how when one of the sultan's grand ships came close to the shore, a stone of the cannons of the Turk fell on it and sank it; the ship was not far from the shore, and it was quickly stripped of its goods and its weapons.

Day and night, the father did not stop. He ran through the camp; by night he brought soldiers into the camp, and by day exhorted the army to defend, to attack, and to embrace martyrdom. In truth, I can write that in fifteen days the father did not sleep eight hours, day or night. All had respect for him. He was the leader of all. They did not care for John Hunyadi. They only obeyed the father. And it was most inspiring to see the crusaders kneeling before the father: he could do more with these crusaders than the king of Hungary!

The Turks did more by night with their cannons and other malicious designs than by day. And the father was always gathering more recruits, so much that through His Paternity there came together some twelve thousand persons in all, who were like a wall and an obstacle to the enemy, since the walls were already torn to the ground. And the governor [Hunyadi] and the castellan [Michael Szilágyi] asked aid from no one else but the father and took counsel from him. I could not write all of this down, because it would take up a large volume.

The Turks sought to engage in a long and bitter battle at the walls, all of which had already fallen to the ground. On the night of the vigil of the most glorious Magdalene, the Turks offered their intolerable prayers, calling out and shouting out to the devil Muhammad. Then came the sound of an astonishing drum, and from this the governor John – who knew their customs – understood that they were about to launch their final assault. He sent for the father, asking that he come with all the troops and all the ships to the shore of the river nearest the fortress. And the father, who never slept, bearing the banner of Saint Bernardino and the cross, did what John had commanded, and when the father arrived the battle had already begun. Many thousands were also gathered within; and then he went out to set the ships in order against the galleys that had surrounded the land on all sides.

This most cruel battle lasted through the night until the third hour.[13] It was fought before the walls, all across the land; but they could not fight on the water because of our ships. Oh, it was something unheard of! Three times the Turks fought their way in and were repelled. The Turks had made tunnels under the ground, so that they could enter secretly inside the moat. They had gathered together innumerable small objects and things to fill the moats, which were quite wide, and on one side there were already pine planks on the fallen walls. It is impossible to write about the multitude of dead Turks. The third time they entered, there were more than six hundred Turks. Castellans, citizens, men-at-arms drained away from the fight and abandoned the defense. Some jumped from the windows, some from the walls; some ran to the water and waded in up to the waist. Only the crusaders remained, along with certain women, who were as strong as lions, and five of our brothers, who remained in prayer and awaited death and holy martyrdom.

Then God gave to the poor crusaders such ardor and such spirit, such a strong will to die and to become martyrs, and such energy and strength, that, gritting their teeth against the Turks, with fire that was set by many bundles of reeds steeped in pitch, and with molten lead and the powder of the cannons, with the death of innumerable Turks they cast them out a third time. This was on the morning of the most holy sinner [Mary] Magdalene. Read now of a miraculous thing: when the Great Turk saw his troops driven back, and their great slaughter, he lost his treacherous nerve, set fire to his galleys and ships, and by midday they were burned up. Oh God, how quickly he was undone who

---

13 That is, the third hour after sunrise, so approximately 9:00 a.m.

schemed against your name! Many spoils were gathered from these ships by our troops. At the ninth hour, after the Turks had retreated in desperation, they began to abandon the field. Five crusaders against more than two hundred Turks. And they were driven back as if we had been a thousand horsemen. Gathering their nerve, our soldiers struck out – perhaps a thousand in all – and killed many Turks and wounded many more. The Turks were all filled with fear and ran away like madmen. The father, who was on the bank of the river with more than ten thousand soldiers, saw this and commanded the troops to come to the aid of the others, while he himself also went along. Meanwhile the governor waited with the galleys and the ships. In any case I can write that perhaps six thousand crusaders without horses stopped one hundred thousand raging Turks. This was the number, with many of them by now killed and wounded. There is no counting the women, because they had so many. And God granted so much grace to the poor crusaders that as the great multitude retreated, they were able to capture and keep the famous cannons and the many riches that the Turks could not defend. They fled like evil women; and when they stood their ground in one place, with our troops holding the position of their cannons, they suffered a great defeat: our men killed many of theirs with their own cannons. By night they all departed, and by the next morning there was not one pavilion to be seen. All of the cannons, with great fanfare, were brought into the fortress.

In this fight the father sought to be in front and to go before the others. I was very afraid that he would be killed by the famous arquebuses of the Turks; but God protected him so much that, though the arquebuses and arrows rained down, he was untouched. I, like Saint Peter, remained behind,[14] to see the end. When the Great Turk saw that he could not have his way – so I learned through those who later came to me – he cursed all of his posterity should they ever presume to move against this fortress; I also learned that he began to act foolishly, and that he said, "And if these peasants can drive me away, what will real soldiers do?" And so he thought he had reached his end. His principal leaders were dead, and his vice-emperor wounded. On this night, as they departed, they buried their dead along the road. All of the men

---

14 Cf. Luke 22:54–7.

defeated in battle were dead or wounded; they carried the wounded away in 120 carts and buried the dead as they went, as is their custom. And as they went on the following day, some who followed behind stole many of the oxen and cattle they had used to carry their machines. Day and night, they fled as if they were being kicked.

Of the Christians it is thought that in all this time there were two hundred martyred by the Turks. But of the Turks there is no number, for I saw so many of them burned that they seemed like salted meat, and I saw so many of them lying in the ditches that they could not be counted; indeed, you could hardly walk over the battlefield for all of the multitude of Turks that lay dead there. By night they had gathered together the tackle and ropes and machines in one church, and with the powder of the cannons burned it all, along with the church. They are most cruel men, and on the first day they captured seven Christians; they cut off their heads and despoiled and trampled their bodies under the hooves of their horses. And always, after they had captured a Christian, they laid out the body in the form of a cross, and after many torments decapitated it for the love of the cross. And they had great hatred for our father, for they knew he had inspired all of Hungary as well as other lands against them. The power of the Turks is broken. They had gloried in their galleys and ships and sails, and their wondrous cannons, and they were confident that in a short time they would gain all of Hungary and soon make their way to Italy. Yet they have been defeated by one fortress, and by crusaders without horses!

Think now, father, that after [the day of] the glorious Magdalene, none other than our father [Capistrano], with his diligence and labor and sweat, has now defeated the Turk, and yet he still does not rest, and is not satisfied, and never tires from moving all the world against the Turks. For now, he even leaves the heretics and the schismatics be, and indeed treats them well, insofar as they wish to be against the Turks. Many religious have also joined this crusade, and priests, whom the father has not supported if they do not wish to dedicate themselves to pious works.

I have written all of this humbly and quickly, but that which I write is as clear as midday. If I have not written well it is because I write on board a ship. Of the other events that are unfolding, I will continue to advise you. I ask for the love of God that if this letter should come into your hands, you would send it to the magnificent Count of Celano, or to the magnificent Countess,[15] to whom I am not able to write at present. But when I have more time, I will write them eagerly. Please recommend both the father and me to them. We look forward to seeing you, my comforting and pleasing brother (who is ready to suffer evil), and each day seems to me like an entire year. And it should not be otherwise that I recommend myself to you and to all the brothers; and also, especially, I recommend to you the old man, our saint and brother, Ambrose.[16]

On the river Sava at the foot of the fortress of Belgrade, on the twenty-eighth day of July, 1456.

Also, the Great Turk has fled, seriously wounded by an arrow.

13. JOHN OF CAPISTRANO TO POPE CALLIXTUS III
August 17, 1456 (Slankamen)

By mid-August of 1456, reports of the events of Belgrade (the texts in the next section among them) had begun to make their way back to Western Europe. In those same days, after weighing many accounts of the battle for himself, John of Capistrano authored his last and most detailed letter regarding the events.

Source: Trans J. Mixson, from Luke Wadding, ed., *Annales minorum*, 3rd ed. (Quaracchi, 1932), 12: 430–2.

Most blessed father, kisses for sacred feet, humble and devout obedience unto the death of the cross,[1] and its savage torture. Since wherever something is lacking, it ought rightly to be provided, and since I am now in fact able, given more reliable news, to say more about what I could not comprehend at first sight on the day of our Lord Jesus Christ's glorious victory (granted to us by the authority of Your Serenity and by the ministry of those few, signed by the character of the true, living cross), even though the machines, instruments, and terrible devices that the enemy had prepared are indescribable – carriages to transport

---

15 Lionello Accrocciamuro (d. 1458) and Covella da Celano (d. 1471). See Alberto Maria Ghisalberti and Mario Carnavale, eds., *Dizionario biografico degli Italiani*, vol. 1 (Rome: Istituto della Enciclopedia italiana, 1960).
16 Ambrose of Aquila. See n. 10 above in this document.

***

1 This may reference the possibility of Capistrano's martyrdom.

the cannons, iron and wooden casters to transport ships and skiffs over the mountains and hills to move the troops that would despoil the kingdom of Hungary (which in the end God would not allow them to do) – nevertheless I will write about those things which can be described turn by turn, not wasting time with adornments, but in simple truth.

For when I said before that many thousands of the enemy had been killed, the illustrious lord despot [George Branković] (who even if he does not accord with our faith, nevertheless according to Your Serenity's designs is with us in coming together against the faithless Turks) reported yesterday to the most reverend lord legate [Carvajal] and to me that more than twenty-four thousand were killed on the day of the battle. He has asserted that the same number and more had died as they fled, as in the time of Gideon.[2] And it was not without divine judgment that the prince of the Turks himself, along with his most trusted warriors, had thereafter found their way, in stunned flight, to Sofia. And intending to prevent his remaining ministers from fleeing any further, he killed many of them, both by his own hand and by those of his executioners. The same despot said furthermore that the principal voivode of the most damned Great Turk Muhammad, who ruled in Scythia (where there is a gold mine that belonged, and by right belongs, to the despot) was beheaded by the sword, as was his wife, by those who are said by right to be subject to the despot.[3] But [the sultan's] castellans still hold five fortresses which, with God's help, [the despot] hopes to recapture, with the favor and assistance of Your Serenity and the reverend lord your apostolic legate. Moreover, the despot also says that he had sent forty scouts to ascertain what had happened to the most monstrous Turk, that a quarter of them have returned, and that all have said that even though they had applied themselves with all diligence, they were not able to learn anything certain about his status – all of which firmly convinced the despot that he was dead. If only it were so.

I had written, blessed father, that in our first battle I had counted forty-four ships, and so it was; but thereafter, having learned the truth by way of better information, we counted sixty-four, of which we now command some twenty-seven in total, counting the small and the large

---

2 Cf. Judges 7.
3 A vice-regent, in this case perhaps a confused reference to Karaca Bey, who was killed at Belgrade. See document 33.

together. Concerning the size of the army, however, though many say that there were 120,000 soldiers, nevertheless the most reverend lord your legate, after a walk with me over the better part of the space in which the army of the enemy had been located, judged that they could have numbered as many as 150,000 given the evidence of so many camps. In my second letter I had written of thirty-two cannons, because at the time I had not seen more. But thereafter, having counted all of them, great and small, we found over three hundred. And of the small firearms that are set off by hand (called, in our parts, *scopettae*), we have no number for all that were found, because so many have been hidden.[4]

Blessed father, since Justinian's law[5] says that "nothing is done while there is still something left to do," therefore, behold, "now is the accepted time"! Behold, "now is the day of salvation" for the Christian people![6] Now is the time to fulfill the desire of Your Serenity, that we proceed not only to recover Greece and Europe, but to recover the Holy Land of Jerusalem, which almighty God will grant us easily, if Your Serenity will not let go of the holy desire that you have embraced. May Your Serenity, most pious and most zealous in the faith, kindly grant this one most pious thing to the reverend lord your legate [Carvajal]: only send from Italy twelve thousand cavalry, or at least ten, armed in the Italian manner and supported by your wages. If they can persevere with us in the field for six months straight, along with your devoted crusader sons as well as these illustrious princes, prelates, and barons of the kingdom of Hungary, we hope to gain so much from the goods of the pagans that we can sustain ourselves abundantly for a further three straight years without any expense, satisfying the needs of our entire army by means of their spoils. Indeed, the same lord despot strongly affirms that we would be more able to expand the Christian faith and to drive back the pagans with ten thousand soldiers at the present time than with thirty thousand at some other time.

Note also that all those who have, for the name of Christ and out of obedience and devout reverence for Your Serenity, taken the sign of

---

4 The term translated here is *pixidibus*, one of many terms for various kinds of handheld gunpowder weapons. See document 16.1, n. 5, and document 25, n. 15.
5 Capistrano, a jurist by training before his conversion to Franciscan life, here references the *Corpus iuris civilis* of the Roman emperor Justinian, a sixth-century text that had by his day become foundational for European law.
6 Cf. 2 Corinthians 6:2.

the living cross, burningly share this desire of the reverend lord legate. And although it has pleased the Almighty to take from us that unconquered warrior of most illustrious memory, a defender so frightening to enemies of the holy Catholic faith, the Lord John Hunyadi, who lost his life to pestilence on the eleventh of this month, he has nevertheless given us a man who is not unequal: Nicholas of Ilok, under whose strong and powerful leadership John himself established his militia, with only five or six horses. For this same Nicholas is an illustrious prince, excellent in magnificence, wise in counsel, prudent in action, virile in spirit, fervent in faith, in obedience to Your Serenity a humble emulator of your honor and great zeal; in word and deed, one who is thought to be a leader among other princes, prelates, and barons of this kingdom; one whom they hold in high esteem, and to whom all attribute praiseworthy fame – and who accordingly possesses a hereditary title in this kingdom, in the banate.

Now, therefore, most blessed father, let the Christian princes and kings be roused anew! While the furnace burns, the gold thickens; while the enemy is weak, and while the fervor burns in the Christian people, let warfare's arms be raised against the shameless infidels. Let Your Holiness therefore command, as it pleases you, what is to be done. And may it please the Almighty to preserve his holy church forever.

From Slankamen, August 17, 1456.

PART THREE

News and Propaganda

14. AMBASSADOR OF THE BISHOP OF ŠIBENIK TO POPE CALLIXTUS III
July 26, 1456 (Buda)

Šibenik was a port city on the Adriatic coast of Dalmatia (modern Croatia). Though long an independent commune with deep roots in the region's history, by the early fifteenth century the city was subject to the Republic of Venice (Italian Sebenico). Both its geographical position on the Adriatic and its importance as a commercial center ensured that the city, like others such as Ragusa (modern Dubrovnik), was a crucial node in the communication networks that ran across the Adriatic coast and its hinterlands to Italy and Western Europe. In this letter, an anonymous ambassador of the bishop of Šibenik reports hurriedly, almost incoherently, of the events of July 1456. The document presents itself as a rapid list of news items and minor details recorded in the days leading up to July 26, some of them at odds with other accounts. It thus captures something of the fluid, confused flow of rumor and partial information that circulated during and after the siege of Belgrade.

Source: Trans. J. Mixson, from L. Thallóczy and A. Antal, eds., *Codex diplomaticus partium regno Hungariae adnexarum*, Monumenta Hungariae Historica 33 (Budapest: Magyar Tudományos Akadémia, 1907), 2: 469–71.

A copy of a news report sent by the bishop of Šibenik to our most holy lord Pope Callixtus III, from Hungary, before anything definitive was reported or known regarding the victory over the Turks.

Having written and sealed his letters, an ambassador came in from the field after a harried journey. He carried letters and brought the latest word, and said that he was an eyewitness to these things and was in the fortress itself.

A great multitude of Turks occupies the plain and the hills, but as is reported by those worthy of trust, many are women and their number seems to be greater [than it actually is].

There is a great amount of [money][1] in the Turkish camp; one loaf of bread costs thirty aspers (these are a third of one [Venetian] ducat).

Many are dying from famine in [the sultan's] army, and many captives are fleeing to our Christian camp.

Even many Turks are being compelled by hunger to come to us.

It is said that when a certain ambassador came from Asia to announce that the eastern regions had been devastated by his enemies, the Great Turk had him killed in his presence, and said he would do the same to others who brought similar news.

The Great Turk is said to have sworn that in the coming month, August, he would celebrate his fast in Buda.[2] Perhaps with God's help this will happen, but in a prison and not in the city.

He [the sultan] is eagerly besieging the fortress, given that he himself is besieged by famine; he has 150 ships on the Danube, but the Christian fleet is unconcerned about them.

In the Christian camp there is an abundance of soldiers. There are one hundred thousand crusaders, according to a letter dated July 18; on that day I believe many thousands arrived from Transylvania; today, on the day of Saint James,[3] there ought to be some thirty thousand soldiers positioned in the fortress; as someone reported from Buda, from that day alone some three thousand passed through.

The Turks have vehemently attacked Serbia.

Up to that day the Christian army had two hundred good and large ships. Up to this day they have three hundred.

---

1 Here *pecuniam*, but given the context perhaps originally *penuriam*, "need" or "scarcity."
2 Presumably a reference to the end of Ramadan.
3 July 25.

On the seventeenth day [of July] there was a certain naval conflict. Our side defeated ten ships of the Turks; seven smaller ships were sunk; three large ones were retained, full of spoils. Everything in these ships was taken, and a thousand Turks were drowned. We lost twelve empty ships, and twelve of our men were killed.

In the fortress are twelve thousand men; some say ten thousand. But they are well supplied, and up to now they have had no fear, even though some part of the wall has been knocked down by the blows of the cannons but [it is now?] restored.

At first the Turks besieged the fortress and had ships on the Sava River. But now they have [retreated?] and are downriver on the Danube, such that the fortress is no longer besieged from the Sava or the Danube, and Christians have safe passage to enter and exit; the weary are able to leave the fortress, new troops enter, and so we are able strongly to resist the besieging army.

If there were a greater number of knights the battle could have already been joined; there is a large enough number of foot soldiers – indeed it is a miracle. For just as "the deer pants for streams of water,"[4] so this devout and strong people seems to thirst for the blood of the Turks, to save the Christian people and this realm.

After the gathering of the harvest, it is believed that an innumerable multitude will arrive. For that reason, the most reverend lord legate [Carvajal] advised the lord governor and leader of the army [Hunyadi] to wait before joining battle, if he could, until the feast of the Assumption of Mary,[5] since any delay would be both harmful to the enemy and useful to the Christians. Those who write from the battlefield say that they do not think the Turks can long bear a delay. Thus, I would not wish that those who are about to depart should be delayed, because they are never more needed than now.

There was a certain fight joined before the fortress by those who struck out from our ranks against the Turks. In that fight we only lost four of our men, but many among the enemy were killed or severely wounded.

On the day of Mary Magdalene, it was proclaimed in Vienna that any who wanted to be paid to fight the Turks should make their way to the Count of Celje, because he will pay well.

---

4 Cf. Psalm 41 (42):1.
5 August 15.

Many good and well-armed crusaders have come from Mainz and other parts of Germany and are now in Vienna. Many will come from Vienna and will continue [the journey] the following day. Moreover, the Count Palatine[6] has now announced that today seven hundred well-armed students will come to Buda, and that today 150 excellently armed troops will depart from Buda.

Also, from a certain village thirty arrive daily, many [of them?] crusaders, and many women send their men at their own expense.

From Buda, July 26.

15. CARDINAL JUAN CARVAJAL TO FRANCESCO SFORZA
July 29, 1456 (Ilok)

As news of the events of Belgrade spread, Juan Carvajal's duties shifted from coordinating the defense of Belgrade (see documents 3.4, 3.6, 3.7, and 3.8) to finding the best way to capitalize on the surprising victory. To that end, he wrote this letter to Francesco Sforza, Duke of Milan. Born the illegitimate son of a farmer, Francesco soon built a reputation as a bold fighter and came to be called Sforza, "the strong one." After his marriage to the daughter of Filippo Maria Visconti, Duke of Milan, he inherited the title of duke in 1450. As the head of one of the largest and most wealthy dominions in Italy, he was easily among the most important figures to help organize any effort to continue the fight after Belgrade. Carvajal sent the letter from Ilok (in modern Croatia), where an ailing John of Capistrano would soon arrive to spend his last days. The letter succinctly captures a crucial strategic moment – and one as fleeting as it was important – in late July and early August.

Source: Trans. J. Mixson, from L. Thallóczy and A. Antal, eds., *Codex diplomaticus partium regno Hungariae adnexarum*, Monumenta Hungariae Historica 33 (Budapest: Magyar Tudományos Akadémia, 1907), 2: 210–11.

To the most serene prince and magnificent lord, Lord F[rancesco] Sforza, Duke of Milan, etc., our most distinguished father and friend:

---

6 Frederick I the Victorious (1425–76), regent for his nephew Philip.

Most serene prince and magnificent lord, on the day of Saint Mary Magdalene the Turk fought to gain the fortress of Belgrade through the many breaches in the wall that he had made with his cannons. He was driven back beyond the ramparts that protected the cannons, which were captured by the Catholics, and he was forced to withdraw his camp farther back from the place. And on this same night he burned certain instruments designed to carry and move the cannons as well as the ships which he had deployed on the Danube. He retreated so that in the morning not a Turk could be seen in the camps, only the bodies of the dead. This is all the work of the hand of God. The governor [Hunyadi] was there, about whose excellence and prudence not enough can be said. But he only had a few of his people with him, [and] the crusaders who fought [with him] were poor [commoners]. Brother John of Capistrano was there, who called to Jesus, and was heard. If the Turk had waited until the tenth of August, given the multitude of people that came before and after me, even if he had had double the army he would not have escaped! But the lord governor could not pursue him because he did not have horses, and the crusaders were all on foot. The knightly and noble crusaders have not yet arrived, though they have been called. On Sunday I will discuss further with the lord governor and other barons about how best to proceed in this matter, and what is decided there I will pass along to Your Most Illustrious Lordship, whom God may see fit to preserve.

From Ilok near the Danube, July 29 in the year, etc. '56.

16. LETTERS OF JOHN GOLDENER

John Goldener was the author of four early letters, two of which are translated here. Much remains unclear about Goldener's background, but the best argument suggests he was a native of Hainburg, a small town on the Danube near the Hungarian border.[1] *A student and then master at Vienna, he went on to a distinguished career as a scholar and cleric who was active in Vienna at the time of the battle for Belgrade. The first of his letters, to a churchman in Regensburg,*[2]

---

1 See Babinger, "Der Quellenwert," especially 13–14 and n. 3. See the introduction, n. 67.
2 For the attributions of these letters see Hofer, *Johannes Kapistran*, 1: 476. See the introduction, n. 57.

offers evidence of the complex dynamics of communication that surrounded the fast-moving events of July–August: it is in fact a letter within a letter, to which is appended a rapid-fire list of other events. It also enjoyed a wider circulation than his other letters (a German translation of the first letter, for example, was later taken up into local chronicles in Basel and Speyer). The second letter, written a day later, offers yet another account of the battle. It captures both some of the excitement unleashed by the spreading news and something of the resentment that arose from the nobility's lack of engagement.

16.1. JOHN GOLDENER TO FRANZ SCHLICK
August 2, 1456 (Vienna)

Source: Trans. J. Mixson, from A. Bernoulli, ed., *Basler Chroniken* (Leipzig: Hirzel, 1890), 4: 392–4 (checked against Vienna, Österreichische Nationalbibliolithek, cod. 4498, fols. 186–8).

Venerable lord, yesterday there came along with the closed letters we were to pass along to Your Reverence a new and reliable report from Hungary; there is no need for Your Dignity to doubt it, and it can be passed along safely to all of our supporters:[1]

> Eight days ago tomorrow, two former Christians came to us from the army of the Turk. They advised the governor [Hunyadi] that the Turk and all of his leading nobles swore by Muhammad that they would all forfeit their lives or gain the fortress of Belgrade, and that they were prepared to attack on Wednesday [July 21], which was the vigil of Mary Magdalene. On the same night, Governor John Hunyadi secretly deployed by way of the Danube some forty thousand of his foot soldiers and almost a thousand knights. He joined them, and they all entered the fortress undetected. On Wednesday morning [July 21], just as the two mentioned above had said would happen, the Turks, cruel beasts, fell upon the town

---

1 Here Goldener inserts the text of an earlier letter (now lost) that must have been written around July 27–8, that is, around seven to eight days after the events described. The letter then made its way, with a flood of other written and oral reports, from Belgrade to Buda and Vienna and beyond.

before the fortress, and fought with our troops for some time. By the grace of God almost all of them were defeated. A second attack came, this time with fresh troops, who fought once more. Then [came] a third, whose troops seemed to yield, because Father John of Capistrano, standing at the top of a prominent place in the fortress, raising the crucifix high, called with a tearful cry: "Oh my God, oh Jesus, where are your ancient mercies? Oh come, come to our aid! Do not wait, come! Free those whom you have redeemed with your precious blood! Come, do not wait, so that they cannot say, 'Where is their god?'" Note that this [story] concerning Capistrano is not found in the governor's letter;[2] but those who are coming north say [it is true]; and even Lord Michael Balduff affirms it, who came last night from [meeting with] the lord legate [Carvajal], and who saw yesterday that there was such joy, with all the bells and fires. So, my brother, this fight lasted many hours, and they attacked three times. But God was with us, so that the infidel took flight and one hundred thousand were laid low.

This letter was read yesterday to the lord of Passau.[3] And Lord John Mulfelder also related to us what Hunyadi writes: so many were killed that he does not know what number to report. He pursued them eight miles, and the poor of Christ were so eager that they gave no thought to gold nor silver, but leaving behind all the carriages, cannons, and provisions, they pursued the enemy continually. They killed so many in flight that the number to be written is unknown. Concerning all of this may almighty God be blessed.

Also, The Turk lost all of his leading nobles and his vice-emperor.[4]

Also, they recovered twelve great cannons, of thirty-two hands in length, seven wide, and more than two hundred smaller firearms.[5]

---

2 See document 9. Also note how much this account is at odds with the others.
3 The bishop of Passau, Ulrich of Nussdorf (d. 1479), also a counselor to King Ladislaus V of Hungary.
4 See documents 33 and 34.
5 The term here is *huffnitzbuchssen*. The sources invoke a variety of terms to designate various kinds of gunpowder weapons. Their usage was not yet standardized and varied widely, so it is not always clear exactly what kinds of weapons the terms are meant to reference. For further instances see the many references in Tagliacozzo's account in document 25 (for example, n. 13).

The governor wrote this to his son, telling him to then pass along to the king that if His Majesty wished to recover both the kingdom of the Greeks and the greater part of his own land, he should come and not delay. The way is now prepared for His Royal Majesty.

This letter was sent to Baden[6] yesterday. Today at the ninth hour[7] a return delegation rode through the entire city, trumpets leading the way, proclaiming that all who wished to enlist should come forward, and all should give abundantly in their support.

Also, when the Turks saw the great danger that threatened in the galleys, they abandoned their ships and took flight by land. Others fell into the water. So they abandoned the ships to stand alone.

From Vienna, on Monday, that is the day of Saint Stephen, pope and martyr.

16.2. JOHN GOLDENER TO MATTHEW SCHLICK
August 3, 1456 (Vienna)

Source: Trans. J. Mixson, from N. Iorga, ed., *Notes et extraits pour servir à l'histoire des croisades au XV. siècle* (Bucharest: Académie Roumaine, 1915), 4: 141, and Leipzig, Universitätsbibliothek Leipzig, MS 1092, fol. 13. The letter also appears in the same manuscript on fols. 178v–179v.

Venerable lord, regarding the victory which the Christian people won on the eve of [the feast of] blessed Mary Magdalene against the Turks, most savage enemies of the blessed cross of Christ, the bearer of the present letter can inform Your Paternity; where God, not humankind, fought, and more than one hundred thousand, indeed they say two hundred thousand [Turks] were cut down, but very few of our own were lost; they won many spoils, twelve great cannons, thirty hands long and seven wide, and common firearms without number, carriages with gold and silver, provisions and other valuables. Peter can report more on the very many ways the enemy entered the fortress, and by what means, etc. When they made a third attack, where now the strongest and the most vigorous of the Turks fought, as it were, in the middle [of

---

6 A town between Vienna and Wiener-Neustadt.
7 That is, around 3:00 p.m.

the fortress], our troops almost gave in. Seeing this, the blessed father John of Capistrano, standing in a high place in the fortress, called to heaven with tears as he beheld the affliction of the Christian people, and extending a crucifix with his hands said, "Oh God, oh God, oh God; oh Jesus, come to the aid of the wretched. Are you asleep, my Jesus? Oh God, where are your ancient mercies? Come to our aid, come and do not delay, so that our enemies cannot say 'Where is their God?' Come and see the affliction of your people, whom you redeemed with your blood!"

What happened? That very hour God gave us the triumph. This is not reported in the letter by Hunyadi, but truthful [witnesses] report it. In fact, I have heard it just this hour at Saint Stephen's[1] – these things were all confirmed by Lord Michael Paladauf,[2] who just yesterday arrived from Buda. They could hardly express in words what kind of dancing, fires, and bell ringing there was in the cities of Hungary; their clapping and joy are great. And indeed, God is blessed forever and ever, amen! And so, they [the Turks] fled. The governor followed them for seven miles.

Consider, Your Lordship, how zealous were these poor Christians, who do not chase after gold or silver or carriages laden with valuables, but rather act with only the victory of Christ's innocent blood before their eyes as they followed the Turk and his army. By this reason it is a great sign of God that so few people have defeated such a multitude, indeed an almost innumerable force, and put the rest to flight. These things are true, and Your Lordship may safely write to our other good allies about them.

Oh God, enlighten the hearts of your faithful princes, who (as these recently arrived people tell of it) if they were to have [enough] people [to fight for them], would no doubt retake Constantinople. For such fear has taken hold of the Turk and his people in the wake of this battle that one of ours could put ten of theirs to flight. Indeed, Lord Michael says that he would never have believed it had he not seen with his own eyes such a great force in Hungary, piling up like snow.[3] There were

---

1 The main urban church in Vienna, at the time still a parish church but soon to be elevated to a bishop's cathedral.
2 Here an alternative spelling of "Balduff." See the previous letter.
3 The phrase used here is difficult to decipher but is perhaps a reference to the tents of the Ottoman force. Cf. Tagliacozzo, who uses the same metaphor (document 12, p. 98).

very few foreigners there in the fight; it was only the locals who did the fighting. Tomorrow and Friday they will leave from Vienna.

Yesterday and today at least three thousand simple, poor folk took the sacrament of the Eucharist with great devotion. There was not a vassal, magnate, or nobleman among them – shame on so many effeminate knights who, clinging to their pride and chasing after vanities, have neglected the hard and manly work of the soldier! I saw them in procession on Sunday: the priests went first; then black monks, lay brothers, and doctors; then around three hundred bachelors and scholars, acting as the battle line for all of the people; then cobblers and tailors and other poor folk came along, without a head or a captain. What a pity for the king and the higher-ups! I suppose what I write goes against the common saying: "Clerics, you do the protecting; knights, you work and pray." The artisans have become the soldiers![4] Pardon me, Your Lordship. I write this out of compassion for the militia [I have seen in procession], since there has never been such shame, at least in our time, as there is now. Alas for such confusion, that among so many thousands there was not one nobleman to be found! I will say nothing more about such great matters.

Vienna, Tuesday on the Invention of [the relics of] Saint Stephen,[5] in the year, etc. '56.

17. LADISLAUS V TO DUKE FRANCESCO SFORZA OF MILAN
August 3, 1456 (Vienna)

Here the king of Hungary, Ladislaus V, writes to Duke Francesco Sforza of Milan (see document 15) in the wake of the victory at Belgrade. The king recounts news of the battle, taking an opportunity to clothe himself in the splendor of the victory. He also highlights the ongoing danger and his own projected role in the response. The letter concludes with its ultimate aim: an appeal for troops.

---

4 Here an inversion of the traditional model of the "three orders of society," according to which knights were to fight, clerics to pray, and laborers to work, each in support of the other.

5 August 3, a commemoration of the finding of the relics, a day distinct from the commemoration of the martyrdom of the saint (December 26).

Source: Trans. J. Mixson, from Josef Chmel, ed., "Briefe und Aktenstüke zur Geschichte der Herzoge von Mailand von 1452 bis 1513," *Archiv für österreichische Geschichte. Notizenblatt* 6 (1856): 33–4.

To the illustrious prince, Lord Francis, Duke of Milan, our beloved friend, Ladislaus, by the grace of God king of Hungary, Bohemia, Dalmatia, Croatia, etc. and Duke of Austria and Styria, also marquis of Moravia, etc.

To the illustrious prince, Lord Francis, Duke of Milan, our beloved friend, greetings and friendly affections. Illustrious prince and our beloved friend, there is no doubt that by now you have sufficiently inquired into how the Turk, an evil enemy, has begun to scheme toward forever oppressing Christian liberty. And if at this point you should have any doubt about it – or if you could recognize it from the very facts themselves – the fight with us is not about glory, but about life and blood. Indeed, we have fought bitterly in a naval battle no less than with our forces on land, and there was no other reason than that we, who were supported with the troops that had been promised by Catholic princes, spurned the conditions of a truce that the enemy had formerly offered. When he then heard that all of Christendom had been stirred into action for a general expedition, and that we were coming against him with an army, he was struck with fear and sent diplomats to all of the gentile world[1] and begged for their help, not only to guard against the loss of life, but to guard the fortune, safety, and freedom of all the heathen world – all because he thought he was about to fight not only with us, but with all the Christian people, on both land and sea.

With this reasoning, a force was gathered together: one that not only our strength could not match, but that would be difficult for all of Christendom to face. He stirred up all of these forces against us and against our kingdom of Hungary so that, having captured our kingdom, he would more easily be able to break out against others and rule over them. Thus, he struck out against one of our fortresses along the borders of our kingdom and besieged it without any interruption. And had he conquered it, nothing would be left but for our kingdom also to be conquered, and thereafter indeed other Christian kingdoms

---

1 Here meaning, broadly, Ottoman subjects and allies.

would seem defenseless. From all of this you should understand that this Turk would bring to Catholic princes either harsh servitude or the cruelest destruction. The whole matter urges us to avoid this – not only what he has already done against us, but further crimes he is considering.[2]

But now, with the Lord's hand, in whose power are all of the laws of kingdoms, the great part of the enemy's army has been routed; all of the machines of war with which he opposed our fortress have been captured; a few of the enemy who were guarded by the speed of their horses have escaped. And yet the Turk, having suffered such a remarkable defeat, resolves anew to recover his strength as much as possible and to fight with us until either he is victorious or meets his own death. And since we estimate our own forces to be unequal to his, we ask and encourage your friendship that you come to our aid with a great show of force, so that this common danger can be avoided by mutual aid, since the crisis threatens us no less than you. For insofar as it has fallen to us in facing such grave danger, we now gather together not only princes and nobles but every individual to withstand the attack of the enemy. We ourselves are going down in person soon, together with the greatest of armies, gathered together from across all of our dominions, to fight with the enemy, insofar as we are able. But if fortune should begrudge us our strength, and if you should delay in ordering that troops be sent more than the moment and our danger requires, beware lest we fall and you steadily retreat, [and?] our fire be extinguished by your ruin.[3] The rest will be explained to your friendship by our trusted [messenger], the venerable George, provost of Pozsony,[4] our counselor. You may trust in his report, and we ask that you send him back to us as quickly as possible with the response we eagerly await.

Given at Vienna on the third day of the month of August in the year of the Lord 1456, but of our reigns in Hungary, etc. the seventeenth, and in Bohemia the third.

King Ladislaus, by my own hand.

---

2 The letter's phrasing and meaning here are somewhat obscure.
3 Here another obscure phrase in the original.
4 Pressburg, or modern Bratislava.

18. THE CITY OF NUREMBERG TO THE CITY OF WEISSENBURG
August 13, 1456 (Nuremberg)

By the middle of the fifteenth century the free imperial city of Nuremberg was one of the most thriving and important city-states in northern Europe. As a hub of politics, commerce, and culture, it was also a vital point of exchange for news of the rapidly unfolding events of the summer of 1456. Here the city council sends brief word of Belgrade to nearby Weissenburg, another independent city-state some thirty miles (fifty kilometers) to the south. The letter offers another highly condensed account of the battle.

Source: Trans. J. Mixson, from Theodor von Kern, "Zur Geschichte des Kampfes um Belgrad im Juli, 1456," *Anzeiger fur Kunde deutscher Vorzeit* 11 (1864): 369–74.

To the esteemed and wise mayor and council of Weissenburg, our especially good friends:

Our friendly and eager service to our honorable and wise, especially dear friend. If our dear and worthy Christian associates are eager to learn of news that is both a consolation to the Christian faith and useful to the common good, we are pleased to let our dear friends know that we have received a reliable written and diplomatic report. As the Turkish emperor lay siege to the citadel and city of Belgrade with his great power, having assaulted the city with his cannons, with a great many of his troops he fought his way in on the Wednesday before the recent feast of Mary Magdalene,[1] raising (as it has been reported to us) thirteen banners in the city.[2] Then the noble John Hunyadi, governor of Hungary, who still held on to the citadel above the city, though worried about his enemy, boldly attacked them and fought mightily and strenuously with them, so much that he killed a large number of them and drove the rest from the city. The following day, on Thursday, the Turk sent a new wave of troops to storm the city, who then won it anew. But the governor [Hunyadi] withstood the fight with them in the name of God, and once more won the victory with almighty God's

---

1 July 21.
2 Literally "market," without any further specificity as to the exact location. Most likely the Upper Town.

help. The Friday thereafter the Turk undertook the fight anew with fresh troops, and the battle lasted from morning until evening. All the while the blessed father Capistrano was there, and with great devotion he continually asked our Lord God for help and favor. The Turk and his remaining people soon took to flight. During that flight, together with the previous attacks and battles, some one hundred thousand of his troops were killed. Many were drowned in the water as they fled. Moreover, the emperor lost twelve large cannons (many of which are said to be thirty-two hands long and seven hands wide) [...] and firearms without number, together with all of his other matériel, carriages, food, and supplies.

Therefore our merciful lord and king Ladislaus [of Hungary] has [just now, with more to come],[3] publicly called for soldiers in Vienna in order to raise troops and to send them further along to the governor, and with the help of the Almighty will bring a plague against the enemy of Christendom. We did not want to hold back this news from you, our dearest friends, but rather to share it with you to bring you special joy, to thank our Lord humbly and to offer praise and honor for his favor.

Given on the Friday after Lawrence,[4] in the year, etc. '56.

The mayor and city council of Nuremberg

19. POPE CALLIXTUS III TO FRANCESCO SFORZA, DUKE OF MILAN
August 23, 1456 (Rome)

After the siege of Belgrade, Pope Callixtus III, who had made a crusade against Mehmed II a central aim of his short pontificate (see documents 5 and 6), sought to capitalize on the surprising victory. Here he writes to Francesco Sforza, Duke of Milan, sending copies of letters he had received regarding the battle. The pope highlights the importance of prayer in the outcome of the battle, and his own liturgical initiative (document 5). He then concludes (in a rhetorical flourish) by urging the duke, one of the most powerful figures in Italy, to respond.

---

3 The phrasing here is obscure.
4 The feast of Saint Lawrence, August 10.

Source: Trans. J. Mixson, from Josef Chmel, ed., "Briefe und Aktenstüke zur Geschichte der Herzoge von Mailand von 1452 bis 1513," *Archiv für österreichische Geschichte. Notizenblatt* 6 (1856): 34–5.

To the beloved nobleman Francesco Sforza, Duke of Milan, Pope Callixtus III:

Beloved son and nobleman, a greeting and apostolic blessing. To the elation and joy of Your Nobility, we bring the happy news that we have just learned from Hungary (though we suspect that rumor has already made it known to Your Eminence). It is news that has lifted and renewed our spirits from enduring and extraordinary sorrow and pain. We send to Your Nobility, included with the present correspondence, the enclosed copies of letters that have been sent to us from the front. From these Your Nobility can learn of the most glorious victory that almighty God has granted to his people against the most cruel Turk in a fight by ship and on land, and the rout and disgraceful flight of the barbarians. We now urge you that for such happy and glorious news you should render due honor and thanks to immortal God, by whose heavenly power, amid such a great crisis for Christendom, the forces of a most monstrous enemy were struck and ground down. [You should do so] by arranging for processions and prayers throughout your dominion; and having done this, your ineffable piety toward us can be made widely known.

For if one might wish to consider the dangers that threaten the Christian world, to bring to mind the innumerable numbers of the enemy's army, and indeed to take note of the ferocity of this Turk and his obstinate intention to subjugate Christendom, one will surely admit that immortal God has been persuaded by both our prayers and those of other faithful Christians and has therefore granted this great victory to the people. For we are certain that human strength could not withstand the force of such great furor without divine help.

We therefore published our bulls of prayer on the day of the feast of the blessed apostles Peter and Paul in the basilica of that prince of the apostles, and with devotion arranged for processions and prayers on the established days and hours both here in our city as well as in our lands and those subject to the Apostolic See, and we have sent these bulls through all of the Christian world to be carried out and published.[1] We

---

1 See document 5.1.

have urged the Christian faithful that they should beg for divine aid in the face of such a great danger. And through these most devout prayers, and others, offered by the faithful, we trust that God (though otherwise angered because of the great sins of his people) has now been pacified, such that whenever our mortal wisdom and strength should fail us, by his divine power he would finish the fight. And so he has indeed had mercy on us, and gloriously done just that. For on the Friday before the feast of Saint James[2] the Hungarians engaged in a most fortunate fight against the Turks and won the victory. For that reason, worthy prayers and honors are due to so great a creator, who protected his people from such great danger, and who by fair weather suddenly scattered the clouds that seemed about to engulf the orthodox faith.

For that reason, we urge Your Nobility that you offer thanks to the divine majesty, just as we have done in the city, and as we have commanded be done everywhere. We also urge that you both raise up your armies and also meet with us, as we strive breathlessly for the total eradication of the people of Muhammad. Now is precisely the time to pursue the victory promised to us from heaven, as the Christian faithful gather their strength and strike out against the kingdom of the Turks, which (since their leader is defeated and confused and uncertain as to what he should do and turns himself shamefully in flight) should be most easily captured. Even now our fleet is sailing to the East; we are giving our all to continue to strengthen and expand it and are spending all that we have. And because this moment of great victory must be followed through to the final extermination of not only the Turks but of all the damned sect of the treacherous Muhammad, lest all the grace that has been granted to us from heaven somehow be dragged down by neglect, for that reason we are focused on this holy enterprise more and more, day and night – and for its completion we are in need of no small amount of money.

Therefore we urge Your Nobility and, in God, with all the urgency we can, we require you, that you come together with us for this most glorious labor, and that you add your forces to the effort – this is our strongest hope, as it always has been. We do so in order that we may fight for the recovery of Constantinople, the total extermination of the infidel, and the liberation of all of Europe, and indeed that we may aspire for the recovery of the Holy Land and all of Asia, and either the restoration or

---

2 The feast of Saint James, July 25. This places the climax of the battle on July 23.

conversion of the lands of the infidel to the Catholic faith, or the thorough expulsion of the infidel from them, just as we firmly believe and hold from the sincere Catholic faith that is fixed in our heart (as many have heard from us!) that the treacherous Turk should be defeated, that the Hungarians and the Christian people should remain victorious, and we along with them – and we have never doubted that all of it should happen just as it is happening now, with greater things to come. For Christ our Savior said, "If anyone has the faith of a grain of mustard seed and should say to the mountain, move yourself to the other mountain,"[3] etc.

And who is so cruel as to not follow us, who are most firm in our intention and certain that victory in our time will be granted from heaven? Shame, shame on those who think otherwise, and let them beware of the wrath of God! For the one who frustrates our plans in this matter, whoever he might be, will suffer judgment.

Therefore we again urge Your Nobility, and from the depths of our heart's affection we require, that you not let slip by this moment in which the highest God offers the opportunity to Your Nobility to sanctify your name through immortality, and while the shameful Turk remains uncertain about what to do, and while the rout is on, that we charge after him, following our leader, Christ, who as we so often say has divinely ordained a most shining victory and triumph in our time. Let not the Christian powers be absent; let them join their powers with us – we, who have devoted our blood and our life in this divine cause; and let them not abandon the banner of the living cross until victory is happily in our hands, in whatever way, and we will burn with the exaltation of the holy orthodox faith.

Given in Rome at Santa Maria Maggiore, under the ring of the fisherman, 1456, on the twenty-third day of the month of August, in the second year of our pontificate.

20. LETTERS OF BERNARD OF KRAIBURG

Bernard of Kraiburg, trained in canon law at Vienna in the 1430s, was by 1456 a priest who had served in several capacities in the archdiocese of Salzburg, and who would eventually become bishop of Chiemsee in Bavaria. He was also an author with strong humanist affinities and ties to figures like Aeneas Silvius Piccolomini

---

3 Here a conflation of two passages: cf. Mark 4:30–2 and 11:23.

(see document 2) and Nicholas of Cusa. Among his surviving letters are these two regarding Belgrade. The first, to Sigismund I of Volkersdorf, archbishop of Salzburg, is in German. The letter is almost like a bullet-point list of newsworthy items, and at several points it reflects again what was still a very fluid, confusing situation. In the second letter, Kraiburg writes to Henry Rüger of Pegnitz, a leading administrator in the circles of Archbishop Sigismund. In his position as protonotary, Rüger would have been charged with a wide range of legal and diplomatic duties, and especially matters of documentation and correspondence. As such he would have been a central figure in the overall communication network for the vast regions under the authority of the archbishop, and someone with a keen interest in the kinds of information and rumor that are hinted at here – perhaps above all the rumor of ambitious plans to advance against Constantinople.

20.1. BERNARD OF KRAIBURG TO SIGISMUND, ARCHBISHOP OF SALZBURG
August 25, 1456 (Vienna)

Source: Trans. J. Mixson, from Paul Joachimson, *Bernhard von Kraiburg* (Nuremberg: Bieling-Dietz, 1901), 34–5, here compared with both N. Iorga, ed., *Notes et extraits pour servir à l'histoire des croisades au XV. siècle* (Bucharest: Académie Roumaine, 1915), 4: 145–6, and the original text in Munich, Bayerische Staatsbibliothek, Clm 27063, fol. 131r–v.

To the most reverend prince, my most generous lord, Sigismund, archbishop of Salzburg and legate of the Apostolic See.

Most reverent father, most generous lord, obedience, etc. Lord William Truchtlinger and I have just arrived in Vienna today, that is on the Wednesday night before [the feast of Saint] Augustine, and neither King Ladislaus nor the Count of Celje are in Vienna, but rather departed this morning for Pressburg,[1] since John Hunyadi recently died at Petrovaradin,[2] around seven miles from Belgrade.[3] So we along with

---

1 Modern Bratislava.
2 In modern Serbia, on the south bank of the Danube across from Novi Sad. See document 3.6, n. 1.
3 For the variability of premodern measurements of distance, see document 12, n. 5. Bernard is here likely referencing a "mile" that is some 7.5 km, rendering this distance some 32 miles (53 km). In fact, Belgrade is some 45 miles (70 km) from Petrovaradin. His estimate, in other words, was reasonable.

my lord [the bishop] of Passau will also make our way to His Royal Grace at Pressburg. Also, the matter between our lord the emperor and King Ladislaus, which had almost been resolved at Baden, has completely fallen apart, and Duke Albert is here in Vienna. I am also prepared to report the following, and want to let Your Grace know:[4]

There are a fair number of crusaders from German lands here, and notably many who are idle and consume uselessly what they have brought with them. But how the matter stands with them, also on account of the Turks, I actually would rather not write to Your Grace.

King Ladislaus has commanded Jan Jiskra[5] to come to him without any excuses.

Also, Your Grace should know of the defeat of the Turks that I have learned about from a reliable report, from one who saw the thing with his own eyes. First of all, the Turk never had over one hundred thousand soldiers for this campaign. Also, he never had more than twenty-one ships available to deploy on the Danube. Hence, he was in great need and unable to transport his troops; instead, he moved all of his troops by land, and came as he was able by dry land.

In the battle there were perhaps four or five thousand engaged on each side. And the fight was the work of the simpleton crusaders, without a leader or commanders, though John Hunyadi and Brother John of Capistrano were in the upper citadel with sixteen thousand troops, none of whom came to the battle. Those who actually fought there numbered perhaps only eight thousand in all. Along the Danube the Christians had numbered over seventy thousand; but none of them cared to join the fight.[6]

Also, thirteen of the cannons of the Turks have been captured, among them one large one and no more. Almost all of the ships have been burned, the others captured and quite a few [sailors?] came from there.

Also, the Turkish emperor has himself been shot under the left breast. Because of that wound, and also by God's grace, the Turks have been set to flight. He is now in a city in Bulgaria called Sofia

---

4   The phrasing of the German here is obscure.
5   Jan Jiskra was a Czech mercenary who had been active in the Hungarian civil wars of the 1440s in the service of Elizabeth of Luxembourg, mother of Ladislaus V.
6   This account, apparently from an eyewitness, is strikingly inconsistent with many of the others.

and has been greatly shamed. And the city of Belgrade has in fact not been so badly destroyed by the Turks as some others; in comparison it is not so bad, since on one end [of the walls?] the damage is actually not that great. Then around ten days after the battle, two Turkish ships were also engaged and destroyed on the Sava, also by the simple folk, who had come because of the preaching, and who won the battle.

As things stand, it seems astounding that only eight thousand simple folk, unarmed, could defeat and put to flight one hundred thousand Turks. But to tell the whole story of the fight and how the Turks were defeated and fled would take too long to write. So, when I arrive home, I will report more fully to Your Grace.

Given in Vienna, Wednesday evening before [the feast of] Augustine, in the year, etc. '56.

20.2. BERNARD OF KRAIBURG TO HENRY RÜGER OF PEGNITZ
August 26, 1456 (Vienna)

Source: Trans. J. Mixson, from Paul Joachimson, *Bernhard von Kraiburg* (Nuremberg: Bieling-Dietz, 1901), 35–6, compared with N. Iorga, ed., *Notes et extraits pour servir à l'histoire des croisades au XV. siècle* (Bucharest: Académie Roumaine, 1915), 4: 144–5, and the original manuscript, Munich, Bayerische Staatsbibliothek, Clm 27063, fol. 131v.

To Master Henry of Pegnitz, protonotary of the archbishop of Salzburg.

Venerable and esteemed man, beloved brother: I departed on Sunday from Lauffen and on the fourth day thereafter arrived in Vienna. I traveled as quickly as I could, but when I arrived King Ladislaus and the Count of Celje had already departed. On the day I arrived they had gone down to Pressburg, in haste, because of the death of Hunyadi. You will learn of other things related to these matters from the letters of my most reverend lord.[1] Those things which I write in the same letters from the lands of the Turks are true and were seen by and related to me from John Tröster, who is trustworthy. And you can disregard the

---

1 The reference here is presumably to the archbishop of Salzburg, and to the previous letter.

copies of those letters which first came to Salzburg, because you know the customs and the clamoring of the Hungarians.

Also, the new bull concerning processions and bells and many other things has become known.[2] The lord of Pavia had a copy.[3] I do not, but I am trying to get one.

Also, there are many crusaders here and in Buda, but there is no one to tell them what to do. They are becoming bored and consuming all of the provisions that have been given to them – they have cost more than forty thousand ducats! And perhaps, unless someone comes along to give them orders, with all their goods consumed, it is only a matter of time before hunger finally consumes them.

Also the lord of Passau[4] has told me that the lord emperor [Frederick III] wrote to his counselors from Neustadt in Baden how the city of Constantinople [could be] won by the patriarch Ludovico and the king of Aragon.[5] And if that is true, there is nothing more worth hearing. But I myself can hardly believe it. He has suggested a means, by what way it might come into their hands through treason. Also he told me of the very widespread rumor that the emperor of the Turks is dead. This one I will leave alone.

Also, Philip Jänsuch, who alone of the barons of all of Hungary was there with the lord governor [Hunyadi] during the battle at Belgrade, has died. The Voivode Nicholas [of Ilok] is also near death. The bishop of Oradea [John Vitéz] is ill and near death.

Also, Belgrade is no more than thirty-four miles from Buda.[6] The lord cardinal legate [Castiglione][7] is in a certain city called Petrovaradin which is about seven miles from Belgrade. The bishop of Passau has also told me that some six thousand Turks have been killed. But others have told me no more than four or five thousand. Belgrade is around sixty German miles, or twelve days' travel from Constantinople.[8]

---

2   See document 5.
3   Cardinal Giovanni Castiglione (d. 1460) was bishop of Pavia from 1453, papal legate to Frederick III, and then cardinal from December of 1456.
4   Presumably the bishop of Passau, Ulrich of Nussdorf (d. 1479). See document 16.1, n. 3.
5   Reference here to the naval and land forces, respectively, of Ludovico Trevisan and Alfonso V of Spain. See document 3.4, n. 3.
6   Again a reasonable estimate. If the German "mile" invoked here was approximately 7.5 km, this distance would be 158 miles (255 km). The actual distance is some 215 miles (350 km).
7   See n. 3 in this document.
8   Here estimated at about 280 miles (450 km), a distance that is actually some 600 miles (980 km).

I believe and suspect that the lord Count of Celje will try to become governor of Hungary.

From Vienna, quickly, on Thursday before [the feast of Saint] Augustine, in the year, etc. '56.

Postscript:[9]

Master Hans Hinderbach, secretary of our merciful lord the Roman emperor, has just come from Rome and reported to us that he has learned from our holy father the pope how the city of Constantinople might once again be won and recaptured. Then the Venetians, who have been here at the court of our emperor, confirmed that they have taken up a peace treaty with the Turks; and whether or not there will be a general campaign against the Turks from Christendom, the Venetians do not want to be obligated to it because of that peace treaty. Also, after the Turks were defeated at Belgrade, it happened very recently that two ships full of men and supplies were discovered to have been sent by the Venetians to aid the Turks. This caused an uproar among many merchants, and the Venetians answered that they had sent six ships, two of which were attacked and surrendered to the Turks, which was an insult for them.

21. POPE CALLIXTUS III, LETTER TO JUAN SOLER
Late August, 1456 (Rome)

In this letter Pope Callixtus III writes to Juan Soler, papal ambassador to the court of King Alfonso V of Aragon. It is representative of a wide range of diplomatic letters the pope wrote in the weeks after news of Belgrade reached Rome. In them, as in this one, Callixtus III capitalizes on the victory, relishing the story and also encouraging his ambassador to bring it to bear on his interactions with the king.

Source: Trans. J. Mixson, from Cesare Baronio, ed., *Annales ecclesiastici* (Bar-le-Duc, 1864), 29: 83–4.

To our beloved son Juan Soler, our ambassador:

---

[9] While the main body of the letter was written in Latin, this note was added in German, presumably in haste.

Among other letters, we send to you those that our beloved son Brother John of Capistrano has sent to us, and signed with his own hand[1] – a friar, if it may be said, who is a living martyr – so that you, whom we embrace with singular charity and in whom we trust so much, might pass them along and show them to King Alfonso of Aragon and Sicily, so that it might be made known to all that it was through divine power, not human strength, that such a memorable and glorious victory has been brought forth among the faithful.

Oh wonderful mystery! Oh miracle, to be celebrated with eternal heralds! Rustic men held up not by arms, but by faith and devotion alone, with only one athlete of God, the most unconquered voivode John, and one religious friar, John of Capistrano, completely destroyed the great power of the evil Turk, with all of his equipment, all of his marvelous instruments. And having scattered innumerable troops, they turned the most rash and wrathful Turk – who was terrified at the slaughter and uncertain of his next move – to flight. Such a strong army, yet they struck down more than half, scattered the rest here and there, and for the most part captured those who fled. Indeed, more than four thousand were given over to servitude by the most glorious captain and were made to rebuild the fortress of Belgrade so that what they had destroyed with their engines and machines they would rebuild and make more distinguished than before.

Who can admire this divine miracle in all of its magnitude? Who can render thanks worthy of its majesty? Unfeeling, inhuman, detestable are those who do not wonder at what our Lord in his mercy has done for his people, and who do not return thanks for his unspeakable compassion.

Deferring in a certain way to His Serenity the king of Aragon [Alfonso V], we have not sent the same kind of letter to him as the one we sent through our legate of Sant'Angelo [Juan Carvajal] to the emperor [Frederick III], whom we decreed to be excommunicated along with the king of Hungary [Ladislaus V] until they should establish peace with one another and direct all their strength against the treacherous Turk. And having sent our command under the sentence of excommunication, what has happened? Peace and all that we have wished for, as is plain to see from the news passed along to us […].

---

1 See documents 7 and 8.

Oh, if you could have heard those who came to us, who were there in that great battle against the Turk! Sixteen tents of gold and silver, the personal ones of the dog himself, and so many more besides: all of the riches remained among the spoils, because they were barely able to escape, and left everything behind. It may even be that the dog himself was wounded or killed, because no one can say where he is. In any case, the glorious count [Hunyadi] granted everything to the crusaders, keeping for himself only the war machines and cannons and other mobile assets on land and water. We then pursued victory on land and sea by sending to the glorious count suitable reinforcements, almost beyond our capacity. Indeed, God wanted to grant this victory to himself alone, and to the pope and the holy Roman Church, through crusading commoners, barely armed, without an emperor, a king, or any other great leader. And on the Nativity of the Glorious Virgin, which will be on a Wednesday, it will have been a year since we began to give the cross amid the solemnities of the mass at Saint Peter's.[2] And we commanded, for the glory of the Holy Trinity, that everywhere the holy cross should be lifted high which that dog carried like a stole, mockingly, from his shoulders to his feet, and made his subjects do the same, blasphemously joking that if it was pleasing for a small cross to be pressed on the Christians, to impose a large one would be all the more pleasing.[3] And in this we might speak with the words of Paul, regarding the name of Jesus: "By whosoever it is called I rejoice, and will rejoice."[4] But each of us reaps the consequences of either honor or derision – just as happened to this dog and his people. It took almost a month for the Christians to gather together all that remained of the spoils of the Turks.

But enough about this. If we wanted to recite and arrange everything as we are doing just now, without a secretary writing it all down, it would take all night. And have we not said, energetically and in strong faith, that the dog – in the face of whose power even our tepid and cold Christian powers hesitated to take up the fight, unless almost all the world joined in – conquered so much because no Catholic resisted him, but that when he finally faced Catholic resistance, he would be destroyed? I not only

---

2 September 8.
3 The origin of this story is unknown, but the joke, in reference to the "large yoke" of Mehmed's rule over Christians, is clear.
4 Cf. Philippians 1:18.

said this in private but preached it from the rooftops. If only you would now do the same – and with God's help we wish and command that you do so. For it has happened just as we always said and firmly believed it would: the resistance of the Greeks and of Serbia and of other heretics and schismatics could not hurt him, insofar as it came from outside the ranks of the church. But the resistance of Catholics could, just as it has, drain away his power. And more than all of this will come to pass.

22. ANONYMOUS (PSEUDO-JOHN OF CAPISTRANO), TO ALL CHRISTIANS
August–October 1456

Alongside the public and private correspondence that passed along news of Belgrade in the later months of 1456, a swirl of stories, rumors, and other narratives inspired by the battle arose as well. These are harder to access, because they often circulated orally, or in ephemeral written forms that are now lost. This document presents one example of the phenomenon. It appears in a Latin chronicle of the Observant Franciscan movement authored by Nicholas Glassberger. Born in Bohemia, Glassberger was a university student (most likely at Leipzig) when the battle for Belgrade unfolded. He entered the Observant wing of the Franciscan order at Amberg in 1472 and later worked as a missionary against the Hussites. He spent the last decades of his life in Nuremberg, and it was there that he completed his chronicle before his death in 1508. In his account of the rise of the Observants, Glassberger pauses to tell the story of Belgrade. He then appends to his account a letter that he attributes to John of Capistrano. It concerns "the miraculous victory of the Christians, and the wonders that preceded it." Revealingly, the same letter also survives in a German version, a text which has a longer concluding passage that does not appear in Glassberger's Latin work. The letter is notable not so much for its value as an "accurate" account, but as a witness to the wider resonance of the Belgrade story and the association of the outcome with signs and wonders.

Source: Trans. J. Mixson, from *Chronica fratris Nicolai Glassberger, Ordinis Minorum Observantium*, Analecta Franciscana 2 (Quaracchi: Typografia Collegii S. Bonaventurae, 1887), 366–8. The German text, whose concluding paragraph is appended here, is found in Robert Naumann, ed., *Sarapeum. Zeitschrift für Bibliothekwissenschaft, Handschriftenkunde und ältere Litteratur* 14 (1853): 161–6 (here 163–6).

To all who are signed by the mark of the Christian faith, let shine the wondrous mercy and inexpressible great deeds of God, which we have indeed seen and sensed to sparkle in our day, as the mother church has now been given one victory in war in the East against the Turks and pagans. We do not wish to stifle your affectionate devotion [concerning the fact] that on the sixteenth day of the month of July in the year 1456, at the fortress that is in the vernacular called *Griechisch Weissenburg*, between the sixth and seventh hours of the morning, there appeared a great star, outshining all others in its splendor – not in the heavens, like other stars, but close to the earth.[1] This star had above it a cross, bright and of unimaginable size. At the sight of this star we rejoiced with a great joy indeed, knowing that divine aid would come to us – not so much from the sight of the star itself, as from the sign of the cross above it. From that point we offered praise and thanks to God, who does not abandon those who hope in him. Committing to God with devout cries in his name and calling on his aid, we went to battle against the Turks around the eighth hour of the morning. We sang the response *Tua est potentia*, etc. and then the response *Christi virgo dulcissima*, and thirdly *Circumdederunt me viri*, etc.[2]

Meanwhile the enemies of Christ, the pagans and Turks, fought for the fortress and nearly overwhelmed all of the Christians who were then in the fortress. And as we drew near to the Turks, they mocked us and our songs – and no wonder, since there were five hundred of them to every one of us. And so, with divine grace in our favor, we fought against them. They fell down before us as if dead, and of all who had gone forth to fight, not one remained. When they saw this, those who remained in the Turkish camp began to flee, leaving behind all of the arms that they had brought. We pursued them and killed many of them for a distance of about four miles. Thereafter, exhausted by such labor

---

[1] The reference here is to what is now thought to have been Halley's Comet. Modern calculations estimate that the comet's perigee was on May 27, 1456. A later story provided the foundation for the long-standing myth, debunked only in the twentieth century, that Callixtus III had excommunicated the comet as an ill omen for Christendom. See also reference to the comet in document 23.

[2] The references here are to common prayers, sung in response to a versicle. The themes of these particular responses – the power of God, praise of the Virgin, and deliverance from unjust persecution by lying enemies – are consistent with the moments leading up to battle. This is the first in a series of liturgical references that the anonymous author weaves into the story.

and fighting (for the entire day, from the eighth hour of the morning all the way to the [ninth hour of the]³ evening on that same day), we returned to our tent, giving thanks and praise to God for his many mercies, that he granted us his divine aid, and singing *Cantemus domino; gloriose enim*, etc.⁴

On the following day we gathered up arms and supplies. Your Devotion⁵ should also be made aware that when they fled the Turks left behind here five squadrons of ships, along with various arms and gold and silver. We have found more gold and silver here than we are able to write to you; but for the common good and to meet the needs of all those Christians who are either present here now or who will be coming here, we will store it all in the aforesaid fortress. And for four days straight we have dragged the bodies of the dead infidels to the river called Danube and thrown them in. But the bodies of the saints who met their end in this battle we have gathered together with both due devotion and reverence, and with hymns and praises buried them worthily in the Church of Saint Michael. Moreover, the star and cross noted above stood above our camp all day and night, and as we moved, the star moved with us, giving us unfailing light by night, until we returned to our tents.

Meanwhile the magnificent lord and baron, most vigorous voivode [Hunyadi], filled with pious devotion and sincerity, was greatly disturbed at the death of those saints who had been killed in this battle, not killed by lances or swords or arrows, but for the most part trampled by horses and camels. Then, during the night of the following day, a vision came to him in this way: there appeared before him one priest, reading Mass.⁶ When he came to the *Kyrie eleison*, many began to move to the *Offertorium*, and as each placed his offering, the priest signed him with the sign of the cross. Then immediately those who were signed had a place or a seat at the altar, and each took them quickly. When the priest, reading the Mass, came to the *Sanctus*, there came one very

---

3 Reference to the "ninth hour of the evening" is in the German manuscript only.
4 A liturgical response of praise, consistent with a return from battle.
5 The addressee here is unknown.
6 The references which follow concern the main prayers that constitute the different elements of the liturgy of the Mass. For basic context see John Harper, *The Forms and Orders of Western Liturgy from the Tenth to the Eighteenth Century* (Oxford: Clarendon Press, 2009), especially ch. 7.

powerful king with his queen, along with a great retinue of ministers. They honorably greeted those who were seated at the altar and sat with them there. When the Mass was finished, the king and queen rose, and all rose with them. The king said to them, "Come all of you, blessed of my Father," etc.[7] Then all disappeared.

The lord baron [Hunyadi] rose in the morning and began to share this vision with me, asking me about its meaning. I responded to him in this way: "The priest reading the Mass is the supreme pontiff, the vicar of Christ, who has the power to bind and loose, and who out of his great fervor for the orthodox faith sends legates and cardinals to various parts of the world who preach and offer forgiveness of sins to all who fight [on crusade], or who offer a helping hand to that cause according to their ability. Those who take this preaching to heart and who offer their pious vow to God – whether by going [on campaign] themselves personally or sending another at their expense – these are the ones whom Your Lordship saw go forth at the offertory. Then the most holy father and lord Pope Callixtus, through his legates and their commissioners, signs them with the sign of the holy cross. These have fought for love of the Catholic faith and lost their lives. Our Lord Jesus Christ and his most glorious Mother, the Virgin Mary, have now received them unto their eternal reward, which they alongside the other saints will enjoy without end, crowned in eternal blessedness." After this explanation the lord [Hunyadi] was filled with great joy at the crowning of the saints, and he died.[8]

Specifically, the number of saints that Christ the Son of God called to their glory in this battle was 3,043 men. The number of the enemies of the cross of Christ who were slain is unknown to us, and we can therefore not posit a specific number, lest we seem to add false accounts to true ones. But we can affirm that it was around sixty thousand or a little more, whom we overcame with thirteen thousand men.

Oh,[9] you kings of the splendid and beloved Christian faith, open your earthly treasures, as God opens his heavenly treasures! Do not look to your crowns, with their precious stones; let your faith be enough and hasten to work in the vineyard of the Lord God Sabaoth. Oh, you

---

7 Cf. Matthew 25:34, a passage with strong apocalyptic overtones.
8 The German version of the letter omits this abrupt line about Hunyadi's death.
9 This paragraph appears only in the German version of the text. It is not present in Glassberger's Latin version of the letter.

unconquerable dukes and counts, knights and landlords, noble and ignoble, look to our struggle and be mindful; put on the yoke of Christian faith, put on the helmet of Jesus Christ, put on your armor and weapons, come to us in the struggle, help us to fight, that we in our fight and struggle might be those that none can conquer. We will have victory in our struggle against the Turks and pagans, with God's help, if you will offer yourselves, and your money and aid, to the cause. Oh, all of you devout priests of God almighty, and you learned religious, and spiritual lords of the religious orders, and nuns, and all Christian people, pour out to God your pious vows and cries and devout prayers, so that the merits of those devout prayers will bring divine power to aid us in our struggle and fight against the pagans and Turks, so that we can all join with one another in these proclaimed good works to earn eternal glory.

Written and given at the abovenamed fortress on the twenty-first day of the month of July after the birth of Christ, in the year given above. To all Christians, useless servants, but faithful in prayer, Brother John of Capistrano of the Order of Friars Minor, with the other faithful who are with him, the well-prepared warriors of Christ.

23. ANONYMOUS, LETTER TO HENRY OF ECKENFELT
November–December 1456

This letter was addressed to Henry of Eckenfelt, a Carthusian monk of the Austrian community of Gaming and later prior of the Carthusian community in Prague. Because it mentions the deaths of John of Capistrano (on October 23) and of Count Ulrich II of Celje (November 9), it must have been written no earlier than the end of 1456. The author of the letter is unknown, but hints in the text suggest that he may have been a prominent public figure with a leadership position in a large city-state, and someone with ties to the highest political circles in Austria and Hungary. The letter is a compelling example of an attempt to make sense of the events of Belgrade, and of much else besides, at what was for the author a moment of great instability and uncertainty. Its mention of what scholars now recognize as Halley's Comet is also striking.

Source: Trans. J. Mixson, from Bernard Pez, *Thesaurus novus anecdotorum* (Augsburg-Graz: Veith, 1721), vol. 2, pt. 3, 343–7.

In Christ Jesus, who has mercy on all, [to] my brother and dear friend:

It has been quite some time since I resolved to write to you (as if to one who spends his time in contemplation of the divine) regarding the marvelous events of this year. I have been motivated by this reason, namely that insofar as I am (as you know) out in the world, overwhelmed by temporal cares and immersed in these storms, you might be like one aroused from the sweetness of sleep, and pray to God for me. Truly, I have been delayed and prevented from writing up until now, far more than I would have liked, because of the constant press of business that arises from the affairs of the metropolitan and republican citadel over which I preside.

Listen, therefore, what comes to my mind regarding these matters, and what wonders occupy my mind. I have been thinking on the four heavenly plagues which in this year, as I see it, have brought only pain. Throughout the world, in my judgment, there is nothing at all that is not disturbed by unusual trouble or quiet. To take the matter up, that is, to begin with the first thing that comes to mind: at the beginning of the year that ominous comet appeared to me – and not only to me, but to many others – when the court of the most serene lord emperor gathered in Neustadt around the most recent feast of John the Baptist.[1] It was a new thing indeed, not a common occurrence, but a rare one. Back then I would often rise from my bed at the hour of matins,[2] and sometimes in the shadow of the night I would go out with the crowd; sometimes they were even armed. It was such a novelty that there was no one who did not get up to go and see the portent. In every alleyway of the city, through the streets, on the walls, and in the piazzas alike, everyone stood around in bunches. Each crowd said that the comet was a portent of something different. But all were united in sharing this one common opinion: that the comet signaled the fall of Hungary and the Slavic lands, and that future evils would soon come to ours.

While I was staying in the city of the emperor, and I considered these things, I was utterly amazed. Then I grew quiet within, and said to myself, "What's the use of such talk? Or what of all the talk do you think

---

1 Another allusion to Halley's Comet. See document 22, n. 1. The feast of John the Baptist is on June 24.
2 A Christian canonical hour in the round of prayers known as the Divine Office, observed in various ways between midnight and sunrise.

will change what will happen?" But then after a few days, and when the comet had still not disappeared, I saw daily the letters of the father and lord cardinal legate [Juan Carvajal] which he had sent from the Apostolic See to Hungary, and in which he sought aid against the tyrant emperor of the Turks. I saw then and began to sense deeply that even though no one among the Catholics, or very few, would come to the aid of the faith, nevertheless the Author of the Christian condition (insofar as he owed it to his creation) did not want his faith to perish or fade away – and indeed that it could never perish.

Thus, when the army came together at Belgrade with few crusaders, with no leader for the Christian army, without any clear orders, with no properly formed battle lines or clamor of arms, [God] scattered, struck down and destroyed in war and glorious victory the armed ships of the Turk, along with his people. Indeed, he struck down the Turk himself with wounds, and compelled him to retreat, and he fled.

You can rest assured that we embrace the kind of faith that is expressed both in love as well as in words. If the Author of that same faith had not by his power and mercy driven the arrows and arms of the Turk from the walls, all of our fatherland would now be subdued and destroyed by his tyranny. But what more? By God's providence (to whom be the highest praise forever), we have been given victory against the attack on our faith; the persecutor of the Christian religion has been put to flight. And with that, the story of the fight of the faithful has echoed in the halls of princes, in the castles of the nobility, in every house, cottage, and hovel.

But let me ask you, my Henry, to speak truthfully from your conscience: has anyone, up to now, embraced any great act of penance for our evil deeds? Has God been appeased by any kind of devotion we have taken up? Or is it rather the case that the evils of men have grown, and continue to grow, daily? There is no ecclesiastical rank nor secular power that does not daily pile sin on to sin. And although we can see that God fights to bring aid to all of us, still we see no armies arising to lead a new expedition against the Turk.

Therefore our God, who has forever understood our negligence and our human condition, and who foresaw the evils of the current year, took from this world that religious friar John of Capistrano, a man distinguished for his divine teaching and always inflamed with devotion, who after many labors in the faith and after seeing the victory of the Christian people [at Belgrade] was taken up (or so we might piously believe) into the highest heaven. Oh, with how many voices did that brother so often call out across the world! How many times did he try to arouse the people in his sermons, that we might run to God! But the holy man could not do as much as he wanted or desired by the force of his words. He has now passed away and gone far away from us up into the heavens, so that he would not have to see the evils that followed after his death (and which we now pass through, as through storms and tempests).

But what am I to do? I send that friar to the grave in his holy rest because there are many more portents up to this point in the year that I need to relate to you. I speak of that armed man, the magnificent John Hunyadi, Count of Beszterce and regent governor of Hungary. How many victories, would you say, has he enjoyed in his day? How many wars has he waged against the infidels? None knew better than he how to order his troops and to take the field against the Saracens and Asians. He was the terror of the infidels. Italy and Asia can bear witness to you about that more than our household. Horrid death took him from before our human eyes this year, and he departed from us to be buried in a foreign land.

But the tears had hardly dried from the eyes of those who mourned him before their eyes became wet again: this year the distinguished Count Ulrich of Celje was slaughtered by many wounds in Belgrade, in a foreign land.[3] Oh, my brother, who will not feel pity for that same prince in the days to come? He was a magnanimous and powerful prince, full in the abundance of his households. I will pass over the [details of the] circumstances, should someone reprove him.[4] I will say this: with my own eyes I saw him leave everything behind, and sail down to meet the Huns [i.e., the Ottomans]. And I know that he did it in support of the faith. He also made a king out of the innocent Ladislaus. He abandoned his palace, his wealth, and men and followers. It is unparalleled: he restored King Ladislaus to his kingdom, which for

---

3 After Hunyadi's death in August, Ladislaus V had named Ulrich II his successor as captain general of Hungary. Ulrich II came to Belgrade to challenge Hunyadi's son Ladislaus, who had become the commander of the fortress. Agents of Ladislaus Hunyadi assassinated Ulrich on November 9, 1456. Ladislaus Hunyadi himself was then captured and executed in Buda in March 1457.

4 Here likely a delicate reference to the divisive circumstances surrounding Ulrich II's assassination. See document 34.

so long had been deprived of its king, and that had for so long desired to have its king return. To satisfy the kingdom's desire, [the count] therefore took to the water and brought the king to his kingdom. And he brought the king not only to the center, but to the farthest reaches of the realm. [The count] stood boldly with him in the kingdom; he might have departed for his own good, but it was unfitting for a noble prince to do such a thing. He stood firm, therefore, and remained until death, pouring out his blood through so many wounds. But let me stop here and move on in silence to other matters, for these things are known to all.

I will tell you of another wonder. How could I pass over the crusaders, and not marvel at them? Never. Listen. You saw previously, when I began to speak with you, how astonished I was that so many simple, unarmed, and poor men, untrained in war, unskilled with the bow, flew so quickly into battle, and sailed so well in their ships. But now I am struck with even greater wonder: that such a great misfortune should arise in this holy affair, that such a great sloth should begin to creep in along the frontiers (where the defense of the faith ought to be most useful!) that without fruit, without utility, and with only loss, without even laying eyes on the armies of the cross, everyone should turn back to their own business [...].[5]

My Henry, the stars of the heavens have seen an astonishing turn of events in this world, and in this year seem even to have begun to err in their very movements. According to the judgment of those who are learned in this art, Mars, which is in Cancer this year, ought to find conjunction with Jupiter, but seems to me quite distant from that conjunction. And as it leaves Cancer, because it has wandered in this way, it causes the vines and the wine, the flowers and fruits of the vine, to perish across almost all of Germany. And as if that were not enough, there is so much pestilence and death daily that all of Italy seems overrun with human bodies.

These are the things that I have chosen to describe to you in general. The evils that afflict me personally, and which I suffer alone (and many others, no less) are so many that they cannot be captured in a brief letter.

---

5 The letter continues here at some length, offering a survey of affairs of the day, focused mainly on royal and territorial politics across Central and Western Europe.

24. LITURGICAL COMMEMORATIONS OF BELGRADE

24.1. POPE CALLIXTUS III, INTER DIVINAE DISPENSATIONIS
August 6, 1457 (Rome)

Three of the Christian gospels recount similar versions of the story known as the "Transfiguration." Jesus ascends a mountain along with three of his disciples, and while there he begins to shine with a supernatural light. The disciples then see him speaking with Moses and Elijah, and then God speaks to him and claims him as his son. For centuries Christian communities had commemorated the event locally and in various ways, but it was on August 6, 1457, that Callixtus III formally established a universal feast day for it. The opening passages of Callixtus's decree upheld the miracle as deserving of special praise, insofar as it spoke to the reality of an incarnate, triune God. The decree offered a range of indulgences for all who celebrated it as well, and toward the end then tied its celebration to the commemoration of the victory at Belgrade, news of which had reached Rome almost exactly a year before. This key passage from the decree, which was published as the pope continued to struggle to mount a campaign that could capitalize on the victory at Belgrade, suggests the strong connection between the memory of those events and a broader theology of liberation from the Ottoman threat.

Source: Trans. J. Mixson, from Cesare Baronio, ed., *Annales ecclesiastici* (Bar-le-Duc, 1864), 29: 128–32 (here 131–2).

We conducted the solemnities of the Mass in the Basilica [of Saint Peter] and read and published our decree concerning the general prayer to be offered by all Christians, which by the Lord's favor was observed everywhere, so that by the pious prayers and works of his afflicted people the ferocity of that impious and savage Turk [Mehmed II], follower of the detestable Muhammad, might in some small way be mitigated. It was this past summer that he came rushing forward with his almost innumerable army of Turks and infidels (in which he placed great trust) and went against the fortress of Belgrade in the kingdom of Hungary on the shores of the Danube. He besieged it from every side and closed in on it tightly and tried mightily to take it, but the siege was lifted by crusaders and Hungarians, all of them commoners, though few in number and almost completely unarmed. They were led by our orders and instruction, directed to our beloved son and apostolic legate for the region, and with ambassadors and letters sent repeatedly, from sincere faith which we have in our Savior, to whom it falls to draw together what has been dispersed, and to give protection in desperate times, and especially to tear down the power of the proud, and especially of the infidel and of the enemies of the Christian faith, even to wage war against them.

And so they fought, under the fierce voivode John of celebrated memory, who was a most fierce defender of our Catholic faith, and a fighter for it and its faithful, and a most worthy leader of the Christian forces, and who never lost either faith or hope in obtaining victory. Also there was John of Capistrano, professed to the Order of Friars Minor, an excellent man indeed and one of extraordinary merit before both God and men. Faithfully and earnestly he and all the people around him called with one voice on the name of Jesus Christ, in which we find our salvation. And with great cries and tears he lifted up the banner of the most holy cross to heaven, whence came the infallible help that indeed everyone hoped would come. What a wondrous thing! On the memorable day of the blessed Mary Magdalene, a people strengthened by heavenly aid, by an attack of the faithful made manfully against the enemy, put to shame and ruinous flight that wild Turk and his sacrilegious supporters [...].

Therefore let the faithful, wherever they might be found over all the earth, prepare body and soul in support of the Christian faith, and offer appropriate thanks to our Savior for the blessings we have received from him. Let them work piously, solemnly, and devoutly to celebrate each year the day of a victory granted to us from heaven, a day of joy and liberation from the son of pride, that poisonous serpent and foulest Turk Muhammad. Like sons of Israel freed from Egyptian domination, let them offer praise to God and recall a day to be celebrated forever. And so let all who participate in this especially solemn feast of the Transfiguration of our Lord Jesus Christ recall the mysteries, the miracles, and the witnesses to the law of nature and grace, and the holy and undivided Trinity, that are even now to be seen in this victory.

24.2. JOHN BURCHARD, LIBER NOTARUM
August 1500 (Rome)

John Burchard (d. 1506) was an Alsatian cleric from near Strasbourg who by the 1480s had made his way to Rome and entered the service of a series of influential cardinals. In 1484 he became the "master of ceremonies" for the papal chapel, a position that charged him with proper arrangement of all the liturgies and other diplomatic and ceremonial protocols of the papal court. From that vantage point he became a keen observer of the affairs of the Roman curia and of affairs in the city of Rome generally. Burchard's massive multivolume diary, the Liber notarum, *intertwined official records of public and ceremonial matters with his personal (and often satirical or scurrilous) remembrances and commentary. The brief passage below appears in that context. It offers a glimpse of processions associated with the Jubilee of 1500 and how these intersected with Callixtus III's* Cum his superioribus *and the feast of the Transfiguration, nearly five decades after the battle for Belgrade. It is this tradition, inflected and adopted in various ways for centuries to come, that survives today as the ringing of the "noon bell" in commemoration of Belgrade.*

Source: Trans. J. Mixson, from *Johannis Burchardi Liber notarum* XXXII/1, p. 239, repr. Zsolt Visy, ed., *La campana di mezzogiorno: Saggi per il quinto centenario della bolla papale* (Budapest: Mundus, 2000), 202.

On Sunday, the ninth day of the same month of August,[1] a great procession was begun with the image of the glorious Virgin Mary that is kept in the Church of San Lorenzo in Damaso, which made its way to the four churches designated for the indulgence of the Jubilee. If I recall correctly, first in line for the procession were around a thousand men or so, each of them holding in their hand a small flame or a torch. The clergy of the parish of the aforesaid church then followed, and after them the aforesaid image, which was carried on four rods held up by four laity of the parish. A crowd of around a thousand women then followed the image, each carrying a burning candle in their hand. It was said that our most holy lord[2] granted an indulgence to all who participated in the procession.

---

1 Perhaps in error for August 6, the feast of the Transfiguration. See document 24.1.
2 This and other instances of "our most holy lord" refer to the pope in Burchard's day, Alexander VI.

On the same day, at midday, for the first time, the bells rang in all of the parish churches of the city, inviting all to say the Our Father and the Ave Maria against the Turks, just as had been established in the time of Pope Callixtus III of happy memory, and (as I understood it) our most holy lord commanded that the bells were in the future always to be rung in this way, at midday, on every day of the year.

PART FOUR

John of Tagliacozzo's *Story of the Victory of Belgrade*

25. JOHN OF TAGLIACOZZO, *THE STORY OF THE VICTORY OF BELGRADE*
1460

John of Tagliacozzo was one of the closest companions of John of Capistrano during his preaching tour across northern Europe in the early 1450s, as well as on the journey that ended at Belgrade (see document 12). Tagliacozzo was also later present at Capistrano's death in Ilok in October 1456, and he brought his books and personal effects back to the friar's home convent in 1457, where they have remained ever since. Tagliacozzo immediately became a champion of the memory of his mentor, and in that capacity he took the lead in the effort to have the friar canonized as a saint. He returned north of the Alps once more in 1459 to collect testimonies and lobby in Germany and Hungary for the cause. He was ultimately unsuccessful, but he left behind a series of important accounts of Belgrade and of Capistrano's death. The longest of these is printed here. It takes the form of a letter, composed on the fourth anniversary of the victory at Belgrade. It is addressed to James of the Marches, Tagliacozzo's fellow Franciscan and heir to Capistrano's missionary efforts in Central Europe. The work is remarkable for its length, depth, and detail, and for the ways in which it combines what seems to be compelling "eyewitness" testimony of a battle with what is also obviously a

Franciscan author's effort to shape a narrative designed to advance the cause of a potential saint. Using as its foundation the core events of the summer of 1456, and the place of Capistrano within them, the narrative develops a hagiographical text that is best read not merely as a straightforward report of pure fact but rather as a story through which one Observant Franciscan author articulates a complex model of holiness for his audience. Here the vivid events of the battle for Belgrade are read through the prism of Franciscan piety. The suffering of Christ on the cross, defense of the faith, and heroic martyrdom on crusade; the name of Jesus, popularized by Capistrano's mentor Bernardino of Siena; the cult of Mary Magdalene, on whose feast day the key moments unfolded – all of these are core Franciscan themes, here marshaled against what the narrative casts as the diabolical menace of the Turks.

Source: Trans. J. Mixson, from Giovanni da Tagliacozzo, "Relatio de victoria Belgradensi," in Luke Wadding, ed., *Annales minorum*, 3rd ed. (Quaracchi, 1932), 12: 750–96.[1]

To the reverend father in Christ and noble elder brother, James of the Marches, most esteemed member of the Order of the Friars Minor of the Observance, and most fervent and distinguished apostolic preacher, worthy of all veneration, [I] the humble and abject brother John of Tagliacozzo, most unworthy member of the same order, kneeling in praise and fervent obedience, with readiness to serve, etc.

I am not ignorant, my noble elder, of the fact that Your Paternity (who is filled with the adornment of every doctrine) has no need of my uneducated pen. But since in your mature and venerable old age you rejoice all the more joyfully and fervently to the extent that you read or hear of the mighty works of God, unheard of in the present course of time, I have chosen to scribble and to write down for Your Paternity, in whatever manner I am able, the events of that miraculous victory, divinely delivered, over the Turks. I will tell of the beginning, the middle, as well as the end, which took place in that exalted kingdom of

---

1 The history of Tagliacozzo's text is complex, and Wadding's edition of it, though at present the most easily accessible, remains problematic. For an overview of the many unresolved issues, as well as a sophisticated account of the hagiographical dynamics at work in the text, see Daniele Solvi, "Un agiografo osservante alla crociata (Belgrado 1456)," *Chronica* 13 (2017): 247–58, and more broadly the essays in Solvi, *Il mondo nuovo: L'agiografia dei minori osservanti* (Spoleto: Fondazione Centro italiano di studi sull'alto Medioevo, 2019).

Hungary, at the castle of Belgrade, under the banner of the most holy cross, with the acclaim of the name of Jesus Christ, in the time of the crusade, a triumph of victory that can be attributed only to the immortal God, through the merits and the most fervent labors and prayers of that most blessed man, Brother John of Capistrano of the Order of the Friars Minor, who was at that time by commission of the holy Apostolic See leader and captain of all of those under the sign of the cross in the aforesaid kingdom; who was assisted by the goodwill and protection of the illustrious Lord John Hunyadi,[2] governor of the aforesaid realm; and by the magnificent Lord Michael Szilágyi, most diligent castellan of the fortress of Belgrade.[3] And though others could accomplish this much more eloquently and in greater detail than I, most devout father, since Your Paternity has asked this of me (who, as divine mercy would have it, and since Your Paternity compelled it, happened at that time to stand beside the same blessed man!), I now report on the matter more truly and with more dedication than words can express. I will not get caught up in the frivolous charm of words but will instead set out the truth of the story with plainspoken words alone.

May our most merciful God therefore sprinkle me, a sinner, with the dew of his grace, so that I may relate worthily, diligently, and truly those things I have seen with my eyes and touched with my hands; so that from these things that I will say before God, the holy and fearful name of Jesus might be magnified; so that the devotion of those who are faithful to that name might be more ardently inflamed; and so that the celebrated devotion of the most blessed father Brother John [of Capistrano], his zeal and fervor and obedience toward the most holy Roman Church might be made known, along with his most serene martyrdom. Hear therefore, noble elder, the story of the aforesaid victory, and as you learn it, proclaim it publicly to the people, as is your custom, with your most fervent voice.

When the blessed father [John of Capistrano] and his companions arrived at Nuremberg from the diet at Frankfurt in the year 1454, in the month of November, he was in agonizing doubt as to where he should preach next, and where he should do the most good for the Christian

---

2 To distinguish between John of Capistrano and John Hunyadi, Tagliacozzo consistently refers to the friar and priest Capistrano as "father" or "paternity" and the military captain Hunyadi as "lord."

3 Michael Szilágyi of Horogszeg (d. 1461), who was married to Hunyadi's sister Elizabeth.

people. On the following night, after matins, when he had prayed and fallen asleep, he saw his impending bloodless death – indeed he longed for martyrdom in an astonishing way. Then, on the following morning, as he was celebrating Mass, he prayed intently regarding where he should set out, and in his vision innumerable voices in the church sounded from above, "to Hungary, to Hungary!" And while preaching in the square before the great church he often heard the very same from the heavens. Moved in this way from doubt to certainty, he resolved, in keeping with the will of God, to set out for Hungary.

[John of Capistrano] planted the word of God across Germany and established the family of the Regular Observance there; returned some sixty thousand heretics and Hussites to the unity of the church in Bohemia; and with God's permission brought forth marvelous fruits in Poland. Then, in the month of May of the following year (that is, 1455), he hastened toward Hungary. Upon his arrival the whole realm was immediately stirred to action in a miraculous way. He was received by all as a second Apostle. He himself despised such honors, very often departing from his route, and changing the plan of his arrival or departure. But it also sometimes happened that he was unable to keep the appointed day and hour because he was honestly misinformed. All who waited for him were thus frustrated in their desire to see him, and he himself deprived of their honors. Nevertheless, what man keeps silent or hides, God reveals. For when he arrived there were clergy solemnly attired; cardinals, archbishops, bishops, abbots, and prelates of the church with relics; and on many occasions with the sacrament of the Eucharist, with many lamps and with both women and men bearing tree branches and lighted candles, carrying banners. With bells ringing, they came before this lover of humility and led him in with the greatest honors, songs, and tears of joy. Princes, barons, nobles, and commoners loved and honored him exceedingly, and such a great multitude rushed to him that nothing but the most wide-open fields or great city squares could hold them all. And when he preached the word of God to them the people came from the most faraway places, seemingly rushing like a mob, not to hear the sermon of one man, but to find great forgiveness. No wonder then, that when they had tasted the sweetness of his speech, received the salvific doctrine of his public sermons, and seen most publicly so many obvious miracles, all were compelled to admire him. He raged against vices and planted virtues.

He was esteemed and welcomed by each and every prince, and all were blessed who found themselves able to stand near him, to speak with him even for a moment, or to hear him. Yet when honors of this kind were shown to him he always said with a humble heart, "Not to us, Lord, not to us, but to your name give glory."[4] And when the king left the kingdom, leaving the illustrious Lord John Hunyadi as governor and defender of his realm, this man [Hunyadi] was so devoted and loving toward that man [Capistrano] that whatever matters had to be handled for the kingdom, whether in private discussions or in public diets, he along with other barons summoned the friar, admitted him into their circle, and deferred to him; they would do nothing without his counsel.

After the many labors of his preaching, after fertile fruits had been marvelously brought forth in Hungary, by the favor of the aforesaid Lord John [Hunyadi] he [Capistrano] traveled to the lands of Transylvania, to the Vlachs, to the schismatic Slavs and Paterenes.[5] And in a span of three months some eleven thousand among them were led to baptism through his preaching, and were returned to the unity and obedience of the most holy Roman Church. Their teacher and confessor, too (after the burning of his house in Hunyad and the seizure of his goods) was overcome by [Capistrano's] disputation, and with the consent of the most reverend lord legate [Juan Carvajal], was baptized publicly, before the barons and prelates in Buda, in the manner of the Roman Church.[6]

On the fourteenth of February, that is the first Sunday of Lent, he [Capistrano] received the cross sent to him by our most holy lord Callixtus III. He took it from the hands of the most reverend lord cardinal of Sant'Angelo [Carvajal], legate *a latere*,[7] with great devotion and

---

4 Cf. Psalm 115:1.
5 These broad references seem here to refer to the Greek Christian (and hence "schismatic") territories and peoples of southeastern Europe.
6 Here Tagliacozzo makes brief reference to the career of the Greek Christian prelate John of Caffa. For details and context see Iulian M. Damian, "The Greek Rite Transylvanian Church in the 1450's: Archbishop John of Caffa and the Crusade in East-Central Europe," in *Extincta est lucerna orbis: John Hunyadi and His Time*, ed. Ana Dumitran, Lajos-Loránd Mádly, and Alexandru Simon (Cluj-Napoca: IDC Press, 2009), 143–55.
7 A special designation for a papal representative sent on a particular diplomatic mission and granted specific powers. See Antonín Kalous, "Papal Legates and Crusading Activity in Central Europe: The Hussites and the Ottoman Turks," in *The Crusade in the Fifteenth Century: Converging and Competing Cultures*, ed. Norman Housley (London: Routledge, 2017), 75–89; and in more depth Kalous, *Late Medieval Papal Legation: Between the Councils and the Reformation* (Rome: Viella, 2017).

with a most fertile pouring out of tears, after a sermon at Buda. He then preached the crusade and gave the cross to others, both through apostolic letter and in person, with full authority through the commission granted him by the lord cardinal against the enemies of the cross of Christ. He took up the cause eagerly, prepared to die for the one who was willing to die on the cross for mankind. For although he foresaw that the crown of martyrdom through the pouring out of his blood would be denied him, he was nevertheless driven to lay down his life for his friends, and to win the martyr's crown. He preached the cross in Hungary and, in a spirit of solemn preparation, tirelessly pinned the cross to their shoulders with his own hands. He then sent those under the cross back to their own lands, admonishing them to respond whenever they might be called. They in turn joyfully promised to obey the blessed father alone. Meanwhile rumors flew throughout the kingdom, and it was made known that both a Turkish army and fleet were soon to arrive at Belgrade – a fortress of great power and sophistication, and one that when captured would allow the occupation of other parts of Christendom. This was made known to the blessed father through repeated diplomatic missions and letters from Lord Michael, castellan of the same fortress. Belgrade is near the borders of the kingdom and the main gateway to Hungary, bound on two sides by the waters of the great Sava and Danube rivers – a fortress that the Turks had long tried to capture, so that entering and leaving the kingdom of Hungary might be more freely open to them.

 The blessed father himself hastened to call the Hungarians to crusade and to place the cross on them, to impress on their minds the memory of the cross, and to raise both the cross and arms against the Turks. And so it happened that he and his companions, through their preaching over the course of about five months, gathered together a great multitude of those signed by the cross. After giving the cross, he sent everyone back to their own lands. But when our preacher of the cross became more certain (through both the letters and the ambassadors of the distinguished lords John and Michael), that the Turks were drawing near with their astonishing power, and that they would find the fortress without defenders; and when he [Capistrano] was encouraged to set preaching aside, and to hasten as quickly as possible with those under the sign of the cross to the defense of the city, he made arrangements for five ships, sought out provisions, inspired the Christians, and proclaimed the looming danger for all Christianity. He abandoned his preaching, and with the ships and a small band of those signed by the cross he began in the name of the Lord to make his way down the Danube toward the fortress. He did so with a heavy heart, since he knew the great power and strength of the Turks and saw how few and inept were those coming to the aid of the fortress. And although he knew that so few could be defended by God, he seemed rather sorrowful. For there was no one in Hungary who would at that time take up arms against the Turks. The king and the barons remained at home. Lord John remained at the fortress of Kovin with his customary household, so as to prevent the forces of the Turks from passing through. Those under the cross, who had begun to return to their homes, could not be brought up so quickly. Yet the imminent threat meant there was no room for any delay. And so that blessed captain [Capistrano] was pleased that the time of his martyrdom had come, even as he was terrified and saddened that while all of Christendom was asleep, the Turks were awake, poised to destroy Christianity and bring shame to the name of Jesus Christ. He wept for the insults to the Christian religion and lamented the destruction of the Christians, and especially the Hungarians, saying: "Now the tribulation is at hand, and there is none who can help."[8]

But now God himself, wanting to offer some kind of consolation, filled him with happiness and joy, and showed him the future in a marvelous way: when the father [Capistrano] made his way down the Danube with so few soldiers, and when he arrived, mournfully, at the town of Petrovaradin, he celebrated Mass there, praying attentively that God would think it worthy to uphold his cause, paying no heed to the ingratitude of the Christians. And as he celebrated Mass, standing during the second *Memento*, with hands clasped and eyes closed, he had a vision of a certain arrow, sent from heaven, shot quickly in front of him and onto the altar. On it, in golden letters, could be read: "Do not fear, John, but march on and make haste, with confidence, as you have begun, for by the power of my name and the name of the most holy cross you will gain victory over the Turks."

Cheered by these things, the father cast off his sorrow, put away his fear, became joyful, resolute, and agreeable, and from that point on was

---

8 Psalm 22:11.

never seen to be downcast or disturbed. He then spoke openly of his wonderful vision while preaching his sermons; revealed it openly to his confessor; talked of it at mealtimes to many brothers, comforting them; and thereafter showed it to be true by the evidence of his deeds. And for that reason, all who were around him turned their sorrow into joy and their doubt into certainty. Resolved to follow such a courageous leader, they were now ready to be imprisoned and to die with him. Secure in the joy of this vision, and in the certainty of the future it promised, with his own hands the father pinned the cross on the shoulders of those who did not yet have it and signed all things with the sign of a red cross, from the portable altar to the priests' vestments. He also nobly adorned with the cross a banner that had been fortified, or rather painted, with the image of Saint Bernardino, saying: "Since the enemies of the cross ought to be ruined and crushed by its power, all things conceded to our use ought to be signed with the mark of the cross." He also often said repeatedly, "I should glory in nothing but in the cross of our Lord Jesus Christ."[9]

And so, at the request of the castellans, he now hastened to the aforesaid fortress with all those signed by the cross, with five ships as well as a large contingent that traveled on land. Upon seeing him from afar, the castellans as well as the citizens showed signs of their joy in the fortress and came out to greet him with various musical instruments, joyfully welcoming him with the aforesaid soldiers of the cross into the fortress itself, with the banner in front of the procession, on the second day of July, that is, on the feast of the Visitation. Now all who were in such great sorrow rejoice at his arrival; now days of joy come to those who were afraid. In his presence, none fear the Turks. Now those who had seen days of sorrow live in days of joy.

On the First Victory

Meanwhile messengers arrived, announcing that the Turks were very close. The governor, esteemed Lord John, while in the fortress of the town of Kovin (which is on the shores of the Danube some four Hungarian miles below Belgrade) was set up against the galleys of the Turks, lest by coming upriver they should be able to cross over. He also sent

---

9 Galatians 6:14.

word to the holy father that he [Capistrano] should leave some of his followers behind in the fortress and lead the rest to him [Hunyadi] downriver (since at that time Lord John had none with him but his household).[10] The father wished to comply with Lord John's wishes and decided (upon arranging affairs at the fortress [Belgrade]) to go down to him. And so, on the day he arrived [at Belgrade], he celebrated Mass and exhorted all in a sermon on defense, fidelity, manliness, and martyrdom. After a meal, he then prepared to make his way down to Lord John, on three ships marked with the sign of the cross. The castellan [of Belgrade] Lord Michael [Szilágyi], knowing that the Turks would soon quickly appear by both land and water, asked the father not to leave, arguing that he would be safe in the fortress, whereas on the Danube he might encounter the Turks, and that he would be of more use in the fortress than out on the water.

But the father, wishing to satisfy and to serve Lord John (toward whom he was drawn in a marvelous way) began to make his way downriver. Michael then delivered a message to him, sending him a certain kerchief[11] as a sign of reassurance, so that His Paternity would know for sure that he would soon encounter the Turkish galleys. But the father, desiring to make his way down to Lord John, thought little of the imminent danger. For the honor of God and the strengthening of the Catholic faith, he no longer feared for any bodily threat. He now longed for martyrdom even more fervently than was his custom.

But what he desired, God himself arranged for his own glory and honor, and the hand of the Lord was upon him.[12] For around the hour of vespers[13] the air was most bright and clear, the sun burned mightily in its heat and fire, and the Danube flowed most peacefully. But behold, the air then quickly became overwhelmed with the thickest of clouds; the sun was blocked out; great winds arose; the Danube churned and was agitated; thunder sounded, the rain clouds thickened, and such

---

10 *Familia*, i.e., his closest followers and advisers.
11 The reference to a "kerchief" here (Tagliacozzo's word is *sudarium*) is somewhat cryptic. It seems to describe a sash or bit of cloth, apparently sent as a symbol of warning and encouragement. In the middle of this sentence, somewhat awkwardly, the original text inserts an explanatory phrase: "knowing that he gave me this kerchief today."
12 Cf. Ezekiel 37:1.
13 That is, in the early evening, perhaps around 6:00 p.m.

a great storm and commotion followed, as well as darkness, that one could not see the other on board the same ship. All were forced, unwillingly, to make their way to shore. Once they were led to land, peace and quiet soon returned, and the Danube fell quiet as before. And behold, the army of the Turks quickly occupied the place from which such a strong storm had driven the holy father.

What else is to be made of all this, most reverend elder, but that almighty God wished to preserve his most faithful servant to fight against and defeat the Turks, in the name of Jesus Christ, under the banner of the cross? For God did not allow that his body, wearied by such great labors, vigils, and abstinence, should be honored by a martyrdom of blood, but rather by the fire and desire of his mind; and that the martyr himself, full of merit after the glorious victory, should return in peace, and not be without the crown of martyrdom.[14]

Liberated now from the hand of the Turks, he returned to the fortress by night. But on the following morning, that is, the third day of the month, behold: the army of the Turks began to appear. Many among them broke from their ranks and ran here and there close to the fortress, as if they wanted to irritate the Christians. When the father saw them, now incensed in a remarkable way, he said, "Let's go out to them! Who wants to follow me?" and similar things. But the one so longing for martyrdom did not find the same faith among his followers. On the fourth day they then began to lay siege to the fortress from a distance, and in a few days the full power of the Turks was settled there. As we have learned from these events, the Turks had never so powerfully, so cleverly, and so strikingly laid siege to a place as they did this one. Some 160,000 of the very best and strongest Turkish warriors – some say 200,000 – came together there, bringing with them innumerable camels and other animals weighed down with machines of war.

None could count the handguns, arquebuses, and springalds that were there.[15] We also saw enormous cannons, the likes of which had never been

---

14 The phrasing here is awkward, but Tagliacozzo is working to anticipate and to emphasize Capistrano's status as a "bloodless" martyr, since the friar was not killed by the Turks in the battle.

15 The terms used here are *pixides*, *scopetos*, and *spingardas*. A *spingarda*, or "springald," could refer to a wide variety of ballistic weapons that cast large stones or darts. By the fifteenth century, however, they had become long-barreled gunpowder weapons, mounted but also increasingly hand-held, that shot small stones.

seen, that could ground not only a fortress, but also the highest mountains into dust. Twenty-two of them in particular, each some twenty-seven feet long, the Turks had brought only with the greatest skill and expense. The smaller ones were innumerable. They also brought seven other machines that (in a marvelous way) threw great and round stones into the air to kill men day and night, without interruption, both in the fortress as well as in the city. These stones were most horrible when they fell among men standing very close together, or among houses filled with people. But they never killed more than a single woman. And I believe this fact to have been no small miracle, since no one could protect themselves at night. In the daytime, however, upon hearing the great noise, or upon a signal from the great bell tower, people came out of their homes, stood with some distance between them, and looked into the air for the stones. These were thrown, by a most vehement explosion, a full Italian mile in the air, and they came down with the mightiest force. But when they fell to the earth they were broken up by the ground and were seen no more.[16]

The Turks brought forth so many and such an array of munitions that they filled many places. Above all there was one large church, at a distance of an Italian mile from the fortress, said to have been dedicated to Mary Magdalene.[17] This church was packed with gunpowder, enormous ropes, iron weapons, and all the things which they said were necessary for fighting. There were also lofty and grand pavilions, each arranged in a marvelous and beautiful way, and so large that the great landscape seemed to be covered with clouds rather than crowded with tents. There were incomprehensible banners, great, high, of various colors, and differentiated according to the status and dignity of the Turks. There was also the sign of the Great Turk, a half-moon on a field of green. Animals were continually led forth from Turkey, Serbia, and Bosnia, loaded down with arrows, bows, and rations, for the Turks had abundant numbers of camels, oxen, and cattle; these animals carried wood from the forests. The carts of bronze, iron, and wood with which they hauled their mighty cannons (with great ingenuity) could hardly be counted. Their trumpets and other instruments were innumerable.

---

16 Tagliacozzo offers here a vivid description of a mortar attack. See n. 15 in this document and the introduction, n. 27.
17 A suburban church to the south of Belgrade. See Map 2: The City and Fortress of Belgrade, c. 1450, on p. 283.

They brought their household gods, the books that contained their ceremonies, the textiles and other things related to their diabolical cult. Mills to grind grain, ovens to bake bread, and various vessels for their use – these too were infinite. All of these things, and much more besides, they brought forth not in one day, but over the course of many days, and not without great labor.

We also heard, through a most reliable report, that they brought dogs to the siege to eat the flesh of Christians, as well as beautiful women, led forth on horses and in carriages, to soften the Christians' strength. Knights, foot soldiers, carters, miners, sappers, their elite and powerful master bombardiers, chosen from across the Turkish realm – all were there. The vice-emperor (who arrived with the first troops), kings, and princes established themselves there in such numbers that they seemed determined not only to take that one fortress, but to storm Hungary, and other kingdoms, and to live there as conquerors – and that was exactly their intention. For as we heard from those who fled to us, the great emperor of the Turks himself had sworn in the name of his devil Mahumeth, and in the name of his own salvation, that he would capture Hungary within two months, and dine in Buda, not thinking, most miserable one, that all he had brought forward would be turned to the use and triumph of the Christians, and to the death and defeat of the Turks. And so the camps of the Turks were set up not far from ours. And their emperor set himself up on a high place, which they surrounded and fortified with ramparts for his safety, along with the tents and banners of five thousand janissaries – those we in Italian call *"provisionati,"* who were his noblest, strongest, elite, intimate, and faithful followers.

The Turks led sixty-four galleys upriver, with many skiffs and other small ships. Neither Lord John nor any other could hinder their passage from the fortress at Kovin. In these galleys were men of various tongues and various nations, all skilled in naval warfare. The galleys also stored an abundance of arms, textiles, and other valuable things. The construction of these ships was a marvelous thing indeed, and a novel undertaking: cleverly designed for fighting and for assault, they flew through the water not like wooden ships, but like the swiftest of arrows. Among them, one seemed larger and faster than all the others. In this ship, which stood out so remarkably, were the most elite and most skilled fighters. It was decked out with many horns and banners and moved more boldly than the others. Seeking to ridicule and mock the Christians, it often made quick runs close to the city. In this way, the ship stood out as the commander and governor of all the others. To put it briefly, whatever the seasoned cleverness of the Turks could think up in order to defeat that fortress and occupy Hungary, the infidels brought it there both by land and up the Danube. But because the land forces had not yet established their place, the ships remained far from the city.

The commander of the people of God, blessed Father John, signed by the cross, saw the fortress besieged, the throng of Turks that arrived there daily, and how they prepared to overthrow it, so that they might capture all of Hungary. He considered their great power and their unimaginable ingenuity on both water and land, as well as the meager number of those signed with the cross who defended the fortress. He therefore decided he would summon the others whom he had signed with the cross. So, on the fourth day of that month, he celebrated Mass and preached a public sermon exhorting all to stand guard, to resist manfully, and to defend their position. He then took four brothers: the Hungarians George and Francis, Alexander of Ragusa, and Ambrose of Aquila, leaving behind the others in the fortress with instructions to be obedient, with exhortations to martyrdom and to works of mercy and piety. From there he made his way by ship to Petrovaradin, quickly and not without great danger, accompanied by two ships of the lord castellan.

Before leaving he said to the castellans: "Do not be afraid, but resist strongly; for with God's favor in a short span of time I will call together such a multitude of those under the sign of the cross that it will astound both the Turks and the Christians." He then commanded and persuaded us that we should prepare ourselves for martyrdom should the occasion present itself (though he also gave us great hope for a good outcome) and that we should persevere in works of mercy, saying, "Hear confessions, calm discord, heal the wounded and the sick, bury the dead, preach resistance. You who are priests, however, beware that you do not strike any of the Turks, nor that you provide or prepare for others any stones or arrows or even weapons to wound or to kill. Let your weapons against the enemies of the cross be prayers, sacrifices, and works of mercy, and the administration of the sacraments. But I do not place any rule on the lay brothers, or otherwise command them, except insofar as God might inspire them."

But note here, venerable lord, the zeal of this most holy father for the salvation of souls. For when he was hastening upriver, he heard that there were many in a village not very far from the Danube who were fleeing from the Turks. Filled with a divine spirit and contradicting his sailors (for the fear of the Turks was very great), he turned aside to that village. Looking around and searching through the place, he found a certain girl, the daughter of a schismatic, who had been abandoned there. The zealot for souls took her with him and carried her by ship to Slankamen.[18] She was baptized, and he found a spiritual father and mother for her; he gave the girl to them to raise and, in time, to arrange her marriage.

But when the brave and troubled captain of God was at Petrovaradin, he sent word to Lord John [Hunyadi] of the ruin and the danger threatening all of the Christian religion. He asked if, given such a great crisis, he wished to assist, for the love of God and the Catholic faith and for his honor. Lord Hunyadi, meanwhile, after the galleys of the Turks had passed, had withdrawn from the town of Kovin, and had maintained his customary and honorable household in a certain secure plain. He was always a great fighter for the Catholic faith, and a fierce defender and governor of the kingdom of Hungary. But he refused to assist for many reasons: because he was hated at the court of the king, and falsely accused of crimes; because none of the barons of the kingdom were moved in the face of such imminent and great danger; because he knew that such great power as the Turks had could not be overcome by unarmed crusaders; and because he himself did not believe he could trust in the crusaders. He was struck with great pain because of all of this, since the Turks would gain all of Hungary through Belgrade, and the city (although it belonged to the crown of the king of Hungary, who had not yet resigned it) was under his care. He had put Lord Michael in charge of the fortress and Lord John the town.[19]

Besieged by letters and messengers and pleas, however, he came to the blessed father, whom he honored and loved in a remarkable way. After many words (which I don't care to write out) he finally set

---

18 A town on the south bank of the Danube roughly a day's journey (some 30 miles or 50 km) northwest of Belgrade. See documents 8 and 13.

19 Here *bastida* is taken as "fortified town," instead of the editor's improbable reading of the word as a last name ("Johannem Bastidam"). The figures referred to here are Michael Szilágyi and likely John Korogh. See document 11, n. 1.

everything aside and took up the cause of defending the city. They also agreed that as many men under the cross as could be had, and ships besides, should gather at Slankamen. The blessed father himself also wrote letters, sent brothers, admonished barons, and asked of prelates that all should send as many crusaders as they had, and that they themselves should come. And he himself went to Kalocsa to the most reverend lord archbishop Raphael [Herczég], seeking his aid and bearing word of the great danger. The crusaders were directed, and it was decreed under pain of excommunication, that all should gather at Slankamen. They were given hope of victory and a longing for martyrdom, and word of the same began to spread through all the kingdom. The most reverend lord legate [Carvajal], preparing to come south to aid in the defense of the city, called together those under the sign of the cross. At Buda, where he was then maintaining residence, he inspired his followers to rise against the Turks, made arrangements for provisions, and prepared to make his way down. He also sent the lord bishop of Assisi [Francis Oddi] ahead of him to Petrovaradin, so that he might be more certain of events, and so that others would know he would soon arrive.

The crusaders now began to arrive, as they had agreed. The poor rose up; the rich and the noble sat at home. Rumor flew everywhere; letters were sent. The father, on fire with zeal for the defense of the city and seeing such a grave danger to the Christians there, was so burdened with care that he neither ate nor drank, nor even slept. But at his urging Lord John called together ships from nearby regions, and for ten days those crusaders who were close by made their way to the city.

Meanwhile the Turks besieged the city in a most powerful way. They arranged their greatest cannons in a threefold array, such that each part of the walls of the castle could be leveled by one alone. In between they placed ordinary cannons, and smaller ones for the defense of the larger. The towers were assaulted, the ramparts torn down, and over the course of about ten days almost every wall of the city was knocked to the ground (though the interior towers remained intact) since those frightful stones, with their unique strike, destroyed the better part of each wall, however thick. And the larger cannons were set up and placed in such a way that even a lone boy could turn them at will. They were readied to do their killing by day, and were attended to even by night, as it was said, to launch their stones. And all of the masters who worked them were Italians, Germans, Hungarians, Bosnians, and Slavs. They were most learned, chosen for knowing how to strike accurately with these cannons, as if with ballistae.

Nor were the others absent: those who carried the boulders in carts; those who made round stones from them; others who were in charge of the powder, still others the fire. And they made a great mound of earth in front of their position, so that whether firing or standing down (since their masters worked night and day to prepare them to fire) they would not be harmed by the cannons of the castle. For our part, although by day we could flee at the sounding of the bells to the thresholds of the doorways, or to the shelter of the arches of entryways, gates, and windows, by night we committed ourselves to the divine will, awaiting martyrdom and the sword – or the stones – of the Turks to come down upon us.

Then, reverend father, we began with confession and tears, then spiritual conversation, then sacrifices, then prayers, then we embraced contrition for our sins, then we observed strict silence. Oh holy time! Oh day, full of spiritual sadness! But the castellan was of good spirits, and the camp placed their hope in both Johns. He [Capistrano] came to us frequently and said, "Do not be afraid."[20] Then once, when I was in the church that was in the city,[21] celebrating Mass and at the moment of communion, one of the huge stones of the large cannons of the Turks struck the roof of the church. At that moment everyone fled outside, leaving me alone, since I decided, reluctantly, to accept whatever might come, and did not flee with them. Thereafter we set up an altar in the palace and offered our sacrifices and prayers there.

Meanwhile, as the blessed father pressed on with the gathering of those under the cross, look! The galleys of the Turks, coming up most quickly and furiously along the Danube, blocked the crossing of the river. Thus, all hope of reinforcement and rescue was lost, and neither Lord John nor Father John now expected any help. Even though we were fully resolved to embrace martyrdom, all were filled with sadness. No aid could now be had from the Danube. The terror was overwhelming for all.

---

20 Cf. Luke 12:7 and 12:32.
21 The church in the Lower Town. See Map 2: The City and Fortress of Belgrade, c. 1450, location 4b (in the Lower Town), p. 283.

The galleys spread out across the Danube and revel in their glory. They anchor on the shore, and men disembark from them. They cut down the grain and shake out the chaff, wash the wheat, load down their skiffs, and carry it all back to their camps. Thus, in a few days all of the fields around the Danube, which had been filled with wheat, oats, and barley, were laid bare; all of this could be seen clearly from the city. And after this, the galleys landed about one Italian mile[22] upriver, near a certain town called Semlin (this town, it seems, had once been a great city, but now the fires of the Turks had recently reduced it to a village, and after a few days its inhabitants began to flee the Turks). Now the city [Belgrade] is under siege by land and by water, surrounded by Turks on every side. Neither man nor aid could come to it or be carried to it; all hope of any rescue was lost. From among these ships many came downriver quickly against the fortress, or rather against the city,[23] and the residents of the city took to their own ships and joined battle with them.

Then that most ornate ship, noted above, made its appearance: full of banners, horns, and noble Turks who mocked the Christians with their actions – as if they were saying, "Now you are in our hands, now your god cannot help you; now you will not escape; now Hungary is ours!" and similar things. Oh, almighty God! There was a certain most frightful stone, shot from one of the great guns across both the fortress and the city, farther than the ones who shot it intended – and it fell right on that ship of mockers and boasters! And soon, with no one able to escape, one part of the ship was underwater; the other part, broken up and about to go under, floated on the surface. The citizens [of Belgrade] quickly sailed out to it, killed all of those who were still alive, and seized all of the banners, clothing, and other things which had not already gone under. Most honorable father, I believe that stone was sent forth by the hand of God, who does not tolerate those who spurn him!

The pious father heard that the cannons were continually battering the fortress, and that the spirit of the Turks was more and more inflamed against it; that their galleys now held the crossing, and there was neither access to the fortress, nor any way to bring supplies or aid

---

22   1.5–1.8 km. See document 12, n. 5.
23   Here a distinction between the fortified Upper Town and the Lower Town. See Map 2: The City and Fortress of Belgrade, c. 1450, on p. 283.

to those besieged there, no way to come to their rescue, unless the ships of the Turks should be first driven from the Danube, and the crossing recaptured. He advised Lord John [Hunyadi] that he should bring together as many ships as possible from the surrounding area, and have them brought together at Slankamen, a task for which the aforesaid Lord [John] was free. It was done quickly; for in a very few days almost two hundred ships designated for the task were brought there. And these, with the help of many masters,[24] were immediately outfitted with planking for assault and for defense. The ships were also filled with bows, arrows, crossbows, arquebuses, and handguns.[25] Stones were gathered, defense works erected, supplies sent in, the elite and the strong among the crusaders gathered together.

Then, after God's herald [Capistrano] offered a public exhortation on the defense of the Christian faith, the full remission of their sins, and martyrdom, he commanded them to call on and to shout out nothing else but the name of Jesus, both on water and on land. Under cover of night, and not without danger from the Turks, both Johns advised the castellans that on the fourth day of the week to come, that is on the fourteenth day of the month, they should both prepare and deploy the ships and, when the others were seen coming downriver to a given position, they themselves should come upriver with their ships. Immediately [the castellans] brought together forty ships, assigned their command to the citizens [of Belgrade] alone, and ensured that only its citizens should fight on board. For although [Belgrade's] citizens are schismatics, they are nevertheless bitter enemies of the Turks, indeed courageous, bitter fighters against them, and ones that the Turks fear more than others. They are also most skilled fighters on the water, and do not turn their backs. It was for these reasons that the aforesaid ships were filled with their ranks.

But Lord John [Hunyadi], not trusting in this array of ships great and small, designated one great ship as a kind of director, protector, and helper for all the others, filling her with arms, powder, munitions, and the members of his household. All hope was placed in this ship, in this ship was placed all trust and security. After these things had been

---

24 That is, master craftsmen or artisans, here presumably carpenters and those trained in shipbuilding.

25 The terms here are *scopetis* and *pixidibus*. See n. 15 in this document.

arranged, when the established day had come, the greater of these armed ships began to descend boldly on the Turks; not far behind, the great guardian ship followed, as the commander and supporter of the ships that were in the lead. The father, patron of the crusaders, went alongside them on the shore of the Danube, where he could be seen by all and could inspire them with confidence. The nobleman Peter carried his banner eagerly. Lord John, further away, came along with many horses so as to defend the ships by land. When the Turks saw the ships they mocked them because they were so few. They drew themselves together and formed a line by tying their ships together in the manner of a bridge, readying themselves to resist, thinking indeed that they were certain to win the fight. The ships of the city, by now well armed, saw the others coming and began to sail boldly upriver.

Now, as the father, athlete of God, growled within himself, invoking the name of Jesus, the Christians joined battle. But the Lord John, decisively and wisely, turned his attention to ensuring that the Turks would not send any reinforcements from their camps; that they would not jump from their positions on the water to occupy the land, or even flee by land. The Turks resisted the Christians, and one side could not defeat the other. The blessed father, remaining on the shore, waved the banner of the cross in their faces, as if to say, "Behold the cross of the Lord! Be gone, evil powers!" and crying out the most holy name of Jesus in the manner of a most vigorous young man.[26] Forty ships came up from the city, and everywhere the Turks were surrounded, everywhere enclosed by ships, everywhere attacked by them. As the Turkish lines were broken and their ships began (against their will) to separate from one another, the two sides joined the fight. Great noises resound; handguns and arquebuses fire on both sides; voices and cries rise to the heavens; they strike one another with swords, blades, and stones; the blessed father prays, hands joined, and eyes raised to heaven, that God himself would see fit to guard his cause, invoking the name of Jesus in aid of the Christians. There was even fervent prayer in the fortress. The galleys of the Turks were now being broken, scattered on the Danube,

---

26 Tagliacozzo here seems to have Capistrano recite a prayer of exorcism attributed to the Portuguese Franciscan Anthony of Padua (d. 1321). See Bert Roest, "Demonic Possession and the Practice of Exorcism: An Exploration of the Franciscan Legacy," *Franciscan Studies* 76 (2018): 301–40.

attacked with crossbows, arquebuses, and springalds.[27] And so, for a stretch of five hours, this fierce battle raged on the river.

What more is there to say? When the battle was over, three great galleys of the Turks had been sunk, along with their crews; four captured with all of their munitions and adornments. The remaining ships fled back down the Danube to their earlier position, now holding back, with nearly all of their crews mortally wounded. More than five hundred Turks had drowned. Those ships that remained were so debilitated that they could neither pose a threat to the Christians nor be of use to the Turks. And though the blessed father did not know it, what the Christians gained here by plunder was burned in a great fire so as not to allow the nobility, who had not been involved in the fight, to take it all away. They saved from the flames only two most noble vestments that reached down to the ankles and that were artfully wrought with iron, made for battle. They had been seized by one of the crusaders and thereafter presented to the holy father. He in turn offered them to the most reverend lord legate upon his arrival.

There were also two most noble Turks, survivors of the battle, who (among others) were led before the holy father [Capistrano]. Despite so much persuasion, so many prayers, so much flattery, even so many threats, they refused baptism. So they were sent to Lord John [Hunyadi] as a kind of trophy for the naval victory. When that most bitter enemy of the Turks saw them, he commanded that they be decapitated before his eyes. When someone said to him, "Let us hold them for a few days and afflict them with prison and chains; perhaps they will be baptized," he responded quickly: "Take their heads off and baptize them after." And though the Turks argued and said that they wished to hold to the belief of their ancestors, soon their heads were cut off and they died, their bodies left in a faraway field to be devoured by animals and birds. No one accused the great lord of cruelty; rather, he was exalted for his enmity against those who offended the Christian religion. Though he did say they should be baptized after death, he did so jokingly; for he spoke as one who knows a little about the most harsh belief of the Turks, and that they would never convert. By "baptize them," he meant,

---

27 See n. 15 in this document.

cut off their heads and throw them in the Danube. I have said these things, noble father, to excuse the magnificent Lord John.

Here, by the Lord's favor, the way has been recovered; the Danube has been returned to the Christians. Now hope is given to the besieged; now those who had been in distress rejoice; now those who had been downcast cry out in joy; now the besieged have little fear of the mortars; now the ruined walls of the city can be repaired; now food falls like rain, grain and wine pour down; now hope of escape arrives; and so both the city and the fortress show signs of joy, while the Turks are downcast.

But note here, father, what God (wanting to show that this glorious victory on the Danube had been brought about by his hand, and not by human effort) allowed to happen, by his permission: our great ship, so skillfully prepared, and in which all our human hope was placed, caught fire when the powders of the mortars were set alight through imprudence (or rather by divine judgment). It was entirely burned up and dragged to the shore. The victory over the Turks on the Danube was won without it!

On the Second Victory

Meanwhile the Turks did not cease from assaulting the fortress. Much more intensely than usual, by day and night, they hastened in their work to bring down the walls and the towers. And the innumerable banners that our lord Michael had tied all along the walls of the fortress (set in sight of the Turks so as to weaken their courage) were now shredded by the strikes of the cannons; they fell from the walls and lay on the ground, trampled underfoot. Now the Turks gathered wood and dug up earth, carried chaff, put together dung and ashes, piled up stones and wood, all so that having thoroughly destroyed the walls they would now be able to fill the moat, which was great and wide; and having filled the moat that they might then have free access to the fortress. "Not so the wicked, not so! They are like chaff that the wind blows away."[28] For the cannons, as has been said, had been placed in three locations, so firmly and safely guarded by palisades, ditches, and hills that the whole world, if I may say, could not dislodge them.

---

28 Psalm 1:4.

But let me return from this little detour I have rightly made, most holy father. Having won the fight on the river, both Johns then entered the fortress with greatest joy. They see the ruined walls, they consider the enormous size of the Turkish army, and what it intends to do. On the holy father's advice, John [Hunyadi] got ready to make repairs; he is filled with strength and inspired by the words of the father. But on the day in which they entered, when Lord John saw so many Turks walking around outside the fortress, as if they were trying to goad the Christians to fight, he ordered some of his household to take up arms and fight. Among them was one of his closer followers, called Farcas. He came before the father [Capistrano] and asked for his blessing, saying that he wished to obey his lord's command and fight with the Turks. The father said to him, "Have you confessed?" And when he replied, "I have confessed and taken communion," the father blessed him. He went out and fought fiercely, killing many Turks, though in the end he himself was killed, and his death was bitter and troubling to his lord. I have recounted this, father, because many enemies of the truth have dared to say that he went out of the fortress to fight with the Turks at the command of the blessed father.[29]

All who were in the fortress were filled with great joy because of the presence of both Lord John and the blessed father. But it was the blessed father himself who sent forth all who had been signed with the cross, and who brought in new and recent recruits. He also dutifully sent the wounded and the ill to cities upriver, arranging for them to be carried by ship, and hired, for a salary, two hundred Polish crossbowmen, so that the fortress might be guarded more safely. He inspired all to resist; encouraged John [Hunyadi] to repair the walls; consoled the brothers with his words, and enjoyed a brief but cheerful gathering with them. He brought joy to the downcast, assurance to the fearful, certainty to those in doubt. And after he had inspired and taught all, as he had done earlier, and having blessed all, he took me (whom he considered weak) with him and hastened back to Semlin, where the victory had been won. All of the crusaders were supposed to gather

---

29 See the introductory remarks to this document. These lines reflect the highly contested, politicized circumstances surrounding Capistrano's potential canonization. The author is here working to shape Capistrano's posthumous reputation.

there; it was there that the father pitched his tent; there also that Lord John, having repaired the walls, established his camp. This is the place near the Danube and near the fortress, in sight of the Turks who were besieging it.

The blessed Capistrano stayed in this place, calling for, waiting for, and welcoming crusaders from everywhere, even those from distant lands. All of them obeyed the blessed father (and no other!) as their captain, indeed as the vicar of Jesus Christ. No wonder, then, that they were inspired by his preaching and exhortation, that they took the cross from him, and were ready to go with him to suffer captivity or death. And since they saw him leading such an angelic life among the crowd – performing marvelous wonders for the infirm; laying down his life for Christ; embracing those things which are above, not here below; working tirelessly for the liberation of the kingdom while others stood idle – all aspired to obey him; venerated him as an apostle; loved him as one sent to them from heaven in a marvelous way. He was the director, leader, judge, captain, and emperor of all who were signed with the cross.

Certainly it must be noted here, dearest lord, that by way of letters, nuncios, and rumors, all who had been inspired to take up the cross made their way to the blessed father, who had set himself up in the aforesaid place. And they all came in a wonderful, devout, and fervent way, arriving in cohorts from their various regions, lands, and locales, each contingent bearing its own banner. The banners bore the cross on one side, and on the other figures of blessed Father Francis, or of Anthony, or of Louis, or Saint Bernardino, so as to indicate that they had been gathered together as crusaders by one who was an outstanding follower of the Order of Friars Minor; or to indicate that theirs was a crusade only for the poor, and not the rich; or perhaps so as to conform themselves to the banner of their father; or so that by the patronage of these saints those fighting under their banners would be deserving of aid.

Nor did each contingent lack various musical instruments for exciting the spirit. There were tubas, there were horns, there were drums, there were guitars, there were bells in great number; there was a cacophony of sounds more suited to inciting animals than men. There were also two trumpeters with the father at the command of Lord John. Through these instruments our men remained vigilant, swift, and joyful, while the Turks were made fearful and sad. And they only took up their positions after they had first presented themselves for review in procession before the father and received a blessing from him, who as patron of the people assigned to them their place and assigned quarters. And indeed, they came before him so full of joy, so happy, so fervent in spirit, that they seemed to be running not to fight with the most vicious Turks, but to join a dinner party.

Thus, for ten days some sixty thousand crusaders came from everywhere to gather together, all of whom had taken the cross in Hungary, either from the blessed father himself or his Hungarian associates, though among them there were also many Germans, Poles, Slavs, and Bosnians. And among them there was nothing of laziness, nothing of softness, nothing of sexual impurity; there was no drinking, no feasting, no dishonesty, no cohabitation with women; there were no vain words, no games, no theft, no plunder, no backbiting, no murmuring, no whispering, no strife among them. Instead, there was devotion, prayer, and frequent Masses. For although many came to the blessed father's Mass, each contingent had its own secular priest or religious, from whom each received the sacrament frequently. For there were many priests and religious signed by the cross who frequently sang Mass and the divine office. There was fasting; there was frequent talk of steadfastness in faith; firm intent to pour out blood for the love of Christ; frequent proclamation of the name of Jesus. The piety among them all was great, for many who found themselves without food now lived from begging and alms. Great was the patience among them, great was the peace, and great the concord. And all had the highest degree of obedience, for although many submitted to the blessed father, among themselves they also obeyed one another out of charity. And whether the father sent them into water or into fire, they all obeyed – like novice religious – without any sadness.

To note briefly one example of their prompt obedience: when the father cried out, all cried out; when the father lifted his hands, or extended them out in the form of a cross and held them there while praying, they did the same; when the father raised his banner, they all raised their banners; when the father walked, they also walked; and all happily followed the banner of the holy father himself. Indeed, he upheld the rigor of justice to the highest degree, and he allowed no wrong to go unpunished. For although each contingent or people had its own leader, every case was referred to the father himself as if to an impartial judge. And when someone happened publicly to commit some infamous crime, he was punished publicly, according to an impartial judgment, so as to set an example for others.

When one among them happened to have stolen something of little value, soon thereafter, late at night, there was a sermon, and his right ear was cut off. Another, after the crossing of the Danube had been recovered, sold bread at a higher price than usual. As soon as it came to the notice of the crusaders, all of his bread was thrown in the Danube. And if I and another friar (called Georgio) had not rescued him and taken him to safety, they would have drowned him. Instead, he was beaten with the most severe blows. Moreover, the crusaders wanted nothing to be done within their ranks that might distract their spirits from divine worship. "We came to shed blood," they said, "and we have a holy, just, and pious leader; how then are we to commit such evil deeds?" There was a miraculous charity toward God, in that they were prepared to lay down their lives for his honor; and also toward each other, through service, through mutual obedience, in learning of doctrine, and in mutual defense. And in all of this the dictum of Ecclesiastes was proven true: "As the people's judge is, so are his officials; as the ruler of the city is, so are all its inhabitants."[30] For the father was leader and judge of all the crusaders.

When some sixty thousand crusaders had arrived, and as they continued to arrive daily in their various contingents, the herald of God preached to them the way of salvation, exhorted them to martyrdom, to courage, and to the defense of the Christian religion. And with the voice of a herald he commanded all of them, whether they were coming or going, striking or being struck, that they should often call on and cry out the name of Jesus. The man of God affirmed that there was no salvation in anything else but this most holy name. He commanded them to fight manfully with the enemies of Christ, and to take no part in robbery or plunder. He proclaimed that everything was to be set on fire, and that anything they captured, except those things taken for self-defense, was to be considered stolen. Indeed, the leader of the camp said this:

---

30 Sirach 10:2.

Keep your hands clean from plunder; fight against the enemies of Christ; drive them out; do not allow them to occupy Christendom. We will be easily conquered if we insist on plunder alone; we will be overwhelmed by the Turks if we pursue them in the name of plunder. God will deliver them into our hands, and all their goods will be ours. Fight manfully in the name of Christ, and you will see God's aid come to us. When we overcome them, whatever they have brought against us will be ours. *Be strong in war and fight against the ancient serpent, and you will gain the eternal kingdom.*[31] Confess your sins; the holy pontiff grants you full remission. Oh my sons and most devout Hungarians! Oh poor ones! To the Turk!

The patron of the people said these things often, and other things like them. He admonished them, moreover, that they should disturb none but the Turks. "All who wish to come to our aid against the Turks," he said, "are our friends. Serbians, schismatics, Wallachians, Jews, heretics, and whatsoever infidels who wish to fight with us in this storm, let us embrace them as friends. The fight now is against the Turks, against the Turks." And so the father, inquisitor general of heretical depravity, although one who had always persecuted, uprooted, and confounded these kinds of people most severely, now refused to make any trouble for them as long as they took up arms against the Turks. He also made them proclaim the name of Jesus as often as possible. All these things he did in the open field, with the Turks looking on and listening in from their camps and siege positions.

Moreover, most fervent herald, it must be noted that although such a great crowd came together in this place, no baron appeared there apart from the illustrious and distinguished Lord John the governor of the kingdom, along with his household; for he had not yet reinforced the army – with God and his angels as my witness, I am not lying about these things – although some of his subjects and vassals and nobles remained with the army at that time. But his counsel and aid alone were enough to take the place of all the others. The distinguished baron Lord John Korogh (perpetual Count of Cassellis and the ban of Macsó, also Count of Vrbas and of Pozsega) offered aid. He came with many

---

[31] Tagliacozzo here invokes a liturgical song, *Estote fortes in bello*, which had apocalyptic overtones (cf. Revelation 20:2) and a broad resonance in sacred music and drama.

knights, since Belgrade was under his ban.[32] Here he proved himself a man of great fervor, of wise counsel, and great discretion and devotion.

Regarding the nobles and vassals, although many had been signed with the mark of the cross, since it is the custom in Hungary for those under the authority of a lord to go out to battle while the lords themselves do not, none of them came; or to say it more accurately, very few of them appeared. Rather, all who came were commoners, rustics, paupers, priests, secular clerics, students, monks, brothers of various orders, mendicants, those from the Third Order of Saint Francis, hermits. Among them hardly any weapons could be seen, unless among the vassals. We saw no horses there except those used to carry supplies, and no lances. Those who appeared covered in armor looked like David armed by Saul against Goliath. They were fully armed with swords, clubs, slings, and staves like those that shepherds usually carry, and they all had shields. They had among them crossbows, bows, arquebuses, lead-ball springalds, iron hooks for grappling.[33] Oh, if you could have seen a certain prior of the Order of Hermits[34] with seven brothers of his convent, burning with the zeal of the faith and love of the martyrs, wearing armor under their habits, girded with swords, protected with helmets, and shields across their shoulders, running to martyrdom – father, you would have wept for devotion! And as has so often been said, the leader and director of them all was the blessed father, like a second Moses or a second Joshua. Oh, if only Your Paternity could have seen so many of these men arrive – so well-equipped, some of them singing, some of them saying the *Pater noster*, others begging – you would have indeed judged them to be armed by the grace of the Holy Spirit and the zeal of martyrdom!

Meanwhile the Turks did not cease from besieging and leveling the fortress. They now began to fear, as we later learned from the Turks themselves, when from their camps they saw the crusaders begin to

---

32 "Cassellis" corresponds to no known county in the region, so it may be a scribal error. For Korogh's role on the defense of Belgrade, which was under his authority ("ban"), see Pálosfalvi, *From Nicopolis to Mohács*, 168, 179, and 183. See the introduction, n. 5.
33 See n. 15 above in this document.
34 Presumably the Augustinian Hermits, an order of mendicant friars established in the thirteenth century. For an overview see Gert Melville, *The World of Medieval Monasticism: Its History and Forms of Life* (Collegeville, MN: Liturgical Press, 2016), 256–62.

come together. They saw not the few and the poor, not the unarmed, but the whole world, resplendent and armed with every kind of weapon, now united against them. They thought that the father himself was the emperor of the whole world. Oh God, how the Turks were struck down with fear! They now worked all the more quickly to destroy the fortress, and they pretended to be joyful from time to time in order to strike fear in the Christians.

One night, trying to frighten the Christians, though in fear themselves, they built many large fires throughout their camps. In doing so they tried to show that because they had destroyed the walls of the fortress, they would be victorious. On another night, the captain of God then commanded that many fires be lit in his camps. The people obeyed and lit so many and various fires that when they had been lit in various places the whole great plain of the Christian camps seemed like one great fire. The man of God then turned to the Great Turk and said: "Greatest dog! You wanted to frighten us with your fires; by fire you will now be terrified, by fire expelled, by fire you will flee!" – as if he were able to tell the future. In this way he comforted the people and persuaded everyone that they should not say "emperor of the Turks," but "greatest dog," and took it poorly if he was called by any other name.

Then on the following night the sounds of various instruments could be heard in the camp of the Turks, with such joy that it seemed they were on the verge of victory rather than defeat. Then the commander of the crusaders, inflamed with holy envy, ordered with a herald's cry that everyone in the camp should have an instrument to play – or rather, to terrify; that after midnight they should play, and terrify, and keep watch until the morning. Those who did not have instruments were to make their own enormous and most frightful noises by striking mightily on their shields and pole arms with sticks and stones, and they did not forget their slings. With the light of day, all of the army then lifted their banners in the sight of the Turks, and shouted with joy and delight. And so it was not some little crowd that was seen there, but rather what seemed like all the world, spending a sleepless night making sounds and noises with different and varied kinds of instruments, and with loudest acclamations of the name of Jesus Christ.

When the day had become bright, at the command of the man of God they lifted their banners before the eyes of the Turks and sounded their flutes. Some sang, some cried out, others led dances, others lifted their hands to heaven with cries and jumped about. In doing so they softened the boldness of the Turks, struck fear into their hearts, and showed contempt for their pride. When the Turks saw and heard these things, they suggested to their emperor that he should retreat, saying, "Let us withdraw, since it seems that the whole world comes to the aid of the Christians, and as we can see, they mock our power." But that most savage dog, fired with greater and greater anger and fury against the Christians, commanded – more fiercely than was his custom – that the bombardments continue, and that the task of leveling the walls to the ground should be hastened. He commanded that underground tunnels be made, and that the earth removed from them should be hauled out and placed alongside the moats, so that on the established day the moats could be filled to allow them a level path and free access to the fortress.

And here it must be noted, most illustrious elder, that in these nine days after the naval victory, when the blessed father was in this place with the crusaders, as has been said, he often went into the fortress. He sent the weak, the timid, the sick, the wounded, and the poor away; and if any died, he had them buried. He also led into the fortress new crusading troops, lively and strong and resolute, whom Lord Michael recommended. He preached to them, as to the others before, to guard the fortress, to embrace martyrdom, and to remain steadfast. And having properly arranged affairs in the fortress, he always returned to the [crusader] army.

What kind of army he had in his camps can be surmised from this: that he did not eat; that if he happened to find an occasion to rest, the naked ground served as a bed for his weakened little body; that if he was thirsty, he drank either wine made scalding hot by the sun and mixed with muddy and stinking water, or water alone. He did not sleep. And although he was seventy years old, in his labors, his vigils, in the evils he suffered, he was like the strongest of young men. By turns he went into the fortress and came out of it; by turns he taught, admonished, encouraged, corrected, commanded. It was also his duty to watch over the people both in and beyond the fortress, to post guards, to set watches, and to send scouts. He had so many labors, hardships, worries, and cares that there was no strong young man, especially in these times, who could keep up with him. Not even the knights could match him in such great labors. The strongest and most experienced failed in their efforts.

What more? Lord John the governor, seeing him burdened with such great labor, and seeing that so many cares weighed him down, gave him a horse better than any other as a gift. Within a few days, it was so exhausted by its incessant labor that it collapsed, skinned raw, in the middle of the crowd, not without inspiring great astonishment and compassion among them all. And although he too should have been worn out by such incessant labor, as the days wore on, he only seemed to grow stronger. He celebrated Mass every day, and with their collects: "Do not despise your people, Lord, etc." as in the missal, *Pro quacunque tribulatione*, or "Crush, Oh Lord, we beseech thee, the pride of our enemies," as in *Contra persecutores et male agentes*; or "The Holy Spirit, most pious God, in whose hands, etc." as in *Contra paganos*.[35] He also exhorted the people in the same spirit, as noted above. Oh father, consumed with age, yet most unwearied! Oh blessed man, worthy of being followed with all honor and reverence! Oh athlete of Christ, conquered by no task! Though you are failing with age, yet you do not grow old in your constant labor! In you is love, in you hope, and in you the strongest trust; in you an inexplicable faith, in you the zeal for martyrdom, in you shines forth that most ardent fervor, which shows us the way.

Lord John stood strong with Lord Michael. And whatever the Turks' siege engines destroyed in the night, they repaired the next day. He was busied each day with repairs, spent sleepless nights in his tent, and worked tirelessly to save the fortress. And however many crusaders were needed for the defense of the fortress, he made it known to the holy father either personally or through an emissary. Meanwhile the father gathered defenders and led them into the fortress by way of the Danube or the back gate of the fortress. In this way the fortress was saved in these days. But Lord John, even as he continued to work to repair the destroyed walls, believed along with Lord Michael that the fortress would soon fall into the hands of the enemy, and he told the blessed father so. The father, knowing what would come, assuaged his fears and offered hope of victory and liberation; moreover, he exhorted him to continue the work of repairs, saying, "Do not fear, noble lord! God is able to liberate his people," and similar things.

---

35 Here Tagliacozzo cites a series of standard prayers associated with particular Masses. For general context see Gaposchkin, *Invisible Weapons*. See the introduction, n. 37.

It must be noted here that in these days the reverend lord legate [Carvajal] sent letters to both Johns from Buda. In them he announced that they should under no circumstances join in battle with the Turks, since he himself was about to move south with great force. His concern, namely, was for so many, unarmed and unaccustomed to war, that were said to be gathered there; he feared that all would fall into the hands of the Turks. It is certainly reasonable, and with good reason it was thought at the time that two things should happen: that is, the movement [of troops] south should be made quickly, and that it should be done with a strong hand. (I would add a third: that the Turks not begin an assault, and of course not enter the fortress. But since, etc. therefore, etc.)[36] It is for this reason, father, that the detractors of the blessed father argue he was disobedient, insofar as he attacked the Turks by divine impulse. Oh! If the crusaders had been conquered, what these barking dogs would say against this most obedient father! But these people do not take note that it was only by the diligence, prayer, preaching, encouragement, and labors of such a father that all of Christendom has been liberated. Certainly, the most reverend lord legate is owed obedience as much as the holy pontiff. But because he [Capistrano] was provoked by God and by the Turks, God allowed his case to be made, as is explained below.[37]

Now to return to my purpose: when the blessed father heard from Lord John about the preparations of the Turks, and that the Turks would soon obtain the fortress, he still sought to extend charity even toward his enemy. Moved by divine spirit, he gathered together a very few crusaders and went alone with a Hungarian friar, Brother Francis, Brother Ambrose [of Aquila], and Brother Alexander of Ragusa. He went to the Sava and, standing on the bank of the river, alongside a small boat, he cried out with a mighty voice, speaking through an interpreter to the Turks who stood across the river: "Oh, enemies of the Lord Jesus Christ! Send word to your great dog that he should reconsider his most evil intention, retreat, and abandon this fortress. And that if he does not do so, the hand of the Lord will soon be upon him, and he will be torn by a twofold sorrow: that of defeat and damnation,

---

36 The parenthetical phrase seems to be an odd addition to the text.
37 Tagliacozzo is again working here to preserve Capistrano's reputation. See n. 29 in this document.

the likes of which Christians have never seen!" These words were said on the day before the vigil of the glorious Magdalene.[38] On that day, when the Turkish bombardiers saw him returning by way of the plain, immediately they sought to kill him with the stones of the larger cannons. But the servant of God returned to the Christian camp and did so joyfully. And although he said these words in a way that foretold the future, he nevertheless did not intend to engage in warfare with the Turks, unless God should otherwise dispose, both because of the letters of the lord legate (which, as has been said, he sought to obey) and also because it was thought rash (by human judgment) to deliver such a multitude of people into the hands of the more numerous Turks.

By now every wall had been leveled to the ground, and the great tower, though like lead, had been cut in two. This was the tower where they kept watch and sent out warning signals for incoming rounds, from which they mocked the great dog by shouting words through a kind of great horn, and from which they inflicted great loss on the Turkish camp; in fact, in my presence a certain priest and chaplain of the fortress killed seven Turks with three rounds from a springald. Now the most cruel Turks resolved among themselves to capture the besieged fortress with all of their power. They announced that those who first entered would receive great gifts, the second and third smaller prizes, and so on, and they resolved to do it quickly. They saw the army of the Christians growing and (as has been said) it seemed to them that the whole world was coming together there against them. Thus, they armed themselves, so that on the following day, that is, on the vigil of the holy Magdalene, it would be done; and yet those miserable ones did not think of the fact that in arming themselves to take the fortress they were readying themselves for death, confusion, and defeat.

Now the cannons and handguns fell silent; now the enemy ran anxiously throughout the camp. Seeing and considering these things, Lord John abandoned the repair of the walls and, quite exhausted from the night before, came to the blessed father, saying: "Oh! Behold, father! We are conquered; we will indeed yield to the Turks. Many times now I have brought news of our victories over them, and I have worn them down not with a great number of soldiers, not with the strength of

---

38 That is, on July 20.

warriors, but through industrious talent, wise effort, and cunning attention to detail – and I know well their ways of war. But now I have no genius, no effort, and no attention to detail left to use against them, and I have no plan left for either offense or defense. I have done what I could. Now I have nothing at all left, and there is no longer any way of defending the fortress. It can no longer be repaired; its walls and towers are destroyed, and the way is open for the Turks. We are so few against such a great multitude, and we have inexperienced men – poor, weak, and timid; the barons [to fight] only when they arrive. What more can we do?" To which the father responded with words of consolation, "Do not fear, noble lord! God is able to overwhelm the power of the Turks with the few and the unarmed, to defend our fortress and to defeat his enemies," and similar things. But almighty God wanted the stern and noble Lord John to say these things so as to show that the wondrous works of God cannot be comprehended by human power, experience, or wisdom; and that the hidden judgments of God cannot be known, because they are a great abyss. God himself wished that through these words it would be made clear that the future and excellent miracle would appear more clearly, certainly, and wonderfully to mortal minds, and that a thing which would be done by the right hand of God, not man, would be seen as the result of divine power.

John [Hunyadi] no longer came into the fortress, but a number of his followers remained behind to defend it. He himself said, "Tomorrow, indeed, the fortress will no longer be ours; the Turks will take possession of it." When the father heard and understood this, he said joyfully "Do not fear! It will still be ours," often repeating that "God's cause will be advanced, the name of Christ will be defended; I am certain that God will take good care of his cause." Oh, most confident father! Who does not shower him with praise and acclaim? He then summoned, strongly, four thousand of the crusaders, and especially those who seemed stronger, more spirited, more faithful, and better armed. He reviewed them, and led them into the fortress, with his banner going before them. And no wonder they followed the banner of the blessed man with such joy, so much that it seemed they went forth not to shed their blood and to die, but as if they were servants who had been invited to a meal, or to receive great wealth. And so it was indeed, since earthly things were exchanged for heavenly things, and bodily for eternal things. When the blessed father led them there, both the citadel and the city met them willingly and with great joy. Everyone was also filled with great fear, but the father exhorted everyone to diligent watchfulness, to martyrdom, to defense, to perseverance, and to fidelity, as he was accustomed to do before, but now even more fervently, asserting that the Turks were now about to join battle and to besiege the fortress with clever tactics. "Therefore," he said, "fight manfully, be strong, and obey the commands of the castellan Lord Michael." He then sent away the weak, the wounded, the timid, and the useless. Those who were ill he sent to the cities to the north to be cared for, as it had been earlier. Those who remained he commanded to invoke and cry out the name of Jesus, preaching to them in the power of this most holy name that the Christians would indeed have victory over the Turks.

With all that he had, he inspired Lord Michael through exhortation and preaching. He then entrusted the crusaders to him, directing him to assign and establish them in the proper defensive positions. Lord Michael himself was a stern man, well experienced in arms, a spirited warrior who for many reasons was a most fierce defender and champion of the fortress – by reason of his Christian faith; by reason of his kingdom; by reason of his close ties to Lord John (whose wife, Lady Elizabeth, was Michael's sister) – as well as by reason of his own honor and fame.

As has been said, Lord [Sesch] was also there, a most noble knight and a man distinguished for his talent, cunning, and instinct.[39] But the father also left behind five brothers whom he commanded, as before, to continue to do works of mercy and to accept martyrdom quickly should it come to pass, since the time of its crown was close at hand. When he had properly ordered all of these affairs, he offered a blessing to the city, and to everyone in it. He then proclaimed the name of Jesus publicly and loudly, and with his banner going before him he returned safely and happily to the army of the Christians that was waiting on the nearby plain. All the while his hope remained in the one who does not abandon those who trust in him.

It was on that day as well that women made their way from the city to the citadel, especially the stronger women and the virgins, so that they would not be taken captive and given as gifts or abducted along with

---

39 The editor's rendering here is unclear. Perhaps a reference to Szilágyi.

the others. In their judgment, they would be safer in the citadel than in the city, by virtue of both the protection of the crusaders as well as the presence of the friars, and also because they did not believe that the citadel, which the holy father had strengthened with so many defenders, would fall easily into the hands of the Turks.

And no one should wonder, most distinguished lord, that the blessed father wanted to stay that night in the camp. For since the great army obeyed none but him, he drew from those who were stationed outside and deployed them among those who would guard from within, as needed. He also knew that the great army was disordered and ignorant, constantly in need of a teacher and a leader, especially since in his absence (the one, as has been said, to whom they referred all judgments) any quarrels that might arise among them would become a scandal for the crusade. Moreover, he had been present for those in the camp both in spirit and prayer as well as in body, aiding them through prayer, correcting them, and reining them in by his most pleasant commands. For he said to them fervently, "Oh Lord, save thy people."[40]

Around the third hour of this vigil the Turks prepared for the main fight to take the castle.[41] As was their custom, they sent up prayers and poured out petitions to their devil Mahumeth. Then, after sounding their various instruments, they cried out as loudly as they could, with sounds more like the lowing of cattle than human voices. In the camp of the Christians, on the contrary, there was the singing of songs with acclamations of the name of Jesus, with banners lifted high. Then in the fortress there was also the loudest of cries, and the crusaders deployed themselves on the walls of the ruins, readying themselves to give their lives for Christ and to stand their ground until they either died for Christ or saw their fortress liberated from their enemies.

Finally, around the hour of vespers on the same day,[42] by squads and with great cries the Turks rushed the castle from all sides like bees, running like roaring lions ready to pounce on their prey, one after the other, so that they could attack with the others who waited behind.

---

40 Cited here is another common liturgical song, a portion of the ancient hymn attributed to Saint Ambrose, the *Te Deum*. Cf. Psalm 27:9.
41 That is, around midmorning on July 21.
42 That is, toward evening, around 6:00 p.m.

And so the Turks reach the moats.[43] Some throw in bundles of wood, others straw, some throw in earth, others manure, some ashes, others place beams and timber. There are even many who come up from underground tunnels, starved, like rapacious and hungry wolves, to bring down the walls. In this way they tried to fill the moats and gain access to the fortress. But the crusaders held their positions on the wall, and at the orders of the castellan, fought back with handguns, cannons, arquebuses, and crossbows, wounding and killing many of the Turks. And though many were killed by the Turks, the Christians were not able to stop them from filling the moat about halfway (though not yet all the way to the top).

Thus, the Turks joined battle amid the ruins of the walls, and filled the moat like so many innumerable ants. They shot arrows and handguns; others threw stones and rocks by hand; others dug out the earth or excavated hidden tunnels, while still others lowered beams across the ruins. Some tried to climb the walls, while others sought to strike the Christians with lances, javelins, or terrible swords. Archers, too, stood at some distance and never ceased to launch their arrows, wonderfully crafted, against the Christians, some casting two, even three arrows at a time from one bow, such that the air seemed clouded with arrows. And thus, the most hostile Turks struggled bitterly in the fight to enter the castle all the way to the first hour of the night; and many of them were killed or mortally wounded by the Christians through arrows and other weapons, as noted above.

As for the Christians, while they were on the walls and ramparts few of them fell, since they stood above the Turks and could only be attacked by stones. But when the walls were gone the Turks rushed in, not without great loss to their own ranks, and surrounded the fortress closely on all sides. They fought harshly and closely with the Christians, and after killing many of them gained entrance to the fortress. Some of the city's defenders were wounded; others, protected by the name of Christ, remained uninjured, and rushed upon the enemy, invoking

---

43 Reference here is likely to the southern and eastern walls of the Upper Town, which at this time rose above both a glacis and a moat that was some seven meters (about twenty to twenty-five feet) deep. See *Beogradska Tvrdjava* [*The Fortress of Belgrade*] (Belgrade: Beograd Arheološki Institut, 2006), especially the three-dimensional reconstruction on p. 126 and the English summary at pp. 325–6. See the introduction, pp. 10–12, as well as Map 2: The City and Fortress of Belgrade, c. 1450, on p. 283.

the name of Jesus. Many Turks were killed and were forced into a confused retreat. The cry among those who were in the fight was great; those outside called on the name of the devil Muhammad, those inside cried out the name of Christ. The father stood amid the crusaders like a second Moses, praying and speaking: "Lord, save your people," and similar things. The people stood and prayed with him. But the Lord John, as has been said, was quite convinced that the fortress would soon fall – and in truth, at least by human judgment, he was right to think so.

They tried a third attack around midnight on the vigil of the most blessed Magdalene. All of them arrive with their various instruments and machines, surround the fortress on all sides, engage in the fiercest of fights, and do not fear death; these Turkish fighters, who now seem infinite in number, long to be struck down. The Christians resist, and they, too, long to be struck down and to die for Christ. They drive back the Turks, break the Turks with stones, do not cease from pressing the Turks. And coming repeatedly to their aid were women, who seemed to be not human but like lionesses, for they were armed, and carried themselves in a certain distinguished, manly way. They aided those in the fight by providing arrows, stones, and other instruments of war. They inspired the men, whether attacking or defending. They also carried the wounded down from the walls and into the castle, using their hands and their teeth to pull out the metal of the arrows. These women appeared often, engaged for long hours in this warlike work. They did not move about in the way typical of women; rather, they pressed on about their business in the fortress with manly strength. And no wonder, since "necessity makes for good soldiers."[44] For in such business they defended the modesty, chastity, and virginity they feared to lose, because they knew the ways of the Turks. Meanwhile the friars within the castle, for their part, focused all the more fervently on their prayers.

And because the Christians, continuously engaged in the fight, could resist no longer – worn out now through labor, sleepless nights, and hunger, exhausted and afflicted by all of these things; many among them killed in the fighting, and all of them rendered weak – the Turks again came in waves (though many were struck and killed) and began to enter and to occupy the castle – or rather the field – of

---

44 Tagliacozzo renders the phrase in Italian: *"per che la necesitade fa buoni fanti."*

the outer castle.[45] Here it must be noted, though it is difficult, that the fortress of Belgrade (as Your Paternity knows) has a three-part structure.[46] The first consists of a great outer wall enclosing a plain, where there are many dwellings for noblemen. The walls of this outer fortress were destroyed. And since the approach (or the descent) to the city is from here, as well as the approach to the two inner fortresses (without which nobody can occupy the others) the Turks fought to take this position, to enter here, and to occupy the plain. The second is small, but it is extremely well fortified and sits beside the first, guarded with great ditches and difficult towers and ramparts, to which there is no access from the broader plain except through one gate with a drawbridge.[47] And here is that tower called "Do Not Fear," which was noted above.[48] It is here that the royal lodgings are found, as if it were the most secure of places. Here are also high windows facing the city, as well as the rear gate, through which there is a way down to the city and also access to the Danube. Here were the books of the blessed father, the relics, and here the larger cannons. Were the citadel to be captured, the people could be saved through this gate; and through this gate, if the city were not taken, reinforcements could be sent to the besieged. Here the brothers made their stand, and here they stood guard over all things.

The walls of the first fortress had been flattened to the ground, though some portions of the towers still stood in ruins. The towers of the second fortress, though badly damaged by the blows of the cannons, had nevertheless not fallen.[49] The Turks now stormed into this outer plain, with great slaughter from their strike. Yet the Christians did not retreat from their assigned positions; although

---

45 A wordplay (*castrum/campum*) that first appeared in Hunyadi's earliest letter. See document 10, n. 1.
46 See Map 2: The City and Fortress of Belgrade, c. 1450, on p. 283.
47 Reference here is to the drawbridge that guarded the eastern entrance to the inner fortress. See location 1 on Map 2: The City and Fortress of Belgrade, c. 1450, on p. 283.
48 Tagliacozzo here references the main tower at the center of Belgrade's inner fortress. See location 2 on Map 2: The City and Fortress of Belgrade, c. 1450, on p. 283. After its destruction, another tower was built around 1460, protecting the Danube port in the Lower Town. It survives as the Nebojša Tower ("Fearless" in Serbian), now a museum in modern Belgrade.
49 The reference here is to the citadel – see locations 1 and 2 on Map 2: The City and Fortress of Belgrade, c. 1450, on p. 283.

they were more spread out than usual as the Turks poured in, they did not hold back from slaughtering and brutally massacring them. Now there are around seven hundred Turks on the outer plain, some of them wounded, others paralyzed by fear because they could not move forward without death raining down from above. But they now believe they have taken the outer fortress; they fix five of their banners on the ruins of the walls; they encourage those who remain outside, and cry loudly. The Christians do not retreat, but resist manfully and hold on in the fight, impeding the Turks' entrance as they are able. They do not stop striking them and cutting them down.

When Lord Michael and the other nobles and followers of Lord John saw all of this, they arranged to have all the goods in the interior fortress loaded into boats, sought to save themselves by way of the back gate of the citadel, and fought to make their way to safety. The guards stopped protecting us; knights fled; vassals made their way to the Danube; and those to whom the gates were not accessible for escape willingly jumped from the highest windows. The women who with such great labor had fled there from the outer fortress now stood firm, their locks of hair resolute: "Alas," they said, "we fled the Turks, and now we will fall into the hands of the Turks." Meanwhile the friars, praying on bended knees and with covered faces, awaited martyrdom. So now it was only the crusaders inside who held and protected Christ. The number of Turks on the outer plain began to grow, although many were killed by the Christians as they entered. But the lord John, hearing that the Turks had begun to enter the fortress and that it would now be lost, was disturbed and saddened. He said to the blessed father: "Alas, now the fortress is lost; now the Turks, as I have always said they would, are taking hold of it!" But the father comforted him and retreated in silence. Again he chose several thousand crusaders from among the people and led them with him right away, entering the fortress through the [rear] gate. Returning to the army he placed all of them at the ready and commanded them to watch and to pray; he himself also commended the cause of God to God himself, through both silent and verbal prayer.

But as the Turks grew in number on the outer plain, and when they saw the citadel held only by unarmed commoners, believing they could now capture it, they rushed the drawbridge (which had not yet been raised) so that they could capture the inner fortress.[50] There was no other way to approach it without violence other than by way of the bridge. The crusaders stood their ground inside, especially those whom the holy father had just recently led in, and resisted mightily. At this bridge, the fiercest of fights was now joined, the greatest of battles. The Turks struggled to take it, the Christians to guard it fiercely, and indeed to be killed by the Turks in defending it – because if the Turks were to obtain this bridge, without doubt they would be victorious indeed.

As dawn approached, when the crusaders who remained along the circuit of the outer fortress saw and heard of the bitter fight at the drawbridge; that there was such a great force of Turks now in the outer plain; that the moat now seemed completely filled with Turks; and the number of invaders was constantly growing, they feared that they would be able to resist no longer. Led inwardly by the Holy Spirit, they began to take countless bundles of timbers, branches, vines, and other flammable things, to set them alight with sulfur, and to cast them – as if with one hand, as if every bundle were held in one hand – onto the Turks, both those standing in the moat as well as those climbing through the ruins. Oh, God! None could flee from the face of the fire; all who were in the moat, a number that could hardly be counted, were consumed by flame, and not one of them remained alive. Those who were about to descend into the moat all retreated in fear. But those who were already in the fortress and who were struggling so mightily to take the drawbridge, seeing that they were now surrounded on all sides by such walls of flame, abandoned the fight. Terrified, and with great cries, they rushed to escape the fortress. Some, struck by a certain fear and blindness and confusion, believed that they could escape by leaping off the walls; they jumped into the fire, and were consumed there. Others, who feared to make the jump, were miserably cut down by the crusaders in the outer plain. But those who had not yet descended into the moat, those who manned the diabolical instruments for the attackers, gave a great bellow to the heavens and ran in retreat back to the positions of the cannons, as if they were the safest of strongholds.

As the Turks saw all of these things unfold, all of their camps were struck with sorrow; their audacity crushed; their pride cast down. Now

---

50 See n. 43 in this document, and location 1 on Map 2: The City and Fortress of Belgrade, c. 1450, on p. 283.

there are not a few who begin to say among themselves, "Let us fall back, because the god of the Christians fights for them." They are mired in confusion and struck by fear. Nor are they singing now or calling out. They are keeping silent, and their trumpets and other instruments cannot be heard. Oh, father and elder! Where do we think that fire came from, unless from the bosom of our great God at the intercession of the blessed father [Capistrano], who was one with his people in praying without ceasing, asking God to uphold their cause and to save his people? Who does not believe that glorious Mary Magdalene was there on the ruins of the walls to aid the Christians in casting the fire? Who doubts that you were the defender of this cause against its enemies, you who after your conversion were such a sweet disciple, and who were worthy of receiving such blessings, oh most blessed father John of Capistrano? Was it not your ministry, your industry, your work, your command, and your prayer that did all of these things? Who could be tempted by such a satanic suggestion that they would dare detract from your sanctity, or bury you in their own fictions? It is only to fulfill what is said through the prophet: "The wicked (that is, the detractor and the envious one) watches the just (or just deeds, virtues, etc.), and seeks to put him to death (that is, to afflict with pain)"; but God does not allow it. He says, "The just shall be in everlasting remembrance," etc., and Proverbs 10: "The memory of the just is with praises."[51]

This glorious liberation of the fortress and this naval victory, beyond all human understanding, prudence, and reason, was accomplished by God alone, reverend lord! And all the world is compelled to acknowledge the virtue of the most blessed father, through whose happy prudence, skill, care, persuasion, confidence, and most fervent prayer it happened that Hungary and the other nations of Christendom were liberated from the Turks. For if that fortress had fallen into their hands, without doubt they would have first taken Hungary, and then other nations.

Now there is great joy in the fortress and in the camps of the Christians. Those who had left returned. Michael took heart, and others embraced their resolve and strength anew. Those who were sad now rejoiced; now there is joy where before there was fear; now the women

---

51 Psalm 36 (37):32; Psalm 111 (112):7; Proverbs 10:7.

who had been lost in fear rejoiced, while the brothers gave thanks to God. In the growing light of the new day, oh most noble elder, we could see the Turks burned and slaughtered, blood splattered everywhere. Indeed, the moats were full of piles of Turkish bodies. In only a small area you could see many Turks charred by fire, and indeed there was no easy way to approach or cross for all of the bodies. Among the Turks the powerful, the brave, the noble Turks were all dead indeed. But among the Christians hardly sixty won the crown of martyrdom for Christ, with many more struck and wounded. And no wonder: they had fought so bitterly, resolutely, tirelessly with the Turks, these unarmed, inexperienced ones; to those who are of sound mind, it is only because they were guarded from above (which is miraculous) that they were not killed. They themselves were the walls, the towers, the bulwarks. Oh, most glorious father! If you could have seen the multitude of arrows that they shot, so skillfully, in the fight against the Turks! Indeed, the whole outer suburb of the fortress was so filled with arrows that you could not walk without stepping on them. For the women as well as the others gathering them made quite a number of bundles, as they are accustomed to do when collecting small reeds into larger sheaves. The walls, or rather the ruins of the walls, were so stuck with arrows, and so thickly, that you would think it had been done on purpose. Trunks, beams, and other wooden objects were sticking out in countless numbers. I will say nothing of the other machines of war, which could not be counted.

On the Third Victory

Your Paternity has now heard the story of the liberation of the fortress, and the victory brought about there by divine intervention. I have perhaps told the story in a more verbose way than Your Paternity might have desired. But I have omitted many things, and I have only touched on those things which without doubt are lacking, and which others might have reported in a confused or inconsistent way, so that Your Paternity might avoid any disdain and have what you asked of me. I now come to the victory over the Turks beyond the fortress, in the great field. In this victory the omnipotence of God will appear much more marvelous than in the first two, and in it will be revealed the power of the most holy name of Jesus and of the holy cross, as well as how much favor the oft-mentioned blessed John of Capistrano (through whose ministry all of these things came about) found with God.

But here it must be noted that after the liberation of the fortress, so wondrously brought about by divine intervention, very early in the morning Lord John [Hunyadi] entered the fortress. He was filled with amazement and admiration and considered the events to mark the liberation of all of Hungary. He also considered them to be to the glory and honor of God, and an enhancement of the reputation, praise, and merit of the blessed father. But because he was afraid that this moment of honor could be turned into one of confusion and fear, like a good governor and defender of the kingdom he directed Lord Michael that no one should be allowed to leave the fortress and move against the Turks. He also commanded the sailors that they should carry no one across the Danube or the Sava. The fear, as has been said, was that such a great crowd of unarmed and inexperienced people should be destroyed by the Turks, who were now driven by anger and desperation. All believed as well that the Turks would soon return to the fortress once more and try to conquer it. Oh, man resisting with all prudence! Oh, man full of shrewdness! For in order to defeat the Turks, he did not wish to lose Christians. But in this case, in a way beyond human understanding, by divine will, things turned out differently. Instructing Lord Michael to guard the fortress diligently, he put on armor and with two men set out in a small boat and moved now on the Danube, now on the Sava. Here he was scouting out the extent to which these might be blockaded, thinking it would be safer for him on the water than in the fortress, even as all the crusaders believed he would remain in the fortress to arrange a response against the Turks.

Meanwhile, the most blessed captain [Capistrano] came with all the army of crusaders, with all of their banners raised, and his banner going before them, not without various sounds and noises and the loudest acclamations of the name of Jesus. And all took up positions in the field by the Sava and the Danube, precisely where the Sava enters the Danube. Here they fixed their banners, shouted insults at the Turks. The Turks were mocked by the Christians, and a great terror took hold of the Turks. Although their cannons were at this point still in their possession, since we were so close to them they stood still, as if there was peace between them and us; but the Christians did not stand still, nor did they keep silent.

Meanwhile outside the fortress some crusaders were seen armed with bows and arrows. A great multitude of Turks rushed against them on horseback with lances lowered; the crusaders, however, standing on a certain mound of earth, drew their bows and repelled the Turks with volleys of arrows. The Turks, turning their backs to the blows of the arrows, returned to their lines pierced and defeated. Others attacked to cries of the name of Jesus, which the most blessed father made and to which all responded. They [the Turks] either fell from their horses or their lances fell from their hands, or the horses themselves fell prostrate to the ground. And no wonder, since at this name, "every knee shall bow," according to the Apostle.[52] Most glorious father! The acclamation of this most holy name was so great that when all responded at once to the voice of the blessed father, it seemed like the sound of thunder. Many more now went out, without the knowledge of the castellan, and when the Turks came near them, they were not only unharmed by the Turks but indeed seemed to walk unharmed before their eyes. They went forth boldly, as if they had weapons before them, and they remained unharmed, like angels, although they appeared as men. Who doubts that they were indeed angels showing the Christians the victory that they would have over the Turks, and on that day drawing them into the fight with the Turks?

But the blessed father, commander of the people, looked out on these things and, while burning for martyrdom in a marvelous way, said, "This is the day of victory we have been waiting for; let us cross over and go up! Do not fear the Turkish people since we can devour them like bread!" What else should we think, noble elder, but that a voice spoke divinely to him – the same one which Gideon heard, that is, "The Lord is with you, strongest of men. Go, and in that strength and faith of yours, you will save Israel, and the Christian people, out of Midian's hand," that is, of the Great Turk.[53] And when he doubted, in humility, because of the paucity and inexperience of his fighters, Gideon heard, "Do not fear; I will be with you, and you will strike down all the Midianites as one."[54] And so the father took with him two brothers as well as the nobleman Peter as his standard-bearer, and had two sailors

---

52 Philippians 2:10.
53 A paraphrase of Judges 6:12–14.
54 A paraphrase of Judges 6:16.

carry him on a small ship across the Sava to the opposite shore, where the Turks were positioned.

Here, most religious father, a most astonishing miracle must be noted: when the father had made it part of the way across the river with the two friars (that is, John of Tagliacozzo and Ambrose of Aquila) it seemed to the Turks that an innumerable multitude of soldiers was moving against them, even though it was in reality only six people: the father himself and the two friars, the standard-bearer, and two sailors. For although there were many friars present in the camp, none had crossed over with the father. The aforementioned Brother Alexander of Ragusa was there, and to him the father said, "Wait here and take care of the equipment," etc. There were also others from Hungary, who did not cross over.

One might wonder why the army of the Christians did not follow its prince and its captain in crossing the river, since it had always followed his command and advice. It must be said that God arranged it such that the sailors, bound by the commands of their superiors, took no one across, so that the miracle to come should appear more marvelously, and so that the glory of such a father would be more clear – the one who, with the few and the unarmed, under the favor of our Lord Jesus Christ, was destined to crush the great power of the Turks.

When the future confounder and destroyer had made his way across with the abovementioned two friars and his standard-bearer, he began to climb on foot from the riverbank to the moat of the fortress. He was fasting, or rather had for many days taken very little food, and was exhausted from his labors. All through the night he had run here and there, never able to sleep, and for many days and nights he ate nothing except as a little child might eat, and took no rest at all. It was around 4:00 p.m. When those who were outside the fortress and who had first gone out now saw him, they were soon filled with joy and ran to him like a father. And when those who were inside saw this, although forbidden by command not to exit the fortress, they began to make their way to the blessed father – some climbing over the ruins, some through the holes in the walls – and before long many had joined him. He first made his way to the moat and saw the wonders that had taken place there, both in the night and on the following morning. He saw the innumerable bodies of the Turks, which lay there burned and reduced to almost nothing, in the ashes of the extinguished fire. He also thought of the great danger that all of Christendom had escaped on the previous night, and joining his hands and raising his eyes to heaven he glorified God, giving him thanks and saying repeatedly, "He who begins it will also bring it to an end."

He then took up a position between the fortress, or the moat of the fortress, and the cannons. When the Turks saw him, they seemed more and more afraid, restricting themselves to the area of the tents and of their emperor and of the cannons. They also readied themselves to defend in the event that the Christians chose to either attack or to seize their cannons. They took up arms, arranged their arquebuses, and joined together their handguns. But the number of crusaders approaching the father continued to grow, and it could not be helped that soon perhaps two thousand were gathered around him. He then sought out an interpreter, and a certain old priest who had taken the cross by the name of Paul, a canon of the greater church of Székesfehérvár who had long been devoted to the father, offered his services.[55]

The leader of the army of God now looked at the great number of crusaders following him, knowing that "It is not on the size of the army that victory in battle depends, but strength comes from heaven."[56] With his banner going before him, he began to walk slowly toward the forward position of the cannons, propped up by a little staff on which was carved the name of Jesus, the same staff that the blessed old man had always used, whether riding or walking, exhausted by such long labor and unremitting sleeplessness, with his old head uncovered, crying the name of Jesus as loudly as he could. He was the first to go, and then perhaps a thousand crusaders followed behind. When the Turks, holding their ground, saw and heard him, they were terrified. They retreated to the more secure cannons and camps and tents. Thus, the forward cannons were captured and held, and upon seeing that, all were filled with astonishment and joy. Oh, who might then have seen the blessed father, full of joy, happy, rejoicing! Who could have put a worthy price on the value of these things? Certainly, if nothing had been captured beyond these forward cannons of the Turks, it would have been to the great honor and enrichment of the renowned kingdom of Hungary.

---

55 This same Paul is mentioned later in the narrative. See p. 198 in this document.
56 1 Maccabees 3:19.

After taking these first cannons, this tireless plunderer of the Turks made his way to the next. Again the Turks, unable to resist the name of Jesus, the father, or his banner, abandoned them without resistance, along with their apparatus, and retreated to a third group.[57] But the father, as fierce as a lion, made a gesture of enormous joy before the eyes of the Turks and now moved toward these [cannons], which were defended by various guards. Mortars and various machines were also set up in this position for their defense, and it was also most strongly defended by the ditches, palisades, and earthworks that surrounded it on all sides. Everyone was afraid to approach it, both because the Turks were so near and because they [the crusaders] were so few in the face of such mighty defenses. But our intrepid captain, calling many together, inspiring them with thoughts of plunder and profit, sent his banner before him, called mightily on the name of Jesus, and made his way toward the third position. When the miserable Turks saw him, they put up no resistance; with iron keys they closed the openings through which they usually fired their cannons, called out as if cursing themselves, abandoned the cannons and many other things that cannot be written about, and then these sorry ones retreated back to their emperor.

Oh, holy and fearful name of Jesus Christ! Oh, aged and unarmed father, beloved by grace of every holiness! Oh, marvelous power of the cross, with whose imprint were marked the blessed father, all of the others who stood with him, and his banner! Oh, sweetest name of Jesus! Oh, most holy Bernardino![58] His image is depicted on the same banner, offering the name of Jesus by his hand – and it was this image that the holy father showed to the Turks, and that terrified them.

Think of this, Your Paternity: how great the joy was toward the father; how great the sadness of the Turks; how great their confusion, their loss, about which there will be more discussion below. But here it must be noted above all that though the Turks be most spirited and warlike, and

---

57 "Apparatus" here is a loose translation of *attinentiis*, designating what must have been the housing and other elements put in place to guard and to operate the cannons during the siege.
58 Bernardino of Siena (d. 1444) was a leading Franciscan preacher and reformer and John of Capistrano's mentor, and also an avid promoter of the cult of the Holy Name. After Bernardino's death Capistrano took the lead in working for his canonization (proclaimed in 1450) and Bernardino's posthumous miracles were central to Capistrano's preaching campaign across northern Europe in the early 1450s.

because of their overbearing pride they are willing to yield to no one, nevertheless they chose to flee from the furor and the face of the most blessed father rather than to fight, and this because, as the Turks themselves later confessed, it seemed to them that bright and shining rays of the sun went forth from the face of the man of God, striking them in the face, and they could in no way withstand it; nor could they withstand the banner, which seemed to them filled with the rays of the sun. It was for this reason that they fled from the face of the holy father.

Yet there are others, most pious father, who disagree concerning the capture of the cannons. There are some who say what I have proposed here: that the Turks fled from one position to the next and were expelled from each one in turn, as has been said. Others say that when they saw the father cross the river with a countless multitude of armed soldiers, and saw those soldiers taking up their position next to the moat, banner raised high and prepared to attack in such great numbers (when in truth there were not two thousand of them all told) the Turks became terrified and abandoned the cannons and retreated to their army.

The friars who were there in person are more of this opinion than the first: although they walked with the father and heard great cries, they did not see the Turks fleeing from the positions of the cannons; but almost without any delay they [the Turks] went from one to the other. In fact, they think that while the father moved alongside the Sava after crossing it, and when he moved from the river to the moat and looked in astonishment on the burned bodies and thereafter stood with the banner about to move against them, the Turks were filled with fear and abandoned the cannons. Both opinions are wonderful and both are circulating among the people. Your Paternity can believe whichever one you like.

Now that the Turks had retreated, the Christians held cannons that were as great as they were secure. The Turks were now in part deprived of their munitions and machines of war. Now they shamefully lost all the things in which they trusted. Great carts of bronze, wood, and iron, along with the apparatus with which they had operated their great machines, where the powder and stones and fire were prepared, and everything related to this – all of this was found there.[59] There was

---

59 For "apparatus" see n. 57 above in this document. The word translated here as "operate" is *conduxerant*, literally "joined" or "assembled," perhaps a reference to the joining of multiple chambers as part of the firing process.

great joy among the Christians before the eyes of the Turks; there was singing, there was rejoicing, there were cries of the name of Jesus. The Turks, seeing and hearing all of this as they came from other places, both fleeing and gathering together, were met with great pain and confusion. Those compelled to flee had no place to make a stand. In fear that they might fall into the hands of the Christians, they were so desperate while fleeing that they were almost compelled to arm themselves to fight (though here I have some doubt: I do not know if they first intended to attack the Christians, or rather to defend themselves if they were attacked; I tend to believe the second opinion).

Those who had been far away now came near, and the unarmed now armed themselves with their typical weapons, that is, arquebuses, bows, and quivers of arrows, slender lances and the sharpest of swords, according to their custom, unimaginable and indeed so terrible that they could cut a man in half with one blow. They mounted their incredibly swift horses, sounded their trumpets, sought to restore their spirits, and drive away their mournful fear. They accepted the arms ready for them and feigned joy as if they were victors who were soon to escape, when in truth all of them were petrified with fear and stood there like deserters.

Meanwhile the number of crusaders coming to the father from both of the other groups continued to grow. They were in three different positions: in the fortress there were about four thousand; with the blessed father, in the field beyond the fortress, perhaps three thousand; and the rest around the Sava and the Danube. These were quite close, though they were separated by the water. But there were others, especially the nobles, who roamed on the two rivers while they awaited the outcome of the events. Lord Michael (who is most cunning and gifted with astonishing talent) remained in the fortress, thinking through how he could harm the Turks if the fight should be joined again. The governor Lord John as well as Lord John Korogh were on board a ship moving here and there on the Danube and were being advised regarding the losses of the Turks.

Thus, from the other two positions about three thousand came to the father, all of them quite inexperienced in war, poor, unarmed, shoeless, old, decrepit, beggars, some priests and some religious – in brief, from the groups of crusaders mentioned above. These were the most incapable and incompetent, such that some Italians call them the "little stick brigade."⁶⁰ The nobles did not bother to come, lest they be cut down alongside the few and the poor. And this is not without mystery, that God should choose the poor, the sick, and the weak in order to break and confound the strongest with the right hand of his power. But this little army had a great many wooden slings and metal staves, and there were crossbows and bows among them, etc., as I have described above. Father, I can say with a clear conscience that they had no arms that would cause even an animal to flee, as I say; nor did it seem that anyone should fear them.⁶¹ But God, as has been said, wished to demonstrate his power through men of this kind, and they did all of these things, according to the Lord's will, so that the triumph of the future victory for the glory of God through the power of the most holy cross and the shining merits of the most blessed father Friar John might appear more gloriously and more marvelously to all mortals.

After capturing the cannons and their apparatus, when the father saw the nature and size of the force that now surrounded him, driven like a hungry lion he now resolved to go against the Turks with this little force. But there were certain ones standing there to whom this seemed unwise, due to the Christians' small numbers and ineptitude. They were astonished, as if they might have said what the people of God said to Judas Maccabeus: "How shall we, being few, be able to fight against so great a multitude and so strong, and we are exhausted by labor and fasting?" And then as if the father responded in consolation, "It is an easy matter for many to be shut up in the hands of a few; and there is no difference in the sight of the God of heaven between many and few. For the success of war is not in the multitude of the army, but strength is from heaven. They come against us as an insolent and arrogant multitude, to destroy us, and our wives, and our children, and to take our spoils. But we will fight for our lives and our laws: and the Lord himself will overthrow them before our face; but as for you, fear them not."⁶²

And so, leaning on his staff, forgetting his old age and his labor, thirsting for martyrdom, he ran as if he feared nothing from the infidels, aflame like one of the seraphim, and with an incredibly intense

---

60 Tagliacozzo notably renders his vivid phrase in Italian, "*la brigata della mazeta.*"
61 Perhaps for rhetorical emphasis, Tagliacozzo renders this sentence in Italian.
62 Cf. 1 Maccabees 3:17–22.

passion. But a certain brother[63] from among his associates, seeing him start to move so boldly against the Turks with the kinds of fighters he had and so few of them; seeing the innumerable Turks so ready to fight and raging more bitterly against the Christians than usual; seeing them flood in from all sides, gathering for the attack, joining one to another; and uncertain of the future, said to the father: "Don't go, don't go! Stay! Look, the Turks are preparing to devour us like lions; we will all be killed, and there will be great confusion and loss." The father responded to him, his face all afire, and in a terrifying voice: "If you are afraid, run away! If you are afraid, run away! I have longed for, waited for, sought this moment for forty years." He had in fact served God that many years in religious life, and for that whole time he had longed for martyrdom. But this friar, even though he had often heard from him how there would be a great victory over the Turks (first on the Danube and then two victories, glorious ones indeed, in the fortress), now could not be turned from his belief that the father would die and that the Christians would not escape without great slaughter. Most terrified and uncertain of his future, he found himself like Peter, who tried to turn Christ away from saving humankind.

When the father discerned that the hour divinely appointed for him had come; saw that the full power of the Turks was now deployed; and saw that he had with him around three thousand crusaders; he climbed on to a certain elevated place, where he could be seen by the Turks and heard by the Christians. With many words he again exhorted his army to be fervent in their defense of the faith and to embrace martyrdom. Above all he said, "Behold, my sons, now is the acceptable time, now is the time of the crown, now is the time of redemption from sin. Defend the name of Jesus Christ manfully and boldly; charge against the enemy of Christianity; fight to defend the Catholic faith. Behold, the dogs are ready to erase the name of Christ from the earth, and to invade, occupy and strike down Christendom. Trust now that God will help his cause. They are in disarray and have lost much. But he who has begun it will see it through to the finish. Do not fear those who kill the body, but who cannot kill the soul." He then added, "Blessed is the one who is struck for the love of Christ; more blessed is the one who sheds his

---

63 In these dramatized lines Tagliacozzo refers to himself.

blood for Christ's defense; and most blessed is the one who lays down his life and dies for Christ's honor. Whether you conquer on earth or are conquered, you will be victorious in heaven. Oh Hungarians! Oh my poor sons, strengthen Christians in their weakness; come to the aid of Christendom; take a stand against your enemies. All of you have now confessed; and if by chance there are some who have not, though they have committed great sins, let them be contrite and well-disciplined, avoiding plunder and rape, turning instead to defense and resistance, because 'charity covers a multitude of sins.'"[64]

When he had said these and many other things, he took his banner and said, "Follow me; the Lord has given our enemy into our hands." Then he gave the banner to his standard-bearer Peter and said, "Lift up the cross and put it before the eyes of the Great Turk, the enemy of the cross," as if he had said, "Behold the cross of the Lord! Be gone, evil powers!"[65] Then, standing on the same elevated ground, so that the soldier of Christ might join hands with all in the fight, he blessed and cried out the name of Jesus. As he did so, the crowd wept bitterly with devotion, though more at the words of the interpreter, that is the aforementioned Lord Paul, who had been the interpreter of all these things. Each prepared himself to fight. But I myself, confessing the misery of my condition, stood far off, like Peter, so that I could watch the outcome – I who, when the blessed father had so often asked me whether I wished to follow him, and especially when he wished to give me the cross, was accustomed to respond in earnest, "I am ready to go to prison with you, and to die."[66]

It must be noted that the father was never heard to say "Kill, strike, wound, destroy," and so on, but "Resist the Turks; drive back the injuries of Christ that the Turks are trying to inflict." The pious father loved the conversion and humiliation of the Turks, but not their death.[67]

As the father was saying these and many other things, the Turks who had been standing far off were now closing in on all sides. Their arrows came first; knights bearing lances came next; others came with

---

64 1 Peter 4:8.
65 Another invocation of Saint Anthony of Padua's prayer of exorcism. See n. 26 above in this document.
66 Luke 22:33.
67 Another instance in which Tagliacozzo is at work curating Capistrano's reputation. See the introduction to this document as well as n. 29.

swords unsheathed, still others armed with harmful machines, roaring like swift lions. And though they strove to wound all Christians, everyone sought with arrows and other machines to kill the most blessed father as their special enemy. But the prince of Christ stood on a higher place near the Turks, in sight of all, like a "target for their arrows."[68] He prayed and cried out, now joining and lifting his hands to heaven, now extending them out in the form of a cross, all the while anxiously awaiting martyrdom. The Turks tried to strike and to kill him with arrows and arquebuses, but their arrows were driven away as if by the wind and missed the father, as if they were guided by a kind of reverence and reason. These same arrows were indeed joined together so thickly in the air that only the arrows could be seen. I think, reverend father, that this was a special miracle: though the father was close to the Turks, elevated above all, and holding his banner high, such an abundance of arrows could harm neither him nor the banner. And when the aforementioned canon[69] offered his shield so that the father would not be wounded, the father, consumed by a certain most holy furor, tossed it away, as an obstacle to his martyrdom. And in fact, when the people of God who were with the father saw the Turks near them, they were armed with the zeal of faith, afire with divine honor against the enemies of Christ. They now shoot arrows and crossbows, cast spears and stones, throw, strike, wound, kill, behead, and drown. Meanwhile the father stands like a second Moses, his hands joined, and eyes elevated to heaven. And when he cried out the name of Jesus in the strongest of voices, like the strongest of young men, such that all around him responded, whether in the fortress, in the camp by the Sava, or nearby, the Turks turned their backs.

The Turks now came against the Christians in a great wave, their lances lifted up, or lowered under their arms and poised to attack. With the swiftest of horses and their terrible noise they hurled insults and ran about, crying out. Meanwhile the blessed captain called on Jesus, and when everyone around responded – oh, God, how wonderful! – some Turks fell from their horses. Others were lifted from their horses. Others let go of their lances unwillingly. Others have their heads pressed

---

68 Cf. Lamentations 3:12.
69 See n. 55 above in this document.

down and hang over their horses. Others suddenly died, and still others became so weak and deprived of strength that if they were on horseback, they were no longer able to direct the horses, or if they were on the ground, they could no longer get up.

And it is no wonder, for it has been learned from a reliable report that the brightest rays of light, like terrible lightning, went forth from the face of that servant of God and struck the Turks, and that a horrible darkness followed. They were terrified because of it, and it could truly be said that "fear and trembling are come upon me, and darkness hath covered me."[70] But they did not dare flee. They saw their death and destruction. And since they could not escape, they said among themselves, "Woe to us, because the God of the Christians fights for them." And so, in their confusion, they held back. And as further insult to their pride, as their great numbers pressed in and they came close to the Christians, behold, the unarmed people of Christ, armed with a most faithful confidence, rose up against them. Some attacked them with dung,[71] some with powder; and with the iron or wooden hammers that were carried in the hands of the Christians, everyone either killed or left [the enemy] robbed of strength.

With God as my witness, for whose honor and glory, beloved father, I have written these things, I am not lying, nor do I suffer from a guilty conscience, except insofar as I am unable to capture in an appropriate style all of the things that I have seen with my own eyes and touched with my own hands. Oh, poor, miserable me, who when I should have gone forward, pitifully retreated! Oh, judgment of God, fathomless abyss! Such is my state after all of these things have come to pass.

The Turks now fell into confusion and did not know what to do. They remained pressed together and tried to charge at the Christians. But in the meantime, the cannons they had left behind had been secured and readied. Stones were hurled toward them, using the powder and fire that were found there prepared. And thus, the Turks suffered a great slaughter from their own instruments of war. For at this point they were still so close by and joined together that the shots could hardly miss. The eminent father stood fast in the same place, his eyes and hands

---

70 Psalm 54 (55):5.
71 The wording as it appears in Wadding's edition of the text: "alii fimo ... eos affligunt."

lifted up, while the most vigorous Lord Michael, in command of the fortress above, directed the fire of the cannons. Their terrible stones flew over the heads of the Christians and miserably devastated many Turks, who stood close together in their formations – so much so that from one and the same shot or stone many Turks and many tents were thrown here and there into the air and destroyed. These shots came indeed not from the cannons of the Turks, but from the castle. And by the divine will they seemed to cast their stones much farther and more fearfully than usual. Perhaps it was Mary Magdalene, on whose feast day these things were done, who prepared the fire and the stones for the cannons. Now the banners, and especially the most valued ones, once abundant, were no longer seen; and those who buried the dead, or who tried to, as was their custom, were either killed or wounded.

The victory grew, as the father continued to pray and to cry out; he himself in fact awaited martyrdom, and God brought death upon the enemies of Christ. He stood his ground, joyful, defenseless, and like the strongest of men. Then there came a fresh charge of most terrible and swift horses from the more distant parts of the enemy camp. With their lances extended they sought to fall upon the Christians, and while charging seemed to want to tear down mountains, making such a tremendous noise that it seemed there was an earthquake. Then the blessed father set himself against them again, crying the name of Jesus, and all the Christians responded. The Turks were suddenly confounded and turned back, unable to come near the blessed father or the Christians across such a great plain, as if there were a ditch or an obstacle between them. And from this it was proven true: "A thousand will fall by your side," etc.[72]

Here is another miracle, and an astounding one, that was gathered from the reports of the Turks themselves: at the acclamation of the name of Jesus, they were struck not only by the greatest fear and terror but were also struck down and killed by that most holy name, as if from javelins cast down from heaven. And indeed, it seemed all the more miraculous to them that what seemed like liquid lead rained down on them, and they fell dead without the work of any machines of war. Again and again the Christians clung to their faith in the Lord and came against them boldly in hand-to-hand combat. And so this

---

72 Psalm 90 (91):7.

vicious battle raged on, across the space of some five hours; and with God protecting his own, though they were unarmed they emerged as the victors; and after suffering such a great slaughter the Turks stood off at a distance, in disarray.

As these events, with the Lord's favor, were so happily unfolding, the Turks began to tear down their pavilions. Others began to prepare their carriages, still others to gather together their baggage and tools, all of them crying out for fear, in confusion, and for the losses they had suffered in such a short time from such an unarmed rabble. I myself was absent for a time from the blessed father for fear of death, weakened by fatigue, and even more by fear, having left the father in the field.[73] I now returned in great haste to the fortress, like a second John, who had fled alone and naked. I found beloved Ambrose [of Aquila] there, who was both my companion and also one most dear to the father himself, whom I thought had stayed in the field with the father. I said, "Oh my! We have both left the father alone!" But when we wanted to return to him there, we came across him near the moat, returning from battle like a second David after the slaughter of Amalek, so happy and joyful in the victory that God had brought about in his presence. And so, it seemed as though he was not worthy of martyrdom; but giving thanks to God, he often repeated that verse, "I will praise thee, for thou art fearfully magnified; wonderful are thy works, and my soul knoweth right well."[74] Oh arrows of the Turks, why among so many did you not find me, so that I could pay more fully for the miseries of my life? Why did you not kill me, so that even if I could not voluntarily be a martyr, at least I would be deprived of life?

But after the slaughter of the Turks, and their confusion and fear, the father returned to encourage both Lord John and Lord Michael to pursue them with all of the crusaders. He said, "He who makes a beginning will see it through." For when he saw the slaughter and fear of the Turks, and that they were now preparing to flee, he wanted to insist that they be pursued. And it was an idea that would not leave his mind. When he said this to Michael, when John was absent, Michael responded through his interpreter, the Polish priest, that this kingdom

---

73 These lines are key for judging the extent to which Tagliacozzo can be read as an "eyewitness" to the events he describes.
74 Psalm 138 (139):14.

of Hungary had never had a greater victory over its enemies, or greater gain, and that this was by divine power and the merits of [Capistrano]. But if he commanded such an unarmed and unlearned crowd to go after the Turks, the kingdom would suffer infamy and loss as it had never seen, nor ever would see. And he attributed it all to [Capistrano], adding that this would not be pleasing at all to Lord John. When the father heard these things, he abandoned his proposal and climbed the walls to recall the crusaders from the field, with Brother Blasius acting as an interpreter. And when some of them, unwisely, went against the will of the father and came too close to the Turks, around ten of them accepted the crown of martyrdom.

That evening, in the camp and among the troops there was great joy, singing, solemn and celebratory dances, and the sound of both drums and other instruments. And all the crusaders hoped that in the morning they would give chase to the frightened few who remained, wear them down, and finally destroy them. All were in the spirit of lions on the prowl, and like elephants reddened with blood. And that night, after such tremendous and terrible slaughter, the Turks buried those they could and left behind almost all of the things they had brought with them to fight the Christians. They ran in retreat, terrified and confused, and in a carriage took along with them the Great Turk himself, who was wounded in the left side by an arquebus. They also drew along with them 140 carriages weighed down with those noble Turks who had been mortally wounded, many of whom they buried wherever they could along the way. They did not stop for a full ten days, until they had returned safe and sound to their own lands, constantly in fear that while on the run they would be attacked from behind and reduced to nothing by the Christians. They also either destroyed or set on fire the many goods they could not keep or carry with them, so that they would not fall into the hands of the Christians – especially all the galleys that remained from the battle on the Danube. They also took special care to set fire to their great store of munitions, from powder to arrows to ropes, as well as the Church of Saint Mary Magdalene, in which they had stored these things.[75]

But the father, now in the fortress and seeing the slaughter there, gave thanks to God. He was deeply astonished at all that had happened

---

75 The suburban church to the south of the city. See Map 2: The City and Fortress of Belgrade, c. 1450, on p. 283.

and all that was told to him by others. He saw the Christians who had won the crown of martyrdom, whom he now commanded to be buried in three mass graves. The most holy victor then consoled all with joy and said, "This is the day that the Lord has made; let us rejoice and be glad in it!"[76] He then went to find his brothers inside the fortress, and as he approached them, they all rejoiced. He glorified God's power, the power of the cross and the most holy name of Jesus.[77] Lord John [Hunyadi], most worthy governor of the kingdom, came thereafter, and was surprisingly astonished that all of these things had happened, in defiance of all human prudence. Together with Lord Michael and the magnificent Lord [John] Korogh and with many other nobles, they were flooded with great joy, and filled with glory; they also proclaimed the blessed father most worthy of all praise, honor, and reverence.

On the following morning, the day after [the feast of] Mary Magdalene, that is on Friday, the blessed father himself together with the aforementioned nobles made their way with all of the crusaders to the place of the victory, where they saw the wonders of God and were astounded.[78] They saw the tents of the Turks wonderfully arranged and variously adorned. They also saw all the things that the Turks had brought with them with such labor and industry in support and aid of the [fight against the] Christians, and which they had to leave behind against their will. They saw those twenty-two astonishing cannons, the likes of which (so they said) they had never before seen, as well as countless munitions. There were stones arranged or ready to be arranged in marvelous ways; frightful carriages of wood, iron, and bronze; the church full of powder, rope, arrows, iron bows, and wooden instruments, all of which had been destroyed in a great fire. The ships so wonderfully arranged along the shore of the Danube had also been set on fire. There were tents and marvelous banners, and such an abundance of wood carried from the forests in support of the Turks that there was enough to support all of their needs for repairs and fires for quite a long time. There were shields, bucklers, arquebuses, springalds, handguns, and various other equipment; mills (which they had now destroyed) to grind grain; clothing; ornaments; books containing their

---

76 Psalm 117 (118):24
77 Cf. document 7.
78 Friday, July 23. See document 8.

diabolical deceptions – one of which I kept for myself, and which thereafter astonished all who saw it. There were various and costly garments, tools, and herds of beasts – cattle, camels, buffalo. Thereafter they saw the countless graves of the dead, and the innumerable bodies that lay across the great plain. Many leaders were among the dead there: their vice-emperor and kings, as they acknowledged, as well as janissaries, who were both buried and also crushed under the stones of the castle. Among the dead were the more noble, the princes, the stronger, the wealthier, the more faithful. Many of them had been exhumed and despoiled of their goods, and now lay there naked, allowing all to see their circumcisions, and their weakness.

And so that I might sum all of it up briefly, all of the strength, the power, and the bravery of the Turks, all of their defiance and pride, their nobility, effort, and malice were now so shattered by the right hand of God that after this battle the Turks were never able to fully regain such great strength.

So here we can exclaim: Oh, glorious victory! Oh, great conflict, never to be forgotten in coming ages! Oh, most holy father! Oh, tireless old man! By your energy, zeal, prudence, initiative, and labor, you in your old age – with cries of the name of Jesus – have freed all Christendom from the brutality and savagery of the Turks! Oh, noble, exalted, and faithful kingdom of Hungary, to be truly honored by all Christians and lifted up by the praises of all! Oh most holy and fearful name of Jesus, holy indeed to the faithful and fearful to the infidel, under which the Turks, wondrously, lie dead. Oh, banner of the most holy cross, under which the crusaders, fighting tirelessly, emerged the victors! Oh, most illustrious prince, true protector of the Catholic faith and strong governor of the kingdom of Hungary, John Hunyadi, who through your labor and energy restored the walls of the fortress of Belgrade, which the Turks had leveled to the ground; whose command sent those small ships against the galleys of the Turks; in whose presence those galleys were driven away and sunk; by whose counsel and through whose anxious letters, sent to the father, saved the fortress! Oh, most illustrious Lord Michael Szilágyi, most tireless and most spirited guardian of the same fortress, who was even wounded in the fight! Oh, you poor soldiers, signed with the mark of the most holy cross, to whom God saw fit to grant the triumph of victory over the enemies of the cross of Christ! Let all offer their praise and say, "Great is the Lord and great is his power," etc.[79] Then the aforesaid Lord John, together with Michael, not without great solemnity and joy, had the cannons led into the fortress, where they remain still today, to the astonishment and admiration of all who see them.

Such a distinguished victory as this, reverend elder, can be compared to the victory of Abraham, who with only a very few of his allies fought against four powerful kings;[80] to the victory of Joshua, with Moses praying, against Amalek, who stood against the sons of Israel, in which Moses did more by praying that Joshua did by killing;[81] to the victory of Joshua, who [was] against the kings, who came to destroy the Gibeonites, when "the Lord hurled large hailstones down on them from heaven, and more of them died from the hail than were killed by the swords of the Israelites,"[82] and then, at Joshua's command, the sun stood still; to the victory of Deborah, who said to Barak, "Go! This is the day the Lord has given Sisera into our hands" and "the Lord routed Sisera and all his chariots";[83] to the victory won in the time of Gideon, when through the three hundred men who drank water by bringing their hands to their mouths the Lord delivered Israel from the hands of Midian and Amalek, whose force was a great multitude;[84] to the victory won when Samuel cried to the Lord for Israel and offered a sacrifice, and "the Lord thundered with loud thunder against the Philistines";[85] to the victory won in 1 Maccabees 3 and 4. Certainly, when considered carefully, this victory without doubt seems similar to or even more wonderful than all of these. Happy was this day, on which the enemies of the cross of Christ retreated and Christendom was liberated! For if the Turks had been victorious, first Hungary would have been occupied, and then they would have invaded other lands the very next day.

And now, honored elder, hear the truth concerning all of the dead on both sides. First it must be noted, as has been said, that in this storm of events the Turks were met by the Christians with a threefold noble battle – that is, on the Danube, in the fortress itself, and outside the

---

79 Psalm 146 (147):5.
80 Genesis 14.
81 Exodus 17.
82 Joshua 10:11.
83 Judges 4:14–15.
84 Judges 7:7.
85 1 Samuel 7:10.

fortress on the wide plain – each of which has been treated in turn above. The power of the Turkish ships was broken and crushed. In the fortress, the inestimable multitude of those killed by both fire and iron, as well as those crushed by stones, could never be counted. For in the smallest of spaces there were four and five Turks whose bodies lay burned up and broken into small pieces. And in the field beyond the fortress there could be seen many Turks whose bodies lay there like animals shredded by wolves in a sheepfold. Some were decapitated, others slashed by swords, others killed by arrows or cannons, others shot through by arquebuses; many who died seemingly without any wounds; others missing arms and legs; many killed by wooden hammers or by earth and powder; others killed by catapult stones; others who had been overcome by the intense heat of the summer and who lay scattered across that broad field. Still others had drowned in the water, for at that time the turbulent waters of both the Sava and the Danube ran red with blood. Graves were also dug here and there, in such a way that no vintner who had ever planted vines could have made a straighter and longer row; these graves were then filled with the bodies of the Turks. And since it is their custom to bury their dead with all of their belongings, when they were buried, the bodies were exhumed and despoiled by the Christians, then left to be consumed by beasts and birds. It was then that all could see their circumcisions, their softness, the effeminate fatness of their flesh.

Having seen and considered all of these things, and taking into consideration all of those who died in the fortress, on the morrow of the Magdalene, or the day after the victory, some five thousand Turks (without any certainty) had been killed. Many wondered at the time that the number of the dead was so small, and no one could be persuaded to believe that the number was not greater, whether because of the innumerable multitude of the Turks; or because so many had been struck down right before the eyes of the Christians, who saw many more killed than this; or because from such a small number of losses the Turks would not have fled in fear, nor would they have retreated from the siege of the city, leaving behind so many things and so many of their goods, though all ascribed their fear and flight to a great miracle. Accordingly, the blessed father himself wrote to the pope from Slankamen.[86]

---

86 See document 8.

In fact this letter, reverend elder, was the one in which the father claimed to lead the army of the crusaders as a poor man, like Joshua.[87] And many enemies of the truth ascribe this claim to the pride of this humble father; but these miserably envious ones do not recognize that the blessed father said this in order to speak the truth, to exalt the glory of a great God, to hold dear this divinely authored miracle, and to bring joy and happiness to the pope by whose commission and command all of these things were done. For this preacher and defender of truth would never cling to a lie; nor was there ever a hurtful word to be found in his mouth. He spurned honors and abhorred pride, knowing that those who put on prideful airs never dwell in the house of the Lord. And whenever he was honored by the world, reluctantly and unwillingly, he said, as it is said, "Not to us, Lord," etc.[88] Let the dogs stop their barking, then, since by virtue of all of the wonders that, with God's favor, this blessed father worked while he was still alive, after he began to serve God, all Christians now lift him up, honor him and proclaim him a distinguished man worthy of every veneration.

There was a certain noble youth among the Turks who secretly slipped away while the rest were in retreat.[89] He fled to the Christians and was baptized on the morrow of the Magdalene, and from him we have a most reliable report that in these days most of the Turks were killed and hastily buried apart from the rest in the forest by night. Those who remained and who were in flight were so struck and shaken by such fear that the smallest of armies utterly destroyed them.

Here he says[90] that the Great Turk was wounded in the left side by an arquebus and has gone insane.

Here he says that the same great dog had furiously decapitated five of his men, whom he had sent as scouts to discern whether an army would be raised against his move against Hungary. They had reported that no army was to form in Hungary, only a certain monk leading many

---

87 See document 8, p. 90 and n. 1: "like a Joshua working among the ruins of the walls of Jericho."
88 Psalm 114 (115):1.
89 See document 8, p. 90, and p. 210 and n. 92 in this document. The discussion here concerns the "noble boy of Bosnia" that Capistrano sent to the pope.
90 "*Hic ait*," repeated throughout this section of the text. It is a curious phrase in this context, perhaps indicating some kind of written testimony or record of hearsay, now lost, that Tagliacozzo inserted into his account.

Hungarian commoners under the sign of the cross. But he sent them back because it did not seem true to him. And indeed, they encountered no unarmed rabble but a great one: the most learned captain Friar John with his crusaders, an innumerable multitude of people and arms, had been seen by the Turks themselves.

Here he says that the vice-emperor was killed by the stone of a cannon before the conflict,[91] and that other kings and most noble leaders across the whole army had been killed by the various war machines of the Christians.

Here he says that five thousand janissaries, with whom (as was noted above) the emperor of the Turks surrounded himself, and in which he trusted greatly, were killed to the last man by fire, iron, and cannon.

Here he says that many Turks said – as he himself heard – that the faith of the Christians was the true faith because their God fights for them, as we have clearly seen.

Here he says that many Turks long to come to the Christian faith, and that they would do so indeed, if they were not afraid: "But I say this having seen and heard such things, and though I have not disclosed it for fear of death, I have decided to become a Christian; and many of my companions long to join me, though I have not called them, lest they betray me."

But here he says that as he retreated the Great Turk himself cursed his posterity, if they should ever thereafter presume to move against the fortress of Belgrade, since his predecessors had gone against it and were never able to conquer it despite their great power. [He says] "But I, with all my power and genius, with all of my skill in war and even with all of my industry and countless numbers of knights and cavalry and a multitude of foot soldiers, have arrived here stronger than any who came before. And look: I am in retreat, in disarray, crushed and destroyed and deprived of all my goods. Woe to me, driven away not by Christian princes and dukes, nor even by knights, but by a man who is a monk, by farmers, commoners. I flee from tricksters and from an unarmed rabble."

Here indeed the youth, who told of these and many other things aboard the ship of the blessed father in the presence of the lord

---

91   Reference here is to Karaca Bey, whose death is mentioned several times in Ottoman and other accounts. Among others see the account of Jacopo Promontorio in document 29, n. 8.

governor John, was perhaps fourteen years of age, though in manner and gesture he was like an old and mature man. He came from the innermost circle of the court of the emperor of the Turks. And all of these things were later confirmed by many others who were more advanced in age. And in fact this young man, as if a reward for the triumph of victory, was first given a golden cross, and then baptized by the father's own hand. Thereafter he was sent to the lord pope with the lord Jerome of Padua, from whose holiness he was most gratefully received, endowed with many goods, and established [in a castle].[92]

After the great battle discussed here, the most illustrious lord despot of Serbia, George [Branković], announced to the blessed father that three of his scouts had returned to him from the camps of the Turks. The scouts brought word that such a great multitude of the Turks' leaders had been killed in the siege that they had been reduced to almost nothing, and that they had fled, filled with fear, from before the Christians. The scouts added that the Turks were never so weakened and close to their ultimate destruction than after this conflict. The most serene king of Bosnia, a tributary to the Turks, in these days gave letters to the blessed father in which he announced that the power of the Turks, with all of their nobility, had been completely overthrown; and that if the Christians should now pursue them, they would be victorious over them. And though it is asserted by many who are most worthy of faith that the great part of the Turks died in the conflict, nevertheless for greater certitude of the truth it has been confirmed that twenty-four thousand Turks, and indeed many of the more powerful among them, were killed by water, fire, and iron and various other machines during the siege. Indeed, Lord John Hunyadi asserted this, along with the castellan Lord Michael. And so the blessed father himself wrote to the same pope a second letter from Slankamen,[93] asserting that twenty-four thousand Turks had been killed at the time, with the rest struck with fear and in disarray, and leaving behind all of their clever machines and their goods and taking flight with rapid steps back to their own lands.

Indeed, experience shows that many [Turks] died from these events; for from that battle up until now, the Turks have never been able to accomplish or even to plot anything against the Christians militarily, even

---

92 See document 8, p. 90.
93 See document 13, pp. 104–7.

if from time to time, according to their custom, they run around here and there like robbers, despoiling those whom their malice finds unawares in the dark of night. But because we Christians lie sound asleep, and no one raises a single weapon against the Turks, they are renewed; they become bolder; they recover their strength and are inspired again to rise up against the Christians. But in this threefold conflict hardly three hundred Christians, killed in various ways, received the crown of martyrdom: forty-nine who, as noted above, fought the Turks from the bridge, were wounded in the great press of the battle, and fell dead, and all of their souls returned quickly to heaven. The rest, whom the Turks were able to kill grimly, were staked to the ground in the form of a cross and decapitated. To these their executioners said, "You have taken up the cross against us, carried it and fought for it; so you will die in the shape of a cross." But the first seven, seized when off guard, were taken from the walls of the castle, first decapitated, then despoiled, and thereafter trampled under the hooves of horses, their shredded bodies left to be eaten by dogs, who did indeed quickly eat them down to the bones, while the Christians watched from the fortress.

Indeed, there were among the aforementioned martyrs many religious and priests who, fighting manfully in the defense of the name of Jesus, found themselves worthy of the crown of martyrdom in various ways. Oh, how happy are those who, in this fleeting life, fought for Christ for such a short period of time, and who by his blood accepted a life that will have no end. The faithful were distinguished from the infidels by the manner of their deaths, by their dress, by the cross, by circumcision, and similar things. Of those who were in the fortress and in the citadel, countless among them were struck and wounded, but they had the iron of the arrows removed from their wounds and were soon healed. Oh, most fervent and truly Catholic Hungarians, who neither fear being wounded, nor fear suffering death for Christ!

After such a glorious victory against the enemies of Christ, the crusaders saw that they would not be allowed to pursue the Turks as they fled – and they did not take it well. In fact, on the day following the victory they had it announced publicly that the victory the Lord had given them on the previous day had not been by labor or effort on the part of any baron of Hungary, but by the power of the most holy name of Jesus alone, and of the most holy cross, and by the merits and labor and sweat of our most blessed father John of Capistrano. And when some who were standing there heard this, they took it hard, became quite disturbed, and wanted to rise up against the lords.[94] The blessed father, who was at that time having a private conference on board a ship with Lord John [Hunyadi], sensed the commotion among the people. Not wanting Lord John to leave the ship, the father slipped away and left him behind. He went out and sought after the cause of the disturbance, rebuked the lords, calmed the disturbance, and commanded all to keep silent. And unless the holy father had been there to stop it, many crusaders would have been killed. And the lord Jerome of Padua, noted above, can very well attest to all of these things, since he was there to witness them.

Then finally the crusaders received from the most blessed father, as if he were their captain, license and blessing to depart. All returned to their own lands filled with joy, in wonder and amazement over all these things which God himself had done through the ministry and service of the most blessed father. And so, the crusade came to an end.

The most reverend legate, cardinal of Sant'Angelo, then came down from Buda. He was armed with a most ardent zeal and desire and equipped with all things necessary for war against the Turks. But seeing that the crusade had already come to an end, he did not take it well. Seeking to restart it from Petrovaradin, where he was then established, he now came down to the place of victory. But neither he nor the father himself were able to accomplish anything. Now all the crusaders went away tired and weakened from their labors, and indeed many of them had no food. And yet they would have patiently borne all of these troubles, and others besides, had they been able to pursue the Turks after the battle.

And here let no one doubt the father's choice to grant the crusaders license [to disband] and his blessing. He would never have given them license to leave had they wanted to stay, even as they suffered from hunger, thirst, and many other unpleasant things. And let no one accuse the father of disobedience, insofar as the reverend lord legate instructed him not to join battle with the Turks, as was noted above, and yet it came about by his deeds that they were so miserably and wonderfully defeated, both in the fortress and in the open field, as has been written. If someone is so consumed with envy that he must object

---

94 Here *banditores*, "bans," i.e., secular princes.

to the holy father in this way, let him close his mouth, beat his breast, look at himself, and ask God for mercy, since he seeks to cast blame on someone he ought to join with others in magnifying and lifting up. Anyone who would not wish for the holy father, led by the spirit of God, to succeed, is surely guilty of wanting Christianity to perish.

Here, that is in Petrovaradin, at that time the bishop of Assisi, colleague of the lord legate, fell ill, died, and was honorably buried.[95] From there the reverend lord legate and the father himself made their way to the fortress of Belgrade, where after the victory the governor Lord John had established himself after the dispersal of the crusaders. When the lord legate saw such destruction in the fortress, and the cannons and all of the other things that had been done in his absence, he was struck with both grief and wonder. Thereafter he went out to see the positions of the Turks and the places where the slaughter had been the greatest. In admiration he said, "Truly, there were more than two hundred thousand Turks here." But the rumor was that there had been 140,000. He praised the divine power and the right hand of our exalted God.

Then the barons, upon hearing the rumor of the defeat of the Turks, began to arrive: the illustrious Lord Nicholas of Ilok, voivode of Transylvania; Paul [Sechar]; and many others. But it was all over.[96] The lord governor, who had led the cannons and other war machines abandoned by the Turks into the castle with great solemnity, and who had just begun to repair the castle, fell ill of disease on the fourth day of August, and on the eleventh day of the same month passed from this world and received his eternal reward for his tireless labors. Let all of faithful Hungary lament the loss of such a protector; indeed, may all of Christendom lament his death, for he was a terror of the Turks and a most faithful protector of the cause of the faith. But let there also be rejoicing, for he has been crowned and now claims his most faithful reward.

By now such a stench had begun to rise from the bodies of the Turks lying all around, and such a multitude of birds of prey had begun to flock there, that the lord legate and other leaders were forced to leave

---

95 Francis Oddi. See document 3.6, n. 2, as well as documents 3.9 and 3.10.
96 The phrase here, given in Italian, seems to be an idiomatic expression: "*Ma date erano le candele.*"

the fortress. The holy father, too, though he had begun to fall ill, followed the lord legate on the sixth day of the month, and they both stayed many days in the oft-mentioned Semlin. In that camp, too, there were many who had taken ill from the most horrible stench. At the command of the lord legate, I myself once went out into the field to see if I could find any place beyond it where both the lord legate and the blessed father might escape the stench; but I only got so far before I had to come back in, on a galloping horse, hardly alive.

Finally, most reverend father, it would be necessary to bring forth the witnesses and various confirmations of this most astonishing victory, since so many – whether in reporting about it, writing about it, or even reading or hearing about it – ascribe it to someone other than God and the merits of the blessed father. For I have discovered many letters and various songs in which, as if he had never existed, there is no mention of the blessed father; and which are so stuffed with lies and with usurpations of his honor that they should be thoroughly disregarded and, for the lies they contain, consumed by fire! But because there are innumerable confirmations and attestations of this kind to be had beyond those recorded in this letter, for the sake of brevity I will not bother to note them here at present. I will, however, not omit this: that this great victory is attributed to the merit of the blessed father John of Capistrano by all: by the Turks; by the schismatics; by the Greeks; by the infidels; by the Roman emperor; by kings, and especially by the most serene lord King Matthias of Hungary;[97] by the prelates and all of Hungary. All of this is made most abundantly clear from all that has been said, and from all of the letters of witnesses carried from Hungary to Italy.

But here the magnificent Lord Paul, mentioned above,[98] does not allow me to remain silent: for when he came here at that time right after the victory, as I have described, and I asked him why, in a time of such great difficulty, the barons of Hungary never came together, he answered me in Latin that it was God's judgment that we [the barons] should all stay at home and that none should come, so that such a triumph and such an honor should be ascribed to God alone, and to the power of the most holy name of Jesus, and to his most holy cross, and

---

97 King Matthias Corvinus (d. 1490), son of John Hunyadi and successor to Ladislaus V as king of Hungary from 1458.
98 Reference here seems to be to the baron Paul mentioned on p. 213.

alone to the merits of the most blessed father, Friar John. For if we [the barons] had fought here militarily, everyone who had fought with the Turks would have wanted to claim the honor of the victory for himself. Thus, he [Capistrano] would have been deprived of his glory, and his labor and efforts and the zeal of this blessed father would have been deprived of their due honor and reward, which God did not want. And so all Hungarians believe that this blessed father was the liberator of the whole kingdom.

Thus, may the tongue of every detractor stay stuck in his throat, if he will not remember such a most holy man; a man who – just as he was distinguished while on earth with every gift of grace, now, having returned to heaven to be among the crowd of the blessed – remains glorious and praiseworthy, to be imitated by all the faithful.

Certainly, reverend elder, I could have satisfied Your Paternity with fewer words. But what I have related here is true. I have recorded nothing that I have not seen with my own eyes, touched with my hands, or that I myself have not received by certain report, either from the most holy father himself, or from others who are most worthy of trust. I obligate myself to be thrown rudely into prison, or to suffer some other woeful penalty, if each and every thing that I have written here is not found to be true. I want this letter to be read by those who were present for all that has been described here, and who are dispassionate about these events; they will agree that every single thing is most true.

I ask those into whose hands these writings may perhaps come that they neither cut anything out nor diminish them. They might expand or add to them, should they learn something from me in fuller detail, but they should change nothing of the substance of these things. And because I am accustomed (both because of inertia and because of the truer style of my teachers) to write in plain and rough and common grammatical terms, those who wish, and who know how to, may transform this work into a more polished and graceful style. Before God and his angels, I have written these things to Your Paternity, and I humbly pray and beg that you at some point pour out prayers, at least mentally, to the highest God for this most unworthy servant of the servants of God; for now, more than ever, I am in need of the support of your prayers and those of others.

Thus, most pleasant father, you now have enough to further exalt the sweetest name of Jesus and the power of the holy cross, as I have always done. You also have a witness to the holiness of the life of the most holy man, Brother John of Capistrano, a venerable man like you, your associate and your companion, one with a burning passion for the Catholic faith and a burning desire for martyrdom, through whose ministry, diligent care, and energy the power and the malice of the pagans was brought low, and in whom ancient miracles were renewed. Exalt him, too, father, in the church of the people, and praise and magnify him "in the cathedral of the elders."[99]

It now remains for me to write to Your Paternity concerning the most faithful passing of the most blessed man, at which (by the Lord's will and with your power encouraging, indeed compelling me) I was present. But at present I do not wish to take up the task. I will wait to write about his death, one filled with all sanctity, and in doing so hope to do right by Your Paternity, to please devout men, and to receive intercession from the one whom we know rules with God in heaven.

---

99 A phrase from liturgies associated with the feast of the Chair of Peter.

PART FIVE

Memoir and Chronicle

26. THOMAS EBENDORFER, *CHRONICLE OF AUSTRIA*
c. 1463

Thomas Ebendorfer was an Austrian theologian trained at the University of Vienna, where he rose through the ranks to become a renowned professor and dean. He was active as a priest and church administrator in Vienna as well, and in the era of the Council of Basel became a trusted counselor and diplomat in the service of Frederick III. As a scholar, Ebendorfer authored a series of tracts, sermons, and commentaries, as well as a number of historical works, including an account of the Council of Basel, histories of the popes, the German emperors, and the bishops of Passau, as well as a work on the early crusades. His most famous work, however, is his chronicle of Austrian history, which he completed shortly before his death in 1464. Its treatment of the battle for Belgrade offers a concise, vividly dramatized account of the events.

Source: Trans. J. Mixson, from Thomas Ebendorfer, *Chronica Austriae*, ed. Alphons Lhotsky, MGH Scriptores Rerum Germanicarum, N.S. 13 (Berlin-Zürich: Weidmann, 1967), 432–6.

When he had done these things Mehmed, the wicked persecutor of the name of Christ and most fierce tyrant of the Turks, puffed up with pride after the capture of Constantinople, climbed into his chariot. He aspired to the destruction of all the Christian people and labored to erase the holy name of Christ from the earth. He sought to spread the damned blasphemy of the wicked dog Muhammad, and to claim for himself rule over all the West, with an endless number of Tartars, Saracens, and Teucri[1] as partakers in his wickedness. Along with a fleet of ships and galleys, hostile and armed, he came into the region of Serbia, crushing all under his feet. There he first encountered the fortress of Smederevo, but the right hand of God protected it; the sultan lost many of his stronger troops and was forced to withdraw in defeat. And because the Lord struck his entire army with hunger and disease, he turned his forces against the fortress of Belgrade (called *Kryechsweissenburg* in the vernacular tongue), confident that if he gave an effort commensurate with his strength, and obtained it, he could advance farther [into Hungary]. He brought his wives and children along with the army, and also firmly commanded his subjects to bring their wives and children on the expedition as well. And so that none might be tempted by any desire to return to their homes, he commanded that all be set on fire, promising that in Christendom they would, as payment, exchange their cottages for fortresses, their villages for opulent cities fortified with bars and gates. Trusting in this empty confidence and puffed up by his swollen pride, this Mehmed, public enemy of the Christian name – as he, first among tyrants of the faith, presumed to style himself in his inscriptions – turned against the fortress of Belgrade with all of his machinery of war.

With his large cannons (certain ones of which, they say, were some thirty hands in length, or more accurately seventeen feet, as those who saw them report) he so destroyed the towers and cast down the walls of the city that it more resembled a plain in the countryside or a field, rather than a fortress or a town.[2] And when the impious one saw that this had been accomplished, on July 21, 1456 (which is the evening of the feast of the blessed Mary Magdalene), around the hour of vespers, he made an assault on the city so cruel, terrible, inhuman,

---

1 Ebendorfer here uses classicizing names to denote the ethnic diversity of Mehmed II's forces.
2 See documents 9–10, n. 1. Ebendorfer may well have had a copy of one of those letters as a source for his account.

and fierce, with cannons never before seen in those regions, crammed full as much with violence as with trickery, continually, as days joined incessantly to nights, such that no writing has ever recorded, nor any age ever learned from the tales of forbears and ancients, nor indeed (as they say) has any mortal eye ever seen or observed anything like it. Indeed,[3] the wicked [Mehmed] ordered this fiercest of attacks and the bombardment with cannons to continue without any pause, for all of the remainder of the day and continuing on into the following night, and indeed – which seems impossible for human strength to bear – for all of the day of the blessed Magdalene, all the way to twilight, until the Christ-following Hungarians, with a few others unarmed in body but armed in faith, left behind the houses and fortresses from which they fought and – with the help of the favoring right hand of God – once and then again powerfully drove out the wicked from the city (which they had partly entered). With the strong John Hunyadi, Count of Beszterce, as their captain, they began to fight them on foot. And though the outcome, in the hands of Mars,[4] was very much in doubt, they fought manfully and struggled strongly in the faith of Christ, until (beyond human hope!) victory was granted from heaven to these soldiers of Christ (forever to be crowned in all glory!). And it was granted not only without much Christian blood, but [by] incomparably [more blood shed] by even the more powerful Turks, and even [the blood] of their leaders.

In any event, heaven happily granted victory to the Christians, and for that reason every person in the Christian world, whatever their age, sex, and rank, should rise to give thanks to almighty Christ, to the all-blessed Trinity, and to all the heavenly court of the saints, by whose merits and prayers, no doubt, holy mother church has given birth to this victory, even though in this regard our sins (both in a church filled with so many who boast of their festivals, and with so many dissimulating nobles) would have demanded something else.

Indeed, if I may, I would rightly sing out this mournful song from the depths of my soul:

---

3 This passage is one very long sentence, deliberately crafted to capture the drama of the events. The translation here is an attempt to recreate the energy of the sentence, and it at times takes small liberties for the sake of rendering it readable in modern English.
4 Ebendorfer is again deliberately clothing the account in classicizing language.

> Where is the Roman empire, that once so thoroughly tamed the barbarian nations?
> Where are its electors, those fearsome princes?
> Where is the king of France, who wanted to be called "most Christian"?
> Where are the kings of England, Denmark, Norway, Sweden, Poland, and Bohemia?
> Where are all the powers of Germany and the East?
> Behold the unarmed farmers, the blacksmiths, fullers, tailors, and shoemakers, artisans and scholars, inspired by God, so it is believed, to their distinguished and strong acts in defense of the faith, and who in this way prove their worth as soldiers!

And no wonder that [God] should forever condemn these powers if they do not put up a fight, and [cast into] infamy especially those who, passing with a deaf ear over insults to the faith, think of no other business from day to day than styling their hair with the craft of the barber; washing their hair like girls; and, when washing, taking good care and experimenting with new colors; and after dying their hair turning to curling it; and in this way find their way to crying out in adulterous beds, in betrayal of their neighbor's trust!

And when this victory had been won as a gift from heaven, on Friday evening, the enemy of God and the faith, in his arrogance shamefully humiliated by the humble of Christ, left behind all of his machinery of war and began his headlong flight, leaving behind four of the tents he had erected – and for this may all praise and glory be to God forever! And after this, Christ's humble ones turned to killing the infidels and carrying away their spoils – starting first (as it is said by those who saw it happen) with eleven large cannons, with three cannons suited for assault and called "quarters" – with which he attacked the walls of the city so fiercely and cruelly. These they collected, along with the small cannons without number, and the gold, silver, vessels, and clothing that they found in the galleys and ships. All of this they calculated to be of no small value – and they set it all on fire. Then, returning to the fortress, they offered up hymns to God, whose tone was "For his mercy endureth forever."[5]

The enemies, therefore, who wanted along with their tyrant to avoid the punishment of the sword of God, fled from the river Danube,

---

5 Psalm 135 (136):17.

running (so it was said) for some fourteen miles under a hail of arrows, spears, and cannon fire. But first they set fire to their own ships and cast what they could not carry with them into the churning Danube. These things were done first, and then slowly there followed an infection of the air because of the stench of the human corpses. Then, in the fortress on the morning of Saint Lawrence,[6] the abovementioned captain, John Hunyadi, received all of the sacraments of the church, finalized his will, and met his fate. A few days after, the most reverend father and lord [bishop Raphael Herczég] of Kalocsa also succumbed to the illness that he contracted from the foul air. But the tyrant of the Turks, who now doubted himself because of all that had happened, fled to more remote lands so that those who were looking for him nearby could not discover his location or movements. It was then that he saw he had lost all of his leaders, along with all of his confidants, guardians, and bravest fighters, all of them the anchor of his trust, and with whose aid he had boldly prepared to destroy the church. Indeed, he had unarmed Christians slain by the sword in his sight, leaving them unburied and thus offered as food to wild animals and dogs and birds of the air. Indeed, by God's will, it was a fully prepared meal, as experience teaches, since the rotting of dead bodies drives away the one who would bury them. In this fight for the faith against the Turks the opinion of all, even our enemies, bore witness to the virtue of the clerics and other learned men from Poland and elsewhere who came running to the defense of the faith, and who (so it is said), when the front of our line faltered because of the strength of the enemy, with great spirit, willingly and steadfastly took the place of the fallen in the fight. The greater part of their number died for Christ. But they first charged like lions against the enemy that stood before them, and by death and wounds incapacitated four times and more of their enemy. Then they rested in glorious victory in Christ.

[The word of salutation of Brother John of Capistrano at the time of the death of John Hunyadi, governor of the kingdom of Hungary, in the year 1456 in Belgrade. "Farewell, heaven's halo! You have fallen, kingdom's crown! You have been extinguished, light of the world! You have been tarnished, mirror, in which we and others hoped to gaze!

---

6 August 11.

Now that the enemy has been safely defeated, you stand in triumph before God and the angels, oh you good John!"[7]]

27. LAONIKOS CHALKOKONDYLES, *THE HISTORIES*
c. 1464

Nikolaos Chalkokondyles was born in Athens sometime after 1430. His father, one of the most prominent aristocrats in Athens, petitioned Murad II for the title of Duke of Athens. His bid failed, and the family was sent into exile at Mistra and the court of the despots of the Peloponnese. Young Nikolaos was raised there, and he soon became a disciple of the renowned Platonist philosopher George Gemistos (d. 1452). Under Gemistos's tutelage Nikolaos became deeply enamored of classical Hellenic culture, and he set for himself the task of writing a new history of his own day. Laonikos Chalkokondyles, as he soon styled himself, completed that work around 1464. His Histories (Apodexis Historion, *the "result of inquiries"*) *cast the story of the rise of the Ottoman empire in a classical light. But it maintained a broad vision, extending even to England and France and the story of Joan of Arc. And as this representation of the Belgrade campaign suggests, for all of its imitation of Herodotus and Thucydides, the author of the* Histories *was able to capture contemporary events vividly.*

Source: Laonikos Chalkokondyles, *The Histories*, vol. 2: Books 6–10, trans. Anthony Kaldellis, Dumbarton Oaks Medieval Library Vol. 34 (Cambridge, MA: Harvard University Press), 227–45. Copyright © 2014 by the President and Fellows of Harvard College. Used by permission. All rights reserved.

When the ruler of the Serbs [Đurađ] learned that Sultan Mehmed was coming against him, he departed and crossed over to the Hungarians and to Hunyadi, fearing that the Sultan might come to Smederevo and besiege it. He asked Hunyadi, as his friend and relative, to defend him,

---

7 This brief but famous passage, a dramatization of Capistrano's reaction to Hunyadi's death, survives in only one manuscript of Ebendorfer's chronicle. It is attributed there to the churchman Paul of Vezsprém, though the editor of Ebendorfer's chronicle suggests it may have been Paul of Székesfehérvár, who had traveled with John of Capistrano as one of his interpreters (Thomas Ebendorfer, *Chronica Austriae*, ed. Lhotsky, 436n3). See the citation on p. 217 above in the introduction to this document.

and he decided to avenge him. At Smederevo the latter negotiated with the sultan to achieve peace. The ruler of the Serbs did not live on much longer, and when he died his principality went to Lazar, his youngest son. But upon the death of the ruler, his blind sons filched away as much money as they could and went to the sultan. The latter provided them with land suitable to maintain them. When Lazar paid him a substantial tribute of twenty thousand gold staters, the Sultan made a treaty with him.

The following year Mehmed marched against Belgrade, the city of the Hungarians. As I said earlier regarding Murad, this city is located by the Danube on one side, but on the other side the river Sava flows past it and joins the Danube; thus, this city is washed on both sides by these two rivers that flow past it. Mehmed, the son of Murad, now marched against Belgrade, having first sent armies against the Illyrians [Bosnians] under the command of Firuz and Ali Mihaloglu. Moreover, a war had broken out in Asia between him and the king of Kolchis, that is, of Trebizond. He dispatched triremes to plunder Kolchis by land and by sea, under the command of Hizir, the prefect of Amaseia. Meanwhile, he sent a herald around to announce that his armies should assemble at Adrianople, and he too marched out with the Porte and the janissaries. A full contingent of bronze for the cannons was conveyed for him by ships and camels as he marched through the land of the Serbs. The ruler of Smederevo provided hospitality for the sultan and his lords, sending them magnificent gifts, but he too made his own preparations: should Belgrade fall, he himself would then be besieged.

Mehmed advanced and besieged the city. There is an isthmus between the two rivers, whose width is about seven stades. He took up his position there, made camp, and besieged the city, bombarding the walls with cannons. The janissaries, under their shelters, approached the walls and shot at the Hungarians. This camp of the sultan was very large. His plan was to gain control of the river and prevent the Hungarians from being able to cross to the defense of the city from the opposite shore; then it would be easy for him to subject the city to himself and for the city to be captured by him. So he prepared a large fleet which had been equipped for him in his territories along the Danube, about two hundred ships strong. He manned the ships with the intention of controlling the river and preventing Hungarian forces from crossing over to the city, so as to cut off the inhabitants of the city and besiege them inside. He brought his ships up to the river from the city of Vidin and within a few days gained control of this part of the river.

As for the king of the Hungarians[1] – for he too had encamped across from Belgrade with a large army – he also manned the most powerful ships that he had in Buda and brought them down the river with the intention of engaging in a naval battle with the sultan's ships. The ships of the sultan sailed upriver far into the land of the Hungarians, and they raided, burned, and plundered. Shortly afterward the Hungarian fleet arrived and attacked the sultan's ships, sinking some and capturing about twenty. The Hungarians killed the crews, placed the bodies of the slain victims in the empty ships, arranging the bodies in a crosswise formation, and let them be conveyed by the current of the river down to the sultan's camp. That, then, was how they perished, while the remaining ships fled in haste back to the sultan's camp. They grounded the ships and disembarked at the camp. The sultan immediately set fire to them to prevent the Hungarians from sailing against them and capturing them.

From that point on the Hungarians held the river and were able to make conveyances from the opposite shore to the city, to strengthen its defenses. Present were Hunyadi and his men as well as the monk Capistrano, a wise man held in great religious esteem by the western peoples. Because of his reputation the pontiff had sent him to the inhabitants of Prague, the great city of the Bohemians, who worshiped the religion of Apollo, for he was a persuasive preacher of the religion of Jesus. He converted many people there to belief in Jesus, and he roused many, including Germans, Hungarians, and Bohemians, to fight against the barbarians, who were the enemies of Jesus. When he came to this war, he brought them with him, but most of them were lightly armed.

When it was announced that the city walls had been demolished by the cannons and the city was at risk of being captured, these men then crossed over to the city – at their leisure, since they controlled the crossing – but they did not despise the sultan's army. As for the sultan, when the city walls had been torn down sufficiently and could be scaled, he prepared to make an attack that would enslave the city. The Turks lit the customary fires on the next day and made their preparations,

---

1 Not Ladislaus V, but Hunyadi.

bringing up their engines and shelters in order to capture the city. It was there that Karaja, the general of Europe and a most excellent man of the sultan's Porte, was killed by the cannons in the city. The sultan took the death of Karaja to heart, and mourned him greatly.

When the sultan decided to make the attack, he sounded the assault at dawn with trumpets, cymbals, and flutes. He led the janissaries and attacked the walls. The janissaries immediately scaled the walls, climbed down from them, and poured into the city. As they attacked the city, they believed that they had already taken it. But the inhabitants of the city and those with Hunyadi were prepared and waiting for the janissaries to enter. For those stationed on the acropolis had arranged for a signal so that when the trumpet sounded it, they should engage with the janissaries. Those on the battlements and the walls had withdrawn, for they had been instructed to do so by Hunyadi, so as to allow the janissaries to freely enter the city. And when the trumpeter sounded the signal on his trumpet, each of them was to race back and take his assigned position; having cut the janissaries off, they would have them at their mercy.

So when the janissaries made their attack at dawn, they immediately entered the city with no one opposing them – the Hungarians had already withdrawn from there, awaiting the signal – and they believed that the enemy had fled. As I already said, they poured into the city and each of them turned in a different direction in order to plunder it. Then the signal was given and the trumpet sounded, and those who were previously on the walls ran to the battlements and cut the janissaries off inside, while those with Hunyadi engaged with the janissaries. When the janissaries saw the Hungarians from the acropolis coming against them, they withdrew to the wall. In this retreat, the Hungarians pressed upon them fiercely and killed a large number of them. But the rest of the Turks, as they rushed to the walls and saw the Hungarians there too on the battlements, forced their way through the Hungarians, ran over the walls, and reached the moat. In this way, then, did the Hungarians repel the janissaries and overcome the barbarians.

Then the men with Capistrano and the other Hungarians made a joint sally against the men at the sultan's cannons, fought them, routed them, and took control of the cannons. When the sultan saw that his cannons were now in the hands of the Hungarians, he was distressed and attacked there and fought fiercely, but was unable to dislodge the Hungarians from the cannons, and was routed. The Hungarians had already encamped there and turned the cannons to fire into the sultan's camp. It was about the middle of the day and the events and turns of the battle had been reported to the Hungarians across the river, whereupon many of their sailors now crossed over not to the city but to the camp. Those in the city came out too and, in elation, they attacked the sultan's camp from both sides and fought. They tore down many of the tents in the camp while the *azaps* were plundering the camp market. But the sultan shouted that he would tear their eyes out. Then he and his men made an attack and routed the Hungarians. He personally killed a Hungarian, but was wounded in the thigh; yet he would not retreat. Later, as he was about to take back the cannons, the Hungarians regrouped and pressed hard against the barbarians, and turned the sultan's men back, all the way to the camp. When this happened for the third time, the sultan was distressed, as he did not have the janissaries present in this battle, and other elements of his camp had gone out to forage and gather supplies.

In the midst of this furor, the sultan summoned the lord of the janissaries, who was named Hasan, and said the following: "You evil man, where have our janissaries gone? Why are they not here with you, for the battle? Or don't you remember what sort of person you were when I appointed you to such a high command? Come then, if I survive I will exact a punishment which all will say was most just." Hasan said in response: "O sultan, most of the janissaries are wounded, while the rest are unwilling to obey. But I am here at your disposal. Instead of being angry at me, watch me now fighting in the midst of the Hungarians and dying on your behalf." With those words he threw himself into the midst of the Hungarians, proving his valor before the sultan, and died at the hands of the Hungarians. Some of his attendants also died there.

When the Hungarians had routed the Turks back to their camp and were pressing hard upon them, having prevailed in the battle, about six thousand of the sultan's cavalry raiders arrived. He had previously sent them to guard his Danubian lands, specifically to guard places where the Hungarians might land with their ships and hinder them from making those landings. They came upon this scene of furor and battle, surrounded the Hungarians, and killed many of them. Then they routed the Hungarians and expelled them from the camp back to the cannons. That was where the battle drew to a close, as it was already evening.

The sultan realized that this had been a disaster for him, with the janissaries wounded and terrified and his armies attempting to desert him. During the night he instructed the camp to pack up and follow wherever he might lead them. He left at night and advanced in fear that the Hungarians might cross over with the rest of their army and press hard upon him, and then his withdrawal and return home would become difficult. It seems to me that the Hungarians would indeed have followed the sultan's army closely had Hunyadi not discouraged and forbidden them to do it, as he knew well that Turks always become stronger by a wide margin and hold up better whenever they are threatened with danger. It seems also that it may have been due to the plague that had broken out in the Hungarian camp and was weighing them down, so that they did not recover from it for a long time.

Janko [John Hunyadi] himself was wounded there and died shortly afterward. It seems to me that this was the chief reason why the Hungarians did not pursue the sultan's army. Janko did not survive for long after the sultan departed, and he died soon after that. He was a man excellent in all respects, having risen from insignificance to a position of great power, performing great deeds against the Germans and Bohemians, and was held in great esteem while he was managing the affairs of the Hungarians. His achievements against the Turks were also numerous. And it does not seem that he would have prevailed over the sultan's power, if it were not for the number and valor of his feats, when the sultan, attacking at dawn, overcame the Hungarian forces. He was hated by the other powerful men of Hungary, who did not want to be ruled by him; nevertheless, he mastered the situation and obtained their consent as they were in no position to resist a man held in such universal esteem, who strengthened the realm and made it much more secure. This man seems to have accomplished everything with ardor, and he handled all situations properly by being present wherever he was required. It is also said that he was carried off by the plague and died that way.

Regarding Capistrano, I will record for posterity what I know. He was a follower of Bernardino of Siena, a great preacher in the religion of Lord Jesus, and he himself attained great fame and glory throughout almost the entire west, reaching the highest degrees of wisdom and contemplation. When Bernardino died, the Italians bestowed on him the honors of a hero and built shrines for him. There are many statues of him throughout Italy that are sanctified as to a holy and supernatural man. It is said also that the man performed verifiable miracles. Giovanni [John of] Capistrano, then, was his follower, as I said, and he traversed many lands and went around preaching in public. Among other places, he came also to the Bohemians who believed in a heretical cult, in that they mostly worshiped fire; they still did not at all accept the religion of the others in that region as they had different beliefs, and they were not persuaded by the others who lived in the weak parts of Bohemia.[2] Capistrano came to them and brought them over to the doctrines of the rest of the Bohemians. He was greatly esteemed for wisdom and prudence and was on close terms with the king of the Hungarians [Ladislaus V], which is why he joined the war against the Turks, as I said earlier.

28. MICHAEL KRITOPOULOS (KRITOBOULOS), *HISTORY OF MEHMED THE CONQUEROR*
c. 1467

Michael Kritopoulos was a native of the Aegean island of Imbros, west of the Dardanelles (now Gökçeada in modern Turkey). By the 1450s he had risen to prominence as a leading political figure on the island and was among those who helped negotiate its peaceful transfer into the hands of Mehmed II immediately after the sultan's capture of Constantinople. Thereafter, under the classicizing pen name Kritoboulos, *he authored* The History of Mehmed the Conqueror, *his only surviving work. It is incomplete, covering Mehmed's reign only to 1467, and it survives in only one manuscript. But it is noteworthy in several respects. Classicizing in language and spirit (its story's places and peoples are given classical names, for example, and there is virtually no discussion of matters of religion), the* History *offers not only one of the most vivid and detailed descriptions of the siege of Constantinople (§§ 117–257 of Book I) but also this brief sketch, from Book II, of the events surrounding Belgrade. In its studied neutrality, Kritoboulos's terse, straightforward account offers a striking contrast to the narratives of Western churchmen, in particular that of his contemporary, Tagliacozzo.*

---

2 This clause is obscure.

Source: Kritovoulos, *History of Mehmed the Conqueror*, trans. Charles T. Riggs (Westport, CT: Greenwood, 1970), 112–16. Reproduced by permission of Princeton University Press.

The Defenses of Belgrade

§ 89. Crossing through [the Sofia Pass], [the sultan] invaded the land of the Triballi and, marching rapidly through it and ravaging most of it, reached the city of the Paeonians that lies on the banks of the Ister. This city is called Belgrade. It is very well fortified on all sides and very safe, almost impregnable, partly because of the way it was built but especially because it is shut off on two sides by the two rivers, the Ister on the north, and the Save [Sava] on the south which here flows into the former. The city is protected by its lofty and steep banks, and by its very rapid currents.

§ 90. On the landward side, where it was much more vulnerable and could be captured with the aid of cannon, it was defended by a very lofty double wall and a deep and marshy moat, full of water. It also contained a fairly large garrison of Paeonian warriors, all well-armed. It was thus impregnable.

Siege of Belgrade

§ 91. The Sultan pitched his camp there, surrounded the city, placed his cannon against it, and besieged it.

Flight of Lazarus to Dacia

§ 92. Lazarus, chief of the Triballi, who had known from the beginning about this attack of the Sultan against his town, immediately crossed the Ister with his wife and children and all his goods, and fled into Dacia. There he remained waiting for the war to cease.

Look!

§ 93. The Sultan in his siege of the city partly shattered and partly destroyed the wall with his cannon. Then he divided his army into sections and filled up the moat so that it would be easier for the heavy infantry to get to the wall. This work was quickly done because there were so many hands.

§ 94. Those inside the city fought bravely, bringing up stockades and all sorts of defense materials, stones, wood, and other things to the wrecked part of the wall, digging a deep ditch on the inner side, heaping up the earth high, and using every other device for defense. But they never had a chance to complete the work, for the stones shot by the cannon scattered and demolished the materials they had gathered, and broke down the wall.

§ 95. John [Hunyadi], the commander of the Paeonians and Dacians, was encamped beyond the Ister, opposite the city, with four thousand heavy infantry, watching events. When he saw that the wall had been broken down and the moat already completely filled and that the grand battle and the assault by the Sultan and his whole army were very shortly to be expected, he feared lest the city should be captured by force of arms in the attack. Therefore he secretly crossed the river with his soldiers and entered the city and halted, without anybody outside knowing of his crossing.

§ 96. Since all was going in his favor – for the wall had been broken down to the ground, and the moat filled up, and everything else now awaited the assault on the inner wall – the Sultan thought he should no longer delay or put it off at all, but should swiftly attack the city with all the power of his army.

§ 97. Hence, after carefully arranging all his forces, be harangued and exhorted them much in advance, encouraging them to fight, giving orders as to what should be done, and urging them to show themselves heroes. He then led the assault on the inner wall.

The Sultan's Attack on the City, Heavy Fighting

§ 98. The soldiers with a loud and fearful battle-cry rushed shouting against the demolished part of the wall, ahead of the Sultan. Climbing over this they fought valiantly, trying to get inside.

§ 99. But the Paeonians met them bravely, withstanding the assault and fighting valiantly. There was a fierce struggle there and many were killed in a hand-to-hand fight just in front of the Sultan, his men trying to get inside the walls and capture the city, while the Paeonians tried to repulse them and guard it.

§ 100. At last the Sultan's men prevailed, forced back the Paeonians, and gallantly scaled the wall. In desperate fighting they [the sultan's forces] beat them back, drove them into the city, and poured in themselves. They drove them back in disorder and confusion, and killed mercilessly.

Attack of John against the Sultan's Forces

§ 101. Just then John suddenly appeared there, rushing up with his men. With a great shout he quickly frightened and greatly perplexed the Ottomans, repelling the advance. There was a sharp fight, with anger and wrath and great slaughter, both of the heavy infantry and of the Paeonians. Both sides fought well, and excelled each other in determination, acting heroically, the attackers believing they nearly had the city and that its loss would be a disgrace, while the Paeonians were ashamed to be beaten or to lose such a city out of their hands.

§ 102. But the Sultan's troops at this point suffered heavily. They were hit in front and from above from the battlements, and from the houses on the wall they were attacked on the flank. Indeed, on every side the Paeonians attacked them. So, unable to hold out any longer, they gave way, and the Paeonians fell on them immediately with fresh courage and more vigorously drove them back foot by foot, taking some of them prisoner.

Repulse of the Sultan's Men, Flight, and Pursuit by the Paeonians As Far As the Camp

§ 103. Driving them back from the wall, they [the Hungarians] followed them clear to the camp and killed some. And when they reached the cannon, they threw some of these into the river and others into the moat, while most of the men turned to looting the camp.

Later Attack of the Sultan on the Paeonians; Severe Battle, Their Flight and Pursuit, and Their Being Again Besieged in the City

§ 104. They would have wrought great havoc and looted most of the camp had not the Sultan attacked them in the center with his guard and stopped their onslaught. Fighting desperately, he drove them back brilliantly and pursued them to the walls, pitilessly killing and slaughtering them. Then with vigorous blows he drove them inside, and again besieged them in the city.

§ 105. After that, he left off pursuing them and went back to the camp. Not much had been removed from the camp, since, as I have said, the Sultan fell upon them so suddenly and put them to flight and chased them.

§ 106. A large number of other soldiers had been killed as well as several from the Sultan's guard, brave men. The Governor of Europe, Karaja, also fell, struck by a stone cannon-ball. He was a fine man, one of the most powerful of the Sultan's entourage, renowned for his courage and military skill and valor. It is also said that the Sultan himself was hit in the thigh by a javelin as he fought, but the wound was not severe, merely superficial.

§ 107. The Sultan gave up all hope of storming the citadel. It had already been very strongly garrisoned, and now many more had got in. Therefore he withdrew his army from there. After overrunning a part of Triballia [Serbia], he plundered it and captured forts and devastated villages, carrying off great quantities of booty for himself and giving much to the army. Then, having reinstated Ali there as governor, he returned to Adrianople, for the harvest season was now over.

§ 108. After spending all the autumn there, in the beginning of winter he came to Byzantium. So the 6964th year [1456] from the beginning drew to its close, being the sixth year of the reign of the Sultan.

29. JACOPO PROMONTORIO, *RECOLLECTA*
c. 1475

Jacopo Promontorio was a Genoese merchant who over the course of his long life developed extensive ties with the Ottoman world. Along with his brother Gian-Andrea, he spent nearly two decades at the court of Murad II before his return to Genoa in 1448. He then returned to the East after 1453 and became a merchant in the orbit of the court of Mehmed II. In that capacity he accompanied the sultan on the campaign that ended at Belgrade. Some years later, he returned home to Genoa to retire, and there around 1475 he recorded his Recollecta, *a wide-ranging memoir that stands as a key early witness to life at the Ottoman court. The passage in which he recalls the battle for Belgrade is translated here.*

Source: Trans. J. Mixson, from Franz Babinger, "Der Quellenwert der Berichte über den Eintsatz von Belgrad 1456," *Sitzungsberichte der Bayerischen Akademie der Wissenschaften* (Munich: Bayerische Akademie der Wissenschaften, 1957), 1–69 (here 64–8).[1]

And so it was [that] in the aforementioned year, 1456, he [Mehmed II] went in person to Belgrade on the Danube with a great army, its great force made of men-at-arms and *azaps* on foot, drawn from all of Turkey and Greece. During the previous winter, he had arranged the construction of one hundred trireme hulls in the forests of Serbia, on a river called the Morava, around 760 miles to the south.[2] He outfitted these ships in every way like those worthy of sailing on the sea, launched them into the river, and had them row toward the Danube where that river joins the Morava. He also arranged for the transportation of metal ore to the city of Skopje, some eight hundred miles to the south, where he had cast twenty-eight large cannons, the smallest of which shot stones weighing four *cantari*, some five, some six or seven.[3] Other cannons and guns were also cast in great numbers and were transported to the city of Belgrade.

The force surrounded the city. On one side, the one hundred aforesaid galleys moved to block the passage of the Hungarians, and also to transport their soldiers to land across the water, where the army of the aforesaid Hungarians was positioned. This was because Belgrade is in fact located in Greece, that is, on the Danube River [on its southern bank], beyond which the country of Hungary begins. And behold! Suddenly the holy brother John of Capistrano of the Order of Friars Minor, of blessed memory, arrived with his great following of men, almost all of them devout foot soldiers of our holy faith, who were ready

---

1 See also Franz Babinger, *Die Aufzeichnungen des Genuesen Iacopo de Promontorio de Campis über den Osmanenstaat um 1475* (Munich: Bayerische Akademie der Wissenschaften, 1957). The text, which survives in a single copy of a lost original, is in a rambling Italian that is difficult to translate literally. The notes indicate some of the places where the original is somewhat obscure, or where the reading should be taken with caution. I am grateful to my colleague Dr. Jessica Goethals of the University of Alabama for her generous assistance in helping me wrestle with the challenges.
2 See document 12, n. 5. If an Italian mile was roughly equivalent to 1.8 km, making this a distance of some 820 miles, the estimate is inaccurate by an enormous margin. The region referenced (around the city of Skopje) is only some 300 miles from Belgrade.
3 A variable Italian unit of mass, the *cantaro* was anywhere from 50–70 kg. The stones described here thus weighed anywhere from 400–1,000 lb.

to die for it. There were also twenty thousand more in Belgrade. I saw the city bombarded by the strikes of the twenty-eight great cannons, and everything destroyed. I saw the aforesaid Great Turk engaged in a grand battle, from which he derived little honor. They had launched a bold assault and had entered the first and second walls with great fury. But that most prudent and most holy man, the aforesaid Friar John, knew that the Turks, after such a long and fierce battle, were all weak and tired (or a great part of them), and so divided his army in three: one larger force surrounding his person, a second for the beylerbey of Greece, another for the other beylerbey of Turkey. Inspired by the divine cult, he decided to take position and ordered for the attack of the beylerbey of Greece, in which seven thousand died; [he did] the same for the other beylerbey of Turkey, [and] the rest to the person of the Great Turk. And with the name of Jesus Christ going before and the holy banner of the holy cross, they drove them back,[4] so that immediately all [the sultan's troops] and both beylerbeys were put to rout, and a great part they cut to pieces and drove them away from the aforementioned cannons, whose firing now ceased. Similarly, all of the hundred galleys were destroyed in this way, namely that in fear the Turks set them on fire and moreover (so that Friar John could not take them) they burned all that remained in their possession.[5]

All the people who remained unwounded now fled to where the sultan has been, to gather around him. But the Grand Turk was no longer there, first because night had fallen, and second because in battle they had captured a few Hungarians who advised them that Biancho,[6] the captain general of Hungary, was nearby on an island in the Danube some eight miles from Belgrade with ten thousand men-at-arms, all on horseback, who were well-positioned to launch a counterattack in the morning. The Great Turk was terrified, firmly believing that our Christians would not be moved for anything, and so by night fled secretly with all of his army toward Turkey, in great silence and great fear. Thus, through the whole night and for three days after, they fled like hunted rabbits along the highway, with great shame. The loss and cost were

---

4 Here an approximation of an obscure phrase.
5 This passage, particularly obscure in its details, is paraphrased here for its general sense, which is clear enough. The overall prominence of the role of Capistrano in this account is striking.
6 A garbled Italian rendering of "Janko," or John Hunyadi.

great: one hundred galleys and twenty-eight large cannons with nearly all of his pavilions and carriages left behind in flight, to his shame. And the Great Turk himself was dangerously wounded by an arrow in the left leg, indeed to the bone, and was already in great flight, seeing that the *ağa*, captain of the janissaries, had been cut to pieces, not knowing that he would be wounded in turning his back, as noted above. For he was wounded in the other, but in this one did not suffer a great injury.[7] The belerbey of Greece, called Charagiabei, was killed.[8] He was a leading general, the most valiant, most wise, most intelligent, most valued, most accepted, and greatest of the sultan's men. The leader of the janissaries, too, as noted above, was killed, along with more than thirteen other Turkish men, apart from those taken captive. Altogether he suffered losses of more than 500,000 ducats, and after it all he remained wretched, malcontent, and irritated. There in person with the Great Turk was the aforementioned Lord James, his trading partner, who was witness to the campaign and to the fight.[9]

30. ÂŞIKPAŞAZADE, *MEMORIES AND CHRONICLES OF THE HOUSE OF OSMAN*
c. 1484

From the early years of the fifteenth century, the rise of the Ottomans began to inspire what quickly became a rich tradition of literature and historiography. In a wide variety of languages, styles, and genres, Ottoman authors began to experiment with how best to explain the new order of their day within the wider sweep of an increasingly global vision of Islamic history. The text translated here, along with two more selections below (documents 32 and 33), offers a small sampling of this tradition. The Ottoman author known as Âşıkpaşazade (d. 1484?) was born in the Anatolian region of Amasya at the beginning of the fifteenth century. By his teenage years, he had entered the ranks of ascetics known as dervishes. He was also recruited to take up arms as a gazi warrior in the service of Mehmed I, who emerged from the disruptions of a decade of civil war (1402–13) to rule

---

7   Here is another obscure passage. It seems to indicate that the sultan suffered two leg wounds, one more severe than the other.
8   Karaca Bey, commander of Thrace, here "Greece."
9   Jacopo here makes reference to himself.

as sultan. *Over the next decades, Âşıkpaşazade continued his adventures as a soldier under Murad II and Mehmed II and was present for several major campaigns, including the Second Battle of Kosovo in 1448, the capture of Constantinople, and Belgrade. Toward the end of his life he also completed the work known as* Memories and Chronicles of the House of Osman (Tevārīh-i Āl-i Osmān). *The work is a rich and layered compilation whose narratives often reflect the perspective of the dervish-gazi world that had nurtured its author.*

Source: Trans. J. Mixson, from Âşıkpaşazade, *Tevārīh-i Āl-i Osmān*, trans. Richard F. Kreutel, in *Vom Hirtenzelt zur Hohen Pforte: Frühzeit und Aufstieg des Osmanenreiches nach der Chronik "Denkwürdigkeiten und Zeitläufte des Hauses Osman" vom Derwisch Ahmed, genannt 'Aşik-Paşa-Sohn*. Osmanische Geshichtsscreiber 3 (Graz: Styria, 1959), 206–8.

127. How the Sultan Mehmed Han Gazi Struck against Belgrade, What He Did There, and How It Turned Out

He raised the army of Islam, dedicated himself to fighting for the faith, and set out for Belgrade. At the same time, he had ships make their way there by way of the Danube. He also had cannons forged from the copper horse and the foolish cross and the bells that he had destroyed in Istanbul.[1] With these cannons, as soon as he arrived before Belgrade, he began the fight. Karaca Bey, the beylerbey of Rumelia, said to his lord: "My glorious sultan, give me, your servant, permission to cross the Danube and set up against the city." But the lords of Rumelia were not in agreement with his plea, because they thought, "If it happens that Belgrade is taken, we will have to live off the surrounding land; in other places, we no longer face any enemies. If we now take this fortress as well, and drive away its handful of infidels, what will become of us?" In this way they crafted schemes in order to thwart the capture of Belgrade. Indeed, they took no joy in the prospect that Belgrade might be taken.

Then one day, in the region that Karaca had wanted to capture, a mighty army of infidels appeared and began to settle in there, with the accursed Ianko [John Hunyadi] as its leader. And at the same time, they brought down innumerable ships on the water. In a word, the fight

---

1 Kreutel, the translator of the Turkish text into German, notes that the "copper horse" mentioned here may have referred to a statue of the Emperor Justinian.

was on. Both sides now fought mightily. And then again one day while Karaca Bey was shooting at the fortress from the trenches, unexpectedly there came from inside a mortar shell that struck the timberwork of his trench. The bulwark collapsed and struck Karaca Bey, and he fell as a martyr.

Meanwhile the ships fought on the water, and unexpectedly many of the ships were destroyed.

The lord sultan gave the order: "Hey, all of you gazi, it's time to storm the fortress!" And so they launched the assault, and the servants of the lord sultan ran toward the walls.[2] But the Rumelians all betrayed us and did not charge. It was the sultan's servants who laid siege to the fortress. As the infidels saw that the attack was being launched from this side, all of them threw themselves against the servants. But the servants kicked them in the rear, drove them into flight, and killed many of them.

Then the great lord climbed on his horse and said, "Hey, all of you gazi, why are we still holding back?" Then right away he charged against the infidels and advanced forward. His soldiers stood ready at his side; they advanced forward with the lord sultan. They drove a contingent of the infidels back into the fortress and slew most of them. There was a mighty battle, but it soon became clear that the Rumelians had committed treason in order to prevent the fortress from being taken.

So the lord sultan retreated from that place, and returned gloriously to his own land […].[3] This campaign fell in the year 860 of the Hijra. And in the same year there appeared two great comets, one in the West, and one in the East.[4]

31. JOHN THUROCZ, *CHRONICLE OF THE HUNGARIANS*
c. 1488

John Hunyadi died shortly after the battle for Belgrade, and King Ladislaus V of Hungary a little over a year later. The successor to their ambitions, and to the leadership of Hungary, was Hunyadi's younger son Matthias Corvinus, who

---

2 "Servants" here meaning the janissaries.
3 The German translation notes here the omission of an extensive passage offering praises to those who fight for the faith.
4 See documents 22 and 23.

was elected king in 1458 and ruled for over three decades until his death in 1490. Those years witnessed the remarkable growth of a "Renaissance" royal court in Buda, and the royal notary John Thurocz (c. 1435–89) was in the middle of it all. Toward the end of a long career at court, he turned his attention to the writing of a comprehensive history that could speak to the strong self-confidence and ambitions of his patron, King Matthias. Thurocz's Chronicle of the Hungarians, *published in 1488, unfolded in four parts. The first three parts of the chronicle were largely compiled or recast from earlier works, but the last, covering the period from 1387–1487, Thurocz completed himself. He had no existing narratives at his disposal, but he did have the advantages of his position, which gave him access to royal charters, books, letters, and other materials, as well as the oral testimonies and memories of key players in events close to his own day.*

Source: John Thurocz, *Chronicle of the Hungarians*, trans. Frank Mantello (Bloomington: Research Institute for Inner Asian Studies, Indiana University, 1991), 173–86.

249. Concerning the Assault on the City of Constantinople Made by the Sultan of the Turks

In the course of the same year in which King Ladislas had come into Hungary,[1] around the first month of summer, Mehmed, sultan of the Turks, turned his arms against the Greeks and waged a formidable war against the whole of Greece, contrary to the treaties he had entered into with the emperor of the Greeks and contrary to his oath. And after collecting countless troops from every source and setting in motion all the instruments of war in his kingdom, with a blockade by land and sea he violently and arrogantly attacked that most celebrated city of Constantinople, formerly called Byzantium, child of the ancient emperors and mistress of the world. And with the unremitting attacks of his arms he so devastated the sad city, which was begging for reinforcements from Christian kings and yet was abandoned by everyone to disaster and destruction, that even women were compelled to come to its defense. But what good was it for the Greeks to raise a mismatched hand against so many countless foes? Devising a new kind of assault,

---

1 Correctly three years before, in 1453.

the sultan had subterranean tunnels and trenches excavated, which he used for an ambuscade; and when the sea had been spanned both with chains and by a bridge, and wooden towers had been erected to such a height that they were taller than the walls of the city, which were exceedingly tall, and from their tops the Turks were with thick showers of arrows striking everything that was being mobilized in the city, he caused, with the additional use of an assemblage of siege-engines and ballistas of many kinds and of unforeseen size, the city's walls to be reduced to debris. At length, with the walls for the most part in ruins on the ground, the sultan, to the exceedingly loud noise of drums and trumpets, set in motion all the main strength of his expedition to invade the interior of the city, and after the [fourth] day of the siege he took the city with the use of the utmost force and in one final struggle. And once its emperor had, when the enemy entered the city, been many times wounded and slain, everything of beauty the sultan of the Turks found in the city, both of God and of men, he handed over to be pillaged by the unclean hands of the Turks. The city's leading citizens were taken prisoner and brought to him, and the cruel prince had them most miserably strangled; the tombs of saints he had overturned, and their relics sunk in the sea. Who can put into adequate words, who can mourn, who can describe the fall of so great a city, the disaster, so very much to be lamented, suffered by the Christian religion, and the countless and enormous crimes indiscriminately perpetrated with brutality and wickedness by a rabid enemy against the sacred and profane, and against men and women alike?

250. Concerning the Siege of the Fortress of Nándorfehérvár by the Sultan of the Turks

King Ladislas was staying in the fortress of Buda and the 1455th year of the Lord was passing, when it was heard that Mehmed, sultan of the Turks, was threatening to invade the kingdom of Hungary and intended to storm the fortress of Nándorfehérvár as soon as possible. This news caused not only the common people of Hungary but also all the neighboring regions and practically the whole of Christendom to become very anxious and apprehensive. For the ferocious blockade of the city of Constantinople was vividly imagined by all Catholic people and seized everyone with great terror. Indeed, once the sultan of the

Turks had obtained his victory over the Greeks, it was as if he had become some other man, and swelling with ambition and a very haughty pride, he thought that the triumphant times of the late Alexander the Great of the Macedonians had come back for him.[2] For he is supposed to have said: "One God rules in the heavens; it is appropriate that only one prince rule the earth."

When these rumors were reported to King Ladislas, at once the young prince became profoundly frightened, and Count Ulrich, whose actions reflected the German spirit of warlike courage and whose advice guided the king, was no less disturbed. They did not therefore discuss the protection of the kingdom nor did they ready their arms to withstand the enemy, but, as if unaware of the rumors, they withdrew one dark night from the fortress of Buda and proceeded to the city of Vienna by an indirect route. And the fortress of Buda remained closed and without appropriate defense beyond mid-month, and although the fearful rumor of the arrival of so large an enemy force daily became more widespread, no one was moved to take up arms against it.

At length, upon the arrival of that part of the next summer when the ears of corn in the fields, brought forth from the living soil, were already turning yellow, and Phoebus was causing his chariot to be drawn through the field of the constellation Gemini, the Twins,[3] the aforementioned sultan of the Turks, along with his terrible and multifarious engines of war and more than 400,000 Turks, attacked the aforementioned fortress of Nándorfehérvár by encircling it with a terrifying blockade. The tops of their innumerable tents, spread out over the level ground of the plain far and wide on all sides, could be seen from the lofty walls of the fortress. Indeed, no one could with his eyes take in the masses of the enemy. What is more, the sultan had brought many ships constructed after the pattern of sea-going vessels, and with these he had so fortified the Danube and Sava rivers flowing alongside the fortress that no one could use a boat to bring aid to it. With the greatest labors he had brought devices and siege-machines

---

2 Mehmed II was known to be an admirer of the ancient Macedonian king, Alexander the Great (d. 323 B.C.).

3 That is, during the zodiacal period between May 21 and June 22. The date is wrong, however, as the Ottoman army arrived before Belgrade in the first days of July and began the siege on July 4.

and ballistas, so many in number, so great in size, and of a kind and magnitude that no one could ever believe they had been transported for the destruction of a fortress. These were with astonishing quickness assembled near the fortress of Kruševac, for because of their size they could not have been conveyed from distant parts. At length these machines were placed opposite that part of the fortress facing the plain. Some of them repeatedly struck the solid walls of the castle; others kept shooting stones the size of a bushel high into the air, which fell down with formidable impact within the walls of the fortress, instantly killing, like a thunderbolt, every living thing they hit.

And so day and night the siege-machines discharged violently and repeatedly, resounding with a thunderous noise, and their terrifying din could be heard as far away as the city of Szeged and in other cities far and wide, distant more than twenty-four Hungarian miles.[4] And the uninterrupted firing of the siege-machines gave off incessant smoke, and the thick murkiness of its clouds darkened the air, once splendidly clear, from the golden radiance of the sun. The swift breezes were tainted with the sulfurous stench, and neither the intensely hot summer's day nor the darkness of night brought any rest to the besiegers and the besieged, for the whole time was spent in deadly struggle.

The tops of the noble towers were collapsing under the massive impact, the walls were being shattered, and the lofty defensive walls protecting the fortress and its inhabitants were being razed to the ground. What more can be said, except that the besieged, utterly dazed by a profound fear of death, were waiting only for their last day?

Rumor of this most bitter and powerful siege spread through all the counties of the kingdom, but the Hungarian lords had fallen prey to a kind of torpor, as if in a deep sleep, and were not bringing any armed assistance to the city that was about to be lost. At last a man of innate courage and military expertise, the aforementioned lord count of Beszterce, went to oppose this awe-inspiring method of laying siege, escorted by a modest number of troops and intending to fight to the finish with an exceedingly numerous foe. A very great number of Hungarians assembled, people who were marked with the sign of the cross

---

4 One Hungarian mile is equivalent to about 8.5 km, and the twenty-four miles given by the chronicler is therefore 204 km or 127 statute miles. In fact, the distance by air in kilometers between Belgrade and Szeged is somewhat less, about 170 km.

by the aforementioned friar Giovanni da Capestrano and were ready to fight for the name of Christ, and from Polish regions there came some three hundred crusaders. Although the lord count, as was mentioned above, had been relieved of the responsibilities of government, he was nevertheless unable to endure not attacking the enemy, impelled as he was by his usual restless energy. He therefore searched for a way by which he could remove the enemy's ships from the aforementioned rivers and bring armed assistance to those laboring under the blockade.

Eventually, after hunting down some ships, he loaded them with armed troops and crusaders and at length dispatched them along the river Danube against the enemy vessels. The result of this maneuver was that both enemies were brought together in a naval battle. Amongst the Turks their loud battle cry abounded, and the Hungarians, too, with loud voices called upon the lord Jesus for assistance. Since both enemies had been deprived of escape routes, there commenced some very fierce fighting. The ships of both sides were conveyed here and there over the deep waters of the Danube, and many men, mortally wounded, were falling from them into the river. The clear water of the Danube turned blood-red from the immense slaughter, the result of the shedding of so much blood, and meals for the voracious fish were made of combatants on both sides.

At length, after the drawn-out struggle of the fight, the Hungarians were victorious; and charging very fiercely against the Turks, they cut apart their ships, which had been fastened together with iron chains, and set them alight.[5] After this became known to the sultan of the Turks, he is supposed to have said: "Now it will be more difficult for us to have our way."

Having achieved a glorious victory in the naval engagement, the lord count at once approached the fortress and brought solace to its captains, who were by now in a state of shock and confusion and awaiting no other fate but death. "Why," he said, "are you terrified? Is it just the Turks you now see? They are the very ones we have very often routed; and we have ourselves sometimes fled before them. Why does the sight of them, whom you have many times seen, upset you? Have you not personally experienced their arms and their fighting power? Let us then

---

5 On July 14, the eleventh day of the siege.

put our trust, my dear sons, in Christ, for whose name we have very frequently shed our blood, and let us fight all the more courageously with his enemy and ours! Did not Christ die for us? Let us then also die for him. Be therefore resolute and courageous in war. The enemy, as we know, is afraid. And if God is with us, this enemy can easily be crushed. For he is in the habit of turning tail, and is not ashamed to give way, take flight, and return home a fugitive. What further need is there of discussion, seeing that you, too, have found out these things by trial while enduring, under my leadership, the long weariness of war?" And so, with these and a great many more words, and by his very presence, the lord count restored them to a state of no little aggressiveness. In addition, he strengthened the fortress with fresh troops and also brought into it a very large number of crusaders. And although they were of common birth and ignorant of the use of arms, the lord count trained them for war as best he could.

Before this, the sultan of the Turks had heard that his father Murad, while alive, had devoted seven months to a siege at the base of the fortress of Nándorfehérvár and had not at all been able to take it, and he had withdrawn from it without a victory and with disgrace.[6] Consequently, with the leaders of his army in attendance upon him, the sultan of the Turks immoderately criticized his father and said that he could capture this same fortress in fifteen days. When the voivode of Anatolia,[7] the most exalted of the sultan's commanders, heard him boasting in this way, he obtained permission to speak first and replied to the sultan's remarks as follows: "Mightiest Sultan, it would be in my best interests to say something agreeable in the presence of your dignity, but I am afraid that the future outcome of this undertaking may convict me of telling your clemency a lie. Yet we should know that the Hungarians surrender their fortresses with greater reluctance than the Greeks."

The tops of the noble towers had by now been knocked down and the defensive walls were largely reduced to rubble on the ground, and the moats and embankments of the fortress were filled up and the ground made level, so that there was no barrier at all to stop the enemy's incursion. When the fifteenth day of the siege, which I mentioned

---

6 In 1440. See the introduction, p. 9.
7 İshak Paşa (d. 1487), beylerbey of Anatolia.

above, had begun to dawn, immediately the sultan, while the sunrise was still glowing brightly, mobilized all his hordes of people with the sounds of beating drums and blaring trumpets all round. And with a frenzied charge, he attacked the fortress, penetrating into its midst with a bloody slaughter. Now although the Hungarians were too few to join battle with so numerous an enemy, they nevertheless defended themselves with all their strength. And very often proclaiming the help of the lord Jesus, they keenly concentrated their efforts on the enemy's destruction. So the lethal war was renewed, with fighting in the streets of the fortress. The bodies of many men who had been killed fell on both sides, and the loud, confused sound of much shouting and of the clanging of countless swords re-echoed in the air. Frequently were both enemies, one after the other, compelled to retreat.

Friar Giovanni da Capestrano was also there. As if in a trance, he and other friars, who with him had prostrated themselves on the ground, were with groans offering prayers, their thoughts and hands raised up for help from on high and their eyes fixed on heaven. Indeed, with the prophet they might have said: "I have lifted my eyes unto the mountains, whence help shall come to me."[8] The lord count of Beszterce was, with threats in one place and warnings in another, urgently pressing his men to fight. Likewise Mihaly Szilágyi,[9] the captain, and Laszló Kanizsai,[10] two young men of surpassing knightly courage, as well as the armed troops that the lord count had brought along with them, and also the companies of crusaders, all took up a position on the ruined walls of the fortress and were fighting with great ferocity.

First the Turks, who had very often been driven out of the fortress and had re-entered it as the result of a dreadful struggle, were stronger than the Hungarians. Now a very great number of houses in the fortress were set alight and were spouting fierce flames. Then a great many of the sultan's standards were held aloft on the walls of the fortress as a sign of victory; and then the Hungarians, deprived of all hope of offering resistance, were forced to withdraw, if there was any place for them

---

8 Psalm 120 (121):1.
9 For Szilágyi (d. 1461) see the introduction, p. 25, as well as Tagliacozzo's account in document 25, e.g., n. 3, and n. 19.
10 Laszló Kanizsai (d. 1477/8), later voivode of Transylvania (1459–61) and Master of the Horse (1464–7).

to retreat to, for the vision of imminent death was for each of them fast becoming a grim reality. Finally, when they saw that flight could not save them but that death alone would be their solution of so great a crisis, they once again loudly invoked the name of the lord Jesus, readied their arms and joined their shields, and rushed against the enemy with as powerful an assault as possible.

The deadly struggle was therefore resumed, with many on both sides pouring forth their blood and their souls. And the help of God was not wanting. For in a short time all the Turkish ranks were thrown into disarray by so strong and vigorous an assault by the Hungarians, and were forced to turn and flee. The Hungarians for that reason regained their fierceness, and as if aided from heaven with fresh fighting spirit, they pursued them at sword point for a very long time, until all the siege-engines and the other catapults that the Turks had employed to destroy the fortress were deprived of the soldiers manning them. The Hungarians therefore set alight all the defense works the Turks had erected, and with iron nails firmly closed the siege-engines' apertures that were designed to discharge fire.

There was no pause in the fighting as long as daylight lasted, but the struggle that had previously taken place in the narrow streets of the fortress was thereafter continued for a time with much severity on the broad plain, until night arrived and with its darkness separated the two foes. But how the sultan, under cover of that night's thick shadows, slipped away by flight below the fortress, no one is in a position to state for certain. Nevertheless, to God's glory and the consternation of the sultan, suffice it to say that, deprived of all his war engines, and having abandoned all his siege-machines and the other kinds of catapults he had brought there, he returned to his own land after a huge slaughter of his own people. And what is more, thereafter any mention of this fortress, made by anyone in his presence, was to him never welcome.

In spite of what has been written here, certain people have said this about the sultan's flight: that he had been wounded in the chest by an arrow during the fierce heat of battle when he was mustering his troops for the fight, and had then fallen to the ground more dead than alive. And his men had picked him up and carried him to their tents. But when it had reached nightfall, the Turks had seen that both the commander of Anatolia and indeed all their nobles had been killed in the war, that they themselves had suffered the greatest of slaughters, and that the sultan himself had hardly any pulse, as if he were half-dead. And terrified they would be attacked by the Hungarians come morning, they had begun to flee. Carrying the sultan with them so that he would not be made more ill by the labors of the journey, they had encamped beyond their fortress called Zrnov.[11] And when the sultan had there recovered consciousness and had asked where he now was, and they had pointed out the place to him, he had said: "And why or how did we come to this place?" "We were decisively defeated," they said, "by the Hungarians, and the commander of Anatolia and practically all the leaders of your army have been killed. We also suffered a great slaughter; and, what is more, we imagined that your serene highness was dead instead of alive. And so we fled until we reached this place." The sultan had in his turn also inquired if the siege-engines and the other devices had also been abandoned there; and when they had replied that indeed everything had been left there, the sultan at once had said, afflicted with profound bitterness of heart: "Bring me poison that I may drink it and die rather than return to my kingdom in disgrace!"

In this way, then, did the sultan of the Turks end his fight with the Hungarians below the fortress of Nándorfehérvár. And he, who with arrogant attitude and proud gaze wished alone to rule the whole world, was decisively defeated by divine judgment at the hands of a rustic band that were better with hoes than weapons. And he who had very joyfully arrived to the sound of many trumpets and many drums, fled shamefully in the silence of the gloomy night.

251. Concerning the Death of Lord Janos Hunyadi, Count of Beszterce

After this victory the lord count of Beszterce fell ill. From the early days of his youth he had completed so many important tasks in wartime, but he had not yet succumbed to old age.[12] He was, however, weary from the uninterrupted burden of bearing arms and the fulfillment of his responsibilities, and he was drained of strength. He fell ill there, and after suffering from the illness for a few days, he was at length taken to the

---

11 The fortress of Zrnov, south of Belgrade, was built by the Turks in the 1440s.
12 Hunyadi's age is not known, but he must have been about fifty at the time.

town of Zemplen,[13] and with the commendation of that man of God, the aforementioned friar Giovanni da Capestrano, he gave his spirit back to his Savior. There arose a loud lamentation throughout the whole of Hungary, and the land was distressed, as was the rest of Christendom, and grieved exceedingly when it heard that its champion had died. Moreover, even the stars fixed high in the heavens announced his death in advance, for a remarkable star with a tail had appeared in the heavens prior to his passing.[14] Even Sultan Mehmed mourned, though put to flight by this lord count below the aforementioned fortress of Nandorfehervar just before his death. When the death of the lord count was announced by Despot George of Rascia to the sultan as if to console him, it is reported that the sultan remained silent, with his head motionless, for a full hour, and that he, although the count's enemy, suffered greatly at his passing and said to the messenger that from the beginning of time there never had been such a man in the service of a prince. That man alone, amongst all the mortals of our generation, demonstrated how correct Solon was in ancient times when he denied supreme happiness to Croesus, king of the Lydians and the richest of all kings, who was questioning him about this. Is it not the case, for instance, that Tellus, the most outstanding of all the Athenians, whom Solon placed above Croesus in happiness after he had seen the latter's treasure-chambers, was provided for by the supreme creator of the world with children, for whom everyone had the highest hopes? Is it not also the case that the count lived a life redolent in all respects of much glory and fame, and that a most illustrious death came to him as his lot just as it came to Tellus, when it brought to a close his life following the conquest and rout of so great a sultan, with the greatest of praise for the victory he was always striving for, when he could still taste the sweetness of his triumph, and with his good name intact?[15]

---

13 Zemplen or Zimony, also Semlin. Today Zemun, opposite Belgrade, a market in Szerem county. Hunyadi died there on August 11, 1456. See Map 3: The Siege and Relief of Belgrade, 1456, on p. 284.
14 See documents 22 and 23.
15 In a confused way Thurocz is here referring to a story he found in a Latin translation of the Greek historian Herodotus (c. 484–c. 420 B.C.). According to Herodotus, the Athenian Solon was asked once by King Croesus of Lydia whom he considered to be the happiest man in the world. It must have been the Athenian named Tellus, Solon answered, whose city was prosperous, who had fine sons and grandchildren, and who died gloriously in a battle in which the enemies of Athens were routed.

At length his body, while his family and followers shed many tears, was carried to Gyulafehérvár[16] and honorably buried. Now the lord count died in the 1456th year of the Lord's Incarnation, when Virgo had the sun as a guest in her heavenly bed. When the aforementioned friar Giovanni da Capestrano observed him laboring to breathe his last, he is reported, after commending him to God, to have repeated this sorrowful epitaph: "Hail, heavenly circle of light; you have fallen, corona of the kingdom! You have been extinguished, lamp of the world! Alas! The mirror into which we were hoping to look has been shattered. Now that your enemy has been decisively defeated, you reign with God and celebrate your triumph with the angels, O good Janos!"[17]

The lord count was a man of moderate height, with a large neck, curly chestnut-colored hair, large eyes, a look of calm assurance, a ruddy complexion, and so appositely and elegantly proportioned in the other parts of his body that he was recognized as a man of the first rank and importance in the midst of large numbers of people. He had two sons, to whom all of Hungary was looking with unrestrained longing. For the merits of their father compelled everyone to love them, and people observed that they had also inherited the courage and character of their father. The elder of these was called Laszlo, who was the same height as his father and a most outstanding young man amongst all his contemporaries for his courage as a knight, the integrity of his character, and his kindness and generosity. The younger son, Matthias,[18] was still a boy when his father passed away. While alive his father was profoundly fond of this boy, and his youthful agility commended him in the eyes of everyone. All who looked at him foresaw that he would be a great man.

252. Concerning the Death of Friar Giovanni da Capestrano

Now those who during life have together fostered a mutual love in Christ are not parted from each other at the time of cruel death's

---

16 Gyulafehérvár (Alba Iulia) in Transylvania, in whose cathedral Hunyadi's tomb is still to be seen.
17 Compare to the account of Ebendorfer in document 26.
18 Matthias I, later surnamed Corvinus, the future king of Hungary (1458–90).

dire examination. For friar Giovanni da Capestrano, the man previously mentioned, whose name deserves to be written in the catalog of saints, and who had been attached to the aforementioned lord count of Beszterce in sincere affection and love, did not live for many days after the passing of the lord count. Greatly desiring to live in a starry dwelling more than in an earthly one, he restored his poor body, now separated from his soul, to the earth of which it had been made, as his spirit flew up to heaven.[19] Buried in the convent of the Observant Friars Minor established in the town of Ujlak,[20] in whose habit he imitated the life of his holy father Francis, his body was renowned because of countless miracles, and its fame has not ceased right to the present day.

32. TURSUN BEG, *HISTORY OF THE CONQUEROR*
c. 1488

Born to a prominent Anatolian family sometime after 1425, Tursun Beg held a series of prominent administrative roles over the course of a four-decade career in the service of both Mehmed II and his successor, Sultan Bayezid II. Tursun Beg was also present on most of the major campaigns of the 1450s to the 1470s, including the construction of Rumeli Hisarı, the capture of Constantinople, and the siege of Belgrade. His History of the Conqueror, *composed at the close of his career, is another rich compilation built from earlier written sources, oral accounts, and the author's own experiences. It reflects his deep familiarity with Turkish, Arabic, and Persian literary traditions, and his often strongly panegyric purpose – strong enough, in the passage translated here, that the author works to frame the events of Belgrade as a virtual victory for the conqueror of Constantinople.*

Source: Trans. J. Mixson, from Tursun Beg, *Târîh-i Ebü'l-Feth*, trans. Luca Berardi, in *La conquista di Costantinopoli* (Milan: Mondadori, 2007), 102–8.

---

19 Capistrano died on October 23, 1456, ten weeks after Hunyadi.
20 Today Ilok in modern Croatia. For Capistrano's death, posthumous miracles, and long-delayed canonization, see Andrić, *Miracles of St. John Capistran*, cited in the introduction, n. 66.

While

> *The shah, father of the conquest, of firm judgment*
> *Shah Mehmed Khan of praiseworthy nature*[1]

was intent on the conquests that have been reported, to his noble ears came word that the infidel king of the "desperate" Hungarians, a notorious wretch named John Hunyadi, burned with desire to become betrothed to the teasing spouse of the country of Serbia. But

> *The gazelle of the king is the worthy prey of the lion;*
> *The dog, who looks after the pigs, goes hunting for carrion.*

The situation required that the sultan had first to kill the rival before being joined with his beloved. Thus, he satisfied himself with the territories he had conquered in this region and turned the bridles of victory toward Edirne, capital of the sultanate. Orders were given to prepare the means to strike the enemy, and the various instruments of war. In this year the sultan had his army, guided by victory, take a rest. He also decided that he, too, would happily take his rest in comfort and amusement, and that both the common people and the nobility would enjoy the blessings of his benevolence. Nevertheless, he remained restless, assailed by doubt over whether he would obtain the bride of the conquest, or whether it would be refused him.

In accordance with the maxim that "all things have a doorway," "enter your houses by their doors" (Qur'an 2:189), the design of the sovereign, which is always accompanied by benevolent fate, hinted at what followed. The key to the conquest of the land of Hungary was the fortress of Belgrade, a celebrated fortress whose reputation for being impossible to assail and impossible to take was well known, built at the confluence of the Danube and the Sava. So his first move was to plan to conquer it. He made generous arrangements for the appropriate measures, in a way that was worthy of the glory of a king who had conquered so many lands: terrifying cannons as large as mountains, and deadly catapults. On the waters of the Danube, he had deployed a fleet captained by renowned and well-equipped *azebs* [light infantry soldiers], sailors, and whatever else was needed.

---

[1] In his account, Tursun Beg frequently adorns his prose with brief poetic passages. These verse passages are signaled here in italics.

In the year 860, the springtime grass decorated the riverbanks, and every flower and every bud took notice.

This is the season of spring, and blessed is he
who is in the company of his beloved, and has a chalice to his mouth.

And so the banners – symbols of triumph – fluttered with waves of success and victory. The soldiers – guided by victory – took to the field, their numbers greater than the waves of the sea. And thanks to the artifice of the engineers, the troops were able to haul the cannons from the city of Skopje.

The same ruler

with triumph, power, and majesty, blessed by God,[2]

resolved to conquer Belgrade, if not to destroy the enemy in a pitched battle, and moved out with the army, boiling, thundering like the sea,

like the surface of the seas driven by a storm.

It was an army that found battle more pleasing than festival. In the face of it, the one bearing the shield could not turn away from the consequence of so many blows of a sword; and the one wearing armor could hardly close an eye amid the swarm of arrows. As it began to settle in before Belgrade, the imperial army deployed itself in the typical Ottoman fashion, and its fearless warriors fought with the enemy before the gates of the fortress. The fleet arrived as well, and so they besieged the fortress, surrounding it on the river and on land, *like a chalice encloses wine*. It was ordered that the cannons and the catapults should open fire, and that the miners should set themselves to work. He showed enormous zeal in carrying out his plan for the city's conquest, working from the breaking of the white light of dawn until the reddening light of sunset. The harp of war sounded from every corner, and battle broke out. Meanwhile the accursed king of Hungary[3] also arrived and arrayed his troops on the opposite shore of the Danube, their camp set up directly opposite the fortress.

---

2 In the original text this poetic line is rendered in Persian.
3 The chronicler here mistakes Hunyadi for a king.

During a consultation, Karaca Bey, lord of Rumelia, who was a brave and expert commander and sailor, said, "The ruler orders and grants license to me, his trusted commander, to cross over to the other shore to disperse the enemy, since his view from there strengthens the defense of the fortress!"

But certain emirs and viziers did not approve this proposal, and countered: "What harm can come from the enemy while he is on the opposite shore? To raid and to destroy crops right before his eyes can only cause his reverential fear of the sultan to grow."

By now the infidel king [Hunyadi] had arranged, at the source of the Danube, for the preparation of a fleet whose numbers by far exceeded the number of the sultan's ships. They arrived by advancing with the momentum of the river's current. The news began to spread: the ships of the ruler of Islam met and fought with the enemy ships, which arrived first, sinking four or five of them. So many infidels were killed that the Danube became a river flowing with blood, so abundantly that it overflowed and became twice its normal size. Finally, the infidel fleet arrived, and it was double the size of the Ottoman one. In keeping with the saying "two kittens are enough for a lion," seeing the superiority of their force, the ruler, yielding to the will of God, withdrew his fleet from the siege of the fortress and followed the direction of the river. Thus, the Hungarian fleet had an open road to the fortress.

Our adversary was the same one who in the time of Sultan Murad had so often led his troops into the territory of Islam, revealing his burning desire "to ruin the crops and the herds" (Qur'an 2:205). And though every time he had come, he went away crushed, defeated, abandoned by God, and deceived, he remained always an infidel, firm in that ancient hatred which waited only for an auspicious moment.

When the game of chance revealed itself to be playing out in this way, the victorious sovereign ordered the assault to be launched, before the forces of the infidel could be carried across to the fortress by their ships. To this end they loaded and prepared the cannons. Before nightfall each detachment placed barricades and ladders at various points against the walls of the fortress, making their advance from the place in which they found themselves. They fought all through the night.

The tent of the horizon was blackened by the vapors of infidel blood, and by the smoke from the lamps of oil. When the laundress dawn began her washing of the tent in heaven's basin with the soap of the sun's disk – that is, when dawn gave way to daylight – the conqueror sultan mounted his steed – the bracelet of fortune – and launched an assault against the fortress. Everywhere there sounded bass and timpani drums, tambourines and brass horns in the guise of a royal band.

> *The cry of the troops and the scream of the cannons,*
> *the sound of the timpani, of the tambourine, and the brass horn.*
> *While the head of heaven rang out,*
> *"To the attack!" said the shah, in the manner of Khosrow.*
> *"God is the greatest!"* [4]

The first to leap forward were the messengers of the fateful hour and the birds of hope, that is, the cannons, now loaded and ready for use. The deadly soldiers and heroic men followed, and with cries of "Allah, Allah!" they assaulted the fortress. Without any delay they threw their misguided enemies from the tower of ostentation into the deadly abyss, and ascended into the fortress. With such an illusion of victory, the avarice of the world began to impose itself on their hearts. And so they poured out and scattered to ransack the city, and failed to remain near to one another. Since the desire of worldly riches caused disunity to fall down upon them, they were unable to confront the enemy, who was ready and waiting in ambush. They turned back, their victory turned into defeat, and were forced to go out where they had come in. At this point many of them became martyrs, and many others fell wounded.

What happened next was this: the accursed infidel king, thanks to his many ships, in one day and one night had been able to ferry across (without their baggage) the soldiers who were on the opposite shore. He now not only placed on the towers of the fortress a sufficient number of infidel troops who were large, strong, and fully armed, but he also deployed a well-supplied regiment in front of every damaged breach. They stayed in this position and drove back the Muslims who, as we have noted, had been scattered in their lust for plunder.

Following the teaching that *"war is cunning,"* the wise counselors of the sultan found an opportunity in this circumstance to draw the infidels into the open field. It was ordered that the servants of His Majesty

---

4 The reference here is to the Sasanian kings of Persia, and to a general Islamic declaration of faith.

should withdraw unarmed from before the walls of the fortress. The infidels became drunk and stunned by drinking the wine of victory. They affirmed resolutely that "The Turks are defeated!" Rushing into an enclosure, they poured out of the fortress and advanced recklessly against the Muslim army. When the Muslims, fighting the infidel advance while in retreat, were approaching the place where the sovereign of Islam held his position, they said, "Let us draw back from the infidels! Don't let a living soul return toward the fortress! The sultan is beginning to retreat!"

The sultan, thinking it foolishness of judgment and weakness of mind among those viziers who said such words, went on a rampage: "To turn from the enemy is a sign of defeat! According to what is sanctioned by God – praise be upon him – the *truthful is the supreme* – great is my fortune. It is for the enemy to retreat!" With that he took up his lance and charged against the throng of infidels that came to meet him. He chose three of the demons who were advancing and struck them down.

> *He took up his lance like Hizir,*
> *Put the bridle to the mane.*
> *He charged, head down, like a roaring lion,*
> *He struck three warriors, and the enemy was filled with fear.*
> *The angel exclaimed, "God will protect you!" (Qur'an 5:67)*
> *The heavens cried out, "God is with you."*

Upon seeing this, the janissaries and the cavalry of the Muslims spurred on their horses and turned back the infidels. They found themselves in a place that was an absolutely level plain, without any kind of harsh feature or irregularity, hills or heights. In the same place they had in hand defenseless infidels, now at the end of their rope – mountain knaves wrapped in armor, caught between their rivers of wine, their exhaustion, and the heat of the sun.

> *When they seized the infidels,*
> *Among a thousand not one remained alive.*
> *At that point the bodies of those pagans began to pile up,*
> *And there were piles of them in every corner.*
> *The land was so filled with the heads of the enemy*
> *That you would have thought them piles of building stones.*
> *The field had become red with blood, the color of a tulip.*

What a tulip! A lake of flowing blood.
The bodies of the enemy lay strewn like rocks;
Their decapitated heads floated in blood.

In brief, they crushed them under the hooves of their horses, so many that not one was able to make his way safely back to the fortress. Among the Muslims there was great triumph. The possibility of now also conquering the fortress with a minimal attack seemed near, as night fell.

The benevolent ruler was satisfied with this clear victory. He said, "My servants are tired and some of them have reported being wounded. The fortress itself is my prey, already struck down. There will be time …" Acting in keeping with the saying "the return is the most commendable thing," he gave the order to depart, with the sweet taste of this military campaign.

A few days after the victorious sovereign had cast his fortunate shadow over his own domains, there came news that the accursed king of Hungary had departed for hell. The cause of his death and of his departure from the world was as follows: when the sultan's servants, as a ruse, had turned as the spit turns, the infidels had communicated to their king: "The Turk has abandoned honor and has been defeated." Convinced by the report, the king also went forth from the city and advanced suddenly toward the field of battle. A gazi struck him in the leg with a lethal blow as he [Hunyadi] turned away and fled directly back to the tower from which he had run out. Because of this wound he was set on his way for the voyage to hell. Better that the enemy is imprisoned in the tomb.

This is what God does with tyrants.

The killing of his rival was the wish of the sultan, and that wish, with God's help, had been granted. And so that shah – of the fortunate banners of the victorious sultan – grasped his reins as swiftly as the north wind, climbed resolutely into stirrups as firm as the ground, on the saddle of a steed that has traveled the world, to return to Edirne, *capital of the sultanate*. Here he would prepare the means and the way to be able to reunite with his beloved, Serbia, like a flirtatious new bride.

With the most sublime conditions and the most auspicious arrival,
With the best fortune following after him, forever.

33. THE OXFORD ANONYMOUS CHRONICLE
c. 1490

One of the most important works in the surviving corpus of fifteenth-century Ottoman histories is known as The Oxford Anonymous Chronicle. *The text, held in the collections of Oxford's Bodleian Library since the eighteenth century, was likely compiled under the patronage of Sultan Bayezid II (d. 1512) and completed shortly after 1484, the year of the last events of its narrative. At its heart is the story of how Bayezid II's predecessors forged their empire and asserted their legitimacy, both by conquering new lands and by surviving internal conflicts fueled by rival claimants to power. The conquests of Mehmed II, as well as his reversal of fortune at Belgrade, are an integral part of that larger narrative.*

Source: *An Early Ottoman History. The Oxford Anonymous Chronicle (Bodleian Library, Ms Marsh 313)*, trans. Dimitri J. Kastritsis (Liverpool: Liverpool University Press, 2017), 182–4. Reproduced by permission of Liverpool University Press.[1]

The Padishah of Islam Takes Novo Brdo and Trepca and All of Vilk-ili[2]

When the year 859 [1454–55] arrived, in spring, the padishah of Islam gathered an army. He cast cannons in Skopje and headed for Vilk-ili.[3] On his first invasion, he went and attacked Novo Brdo, staying there for a few days. He fired cannons and guns and destroyed some of the ramparts of the fortress, so that the people inside begged for quarter and surrendered the castle. Placing men inside, the padishah of Islam moved onward to Trepca, capturing it also within a few days. He took possession of all its mines and placed men in charge of them. Meanwhile, Karaca Bey went with the Rumelian army and conquered

---

1 I am grateful to Dimitri Kastritsis for his advice and support regarding not only this text but the world of early Ottoman chronicles generally.
2 Novo Brdo and Trepca were both important mining centers in the region of Kosovo. Novo Brdo surrendered on June 1, 1455, but its notables were executed nonetheless. Among the young men taken into the janissary corps was Konstantin Mihailović, whose published memoirs are an important source on the period. See documents 3.1 and 34.
3 Vilk-ili, the "Land of Vuk," meaning the lands belonging to Vuk Branković.

Bohor. Having taken all of Vilk-ili, the padishah dismissed his army at Kosovo. Then he proceeded to Salonika with the people of his Porte. After inspecting the city, he moved on to Edirne, stopping there for a few days. Then he continued on to Istanbul. At that time, envoys came from Vılkoğlu,[4] displaying humility and asking for terms of surrender. In exchange, Vılkoğlu took it upon himself to pay a tribute of thirty thousand gold coins per year. That year, the padishah wintered again in Edirne, giving praises and thanks to God.

The Padishah of Islam Marches on Belgrade

When the calendar reached the year 860 [1455–6], the padishah of Islam sent couriers to the people in his army, and a host was assembled the size of which had never before been seen. The padishah of Islam ordered that cannons be cast in Skopje, then with fortune and felicity he proceeded there in person. Mahmud Paşa transported the cannons through the Kaçanik pass[5] and headed for Belgrade, while Karaca Bey had ships constructed on the Morava. Accompanied by an endless army, he passed before Semendria, reaching a location near Belgrade. Finally, the sultan of Islam also arrived outside Belgrade and camped there. Earthworks were constructed and the cannons were brought out, assembled, and arranged behind them. Karaca Bey had transported by ship a large quantity of tree trunks and timber boards. Surrounding every side of the castle, the Anatolian and Rumelian armies began to cast their cannons.[6]

The infidels were worn out from constant battle and were rendered helpless. Few remained in the fortifications; however, a courier had gone to Yanko requesting assistance.[7] In response, he assembled the armies of the Pope and the Hungarians and was headed in that direction. Karaca Bey came and addressed the pashas, saying, "Let us launch

---

4 George Branković, Despot of Serbia.
5 The Kaçanik pass lies to the north of Skopje.
6 This description suggests that some cannons were transported by Mahmud Paşa, perhaps in parts, while others were cast in situ in wooden molds. The wood may also have been used for constructing the earthworks behind which the cannons were placed.
7 John Hunyadi. See also Kastritsis, "Inquiry Six," in *The Oxford Anonymous Chronicle*, 164, 171–2. See citation on p. 256 above in the introduction to this document.

the ships and transport our soldiers to the island. That way, aid will be unable to reach it from Hungary on the other side. Let us surround the castle from both sides." But his words were not received favorably, and such a move was not authorized. Within a short time, the infidel's ships arrived and began to wage battle against the Muslim ships. Hass Ahmed Bey fought a royal battle beyond description, but the infidels were victorious, and the people of Islam were defeated. The infidels arrived, and thus thirty thousand armed men entered the castle. Yanko also entered with them, so that at every battlement, a hundred infidels showed up and began to fight.

When by divine ordinance God did not make possible the conquest of the castle, after that whatever they attempted to do resulted in failure. In fact, the cannons had caused such structural damage to the castle's fortifications that with a small effort it could have been taken. Then the criers proclaimed, "Let no one mingle with the janissaries or join them in their trenches." For that reason, the rest of the army refrained from fighting, saying to themselves, "Apparently the castle may not be pillaged by the Anatolian and Rumelian armies." Nonetheless, on the Anatolian side İshak Paşa fought fiercely, while the janissaries stormed the castle from the place where the cannons had breached its walls. The padishah of Islam dismounted. Horsetail standards and war banners were raised, then they attacked the castle to the sound of drums and kettledrums, crying, "God is great!" At the breach made by the cannons, four or five hundred janissaries entered the fortifications. But the infidels attacked from either side and cut off their rear, injuring many of them with arrows. It was impossible for the remaining janissaries to rush to their aid, and the *Ağa* of the janissaries was martyred there. So the gazis did not proceed with battle operations, but returned to their tents.

When the infidels saw that the people of Islam had been routed, they made a sortie from the castle and overran their cannons and earthworks. In that way, they made martyrs of many Muslims. Seeing this action on the part of the infidels, the sultan of Islam seized his shield and shouted, "I have placed my trust in God." He fought so fiercely that he rendered many infidels lifeless, cutting most of them in half with a single stroke of his sword. The infidels were totally routed, and the padishah went to his pavilion tent safe and sound. At this time, the Rumelian and Anatolian armies had begun to retreat and flee the battlefield. But, as the people of Islam continued to fire their cannons, the Beylerbey of Rumelia, Karaca Bey, was struck by a falling tree and became a martyr. The padishah moved on. At that time, there was severe plague in Rumelia,[8] so he headed for Istanbul. And, in the course of the above battle, an arrow struck Yanko and sent his soul to hell.

34. KONSTANTIN MIHAILOVIĆ, *MEMOIRS*
c. 1490

Konstantin Mihailović was born in Serbia around 1430 and was among Mehmed II's many captives taken at the siege of Novo Brdo in June 1455 (see document 3.1). He was thereafter trained to serve as one of the sultan's janissaries and fought in a wide range of campaigns over the next decades. Over those years he earned enough trust to eventually find himself at the head of a garrison of some fifty janissaries at Zvecaj in Croatia and was captured once more when Hungarian forces took that fortress in 1463. The former Christian turned janissary now shrewdly switched sides again and capitalized on his unique position. He toured many of the leading courts in Central and Western Europe, including France, Bohemia, and Poland, sharing all that he knew of the Ottoman world. In the same years, until at least 1490, he wrote all of it down in a text that he called a "chronicle" and a "report," now known to modern scholars as his "memoirs." The earliest text, likely first written in Konstantin's Serbian, is now lost, but translations in Polish and Czech have survived. In them Mihailović offered his readers a wide range of information about the Ottoman world – its religious traditions, history, diplomacy, government, and military affairs. The passage translated here offers his recollection of the battle for Belgrade. The events took place only a year after his capture at Novo Brdo, so it is not known whether he would have yet been actively serving as a janissary. But the account nevertheless provides a key witness to the events from the point of view of the Ottoman camp.

Source: Konstantin Mihailović, *Memoirs of a Janissary,* ed. Svat Soucek, trans. Benjamin Stolz (Ann Arbor: University of Michigan Press, 1975), 49–55.

---

8 This was apparently one of several periodic outbreaks of the plague, situated between the sporadic occurrences of the 1440s and the great plague that struck Istanbul in 1467.

Chapter 27: How Emperor Machomet Deceived Despot Đurađ under Truce

The Turkish emperor, Machomet, made a truce with the Despot never to bother him before his death and that of his son Lazar and to support him faithfully and truly, as was mentioned previously about this. For Emperor Machomet made the truce with the Despot in order that he might take Constantinople or Stambol more easily.[1] This turned out indeed to be so. And as soon as Constantinople was taken, immediately the next year, without having denounced the truce with the Despot, the Turkish emperor marched upon the Serbian or Raškan land against the Despot with all his might. The Raškans, having heard this, gave the Despot to know that "The Turkish emperor is marching upon us with all his might. What have we to do? Earlier we told you that the Turkish dog would deceive us; know, therefore, Your Highness, this is our view: Rather than give up our wives and children before the eyes of our brothers to be distributed among the heathens, we want to venture our necks and fight them. Therefore, Your Grace, march to our aid with as much might as you can. We have one army in Sitnica and another in Dubočica or Kislina. Therefore, Your Grace, knowing this, do not delay."

The Despot answered them: "I cannot raise troops so quickly, for there is no King Vladislav in the Hungarian land who would gladly help me in this; therefore leave it all as it is. If you surrender to the Turkish emperor I will, by God, free you with God's help." The Emperor, having arrived in Constantine's land at a plain called Žegligiovo, on the border of the Raškan land,[2] hearing about the troops who were in Sitnica and

---

1 Mihailović is undoubtedly right in his assertion that Mehmed II would have kept the truce with the Serbian Despot only as long as convenient; however, it is also true that George Branković made the Turkish attack inevitable by negotiating with Pope Nicholas V (d. 1455), who was trying to organize another crusade. Ottoman intelligence found out about it, and Mehmed II may then have considered the occupation of Serbia a strategic necessity, before another Christian army under Hunyadi headed for Edirne and Istanbul.

2 Mehmed II set out on his second Serbian campaign in the spring of 1455. Starting from Edirne, he followed one of the usual routes westward, via Sofia, Küstendil (still in Bulgaria) and Kratovo (in Serbia). Our author's remark that the sultan arrived "in Konstantin's land at a plain which they call Žegligiovo, on the border of Raškan land," may mean that the Turks passed through the area of Küstendil, where a Bulgarian prince by the name of Konstantin had been confirmed in 1371 as Ottoman governor – hence the new name of classical Ulpianum and Byzantine Iustiniana Secunda. The region of Žegligiovo is just west of there, between Küstendil and Skopje.

Dubočica (Kislina), encamped here four weeks not knowing what to do nor which army to turn against. The army that was in Dubocica attacked his army bravely and fought and killed many Turks and also some famous Turkish leaders. Then the Emperor himself, having arrived with all his might, attacked them beside a mountain called Trepanja. The Turks say that as long as they have lived it is unheard of that from so few men there was such a battle with such a large force. And they say that if that abovementioned army had all been together with them, it would have decisively defeated the Turkish Emperor. And thus the poor wretches were defeated. Some were killed and others escaped. And one lord named Nikola Skobaljić was impaled with his uncle.[3]

And from there the Emperor marched and surrounded a city which they call Novo Brdo,[4] "Mountain of Silver and Gold," and having attacked it, conquered it, but by means of an agreement he promised to let them keep their possessions and also not to enslave their young women and boys. And when the city of Novo Brdo had surrendered, the Emperor ordered that the gates be closed and that one small gate be left open. Having arrived in the city the Turks ordered all the householders with their families, both males and females, to go out of the city through the small gate to a ditch, leaving their possessions in the houses. And so it happened that they went one after another, and the

---

3 As Mehmed II invaded Serbia in the spring of 1454, the Despot fled to Hungary; the sultan did not encounter any real resistance in open warfare in the field, but his chief objective was the seizure of important fortified places: thus he took Ostrovica near Rudnik, a small but important fortification because the Serbian crown treasure was kept there; he gave up, on the other hand, on the extremely well-fortified Smederevo. The campaign ended, the sultan returned with the bulk of his army to Edirne; then only, in the fall of 1454, did the Christian counteroffensive take place: the relatively small force under Firuz Bey, left at Kruševac, was overwhelmed by Hunyadi, who then pushed forward to Vidin and then withdrew to Hungary, while two Serbian groups clashed with the Turks in southern Serbia: this is the double encounter described by Konstantin Mihailović. One group [of Serbs] was positioned on the Sitnica river near Kosovo Polje (just west of Priština) and did not become involved in any significant fighting; the other group, however, under Nikola Skobaljić, was in the area of Dubočica near Leskovac. It was between Skobaljić and a Turkish army which marched in from Macedonia that the two main clashes occurred: at first on September 24 near Vranja, when Skobaljić gained the upper hand; then on November 16 on the Trepanja brook, where he [Nikola] was defeated, taken prisoner, and impaled. In all these encounters there was no question of the main force of the Ottoman troops or of the presence of the Sultan, who had long returned to Edirne.

4 The author presents as one campaign of the Ottoman sultan what were in fact two campaigns in 1454 and in 1455. Novo Brdo was taken in the second.

Emperor himself, standing before the small gate, sorted out the boys on one side and the females on the other, and the men along the ditch on one side and the women on the other side. All those among the men who were the most important and distinguished he ordered decapitated. The remainder he ordered released to the city. As for their possessions, nothing of theirs was harmed.[5] The boys were 320 in number and the females 74. The females he distributed among the heathens, but he took the boys for himself into the janissaries, and sent them beyond the sea to Anatolia, where their preserve is.

I was also taken in that city with my two brothers, and wherever the Turks to whom we were entrusted drove us in a band, and wherever we came to forests or mountains, there we always thought about killing the Turks and running away by ourselves among the mountains, but our youth did not permit us to do that; for I myself with nineteen others ran away from them in the night from a village called Samokovo.[6] Then the whole region pursued us, and having caught and bound us, they beat us and tortured us and dragged us behind horses. It is a wonder that our soul remained in us. Then others vouched for us, and my two brothers, that we would not permit this anymore, and so they peacefully led us across the sea.

And the Turkish Emperor Machomet took from the Despot all the Raškan land as far as the Morava, and left him [the land] from the Morava to Smederevo.[7]

Then the Emperor, having arrived at Adrianople, took eight youths of this same group among the chamberlains. These youths agreed to kill the Emperor on night watch, saying among themselves, "If we kill this Turkish dog, then all of Christendom will be freed; but if we are caught, then we will become martyrs before God with the others."

And when the night watch came, they had made preparations, each having a knife on himself. And when the Emperor was to go to his bedchamber, then one of them named Dmitar Tomašić left them as an ignoble traitor and told the Emperor what was to happen. Then the Emperor ordered them seized and brought before him. The Emperor,

---

5 The fall of Novo Brdo took place on June 1, 1455, after a siege of forty days.
6 Samokovo is a village in Bulgaria between Sofia and Plovdiv, on the old imperial road to Constantinople.
7 Mehmed II thus occupied about half of Serbia – the southern half.

having seen a knife on each one, asked them: "Who led you to this, that you dared attempt this?" Their reply was in a word: "None other than our great sorrow for our fathers and dear friends."

Then the Emperor ordered that hens' eggs be brought and ordered that they be placed in hot ashes so that they would be baked as hard as possible. And having taken them from the ashes, he had a hot egg fastened under each one's knee so that their muscles would shrink and burn. Then he ordered that they be carried by wagon to Persia with the eggs [attached], not allowing them to be removed from them until they cooled off by themselves. And after a year he ordered that they be brought back; and seeing that there was nothing to them, he ordered them beheaded, and several of us, having taken the bodies in the night, buried them beside an empty church called "Does Not See the Sun." And so it happened to those youths in Constantinople. And the one who had warned the Emperor he made a great lord at his court, but later such a serious illness – some sort of consumption – befell him, that he dried up to death. And his heathen name was Haydari. And so the Lord God deigned to visit that upon him for his ignobility and faithlessness.[8]

Thereafter Emperor Machomet did not want to have any Raškan boys in his bedchamber. So he took six boys and had all their genital organs cut off to the very abdomen; and so one died and five remained alive. They are called in their language *hadomlar*, which means in our language "eunuchs." And these guard the Emperor's wives.

Chapter 28: What Incident Happened to the Despot at the Hands of the Hungarian Governor Janko for His Great Acts of Kindness[9]

There was a great plague in Smederevo and because of this act of God the Despot went out of Smederevo to a mountain in the open air near Belgrade and rested there, having put up his tents, until the act of God passed. With him he had a small number of men; nevertheless he had

---

8   This story is unknown to us from other sources. By and large it is not impossible.
9   The events that Mihailović narrates in this chapter took place at the time when he was in Turkish captivity; he must have heard about them mainly after his return in 1463, thus after the extinction of the remnants of independent Serbia.

his son Lazar with him. And he sent a message to the Hungarian Governor and also to Michael Szilágyi, for he ruled Belgrade at that time, and he requested of them that he might freely rest there. Janko [John Hunyadi] the Hungarian Governor and Michael Szilágyi of Belgrade, vowing to him cunningly and falsely, solemnly authorized him to stay there in security both day and night as long as he wished, and what is more authorized him, "Whatever you ask of us we will be glad to do for you." The Despot, relying on their vows, released the chamberlains from his entourage and lay there confidently as befitted the term, having no concern for anyone.

And in two weeks Michael Szilágyi left Belgrade with several hundred cavalry and attacked the Despot in the night and cut off two fingers of the right hand, and the Despot was captured there but his son Lazar escaped. And they carried the Despot to Belgrade. There they assessed that he give one hundred thousand gold pieces. The Despot had to leave them his wife, named Jerina, and he himself rode to Smederevo in order to raise that sum of money. And the Despot promised to pay out that money without delay to a certain knight named Galvan.

This same Galvan, having several hundred cavalry in his reserve, rode with a small number of men to Smederevo for the money, and the money was immediately given to him. But the Raškans, pitying their lord, assembled without the knowledge of the Despot or his son Lazar and rode against the abovementioned Galvan to overtake him, so that they overtook them and attacked his reserve first, and decisively defeated them. And having killed Lord Galvan and having taken the money, they rode away with it and no one knew where those men went with the money.

King Vladislav [Ladislaus V of Hungary], having heard of this ignoble deed of Governor Janko and his brother-in-law Michael Szilágyi, His Grace King Vladislav was grieved by it, and so was the Celje prince, for he had for a wife the Despot's daughter. And the late King Vladislav of glorious memory ordered that the Despot's wife be released without any hindrance, and Michael Szilágyi having heard the King's order released her. And the Raškans, asking their lord the Despot to forgive them for having taken the money without his command, the King himself and the Celje prince had to cause it to be forgiven them. And then they brought the sum of money in its entirety and returned it to the Despot. Then the Despot wanted to send the money to King Vladislav.

The King did not want to take it, saying, "Sir Despot, I have no right to that money." Therefore the Despot sent the King a gift of fifty thousand [gold pieces] and the King gave him in return for this a certain castle in Hungary.[10]

And through such a deed much evil befell the Governor. And the Celje prince was killed by Janko's son because Janko feared him on account of the Despot.[11] And Smederevo together with other fortresses, after the death of the Despot and his son, Lazar, came into the possession of the Bosnian king, Tomaš; for the Bosnian king, Tomaš, had [for a wife] Lazar's daughter. And the Bosnian king was very weak besides, for he feared the Turkish emperor. The Raškans, because of the above-mentioned deed of the Governor, preferred to give Smederevo to the Turks than to the Hungarians.[12] And had there been good will between them at that time, then the Hungarians would have held Smederevo and other fortresses such as Belgrade to this day. For every man will gain more for himself by noble goodness than by accursed evil.

Take, for example, King Matyas [Matthias I of Hungary]. Did he leave much behind him by dint of his fierce struggle and great expenditure? Had he spent half as much against the heathens as he spent here, he would have driven the heathens back across the sea and would have

---

10 Branković was staying at his estate of Kupinik (now Kupinovo) on the Sava just west of Belgrade, when he was attacked by Michael Szilágyi on the night of December 17, 1455. He was taken to Belgrade, and his wife Irina had to stay prisoner until he would pay ransom money and give up two fortified places. The King of Hungary, Ladislas Posthumous, who had reached majority in 1453, was by then sixteen years old and was beginning to show his own will in the face of the power of the Hunyadi party. He invalidated the demands of Hunyadi's brother-in-law and saved the Despot from humiliation.
11 This happened after the siege of Belgrade, on November 9, 1456, thus after Hunyadi's death. Belgrade was then governed by Hunyadi's elder son Ladislas. Intense animosity existed between the "Hunyadi party" and royal authority, at this time represented by the king's uncle, Ulrich II of Celje, ban of Croatia. When a royal army arrived at Belgrade in November, the young king and his uncle were admitted inside, but the drawbridge was raised and the king and his uncle were virtual prisoners of Hunyadi's son. In the ensuing altercation Ulrich II was killed, and the king saved himself only by means of apparent conciliation.
12 Branković died on Christmas Eve 1456, and his son and successor Lazar, on January 20, 1458. During his short rule, Lazar tried to maintain good relations with the Turkish sultan, pay the tribute, and observe the usual obligation of sending auxiliary troops when summoned to do so. It seems that in this period of intense diplomatic activity, there was a "Turkish" party at Smederevo, led by Michael Angelović, who may have been a brother, according to some sources, of Mahmud Paşa, the Ottoman grand vizier. These two seem to have been natives of Novo Brdo.

had a great and glorious name from east to west, and from the Lord God an eternal reward, and from the people, honor and praise. Moreover, all Christians would have interceded for him with the Lord God, and also the heathens would have had him in their memory. Therefore take note: When Christian carries on a struggle against Christian, all of that is loathsome before God and before the world. Also take note of this: The heathens are brave not only in themselves, but because of Christian discord. For Christian discord is heathen bliss and joy, and our hatred and common malice bring the heathens victory.

Chapter 29: How Emperor Machomet Attacked Belgrade but Gained Nothing[13]

Emperor Machomet, knowing the deed that happened to the Despot at the hands of Janko, noted that such discord existed among the Christians.[14] Having prepared himself he marched toward Belgrade and assaulted it and decided to transport himself across the Sava to the other side on foot and to encamp along the Danube, entrench himself securely and emplace cannon so as not to allow the Hungarians to reach the fortress, but certain men dissuaded him, saying, "Fortunate Lord, that is unnecessary for you." Then the Hungarians arrived and encamped beside the Danube and from there as many as they needed reached the fortress.

And that was the first of the Emperor's sorrows, that they had dissuaded him from that.[15] The second of the Emperor's sorrows was that

---

13 The account of Belgrade offered here strikes one as an eyewitness report, or at least as one heard from an eyewitness. Konstantin, taken prisoner at Novo Brdo in June 1455, had by then spent only one year on the Turkish side. His presence at the siege would thus seem most unlikely if he had to participate as a janissary, but possible if he was there in some other capacity.

14 Konstantin is referring here to the attack on the Despot by Hunyadi's brother-in-law Michael Szilágyi, described in the previous chapter. Whether these events were the main spur for the sultan to launch his campaign is at best uncertain. The strategic importance of Belgrade must have been a principal factor in Mehmed II's decision to conquer it. It would shield his possessions to the north and the southeast and open the door to new conquests to the north and northwest.

15 It was Karaca Paşa, beylerbey of Rumelia, who proposed to the sultan this maneuver. The paşa would cross the Danube (not the Sava) and take up a position with his cannon on the northern bank, so as to fight off any aid that would come from Hungary. However, some of the other leaders, especially the *akinji* commanders, dissuaded the sultan from approving the proposal. This is at least how certain

the highest lord after the Emperor, named Karadiabassa [Karaca Bey], was standing on a rampart alongside the great cannon observing, and a cannoneer fired from a great cannon into a wall, and a stone, having torn loose from the wall, struck Karadiabassa in the head.[16] He was not alive for long. The third sorrow was that the Emperor wanted to batter the wall for two more weeks and breach it, but Smagilaga [?] dissuaded the Emperor, saying that it was not necessary, trusting in the janissaries, for he had been appointed highest lord over them by the Emperor.[17] Then the Emperor took his advice and ordered him to storm; and so they stormed until they got into the city. Four hundred and some janissaries were listed wounded, and also some, but not many of them, killed. Then, in a short time we saw the janissaries running back out of the city, fleeing, and the Hungarians running after them and beating them. And so the walls were occupied again more heavily than before. The fourth sorrow was, as far as the cannon were concerned, that the wagons, ropes, racks, and all the accouterments that are required for cannon were in a heap, and all covered by one roof; and someone set fire to it in the night and it all burned to ashes and the cannon were left bare. The Emperor ordered several tents to be left, and himself set off as if he wanted to take flight, in order that they would be enticed from the fortress to those tents, which in fact happened: they ran out of the city to gather up those tents. The Emperor, seeing that foot-soldiers had come a long way out of the city in gathering up the tents, turned upon them swiftly with cavalry and

---

Ottoman historians tell it. Konstantin's account is the same except for the important detail that not the Danube but the Sava river is meant. It is probably a confusion in the author's memory, unless he is right that the Turkish commander was planning to take up a position to the west of Belgrade along the southern bank of the Danube from where he still could shell Christian troops trying to cross the river from the north, and the ships that might come sailing down from Novi Sad.

16 It was the same Karaca Paşa who was killed in this manner. The event is reported in a similar way by Ottoman historians (see, for example, document 33).

17 According to standard Ottoman sources, the janissary commander's name was Hasan Ağa, not Ismail Ağa. Konstantin may be the only source that claims that the Ağa of the janissaries persuaded the sultan to order an assault too early. Altogether, the Turks seem to have tried to storm the city three times, the last assault coming on July 22, the day of their withdrawal. The assault mentioned here should have been the first or the second. There was considerable in-fighting and rivalry among the various commanders and dignitaries around the sultan, and an attempt on the part of the Ağa to distinguish himself and his troops over the others seems quite possible.

here they [the Turkish cavalry] beat them and killed them all the way to the earthworks.[18]

And the same man who had advised the Emperor not to batter the fortress any more, that it was sufficient, fearing lest the Emperor recall that to him, when the Emperor had defeated the foot soldiers who had run out of the city and had ridden away from there, leaving the guns and everything else, this same janissary officer returned. Wanting to show the Emperor some sort of bravery in order that he might come back into favor, he attacked among the infantry along the earthwork, and was killed there.

But the greatest sorrow of all was that the Lord God did not grant that Belgrade be captured by the Turks.

---

18 There are contradictions in other sources about this thrust of the Christians all the way to the Turkish camp, and about the outcome, some claiming that only the personal intervention of the sultan saved the situation. Konstantin's version supports the reports that the Christians were lured by a Turkish ploy. See documents 30, 32, and 33.

Cast of Characters

The following provides an alphabetized selection of brief descriptions for some of the most important figures in the story of Belgrade. Used in conjunction with the index and other general reference aids, it can provide a useful starting point for sorting through what may at first be a range of unfamiliar details. With a few exceptions, the list omits discussion of the authors whose works are translated here, since each of these is introduced at greater length in the documents themselves.

Aeneas Silvius Piccolomini, humanist author, churchman, and later Pope Pius II (1458–64). Piccolomini rose from a position as a teacher in Siena to acting in the service of important Italian churchmen in the era of the Council of Basel, and eventually became imperial secretary to Frederick III. In that position he was a key diplomat during the negotiations over the launching of a crusade after 1453. He was also a prolific and talented humanist author, and he delivered the famous classicizing oration *Constantinopolitana clades* (document 2) at the Diet of Frankfurt in 1454.

Alfonso V, king of Aragon, Sicily, and Naples. Alfonso "the Magnanimous" was one of the most consequential political and cultural figures of his era. Along with Duke Philip the Good of Burgundy, Alfonso was also one of the princes best positioned to help launch a successful campaign against Mehmed II. Alfonso took the vow to crusade in Naples in

1455 and supported the Christian warlord Skanderbeg, but in the end he remained distant from the campaign that ended at Belgrade.

Bayezid, the "Thunderbolt," Ottoman sultan. Renowned for his military leadership, Bayezid rose to prominence after the battle of Kosovo in 1389. He married the youngest daughter of the deceased prince Lazar Hrebeljanović of Serbia and worked to consolidate Ottoman rule in both Rumelia and Anatolia. He defeated the crusade led by King Sigismund of Hungary at Nicopolis in 1396 but was then himself defeated by Timur at Ankara in 1402 and died in captivity shortly afterward.

Callixtus III, pope. Formerly Alfonso de Borja. A Catalan from Xátiva in Valencia, Alfonso was an aging, compromise candidate for pope upon his election in March 1455. But as Callixtus III he took to the crusading cause with surprising dedication and energy. Among his many efforts was the influential call to prayer (document 5) issued just days before the start of the siege of Belgrade.

Constantine XI, last Byzantine emperor. Defender of Constantinople against Mehmed II in 1453, he was killed in the last hours of the siege.

Frederick III, king of Germany and Holy Roman emperor. Frederick was a member of the Hapsburg dynasty and cousin to Emperor Albert V, who died in 1439. Elected king in 1440, Frederick became regent in Austria for the young Ladislaus V (Ladislaus the Posthumous), son of the deceased Albert V. Though in theory a key leader in any effort to launch a crusade against Mehmed II, Fredrick's disposition and the complex political circumstances in the Empire prevented him from engaging fully in the crusade of 1456.

George Branković, despot of Serbia. Designated heir of Stefan Lazarević by treaty in 1427, in return for his title as despot George returned the fortress of Belgrade to Hungary. With complex ties across the region – a wife, Eirene, who was of the Byzantine Kantakouzenos family; a daughter, Katarina, married to Ulrich II of Celje; a daughter, Mara, married to Murad II; and a network of lands and titles in Hungary – for three decades Branković chose his alliances carefully and played a pivotal military and diplomatic role in the events leading up to Belgrade.

John VIII, Byzantine emperor. In 1438–9, John led a diplomatic mission to Italy that eventually settled in Florence, where his delegates negotiated (among many other matters) the agreement enshrined in the decree *Laetentur coeli*. In return for Byzantine recognition of papal authority and technical agreement on other theological matters (purgatory among them), John worked with Pope Eugenius IV to secure a fleet and an army that would campaign on behalf of Byzantium.

John Hunyadi, regent for Ladislaus V and captain general of Hungary. Hunyadi rose to prominence from the 1430s, when he was drawn into the service of King Sigismund of Hungary. After a string of victories that helped put an end to his kingdom's civil war in 1440–2, Hunyadi was awarded broad territorial and military power across southern Hungary. Soon after, he was appointed captain general and led a series of important campaigns against the Turks, culminating at Belgrade. He died there after the battle on August 11, 1456.

John of Capistrano, jurist and Observant Franciscan preacher. After years of leading the reform of the Franciscan order, and after successfully working for the canonization of his mentor, Bernardino of Siena, in 1451 Capistrano was called north by Frederick III to preach in Vienna. At the end of what became a four-year preaching tour, in 1454–5 he was drawn into the service of preaching the crusade that ended at Belgrade.

Juan Carvajal, cardinal and papal legate to Hungary. Born to a distinguished noble family in Trujillo (in western Spain) and trained in church law, Carvajal rose to service in the Roman curia by the 1430s, and through the 1440s he earned a reputation as a diligent and skilled diplomat. He was a central figure amid the complex matters of diplomacy and strategy that led up to the battle for Belgrade.

Karaca Bey, Ottoman beylerbey of Rumelia. Karaca Bey was a seasoned veteran of the campaigns of both Murad II and Mehmed II, including the victory at Varna and the siege of Constantinople. As overlord of Rumelia, he was also a key commander and strategist for the siege of Belgrade. He was killed during the battle.

Konstantin Mihailović, Ottoman janissary and chronicler. A Serbian Christian who was captured at Novo Brdo in 1455, Mihailović converted to Islam and served for many years as an Ottoman janissary. He was later captured by Christians, reconverted to Christianity, and eventually recorded a compelling narrative of his experience (document 34). He may have been an eyewitness to the events of Belgrade.

Ladislaus V, king of Hungary, Croatia, and Bohemia. Son of the Hapsburg emperor Albert V and Elizabeth of Luxembourg (the daughter of Sigismund), Ladislaus was born after his father's death (and is thus often styled Ladislaus the Posthumous). Though his mother had him crowned as king of Hungary already as an infant in May 1440, his authority was repeatedly contested and he was forced to live under a series of wards and regents, including Frederick III and Ulrich II of Celje, until he claimed the throne in 1453. He then reigned only briefly, until his death in 1457.

Lazar Hrebeljanović, ruler of Moravian Serbia. As ruler of one of the most important fragments of an older Serbian empire, Prince Lazar was a key figure in this region during the early years of the Ottoman advance into southeastern Europe. He was killed at the Battle of Kosovo in 1389, as was his rival Murad II.

Mara Branković, daughter of George Branković and consort of Murad II. Mara was married to the sultan in 1435, as part of her father's wider efforts to forestall Ottoman encroachment into Serbia. Upon Murad's death in 1451, Mara returned to Serbia, but after her father's death, she ultimately made her way back to the circles of Mehmed II. He granted her an estate in eastern Macedonia, and she held court there under his patronage and protection until her death in 1487.

Mehmed II, Ottoman sultan. Son of Murad II, Mehmed "the Conqueror" first ascended to the throne at age twelve upon the abdication of his father in 1444. He ruled briefly before his father reclaimed the title of sultan, and then definitively from 1451. Two years later he captured Constantinople, the first in a series of conquests that expanded Ottoman rule from the Adriatic to the Black Sea. Interwoven with and reinforcing these conquests were Mehmed's commitments to strengthening and refining the administration of the Ottoman court and to his role as a patron of arts and culture in the best tradition of the Roman emperors, to which he saw himself as heir.

Michael Szilágyi, Hungarian nobleman from Horogszeg in Temes county, ban of Macsó and Slavonia. Michael was the brother of John Hunyadi's wife, Elizabeth. As castellan of Belgrade, along with Hunyadi and Capistrano, he was one of the most important leaders of the defense of the city during the Ottoman siege. In November of 1456, amid negotiations with Count Ulrich II of Celje, Szilágyi and his henchmen murdered the count. Szilágyi was then ban of Macsó (1457–8) and governor of Hungary (1458) before his death in 1461.

Murad II, Ottoman sultan. Murad's long reign (from 1421) saw the consolidation of Ottoman rule in the Balkans, signaled by diplomatic alliances and institutional consolidation as well as important campaigns, including Thessalonica (1430), Varna (1444), and Kosovo (1448). Murad abdicated unexpectedly in 1444 but reclaimed the title of sultan in 1446 and ruled once more until his death in 1451.

Nicholas V, Tomasso Parentucelli, elected pope in March 1447. Parentucelli rose to prominence in Bologna, where he was made bishop in 1444. As Pope Nicholas V, he became famous for his many efforts at cultural patronage in Rome – among them the formation of what would become the Vatican Library. Nicholas also issued decrees that became foundational for the later history of Atlantic slavery, as well as the first call to crusade after Mehmed II's capture of Constantinople.

Nicholas of Ilok, Croatian-Hungarian nobleman. Ban of Macsó, Croatia, and Slavonia, voivode of Transylvania. As one of the wealthiest magnates in Hungary and Croatia, Nicholas rose to prominence alongside Hunyadi during the civil wars and other campaigns of the 1440s and played a prominent role in the affairs surrounding Belgrade. John of Capistrano died in Ilok in October 1456 and was buried there, and the friar's shrine and purported miracles brought Nicholas and his city great prestige in the years thereafter.

Philip the Good, Duke of Burgundy. One of the most powerful princes in fifteenth-century Western Europe, Philip famously hosted the "Feast of the Pheasant" in February 1454, where he vowed to take up the cross against the Turks. Thereafter he often put forth sincere efforts to honor that vow, starting with his personal attendance at the Diet of Regensburg in May 1454. But the complexities of his political circumstances ultimately placed strong limits on his crusading aspirations.

Sigismund, king of Hungary and Croatia (1387), king of Germany (1411), Bohemia (1419), and Holy Roman emperor (1433). Son of Charles IV and last member of the Luxembourg dynasty, Sigismund led a crusade against the Ottomans that ended in defeat at Nicopolis in 1396. Thereafter he worked to reform Hungary's military and financial affairs and played a central role in the affairs of the Council of Constance, including the execution of Jan Hus.

Stefan Lazarević, despot of Serbia and ban of Macsó. Son of Prince Lazar Hrebeljanović of Serbia, Stefan was a key Ottoman vassal until Bayezid's defeat at Ankara. Thereafter he cultivated ties with both Constantinople and Hungary. The Byzantines recognized him as despot in 1402, and in 1403 Sigismund recognized him as both ban of Macsó and a member of the Order of the Dragon. For two decades and more thereafter, until his death in 1427, Stefan became the patron of a remarkable architectural and cultural flowering in Belgrade.

Timur, or "Tamerlane," central Asian warlord. An ambitious and energetic ruler who styled himself as successor to the legacy of Genghis Khan, Timur launched a series of campaigns across his far-western frontiers, into Syria and Anatolia. Among these was a campaign that ended in the defeat and capture of the Ottoman sultan Bayezid in 1402. A decade of feud and instability in the Ottoman world followed.

Ulrich II, Count of Celje. Ruler of an important network of territories along the Sava River (in modern Slovenia), Ulrich II claimed authority as regent for Ladislaus V and thus a role in the affairs of Hungary. He was also son-in-law to George Branković. As such, he was a key figure in the military and diplomatic affairs surrounding Belgrade. He was also a fierce rival to John Hunyadi, whose son Ladislaus murdered Ulrich II in Belgrade in November 1456.

General Timeline

Warfare and Crusade in Central and Southeastern Europe	Western Europe
	1347–50 The Black Death
1354 Ottoman capture of Gallipoli	
1355 Death of Serbian prince Stefan Dušan	
c. 1361 Ottoman capture of Adrianople (Edirne)	
1371 Ottoman victory over Serbians at the Battle of the Maritsa	
	1374 Death of Francesco Petrarca (Petrarch), humanist author and poet
c. 1375 Rise of Prince Lazar Hrebeljanović and Moravian Serbia	
1376 Ottomans establish suzerainty over Bulgaria; raids begin into Serbia	

General Timeline

1378 Outbreak of papal schism

1381 Peasant rebellion in England

1383 First translations of Wycliffe Bible

1389 Battle of Kosovo; accession of Bayezid I; Lazar of Serbia executed

1395 Bayezid battles Mircea of Wallachia at Rovine

1396 Bayezid defeats Western crusaders at Nicopolis; siege of Constantinople

1400 Death of Geoffrey Chaucer

1402 Timur defeats Bayezid at Ankara; Stefan Lazarević granted title of despot

1406 Death of Coluccio Salutati, humanist chancellor of Florence

1413 End of Ottoman interregnum and civil war; rise of Mehmed I

1414–18 Council of Constance

1415 Battle of Agincourt

1418 Election of Otto Colonna, Pope Martin V (d. 1431)

1420–34 Hussite Wars

1421 Death of Mehmed I; accession of Murad II

1422 Murad II besieges Constantinople

1424 Peace treaty between Byzantines and Murad II

c. 1425 Flowering of Serbian culture at Belgrade under Stefan Lazarević

c. 1425 Bernardino of Siena begins preaching career

1427 Under the agreement of Tati, Stefan Lazarević designates George Branković his successor and returns Belgrade and Golubac to Hungary

1428 Masaccio, *Holy Trinity*

1430 Murad II takes Thessalonica; Despot George Branković establishes exiled court at Smederevo

1431 Election of Gabriele Condulmer, Pope Eugenius IV (d. 1447); execution of Joan of Arc

1431–49 Council of Basel-Ferrara-Florence

1436 Completion of Brunelleschi's dome on the cathedral of Florence

1439 Death of King Albert V and Hungarian succession crisis; Ottoman capture of Smederevo; George Branković exiled to Hungary

1439 Decree of Union (*Laetentur coeli*) proclaimed at Florence

General Timeline

1440 Murad II launches first Ottoman siege of Belgrade

1441–2 Hungarian civil war and rise of John Hunyadi

1443–4 "Long campaign" and Crusade of Varna

1440 Lorenzo Valla, *Donation of Constantine*

1444 Death of Bernardino of Siena, OFM

1447 Election of Tommaso Parentucelli, Pope Nicholas V (d. 1455)

1448 Death of Byzantine emperor John VIII; Second Battle of Kosovo

1450 Jubilee in Rome

1451–6 John Hunyadi regent and captain general of Hungary

1451–4 Preaching tour of John of Capistrano across northern Europe

1452 Construction of Rumeli Hisarı

1452 Frederick III crowned Holy Roman emperor

1453 Mehmed II captures Constantinople

1454 Gutenberg's earliest printings in Mainz

Timeline of the Crusade of 1456

1453 *September 30:* Pope Nicholas V, *Etsi ecclesia Christi*

1454 *February:* The "Feast of the Pheasant" at the court of Duke Philip the Good of Burgundy

April: Diet of Regensburg and Peace of Lodi

October: Diet of Frankfurt; Aeneas Silvius Piccolomini, *Constantinopolitana clades*

1455 *February:* Diet of Wiener Neustadt

March 24: Death of Nicholas V

April 8: Election of Alfonso de Borja as Pope Callixtus III

May: Pope Callixtus III, *Ad summum pontificates apicem* (May 15). The bull reissues and revises Nicholas V's call to crusade in *Etsi ecclesia Christi*.

June–July: Assembly at Győr; beginning of John of Capistrano's preaching tour

August: Beginning of efforts of Juan Carvajal as papal legate in Hungary

November: King Alfonso of Aragon, Naples, and Sicily takes the cross

1456

December: Cardinal Ludovico Scarampo named legate and captain of the papal fleet sponsored by Callixtus III

February: Diet in Buda opens on February 6; Juan Carvajal publishes bull of crusading and commissions Capistrano to preach (February 14)

June 29: Callixtus III issues *Cum his superioribus*, calling on all Christians to pray for the campaign that will end at Belgrade

July 2: John of Capistrano and first wave of crusaders arrive at Belgrade; Ottoman siege and bombardment begins soon after

July 14: Hunyadi's flotilla approaches Belgrade via the Danube; naval battle with Ottoman fleet ends in victory for Hunyadi

July 21–3: Final assault on Belgrade and retreat of Mehmed II

July–August: News of the events of Belgrade makes its way to Budapest, Vienna, and beyond

August 6: News of the events of Belgrade reaches Rome; Scarampo's fleet departs from Naples for the Aegean

August 11: Death of John Hunyadi; his son Ladislaus Hunyadi becomes his heir

October 23: Death of John of Capistrano

November: Rivalry between Ladislaus Hunyadi and Ulrich II, Count of Celje, ends in the assassination of the Count at Belgrade. Ladislaus Hunyadi is executed by King Ladislaus V of Hungary.

1457

August 6: Callixtus III, *Inter divinae dispensationis* commemorates the first anniversary of the arrival of news of Belgrade in Rome. The bull links the feast of the Transfiguration to the victory of a Triune God.

Maps

Map 1. Central and Southeastern Europe, c. 1450

Source: Craig Remington, Amber Chan, Alex Fries, and the Cartographic Research Laboratory of the University of Alabama.

Map 2. The City and Fortress of Belgrade, c. 1450

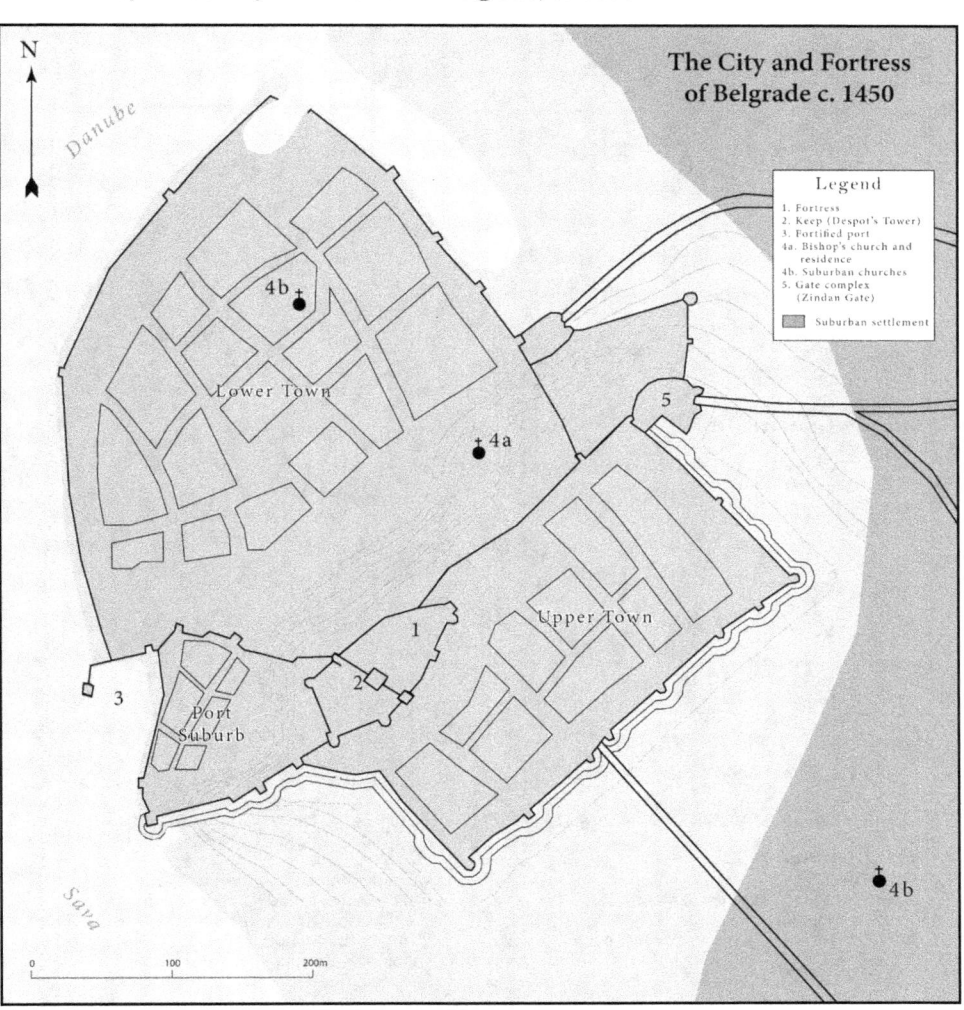

Source: Craig Remington, Amber Chan, Alex Fries, and the Cartographic Research Laboratory of the University of Alabama. After Marko Popovic, *Beogradska Tvrdjava* (Belgrade, 2006), 120 and 145.

Map 3. The Siege and Relief of Belgrade, 1456

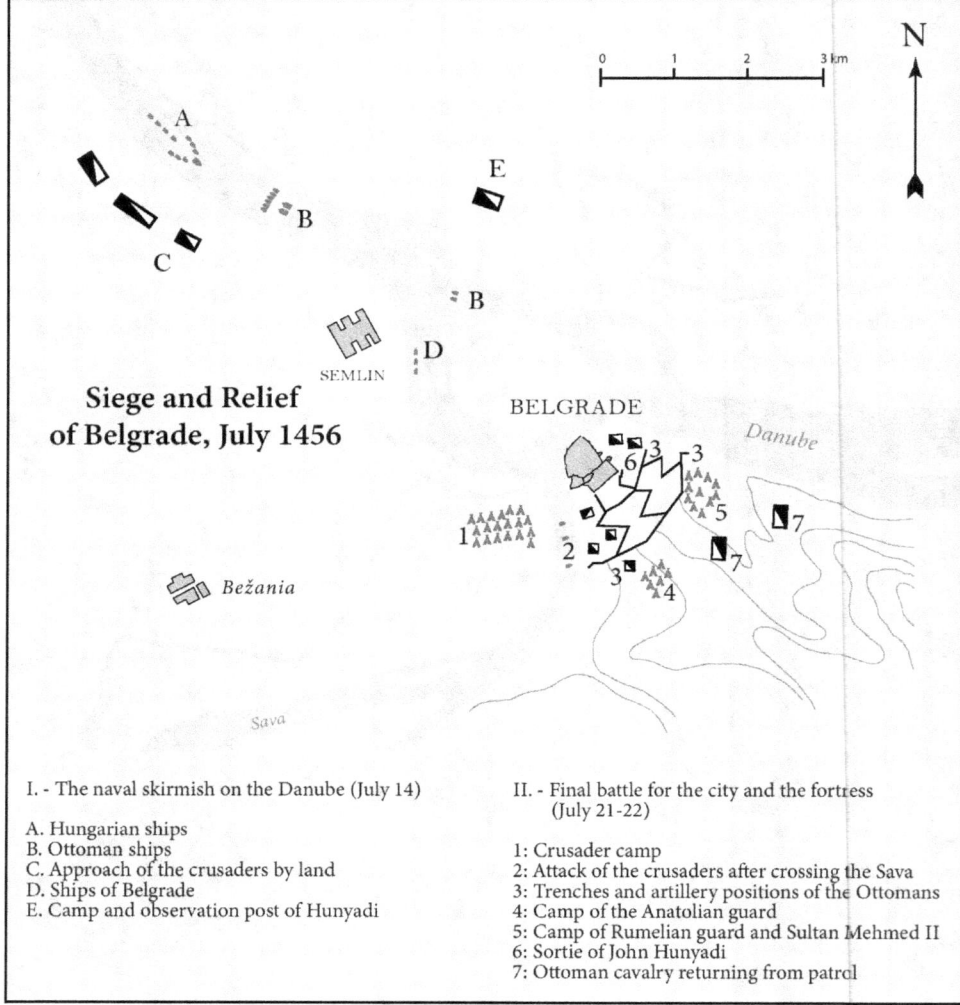

I. - The naval skirmish on the Danube (July 14)

A. Hungarian ships
B. Ottoman ships
C. Approach of the crusaders by land
D. Ships of Belgrade
E. Camp and observation post of Hunyadi

II. - Final battle for the city and the fortress (July 21-22)

1: Crusader camp
2: Attack of the crusaders after crossing the Sava
3: Trenches and artillery positions of the Ottomans
4: Camp of the Anatolian guard
5: Camp of Rumelian guard and Sultan Mehmed II
6: Sortie of John Hunyadi
7: Ottoman cavalry returning from patrol

Source: Craig Remington, Amber Chan, Alex Fries, and the Cartographic Research Laboratory of the University of Alabama. After Leopold Kupelwieser, *Die Kämpfe Ungarns mit den Osmanen bis zur Schlacht bei Mohács, 1526* (Vienna, 1899), 131, and Johannes Hofer, *Johannes Kapistran: Ein Leben in Kampf um die Reform der Kirche*, 2nd ed. (Heidelberg: F.H. Kerle, 1964–5), 379.

Index

Page numbers in *italics* indicate illustrations.

Abraham (biblical figure), 206
Acacius (patriarch of Constantinople), 45
Achior (biblical figures), 75
Acre, fall of (1291), 16
Ad summum pontificates apicem (papal decree, 1455), 76n18
Adrianople. *See* Edirne
Adriatic Sea, 109
akinji, 5, 266n15
Albania, 9, 64
Albert II of Hapsburg, 10
Albrecht Achilles, Margrave of Brandenburg, 22, 50n13
Aleppo, 6
Alexander VI (pope), 144n2
Alexander the Great, 240
Alexander of Ragusa, 159, 177, 191
Alexandria, See of, 49
Alfonso V the Magnanimous (king of Aragon, Sicily, and Naples), 269–70
    post-Belgrade crusading plans of, 129
    preparations for crusade and, 53, 55, 59, 62, 64
    Soler, Juan, papal ambassador to Alfonso, letter of Callixtus III to (late Aug., 1456, Rome), 122–5
Ali Mihaloglu (Turkish leader), 223
Amalek (biblical figure) and Amalekites, 74, 202, 206
Ambrose of Aquila, 99, 104, 159, 177, 202
Ambrose of Milan, 79, 181n40, 191
Ammonites, 75
Anatolia, 4, 5
Anatolian cavalry/guard/army, 6, 13, 14, 25, 257–8
Andronicus III (Byzantine emperor), 3
Ankara, 6
Anthony of Padua, 165n26, 169, 198n64
Antioch, See of, 49
Antiochus IV Epiphanes (Seleucid ruler), 75

arquebuses, 98, 102, 106, 156, 164, 166, 173, 192, 195, 199, 203, 204, 207, 208
Âşıkpaşazade, *Memories and Chronicles of the House of Osman* (c. 1484), 235–7
Assumption, feast of (Aug. 5), 111
astronomy/astrology
  anonymous to Henry of Echenfelt on pestilential alignments (Nov.–Dec. 1456), 141
  Halley's Comet, appearance of (1456), 134, 137, 138–9, 237
  John Thurocz on celestial alignments for specific dates, 240, 248
Atiya, Aziz, 17
Augustine of Hippo, feast of (Aug. 28), 126, 128, 130
Augustinian Hermits, 173n34
azaps, 6, 25, 226, 233

Bacchides, 75
Baden, 116, 127, 129
Baghdad, 6
Balduff, Lord Michael, 115, 117
Balkans
  historiography of, 19–20
  See also specific states
Baloup, Daniel, 18
baptisms. *See* conversions
Barak (biblical figure), 206
Basel, Council of (1431–49), 47, 217
Bayezid I (sultan), 4–6, 7, 9, 270
Bayezid II (sultan), 249, 256
Belgrade, town and fortress of
  citadel, 25, 87, 96, 98, 100, 121, 127, 138, 180, 181, 184, 185, 211, 232
  damage done to city in siege, 128
  drawbridge, 184, 185, 186, 265n11
  fortification and development of, 7–8
  John of Tagliacozzo's description of, 184–6
  Kritoboulos's description of, 229
  Lower Town, 8, 162n21, 164n23, 283
  map of city and fortress of (c. 1450), *283*
  names for, 7, 96n2
  Nebojša or "Do Not Fear" tower, 184
  as new Jerusalem, 8
  siege of (1440), 9–10
  siege of (1456) (*see* Crusade of 1456 / siege of Belgrade)
  as Singidunum (Roman camp), 7, 8
  Upper Town, 8, 25, 122n2, 164n23, 182n43, *283*
Benediktbeuern, abbey of, Bavaria, 68
Bernard of Kraiburg (later bishop of Chiemsee), letters of, 125–30
  to Henry Rüger of Pegnitz (Aug. 26, 1456, Vienna), 126, 128–30
  to Sigismund I of Volkersdorf, archbishop of Salzburg (Aug. 25, 1456, Vienna), 125–30
Bernardino of Siena, 23, 101, 148, 154, 169, 193, 227–8
Beszterce (modern Bistriţa), 12
beylerbeys, defined, 5
biblical citations
  Acts 14:21, 40n5
  2 Chronicles
    20:15–17, 74n10
    20:21–2, 74n11
    32:20–1, 74n9
  1 Corinthians 15:58, 73n2
  2 Corinthians 6:2, 106n6
  Ecclesiasticus 7:36, 50n15

Exodus 17, 206n81
Ezekiel 37:1, 155n12
Genesis 14, 70n4, 206n80
Isaiah
  9:6, 43n12
  40:31, 70n5
  53:9, 82n2
  59:1, 76n15
James 1:3–4, 78n24
Joel 2:13, 76n16
John
  10:11, 82n3
  14:6, 70n5
  16:33, 40n2
Joshua
  6:1–27, 90n1
  10:11, 206n82
Judges
  4:14–15, 206n83
  6:12–14, 190n53
  6:16, 190n54
  7, 105n2
  7:7, 206n84
Judith
  5:24–5, 75n14
  9:16, 75n12
2 Kings 18–19, 41n7
Lamentations
  1:12, 82n1
  3:12, 199n68
Luke
  12:7, 162n20
  12:32, 162n20
  22:32, 42n9
  22:54–7, 102n14
1 Maccabees
  3–4, 206
  3:17–22, 196n62
  3:19, 192n56
  9, 75n13
2 Maccabees 8, 59n1
Mark
  4:30–2, 125n3
  11:23, 125n3

Matthew
  3:2, 79n25
  16:18, 42n8
  16:24, 43n12, 70n4
  25:34, 136n7
  28:20, 40n1
Numbers 17, 69n3
1 Peter 4:8, 198
Philippians
  1:18, 132n4
  2:9, 91n3
  2:10, 190n52
Proverbs 10:7, 187n51
Psalms
  22:11, 153n8
  27:91, 181n40
  32 (33):16, 70n5
  32 (33):18–19, 70n6
  36 (37):32, 187n51
  54 (55):5, 200n70
  60:4, 70n3
  67 (68), 90n2
  90 (91):7, 201n72
  111 (112):7, 187n51
  117 (118):24, 204n76
  120 (121):1, 244n8
  123:8, 69n1
  126 (127):1, 40n3
  135 (136):17, 220n5
  138 (139):14, 202n24
  146 (147):5, 206n79
Revelation, 41
Romans
  10:17, 78n23
  13:11, 67n1
1 Samuel
  7:8, 74n7
  7:10, 74n8, 206n85
  15:22, 50n14
Sirach 10:2, 171n30
Tobit 5 ff., 70n6
Bisaha, Nancy, 18
Blachernae Palace, Constantinople, 13, 14

Black Sea, 11, 20, 48n8
Blasius (Franciscan), 203
Boğazkesen (Rumeli Hisar), 12–13, 249
Bohemond I of Antioch, 28
Bohor, 257
bombards
  in fall of Constantinople (1453), 13, 239
  in siege of Belgrade (1456), 88, 97–8, 157, 177
Borja, Alfonso de. *See* Callixtus III
Bosnia/Bosnians, 3, 6, 89, 90, 98, 157, 162, 170, 208n89, 210, 223, 265
Bosporus, 12, 13, 48
Bratislava (formerly Pressburg), 120n4, 126–7, 128
Buda, 11, 23, 62, 64, 65, 109, 110, 112, 114n1, 117, 129, 140n3, 151–2, 158, 161, 177, 212, 224, 238, 239, 240
Bulgarians, Ottoman Turks versus, 3, 4
Bull, Marcus, 27
Bulla Turcorum or *Türkenbulle* (Callixtus III, 1456), 80, *81*, 129
Burchard, John, *Liber Notarum* (Aug. 9, 1500), 144–5
Bursa, 2, 5
Byzantine empire
  fall of Constantinople to Mehmed II (1453), 12–14, 18, 39, 41, 47–50, 72, 228, 238–9, 249, 260
  historical framework, 3–6, 9
  post-Belgrade plans to re-take Constantinople, 126, 129
  siege of Constantinople by Bayezid (1394), 4
  siege of Constantinople by Murad II (1422), 9
  Turkish cannon forged from spoils of, 236

Callixtus III (pope; formerly Alfonso de Borja), 270
  Ad summum pontificates apicem (1455), 76n18
  biases and ulterior motives of, 27
  Bulla Turcorum or *Türkenbulle* (1456), 80, *81*, 129
  calls to crusade by, 22, 23, 53, 76, 82–6
  Cum his superioribus (papal bull, 1456), 23, 72–80, 129, 144
  election of, 22, 54
  general calls to prayer issued by, 71–80, 122–4, 142
  Halley's Comet, supposed excommunication of, 134n1
  Inter divinae dispensationis (Aug. 6, 1457), 142–3
  liturgical commemorations instigated by, 27, 129, 142–3, 145
  in liturgy for taking the Cross, 71–2
  in memoirs and chronicles, 224, 257
  Omnipotentis dei misericordia (1457/1455–60), 82–6
  peace brokered between Frederick III and Ladislaus V by, 131
  on prayer, role and importance of, in final battle of Belgrade, 122–4
Callixtus III (pope; formerly Alfonso de Borja), correspondence
  letters from
    John of Capistrano (June 21, 1455, Győr), 53–7
    John of Capistrano (Sept. 17, 1455, Csanád), 57–8
    John of Capistrano (July 22, 1456, Belgrade), 87–8
    John of Capistrano (July 23, 1456, Slankamen), 88–91, 207–8
    John of Capistrano (Aug. 17, 1456, Slankamen), 104–7, 210

Šibenik, ambassador of bishop of (July 26, 1456, Buda), 109–12
letters to
  Francesco Sforza (Aug. 23, 1456, Rome), 122–5
  Juan Soler (late Aug., 1456, Rome), 130–3
cannons. *See* firearms
Capistrano. *See* John of Capistrano
Cappel, Hartung von, 50n13
Capranica, Domenico, bishop of Fermo, 54
Carthusians, 78n21, 137
Carvajal, Cardinal Juan, 23, 271
  in eyewitness accounts, 91, 97, 105, 106
  in John of Tagliacozzo's *Story* (1460), 151, 161, 177, 212
  letter from John of Capistrano (Feb. 19, 1456, Pest), 60–2
  letters to
    John of Capistrano (Jan. 16, 1456, Vienna), 58–60
    John of Capistrano (May 14, 1456, Buda), 62–4
    John of Capistrano (May 25, 1456, Buda), 64–5
    John of Capistrano (June 5, 1456, Buda), 65
    Francesco Sforza (July 29, 1456, Ilok), 112–13
  in news and propaganda, 111, 131
Castiglione, Cardinal Giovanni, bishop of Pavia, 129
Catholic Church. *See* Church
Celano, Lionello Accrocciamuro and Covella da, Count and Countess of Celano, 103–4
Černomen, 3
Chair of Peter, feast of (February 22), 216n99
Chalkokondyles, Laonikos (Nikolaos), *The Histories* (c. 1464), 28, 222–8

Chiemsee, Bavaria, 125
Christianity. *See* Church
Chronicle of Austria (Ebendorfer, c. 1463), 28, 217–22
Chronicle of the Hungarians (Thurocz, c. 1488), 28, 237–49
chronicles. *See* memoirs and chronicles
Church
  Callixtus III on importance of Catholic resistance to Turks, 132–3
  Christian unity/discord, 172, 266
  fall of Constantinople and, 47–9
  financing of crusade by, 43–5
  heretics and heresy, 61, 103, 133, 150, 172, 228
  incarnational theology of, 82
  indulgences offered by, 22, 23, 28, 29, 39, 43, 77, 79, 80, 82–4, 142, 144
  reconciliation attempt between Orthodox and Roman Catholics, 11
  relics, 8, 23, 72, 118, 150, 184, 239
  schismatics, 55n5, 103, 133, 151, 160, 164, 172, 214
Church Councils. *See* Councils
Cicero
  De officiis, 51nn19–20
  Pro lege Manilia, 50nn16–18
class. *See* social class
classicizing language, use of, 18, 28, 218n1, 219n4, 228, 247
condottieri, 7
Constance, Council of (1414–18), 6
Constantine I the Great (Roman emperor), 8
Constantine XI (Byzantine emperor), 13, 62, 270
Constantine the Philosopher, 8
Constantinople. *See* Byzantine empire; *specific buildings and locations*

Constantinopolitana clades
  (Piccolomini, 1454), 22,
  46–51
contra paganos (against the pagans)
  Mass for, 78
  traditional crusader prayer,
    76–7, 176
conversions
  baptism/decapitation offered to
    captive Turks, 166–7
  of daughter of schismatic, 160
  of Konstantin Mihailović, 269
  of "noble boy of Bosnia," 208, 209
Corpus iuris civilis, 106n5
Council of Basel (1431–49), 47, 217
  Council of Constance
    (1414–18), 6
Croesus (Lydian ruler), 247
Crusade of 1456 / siege of Belgrade,
  1–29
  attack on city (July 22), 26, 87–94,
    100–3, 114–15, 116–17, 134–
    5, 181–8, 225–8, 230–1, 237,
    244–6, 253, 267
  biographies of persons involved
    in, 269–74
  bombardment of walls, 25, 88, 92,
    94, 97–100, 161–2, 175–8, 218,
    224–5, 229–30, 241, 243, 267
  Christian discord/unity and,
    172, 266
  clerics and religious, involvement
    and role of, 98–9, 103, 159,
    173, 183, 195, 198
  combat events, 25–6
  contradictions, biases, and
    ulterior motives in accounts
    of, 26, 27, 127, 128–9
  dead and wounded in, 102–3, 105,
    111, 115, 116, 122, 135, 146,
    175, 203–5, 208–11, 213–14,
    234, 252
  devotions of crusaders, 118, 162,
    170–2, 176, 180

  disbanding and departure of
    crusaders, 212–13
  encirclement of city by Ottomans,
    24–5, 97, 117n3, 142–3, 156–
    9, 223–4, 229, 240–1, 251, 266
  feigned retreat, 25–6, 93, 94, 101–
    2, 113, 117, 134–5, 192–5,
    227, 253–5, 267–8
  as fifteenth-century event, 28–9
  financing of, 43–5
  fires set along walls and moat, 186
  Halley's Comet, appearance of,
    134, 137, 138–9
  historical framework, 2–14, *275–8*
  historical interpretation of, 14–17,
    26–7
  illness and famine during and after,
    98, 99, 110, 129, 227, 259
  key events of, 24–6
  later crusades, historical interest
    in, 17–21, 28, 33n40
  map of, *284*
  mining of walls, 101, 175, 182
  moat, filling of, 14, 89, 94, 101,
    167, 182, 230, 243
  nobles, lack of involvement of,
    118, 213–16, 220, 241
  numbers of crusaders and Turks
    involved in, 102, 106, 111,
    112, 117, 118, 127, 134, 156,
    195, 213
  post-battle behavior of crusaders,
    127, 129
  post-Belgrade plans and hopes for
    additional crusades, 106, 120,
    122, 124–5, 126, 129, 130,
    136–7
  punishment of crusaders' sins
    during, 171–2
  pursuit of Turks after battle,
    restraint of, 211–12
  relief army, arrival of, 25, 99, 114,
    161, 242–3
  sources for, selection of, 21–8

spoils from, 132, 135, 166, 204–5, 220, 235
timeline, *279–80*
women at, 29, 102, 110, 158, 180–1, 183, 185, 187–8
working people as crusaders in, 118, 127, 128, 141, 173, 195–6, 220, 243
See also eyewitness accounts; firearms; memoirs and chronicles; naval battle on Danube; news and propaganda; preparations for crusade; *Story of the Victory of Belgrade*
Crusade of Varna (1443–4), 11–12, 20
Csanád, 57
Cum his superioribus (papal bull of Callixtus III, 1456), 23, 72–80, 129, 144

Dacians, 230
Damascus, 6
Damian, Iulian, 18
Dandalo, Enrico, 28
Danube River/frontier
  early Ottoman expansion and Western fortification along, 4–11
  location of Belgrade on, 152, 250
  Morava River, junction with, 66
  Sava River, junction with, 189
  See also naval battle on Danube
Dardanelles, 3, 48n9, 228
Dardanelles gun, 97n6
David (biblical king), 60, 202
De placet letters, 85
Deborah (biblical figure), 206
devşirme, 3
dhimmi system, 3
diets or conferences prior to crusade, 22, 46–7, 49–50, 61, 95, 149

distances, weights, and measures, 57, 97, 99, 115, 117, 126, 129, 157, 163, 233, 241
Dmitar Tomašić (Haydari), 262–3
dogs
  corpses eaten by, 158, 211, 221, 250
  as insulting term for Turks generally, 177, 197, 208
  Mehmed II (sultan) as "dog" or "great dog," 132, 174, 175, 177–8, 208, 260
  Muhammad referred to as, 72, 218
Dominicans (Order of Preachers), 63–4
Don River, 48n5
Dormition of Mary, Belgrade, 8
Doukas (chronicler), 13
Dragon, Hungarian order of, 6–7
Dubočica (Kislina), 261
Dubrovnik. *See* Ragusa

Ebendorfer, Thomas, *Chronicle of Austria* (c. 1463), 28, 217–22
Edirne (formerly Adrianople), 3, 5, 13, 223, 232, 250, 257, 260–1nn1–3, 262
eggs, heated, torture using, 263
Elizabeth (sister of John Hunyadi / wife of Michael Szilágy), 180
Elizabeth of Luxembourg, 10, 127n5
Etsi ecclesia Christi (formal call of Nicholas V to crusade, 1453), 21, 39–46, 76n18
Eugenius IV (pope), 11, 47
eunuchs, 263
Europe, geopolitical concept of, 48
Euxine Sea, 48
excommunications in relation to crusade, 44–5, 131, 134n1, 161

Exequatur letters, 85n6
eyewitness accounts, 23–4, 87–107
　complex origins of / motives behind, 2, 26, 27
　of Hunyadi, 24, 91–5
　of John of Capistrano, 24, 87–91, 104–7
　of John of Tagliacozzo, 24, 95–104
　Konstantin Mihailović's possible presence at siege of Belgrade, 266n13
Ezekiel (biblical prophet), 75–6

famine, during and after siege of Belgrade, 99, 110, 129
Farcas (follower of John of Capistrano), 168
Feast of the Pheasant (1454), 21
feigned retreat
　in Crusade of 1456 / siege of Belgrade, 25–6, 93, 94, 101–2, 113, 117, 134–5, 192–5, 227, 253–5, 267–8
　as tactic, 12
Felix III (pope), 45
Ferrara, court of, 18
Filomarinus (captain of Aragonese fleet), 64
financing of crusade, 43–5
firearms
　arquebuses *(scopettae)*, 98, 102, 106, 156, 164, 166, 173, 192, 195, 199, 203, 204, 207, 208
　Belgrade, description of town and fortress of, 184–6
　Dardanelles gun, 97n6
　eyewitness accounts of, 88, 92, 94, 97–100, 106
　in fall of Constantinople to Mehmed II (1453), 13
　handguns, 6, 156, 164, 165, 178, 182, 192, 204

　in John of Tagliacozzo's *Story* (1460), 115n5, 156–7, 161–2, 164, 166, 173, 178, 182, 192–4, 199, 204
　key events in Crusade of 1456 / siege of Belgrade and, 25
　in memoirs and chronicles, 218–19, 225–6, 229–30, 233, 234, 235, 236, 241, 245, 258, 267
　in news and propaganda, 115, 122, 127
　Ottoman use of, 5–6
　pixides, 106n4, 156n15
　Skopje, cannons cast in, 251, 256, 257
　springalds *(spingardas)*, 156, 166, 173, 178, 204
fires
　lighting, in camps, 174
　set along walls and moat, during siege, 186
First Crusade (1095), 16
Firuz Bey, 223, 261n3
Florence/Florentines, 7, 11, 46
Francis (Hungarian Franciscan accompanying John of Capistrano), 159, 177
Francis of Assisi, 169
Franciscans, 22, 24, 29, 54n3, 57, 58, 95, 106n5, 133, 147–8, 165n26, 173, 193n58
Frankfurt, diet of (1454), 22, 46–7, 61, 95, 149
Frederick I the Victorious (Count Palatine), 112n1
Frederick III (Holy Roman Emperor), 10, 12, 22–3, 47, 49–50, 129, 131, 217, 269, 270

Gaddis, John, 14, 15
Gallipoli, Battle of (1354), 48n4
Gallopoli peninsula, 3
Galvan (knight), 264

Gaposchkin, Cecilia, 77n19
Garai, Ladislaus, Palatine of
  Hungary, letters to
  from city of Ragusa (June 11,
    1455), 53
  from Hunyadi (July 24, 1456,
    Belgrade), 91–3, 218n2
Gemistos, George, 222
Genoa/Genoese, 13, 14, 232
George (Hungarian Franciscan
  accompanying John of
  Capistrano), 159
George, provost of Pozsony, 120
George Branković (despot of
  Serbia), 8, 9, 12, 54, 57, 105,
  210, 256–7, 260–6, 270
George of Rascia, 247
German language, 80, 114, 126,
  130n9, 133
German mile, 129
Gibraltar, 48n6
Gideon (biblical figure), 105, 190
Giustiniani, Giovanni, 13, 14
Glassberger, Nicholas, 133
Goffman, Daniel, 19
Golden Horn, 13
Goldener, John, letters by, 113–18
  letter-within-a-letter, 113–15
  to Franz Schlick (Aug. 2, 1456,
    Vienna), 114–16
  to Matthew Schlick (Aug. 3, 1456,
    Vienna), 116–18
Gorgias (biblical figure), 59
Greek Church. *See* Church
Gregory I the Great (pope),
  Epistolae, 76
Gutenberg, Johannes, and
  Gutenberg type, 29, 80
Győr, assembly at, 53–7
Gyulafehérvár (Alba Julia), 248

Hagia Sophia, Constantinople, 14, 21
Hainburg, 113

Halley's Comet, 1456 appearance of,
  134, 137, 138–9, 237
handguns, 6, 156, 164, 165, 178,
  182, 192, 204
Hankins, James, 18, 34n47
Harris, Jonathan, 19
Hasan Ağa (lord of the janissaries),
  226, 267n17
Haydari (Dmitar Tomašić), 262–3
Hellespont, 48
Henry of Eckenfelt, anonymous
  letter to (Nov.–Dec. 1456),
  137–41
Henry of Pappenheim, 50n13
Herculean Sea, 48
Herczég, Raphael, archbishop of
  Kalocsa, 161, 221
heretics and heresy, 61, 103, 133,
  150, 172, 228
hermits, participating in Crusade of
  1456, 78n21, 173n34
Herodotus, 247n15
Hezekiah (biblical king), 74
Hinderbach, Hans, 130
Histories, The (Chalkokondyles,
  c. 1464), 28, 222–8
History of Mehmed the Conqueror
  (Kritoboulos/Kritopoulos,
  c. 1467), 28, 228–32
History of the Conqueror (Tursun Beg,
  c. 1488), 249–55
Hizir, prefect of Amaseia, 223
Hollós, 66, 67
Holofernes (biblical figure), 74, 75
Holy Name of Jesus, populist
  piety of, 29, 132, 143, 148,
  149, 153, 156, 164, 165, 170,
  171, 172, 174, 180, 181, 183,
  188, 189, 190, 192, 193, 195,
  197, 198, 199, 201, 204, 205,
  211, 214, 215, 234
Homer, 21
Hospitalers, 9

Houseley, Norman, 17–18
  Crusading and the Ottoman Threat, 17
  Crusading in the Fifteenth Century, 34n43
  The Later Crusades, 17
  Religious Warfare in Europe, 17
huffnitzbuchssen, 115n5
Hunedoara, 10
Hungarian mile, 241
Hungary/Hungarians
  Balkan historiography and, 19–20
  Belgrade, fortification and development of, 7–9
  civil war (1440–2), 10–11
  earlier conflicts with Ottomans, 6–12
  John of Capistrano, preaching tour of, 23
  Nicopolis (now Pleven, Bulgaria), siege of (1396), 4, 6, 7
  Order of the Dragon, 6–7
  truce of 1451 with Ottomans, 12
  See also Crusade of 1456 / siege of Belgrade
Hunyadi, John, 271
  background and early career, 10–11
  baptism/decapitation of Turks by, 166–7
  death of, 107, 126, 128, 136, 140, 213, 221–2, 227, 237, 246–8, 255, 259
  despair of, John of Tagliacozzo on, 178–9, 183, 185
  eyewitness accounts by, 24, 91–5
  in eyewitness accounts of others, 87, 88, 91, 96, 98–101
  George Branković, ransom of, 263–6
  John of Capistrano and, 23, 247
  key events in Crusade of 1456 / siege of Belgrade and, 25
  in memoirs and chronicles, 219, 221, 224, 225, 230, 231, 234, 236, 241–4, 246–8, 250–3, 255, 257–9, 260n1, 263–6
  in news and propanganda, 111, 113–16, 121, 122, 127, 129, 132, 135–6, 143
  physical description of, 248
  preparations for crusade and, 53, 55–6, 59, 62–5, 67
  pursuit of Turks after battle, restraint of, 212
  as regent of Ladislaus V, 12
  in Varna Crusade, 11–12
  vision of, 135–6
  See also Story of the Victory of Belgrade
Hunyadi, John, correspondence
  letter from city of Ragusa (June 11, 1455), 51–3
  letters to
    Denis Szécsi and Ladislaus Garai (July 24, 1456, Belgrade), 91–3, 218n2
    Ladislaus V (July 24, 1456, Belgrade), 93–5, 115, 116
    Francis Oddi (June 18, 1456, Hollós), 65–6
Hunyadi, Ladislaus/Laszlo, 140n3, 248, 265
Hus, Jan, and Hussites, 61n1, 133, 150

illness during siege of Belgrade, 98, 99, 227, 259
Ilok (Ujlak), 112, 249
Imber, Colin, 19
impalements, 261
indulgences, 22, 23, 28, 29, 39, 43, 77, 79, 80, 82–4, 142, 144
Inter divinae dispensationis (papal decree, Aug. 6, 1457), 142–3
interpreters used by John of Capistrano, 23, 177, 192, 198, 202–3, 222n7
Iorga, Nicolai, 17, 34n43
Irina (Jerina; wife of George Branković), 264

İshak Paşa, 243, 244n7, 258
Islam. *See* Ottoman Turks; Qur'an citations
Ismail Ağa (Smagilaga), 267
Ister River, 229, 230
Italian language, 65, 66, 95, 96n1, 97n4, 158, 184n44, 196nn60–1, 213n96, 233n1, 234n6
Italian mile, 97, 99, 157, 163, 233n2

Jahaziel, son of Zechariah, 74
James of the Marches, 24, 147, 148
janissaries
    conscripted from Novo Brdo, 52, 256n2, 259, 262
    in Crusade of 1456 / siege of Belgrade, 25, 29
    fall of Constantinople (1453) and, 13, 14
    guns used by, 6
    in John of Tagliacozzo's *Story* (1460), 158, 205, 209
    in memoirs and chronicles, 223, 225–7, 235, 237n2, 254, 256n2, 258
    origins of, 5
    in siege of Belgrade (1440), 9
    See also Konstantin Mihailović
Jänsuch, Philip, 129
Jehoshaphat (biblical king), 74
Jerina (Irina; wife of George Branković), 264
Jerome of Padua, 88, 90–1, 210, 212
Jerusalem
    post-Belgrade hopes of recovery of, 106
    See of, 49
Jews, 172
Jiskra, Jan, 128
Joan of Arc, 36n69, 222
John, brother of Matthew Talovac, 9
John V (Byzantine emperor), 3
John VIII (Byzantine emperor), 11, 271

John Hunyadi. *See* Hunyadi, John
John of Caffa, 151n6
John of Capistrano, 271
    call to crusade by, 23, 53, 151–2
    canonization efforts, 147, 148, 169n29, 177, 198n67, 249
    death of, 137, 139–40, 147, 150, 216, 248–9
    on death of John Hunyadi, 221–2
    eyewitness accounts of, 24, 87–91, 104–7
    in eyewitness accounts of others, 96–103
    historiography of, 18
    horse given to, 176
    in Ilok, 112
    interpreters used by, 23, 177, 192, 198, 222n7, 202203
    John Hunyadi and, 23, 247
    John of Tagliacozzo and, 95, 157
    journey to Belgrade, 152–4
    kerchief sent from Michael Szilágyi to, 155
    key events in Crusade of 1456 / siege of Belgrade and, 25, 26
    martyrdom associated with, 57n1, 131, 150, 152, 156, 159, 190, 199, 201, 202
    in memoirs and chronicles, 224, 227–8, 233, 234, 242, 244, 247, 248–9
    in news and propanganda, 113, 115, 117, 122, 127, 131, 143
    as participant in battle, 87, 88, 89, 90, 98–103, 131, 175–8, 189–203, 208
    preaching of, 22–3, 29, 53, 61, 150–1, 171
    preparation for Crusade of 1456 and, 22–3, 149–54
    pride attributed to, 208
    pursuit of Turks after battle, restraint of, 211–12

John of Capistrano (*cont.*)
  Story of the Victory of Belgrade (John of Tagliacozzo, 1460) as hagiographical text for, 148
  success of Christians at Belgrade attributed by John of Tagliacozzo to God and, 214–16
  See also *Story of the Victory of Belgrade*
John of Capistrano, correspondence, 53
  letters from
    Carvajal (Jan. 16, 1456, Vienna), 58–60
    Carvajal (May 14, 1456, Buda), 62–4
    Carvajal (May 25, 1456, Buda), 64–5
    Carvajal (June 5, 1456, Buda), 65
  letters to
    Callixtus III (June 21, 1455, Győr), 53–7
    Callixtus III (Sept. 17, 1455, Csanád), 57–8
    Callixtus III (July 22, 1456, Belgrade), 87–8
    Callixtus III (July 23, 1456, Slankamen), 88–91, 207–8
    Callixtus III (Aug. 17, 1456, Slankamen), 104–7, 210
    Carvajal (Feb. 19, 1456, Pest), 60–2
    Oddi (July 3, 1456, Belgrade), 66–8
  new edition of, 36n66, 54n2
John of Tagliacozzo, 95, 147–8
  eyewitness account of, 24, 95–104
  John of Capistrano and, 95, 157
  Kritoboulos compared, 228
  letter to fellow Franciscan (July 28, 1456), 95–104
  presence at final battle of Belgrade, in *Story*, 190–1, 197, 198, 200, 202

vernacular versus Latin, writing eyewitness account in, 96n1
See also *Story of the Victory of Belgrade*
John the Baptist, 79
John the Baptist, feast of (June 24), 66, 138
Joshua (biblical figure), 90, 173, 206, 209
Jubilee of 1500, 144
Judas Maccabeus (biblical figure), 59, 75, 196
Judith (biblical figure), 74
Justinian, statue of, Constantinople, 236n1
Justinianic law, 106

Kafadar, Kamal, 19
Kalocsa, 161, 221
Kanizsai, László, 244
Kantakouzenos, John, 3
Kar, Margrave of Baden, 50n13
Karaca Bey, 105n3, 135, 209n91, 225, 232, 236–7, 252, 256–7, 259, 266n15, 267, 271
Karaman, 12
Katarina (daughter of George Branković), 9
Khosrow (Persian ruler), 253
Kolchis (Trebizond), king of, 223
Konstantin Mihailović, 272
  Memoirs (c. 1490), 28, 259–68
  Novo Brdo, conscripted as janissary after Ottoman conquest of, 52, 256n2, 259, 262
  possible presence at siege of Belgrade, 266n13
Korogh, John (ban of Macsó), 95, 160n19, 172–3, 195, 204
Kosovo, battle of (1389), 3, 12
Kosovo, battle of (1444), 12
Kosovo Polje, 261n3
Kovin, 153, 154, 158, 160

Kratovo, 260n2
Kritoboulos/Kritopoulos, Michael,
  History of Mehmed the Conqueror
  (c. 1467), 28, 228–32
Kruševac, 241, 261n3
Küstendil, 260n2

Ladislaus III Jagiello (king of Poland
  and Hungary), 10, 11
Ladislaus V the Posthumous (king of
  Hungary), 10, 272
  Bernard of Kraiburg on, 127, 128
  Callixtus III on peace brokered
    between Frederick III
    and, 131
  death of, 237
  Jan Jiskra and, 127
  letters from
    city of Ragusa (June 11,
      1455), 53
    Hunyadi (July 24, 1456,
      Belgrade), 93–5, 115, 116
  letter to Francesco Sforza (Aug. 3,
    1456, Vienna), 118–20
  in memoirs and chronicles, 239–
    40, 264–5
  post-battle military requested by,
    120, 122
  preparations for Crusade and, 58,
    63, 65
  Sigismund I of Volkersdorf,
    archbishop of Salzburg,
    and, 127
  Ulrich of Celje and, 140–1
  Ulrich of Nussdorf as counselor
    to, 115n3
  as ward of Frederick III, 12
Laetentur coeli (papal decree, 1439), 11
later crusades, historical interest in,
  17–21, 28, 33n40
Lauffen, 128
Lazar Hrebeljanović of Serbia, 3, 4,
  7, 223, 229, 260, 264, 265n12,
  272

Lazar, son of George Branković, 223,
  229, 260, 264, 265n12
Leo I the Great (pope), 40
letters-within-letters, 113–15,
  123, 127
Liber Notarum (John Burchard, Aug.
  9, 1500), 144–5
Liegnitz, Battle of (1241), 48n5
liturgical commemorations of
  Belgrade
  bell rung at noon, 77n20, 129, 145
  Callixtus III instigating, 27, 129,
    142–3, 145
  Inter divinae dispensationis (Aug. 6,
    1457), 142–3
liturgical processions for Jubilee of
  1500, 144
liturgy for taking the Cross (1456,
  Germany/Austria), 68–72
liturgy of the hours, 77n20
Lodi, Peace of (1454), 22, 46
Louis IX (king of France), 28, 169

Macsó, banate of, 7–8
Mahmud Paşa, 257, 265n12
Mamluks, 6
Mantua, court of, 18
Manuel II (Byzantine emperor), 9
maps
  Belgrade, city and fortress of
    (c. 1450), *283*
  Belgrade, siege and relief of
    (1456), *284*
  central and southeastern Europe
    (c. 1450), *282*
Mara Branković, 9, 12, 272
martyrs and martyrdom
  crusades and rhetoric of, 63, 99,
    101, 103, 162, 164, 185, 211,
    262–3
  of early popes, 63
  John of Capistrano associated
    with, 57n1, 131, 150, 152,
    156, 159, 190, 199, 201, 202

Mary Magdalene, cult of, 148, 157, 201
Mary Magdalene, feast of (July 22), 88, 91, 100, 101, 103, 111, 113, 114, 116, 121, 143, 148, 178, 183, 187, 201, 203, 204, 207, 208, 218, 219
Matthias I Corvinas (king of Hungary), 28, 214, 237–8, 248, 265–6
measures, weights, and distances, 57, 97, 99, 115, 117, 126, 129, 157, 163, 233, 241
Mehmed I (sultan), 235–6
Mehmed II (sultan), 272–3
  Crusade of 1456 / siege of Belgrade, key events in, 24–6
  on death of John Hunyadi, 247
  as "dog" or "great dog," 132, 174, 175, 177–8, 208, 260
  fall of Constantinople (1453) to, 12–14, 18, 39, 41, 47–50, 72
  in John of Tagliacozzo's *Story* (1460), 158, 174, 175, 177–8, 208–9
  in memoirs and chronicles, 217–19, 222, 223–4, 228–40, 243, 246, 247, 249–63, 266–8
  in Nicholas V's *Etsi ecclesia Christi*, 39, 41–2
  Novo Brdo, conquest of (1455), 22, 52–3, 55, 256, 261–2
  Omnipotentis dei misericordia on, 82, 83
  peace arranged between George Branković and (1455), 57–8
  plot to assassinate, 262–3
  post-battle accounts of, 104, 105, 110, 127–8, 129, 208–10, 245–6
  pride attributed to, 240, 243
  Rhodes, siege of (1480), 27
  truce negotiated by (1451), 12
  truce offered by (1456), 119
  wounding of, in battle for Belgrade, 104, 127, 132, 208, 245–6
memoirs and chronicles, 24, 27–8, 217–68
  Âşıkpaşazade, *Memories and Chronicles of the House of Osman* (c. 1484), 28, 235–7
  Laonikos (Nikolaos) Chalkokondyles, *The Histories* (c. 1464), 28, 222–8
  Thomas Ebendorfer, *Chronicle of Austria* (c. 1463), 28, 217–22
  of Nicholas Glassberger, 133
  John of Tagliacozzo (1460) (*see Story of the Victory of Belgrade*)
  Konstantin Mihailović, *Memoirs* (c. 1490), 28, 259–68
  Michael Kritoboulos/Kritopoulos, *History of Mehmed the Conqueror* (c. 1467), 28, 228–32
  Oxford Anonymous Chronicle (c. 1490), 256–9
  John Thurocz, *Chronicle of the Hungarians* (c. 1488), 28, 237–49
  Tursun Beg, *History of the Conqueror* (c. 1488), 249–55
Memories and Chronicles of the House of Osman (Âşıkpaşazade, c. 1484), 235–7
Merserve, Margaret, 18
Mezid Bey, 11
Michael Angelović, 265n12
Middle Ages, concept of, 15–16, 29
Midianites, 190
Milan/Milanese court, 10, 112, 118–19, 122–3. *See also* Sforza, Francesco
mines
  of Novo Brdo, taken by Ottomans (1455), 22, 52–3, 55, 256, 261–2
  in Scythia, 105

mining of walls
  in fall of Constantinople, 239
  in siege of Belgrade, 101, 175, 182
Mistra, 222
Modestus and Vitus, feast of (June 18), 66
Mongols, 48n5
Morava River, 66, 233, 257, 262
Moravia, 23, 61, 94, 119
Moses (biblical figure), 199, 206
Muhammad (prophet), 41, 48, 73, 101, 114, 183, 218
Mulfelder, Lord John, 115
Murad I (emir), 3, 7
Murad II (sultan), 9–10, 11, 12, 222, 223, 236, 243, 252, 273
musical instruments used in battle, 169–70, 174
Mustafa (uncle of Murad II), 9

name of Jesus. *See* Holy name of Jesus
Nativity of the Virgin Mary, feast of (Sept. 8), 132
naval battle on Danube, Crusade of 1456 / siege of Belgrade, 25
  eyewitness accounts of, 89, 93, 97, 98, 99–100, 105–6
  in John of Tagliacozzo's *Story* (1460), 154–67
  in memoirs and chronicles, 223–4, 233, 240, 242, 252, 256
  news/propaganda on, 110–11, 119, 127, 128
  preparations for crusade and, 60n3, 64, 67, 73
Nebuchadnezzar (Babylonian king), 74
Negroponto, fall of, 18
news and propaganda, 24, 109–45
  correspondence
    anonymous to Henry of Echenfelt (Nov.–Dec. 1456), 137–41

Bernard of Kraiburg to Henry Rüger of Pegnitz (Aug. 26, 1456, Vienna), 126, 128–30
Bernard of Kraiburg to Sigismund I of Volkersdorf, archbishop of Salzburg (Aug. 25, 1456, Vienna), 125–30
Callixtus III to Francesco Sforza (Aug. 23, 1456, Rome), 122–5
Callixtus III to Juan Soler (late Aug., 1456, Rome), 130–3
Carvajal to Francesco Sforza (July 29, 1456, Ilok), 109–12
John Goldener, to Franz Schlick (Aug. 2, 1456, Vienna), 114–16
John Goldener, to Matthew Schlick (Aug. 3, 1456, Vienna), 116–18
Ladislaus V, to Francesco Sforza (Aug. 3, 1456, Vienna), 118–20
Nuremberg, city of, to city of Weissenburg (Aug. 13, 1456), 121–2
Šibenik, ambassador of bishop of, to Callixtus III (July 26, 1456, Buda), 109–12
historical efforts to separate fact from, 27
liturgical commemorations
  Burchard's *Liber Notarum* (Aug. 9, 1500), 144–5
  papal decree *Inter divinae dispensationis* (Aug. 6, 1457), 142–3
Pseudo-John of Capistrano, to all Christians (Aug.–Oct. 1456), in Glassberger chronicle, 133–7
Nicanor (biblical figure), 59
Nicholas of Cusa, cardinal of Saint Peter in Chains, 61, 126
Nicholas of Ilok, 53, 129, 213, 273

Nicholas V (pope; formerly Tomasso Parentucelli), 273
  death of, 22
  Etsi ecclesia Christi (formal call to crusade, 1453), 21, 39–46, 76n18, 83
  George Branković negotiating with, 260n1
  Piccolomini and, 21, 47
  Regensburg diet not attended by, 22
Nicopolis (now Pleven, Bulgaria), siege of (1396), 4, 6, 7
Ninevites, 78
Niš, fall of (1386), 3
"noble boy of Bosnia," 88, 90–1, 208–10
nobler classes, purported lack of involvement of, 118, 213–16, 220, 241
Novo Brdo, Ottoman conquest of (1455), 22, 52–3, 55, 256, 261–2
Nuremberg
  diet held in Regensburg versus, 49
  Glassberger's chronicle completed in, 133
  John of Capistrano in, 149–50
  letter to city of Weissenburg from city of (Aug. 13, 1456), 121–2

Oddi, Francis, bishop of Assisi
  death of, 213
  in John of Tagliacozzo's *Story* (1460), 161, 213
  letter from John Hunyadi (June 18, 1456, Hollós), 65–6
  letter from John of Capistrano (July 3, 1456, Belgrade), 66–8
  preparation for crusades and, 63, 64, 65
Omnipotentis dei misericordia (Callixtus III, 1457/1455–60), 82–6
Orhan (emir), 2–3

Orientalism, 16
Orthodox Church. *See* Church
Osman, dream of, 2
Ostrovica, 261n3
Ottoman Turks
  baptism/decapitation offered to captive Turks, 166–7
  Callixtus III on importance of Catholic resistance to, 132–3
  Christian scouts in camps of, 210
  early regime of, 2–6
  historical framing of siege of Belgrade by, 28
  historiographical tradition of, 235
  historiography of, 18–19
  Novo Brdo, conquest of (1455), 22, 52–3, 55, 256, 261–2
  post-battle famine amongst, 110
  post-Belgrade plans and hopes for additional crusades against, 106, 120, 122, 124–5, 126, 129, 130, 136–7
  Westen portrayals of, 2, 39, 41–2, 50, 72, 82, 83, 103
  women accompanying army, 102, 110, 158, 218
  See also Crusade of 1456 / siege of Belgrade

Paeonians, 229, 230, 231
Parentucelli, Tomasso. *See* Nicholas V
Paul (canon of Székesfehérvár), 192, 198, 199, 202, 222n7
Paul of Vezsprem, 222n7
peace / peace negotiations
  Callixtus III on peace brokered between Frederick III and Ladislaus V, 131
  between George Branković and Mehmed II (1455), 57–8, 257
  Lodi, Peace of (1454), 22, 46
  papal order for peace within Christendom, during Crusade, 46

truce negotiated by Mehmed II with Western powers (1451), 12
truce offered by Mehmed II in siege of Belgrade (1456), 119
between Venetians and Ottomans, 130
Pécs, bishop of, 54
Pedro of Coimbra, 6
Pest, 60, 61, 62
Peter (nobleman), 116, 165, 190, 198
Petrovaradin, 63, 64, 126, 129, 159–60, 212, 213
Philip, Count Palatine, 112n1
Philip the Good, Duke of Burgundy, 273–4
    Carvajal asking Callixtus III to write to, 59
    Feast of the Pheasant (1454), 21
    John of Capistrano writing to, 62
    at Regensburg diet, 22
Philistines, 74, 206
Piccolomini, Aeneas Silvius, 269
    at Basel (1431–49), 47
    Bernard of Kraiburg and, 125
    Constantinopolitana clades (1454), 22, 46–51
    on fall of Constantinople, 21, 47–50
    John of Capistrano and, 22–3, 61
    Nicholas V and, 21, 47
    as Pius II (pope), 18
    as secretary of Frederick III, 22–3, 47
Pipo Scolari, Count of Temesvár, 7
Pius II (pope), 18. *See also* Piccolomini, Aeneas Silvius
pixides, 106n4, 156n15, 164
plague, 29, 227, 259, 263
Plato, 21
Pleven, Bulgaria (formerly Nicopolis), siege of (1396), 4, 6, 7

Poland/Poles, 10, 11, 23, 61, 100, 150, 168, 170, 202, 220, 221, 242, 259
Prague, 61, 224
prayers
    of Anthony of Padua, 165n26
    Callixtus III on role and importance of, in final battle of Belgrade, 122–4
    contra paganos (against the pagans; traditional crusader prayer), 78, 176
    general calls to, issued by Callixtus III, 71–80, 122–4, 142
    responses sung by crusaders in battle, 134, 135
    of Turks at final battle of Belgrade, 101
    used by John of Capistrano, in John of Tagliacozzo's *Story*, 165, 176, 181, 198
    vision of John Hunyadi, Mass prayers in, 135
preparations for crusade, 21–3, 39–86
    Bulla Turcorum or *Türkenbulle* (1456), 80, *81*, 129
    Constantinopolitana clades (Piccolomini, 1454), 22, 46–51
    correspondence, 51–68
    Carvajal to John of Capistrano (Jan. 16, 1456, Vienna), 58–60
    Carvajal to John of Capistrano (May 14, 1456, Buda), 62–4
    Carvajal to John of Capistrano (May 25, 1456, Buda), 64–5
    Carvajal to John of Capistrano (June 5, 1456, Buda), 65
    city of Ragusa to John Hunyadi (June 11, 1455), 51–3
    Hunyadi to Francis Oddi (June 18, 1456, Hollós), 65–6

preparations for crusade (*cont.*)
   John of Capistrano to Callixtus III (June 21, 1455, Győr), 53–7
   John of Capistrano to Callixtus III (Sept. 17, 1455, Csanád), 57–8
   John of Capistrano to Carvajal (Feb. 19, 1456, Pest), 60–2
   John of Capistrano to Francis Oddi (July 3, 1456, Belgrade), 66–8
   Cum his superioribus (papal bull of Callixtus III, 1456), 23, 72–80, 129, 144
   diets or conferences, 22, 46–7, 49–50, 61, 95, 149
   Etsi ecclesia Christi (Nicholas V's call to crusade, 1453), 21, 39–46
   financing, 43–5
   general calls to prayer issued by Callixtus III, 71–80, 122–4, 142
   John of Tagliacozzo's *Story of the Victory of Belgrade* (1460) on, 148–54
   Omnipotentis dei misericordia (Callixtus III, 1457/1455–60), 82–6
Peace of Lodi (1454), 22, 46
Pressburg (modern Bratislava), 120n4, 126–7, 128
Promontorio, Gian-Andrea, 232
Promontorio, Jacopo, *Recollecta* (c. 1475), 28, 66n1, 209n91, 232–5
propaganda. *See* news and propaganda
Pseudo-John of Capistrano, to all Christians (Aug.–Oct. 1456), in Glassberger chronicle, 133–7

Quattrocento, concept of, 18, 29
Quintilian, *Institutio oratoria*, 51n21

Qur'an citations
   2:189, 250
   2:205, 252

Ragusa (modern Dubrovnik)
   letter to John Hunyadi from (June 11, 1455), 51–3
   Šibenik compared, 109
Ramadan, 110n2
Raphael (archangel), 70
Raškans. *See* Serbs/Serbia
Regensburg
   diet of (1454), 22, 46, 49
   letter of John Goldener to Franz Schlick in (Aug. 2, 1456, Vienna), 113–16
Regium placet letters, 85n6
relics, 8, 23, 72, 118, 150, 184, 239
Rennaissance humanism and later crusades, 18, 29, 47, 125–6
Rhodes, Mehmed II's siege of (1480), 27
Richard I Lionheart (king of England), 28
Robert the Monk, *Historia Hierosolymitana*, 68
Rokyczana, Jan, 61
Roman Church. *See* Church
Romania, 10, 12, 17, 20, 23, 57, 66n2
Rome / Roman See, 48, 49, 122, 125
Rudolf (ambassador of Holy See), 54
Rüger, Henry, of Pegnitz, letter of Bernard of Kraiburg to (Aug. 26, 1456, Vienna), 126, 128–30
Rumeli Hisar (Boğazkesen), 12–13, 249
Rumelia, 5, 66, 236, 252
Rumelian cavalry/guard/army, 6, 9, 13, 25, 237, 256–8
Ruthenians, 49

Said, Edward, 16
Saint James the Apostle, 84

Saint James the Apostle, feast of (July 24), 93, 95
Saint Lawrence, feast of (August 10), 122, 220
Saint Mary Magdalene, church of (near Belgrade), 157, 205
Saint Michael, church of, Belgrade, 135
Saint Paul, 43, 46, 77, 80, 84, 86
Saint Peter, 42, 43, 45, 46, 77, 80, 84, 86, 102, 197, 198
Saint Peter, abbey of, Salzburg, 68
Saint Peter, feast of the Chair of (February 22), 216n99
saints Peter and Paul, feast of (June 29), 71
Saint Peter's, Rome, 80, 86, 132, 142
Saint Stephen's church, Vienna, 117
Saladin, 28
Sallust, *Bellum Catilinae*, 49n12
Salonika, 257
Samarkand, 6
Samokovo, 262
Samuel (biblical prophet), 74
San Lorenzo in Damaso, Rome, church of, 60n3, 73, 144
sanjaks, defined, 5
Santa Maria Maggiore, Rome, 125
Saracens, 48, 218
Sava River
  in historical framework, 7, 8
  John of Tagliacozzo writing from ship on, 95
  location of Belgrade on, 152, 229, 250
  in siege of Belgrade (1456), 25, 26, 90, 111, 128, 189–91, 266
schismatics, 55n5, 103, 133, 151, 160, 164, 172, 214
Schlick, Franz, letter from John Goldener to (Aug. 2, 1456, Vienna), 114–16

Schlick, Matthew, letter from John Goldener to (Aug. 3, 1456, Vienna), 116–18
scopettae. *See* arquebuses
Scythia, 105
Sechar, Paul, 213, 214
Şehabeddin Pasha, 11
Semendria, 257
Semlin (now Zemun), 25, 163, 168, 214, 247, 247n13, 284
Sennacherib (king of Assyria), 41, 42, 74
Serbs/Serbia
  Balkan historiography and, 19–20
  conflicts with Ottomans, 3–9, 12, 110, 218, 222–3
  important routes into/through, 66n1, 96
  Novo Brdo, Ottoman conquest of (1455), 22, 52–3, 55, 256, 261–2
  Ottoman campaigns in, 260–3
  Roman Christians and, 133, 172
  as Triballi/Triballia, in Kritopoulos's account, 229, 232
  truce with Ottomans, 12, 57
  See also specific rulers
Setton, Kenneth, *The Papacy and the Levant, 1204–1571*, 17, 34n43
Sforza, Francesco, Duke of Milan, 112
  letters from
    Callixtus III (Aug. 23, 1456, Rome), 122–5
    Carvajal (July 29, 1456, Ilok), 112–13
    Ladislaus V (Aug. 3, 1456, Vienna), 118–20
  post-battle military aid requested from, 120, 124–5
Šibenik, ambassador of bishop of, letter to Callixtus III (July 26, 1456, Buda), 109–12

siege of Belgrade (1456). *See* Crusade of 1456 / siege of Belgrade
Sigismund (king of Hungary), 4, 6–8, 10, 274
Sigismund I of Volkersdorf, archbishop of Salzburg, letter of Bernard of Kraiburg to (Aug. 25, 1456, Vienna), 126–8
Singidunum (now Belgrade), 7, 8
Sisera (biblical figure), 206
Sitnica, 260
Skanderbeg, 64
Skobaljić, Nikola, 261
Skopje, 251, 256, 257
Slankamen, 88, 91, 104, 107, 160, 161, 164, 208, 210
Smederevo, 9, 66n1, 218, 223, 261n3, 263, 265
social class
  nobler classes, purported lack of involvement of, 118, 213–16, 220, 241
  three orders of society, inversion of, 118
  working people as crusaders in siege of Belgrade, 118, 127, 128, 141, 173, 195–6, 220, 243
Sofia, 3, 105, 127, 260n2
Soler, Juan, papal ambassador to Alfonso V of Aragon, letter of Callixtus III to (late Aug., 1456, Rome), 122–5
Solon, 247
Sonnenberger, Ulrich (bishop of Gurk), 50n13
springalds *(spingardas)*, 156, 166, 173, 178, 204
Stefan Lazarević (despot of Serbia and ban of Macsó), 4, 7–8, 25, 274
Stephen (pope and martyr), feast of (August 2), 116

Stephen Protomartyr
  feast of invention of relics of (August 3), 118
  feast of martyrdom of (December 26), 118n5
Story of the Victory of Belgrade (John of Tagliacozzo, 1460), 24, 147–216
  on preparations for crusade, 148–54
  on first victory (naval battle), 154–67
  on second victory (liberation of fortress), 167–88
  on third victory (defeat of Turks in the field), 188–203
  on aftermath of battle, 203–16
  on crossing of Sava by John of Capistrano, 189–92
  on death of John of Capistrano, 216
  "face of battle" represented in, 28–9
  on feigned retreat, 192–4
  on firearms, 115n5, 156–7, 161–2, 164, 166, 173, 178, 182, 192–4, 199
  as hagiographical text, 148
  letter-form of, 24, 147, 148
  miraculous events in, 155–6, 157, 167, 199, 200, 201
  presence of John of Tagliacozzo at final battle in, 190–1, 197, 198, 200, 202
  success in battle attributed to God and John of Capistrano, 214–16
Szécsi, Denis, cardinal archbishop of Esztergom, 56, 66n2
  letter from Hunyadi (July 24, 1456, Belgrade), 91–3, 218n2
Szeged, 63, 66, 241
Székesfehérvár, 192

Szilágyi, Michael, of Horogszeg, 273
  as brother-in-law of Hunyadi, 25
  in eyewitness accounts, 93n1, 100
  George Branković, ransom of, 264–6
  in John of Tagliacozzo's *Story of the Victory of Belgrade* (1460), 149, 152, 155, 160, 167, 175, 176, 180, 185, 187, 189, 195, 201, 202, 204–6, 210
  kerchief sent to John of Capistrano by, 155
  in memoirs and chronicles, 244, 264, 265n10, 266n14

Talovac, Matthew, 9
Tanais, 49
Tartars, 48, 218
Tellus, 247
Teucri, 218
Themistius, 48n10
Theophano (saint and empress), 8
Thessalonica, capture of (1430), 9
three orders of society, inversion of, 118
Thucydides, 26
Thurocz, John, *Chronicle of the Hungarians* (c. 1488), 28, 237–49
Timur (Tamerlane; Asian warlord), 6, 274
Tobias (biblical figure), 70
Tomaš (Bosnian king), 265
Transfiguration, feast of (August 6), 142–5
Transoxiana (modern Uzbekistan), 6
Transylvania, 1, 10, 11, 23, 60, 93–4, 110, 151, 213, 244n10, 248n16
Trebizond (Kolchis), king of, 223
Trepanja, 261
Trepca, 256
Trevisan, Ludovico, 60n3, 73, 129

Triballi/Triballia (Serbia), 229, 232
Tröster, John, 128
truces. *See* peace / peace negotiations
Türkenbulle or *Bulla Turcorum* (Callixtus III, 1456), 80, *81*, 129
Turks. *See* Ottoman Turks
Tursun Beg, *History of the Conqueror* (c. 1488), 249–55

Uljak (Ilok), 112, 249
Ulrich II, Count of Celje, 9, 60, 111, 128, 130, 137, 140–1, 240, 264, 265n11, 274
Ulrich of Nussdorf, bishop of Passau, 115, 127, 129
Urban II (pope), 16, 28

Varna, 11–12, 20
Venice/Venetians, 6, 13–14, 17, 21, 49, 51–2, 63–4, 98, 109, 110, 130
vernacular versus Latin, writing in, 96n1
Via Egnatia, 5
Vidin, 224, 261n3
Vienna, 12, 23, 58, 60, 111, 112, 113, 114, 116, 117n1, 118, 120, 122, 125, 126, 127, 128, 130, 217, 240
Vilk-ili, 256, 257
Visconti, Filippo Maria, Duke of Milan, 112
vision of John Hunyadi, 135–6
Visitation, feast of (July 2), 97, 154
Vitéz, John, bishop of Oradea (later cardinal archbishop of Esztergom), 53, 54, 66, 129
Vitus and Modestus, feast of (June 18), 66
Vılkoğlu. *See* George Branković
vows of crusading or pilgrimage, commutation of, 84
Vrana, 9

Vranja, 261n3
Vuk Branković. *See* George Branković

Wallachia/Wallachians, 4, 10, 11, 172
Weber, Benjamin, 18
weights, measures, and distances, 57, 97, 99, 115, 117, 126, 129, 157, 163, 233, 241
Weissenburg, city of, letter from city of Nuremberg to (Aug. 13, 1456), 121–2
"White City," Belgrade as, 7
Wiener Neustadt, diet of (1455), 22, 46, 61

women, crusader and Turkish, 29, 102, 110, 158, 180–1, 183, 185, 187–8, 218, 238
wordplay, 41n6, 92n1, 184n45
working people as crusaders in siege of Belgrade, 118, 127, 128, 141, 173, 195–6, 220, 243

Žegligiovo, 260
Zemun (formerly Semlin), 25, 163, 168, 214, 247, 247n13, 284
Zlatitsa pass, 11
Zrnov, 246
Zvecaj, 259

www.ingramcontent.com/pod-product-compliance
Lightning Source LLC
Chambersburg PA
CBHW071149070526
44584CB00019B/2717